Edmund Gosse, Thomas Gray

Works

In Prose and Verse

Edmund Gosse, Thomas Gray

Works
In Prose and Verse

ISBN/EAN: 9783744685498

Printed in Europe, USA, Canada, Australia, Japan

Cover: Foto ©Thomas Meinert / pixelio.de

More available books at **www.hansebooks.com**

GRAY'S WORKS

VOL. IV.

Sonnet.

In vain to me the smiling Mornings shine,
And redning Phœbus lifts his golden Fire:
The Birds in vain their amorous Descant join;
Or chearful Fields resume their green Attire:
These Ears, alas! for other Notes repine,
A different Object do these Eyes require:
My lonely Anguish melts no Heart, but mine;
And in my Breast the imperfect Joys expire.
Yet Morning smiles the busy Race to chear,
And new-born Pleasure brings to happier Men:
The Fields to all their wonted Tribute bear;
To warm their little Loves the Birds complain:
I fruitless mourn to him, that cannot hear,
And weep the more, because I weep in vain. ❧ at Stoke. Aug:

THE WORKS

OF

THOMAS GRAY

𝕴𝖓 𝕻𝖗𝖔𝖘𝖊 𝖆𝖓𝖉 𝖁𝖊𝖗𝖘𝖊

EDITED BY

EDMUND GOSSE

CLARK LECTURER ON ENGLISH LITERATURE AT THE
UNIVERSITY OF CAMBRIDGE

IN FOUR VOLS.—VOL. IV.

NOTES ON ARISTOPHANES AND PLATO

𝕷𝖔𝖓𝖉𝖔𝖓

MACMILLAN AND CO.

1884

CONTENTS.

NOTES ON ARISTOPHANES.

	PAGE		PAGE
ACHARNENSES . . .	3	THESMOPHORIAZUSÆ	43
EQUITES	7	LYSISTRATA . . .	46
VESPÆ	11	RANÆ	49
NUBES	17	ECCLESIAZUSÆ . .	55
PAX . . .	20	PLUTUS	58
AVES	26	NOTES ON THE PLUTUS	60
NOTES ON THE AVES	38		

NOTES ON PLATO.

	PAGE		PAGE
BRIEF NOTICES OF SOCRATES		LACHES	116
AND OF HIS FRIENDS .	67	HIPPARCHUS . . .	122
THE COMPANIONS OF So-		PHILEBUS . . .	124
CRATES	69	MENO	134
PHÆDRUS . . .	75	GORGIAS	140
LYSIS . .	87	MINOS	158
ALCIBIADES I. .	90	CHARMIDES . . .	160
ALCIBIADES II.	94	CRATYLUS . . .	164
THEAGES . . .	98	SYMPOSIUM . .	166
EUTHYPHRO . .	101	EUTHYDEMUS . . .	172
APOLOGIA SOCRATIS	104	HIPPIAS MAJOR .	175
CRITO . . .	110	HIPPIAS MINOR .	177
PHÆDO . . .	111	PROTAGORAS . .	178
ERASTÆ . . .	115	IO . . .	198

CONTENTS.

	PAGE		PAGE
THEÆTETUS . . .	205	DE LEGIBUS—	
THE SOPHIST . .	209	Book IV. . . .	297
POLITICUS . .	214	„ V. . . .	302
DE REPUBLICA . .	221	THE EPISTLES—	
Book I. . . .	223	Epistle I. . . .	308
„ II. . .	226	„ II. . .	309
„ III. . .	232	„ III. . .	312
„ IV. . .	237	„ IV. . .	315
„ V. . .	241	„ V. . .	316
„ VI. . .	247	„ VI. . .	317
„ VII. . .	252	„ VII. . .	320
„ VIII. . .	256	„ VIII. . .	330
„ IX. . .	262	„ IX. . .	332
„ X. . .	266	„ X. and XI. .	333
DE LEGIBUS . . .	270	„ XII. . .	334
Book I. . . .	272	„ XIII. . .	336
„ II. . .	282	APPENDIX . . .	339
„ III. . .	287	INDEX	345

NOTES ON ARISTOPHANES

[The original of these notes was contained in a separate manuscript, dated July 1747, in the possession of Mathias, which was presented to him by Richard Stonehewer, one of Gray's executors. They were published by Mathias in 1814, and have never since been reprinted. It has been thought best to print the Greek, in this instance, as Gray wrote it.—ED.]

ACHARNENSES.

Olymp. 88. 3.

IT[1] appears from several passages in the drama itself and in the Scholia, that it was played in this olympiad and year, Archont. Euthydemo, and consequently the year before his Equites. In the sixth line he mentions the fine imposed on Cleon, of five talents; so that it is not true, that his Equites was the occasion of that disgrace (see v. 300), as the author of his life has written, and the Scholia here say.

v. 11. This Theognis, satirized as a bad writer of tragedy, and from his coldness nicknamed Χιων, was twenty-two years afterwards one of the thirty tyrants. Moschus, Dexitheus, and Chæris, mentioned here, were tibicines of this time.

47. Euripides, in his Iphigenia in Tauris, is here ridiculed.

66. The allowance to an Athenian embassy consisted of two drachmæ a day to each person employed.

119. The Medea of Euripides is here parodied. I

---

[1] It was not any oligarchy, or tyranny, which retrenched the chorus in the Athenian comedy, or prohibited the representation of real characters, as Platonius asserts, in his observations entitled Περι διαφορᾶς κωμωδιῶν.—[GRAY.]

read, εξυρημενε, which improves the parody of Euripides.—Effeminate persons began to shave their chins
even in these times. (V. Athenæum, L. 13. p. 565.
and Thesmoph. v. 225.)

233. The action against Pisistratus at Pallene, one
of the Δημοι of Attica, is mentioned by Andocides,
de Mysteriis, whose great-grandfather Leogoras was
Στρατηγος there.

346-47.—   Ανασειειν βοην,
Ολιγου τ' απεθανον ανθρακες Παρνασσιοι. κτλ.
Should we not read Παρνηθιοι?

387. &c. Hieronimus a tragick and lyrick poet.—
Euripides and Cephisophon ridiculed.—The Æneus,
Phœnix, Philoctetes, Bellerophon, Telephus, Thyestes,
and Ino of Euripides, are laughed at, where he had
introduced the principal characters in poor apparel to
move compassion. The sententious pertness of his personages, and the inactiveness and folly of his chorusses,
are all noticed. The poverty of his mother is alluded to.

442.—Τους δ' αυ Χορειτας ηλιθιους παρεστεναι, &c.

Euripides is here satirized for making his chorusses
take little part in the action of the drama, but either
telling long fables, or impertinently questioning and
answering the characters.

504.—Ουτε γαρ φοροι Ηκουσι, &c.

The time, when the contributions of the allies were
brought to Athens, was during the Dionysia τα κατ'
αστυ, (see Isocrat. de Pace, 175,) in spring time in the
month Elaphebolion; the Lenæa were celebrated in
winter pretty late, two months before the other, and in
the country, at which time this piece was played.

529. Περικλεης οὐλυμπιος

Ηστραπτεν, εβροντα, ξυνεκυκα την Ελλαδα, &c.

The fine fragment from the Δημοι of Eupolis on Pericles.

602. Μισθοφοροιντας τρεις δραχμας, &c.

He seems to mean that they sent their Στρατηγοι on various useless embassies, who gladly accepted them, as well to be out of the way of danger, as to earn the publick allowance, two or three drachmæ a day, and to be out of the power of their creditors.

628. Ἐξ οὕγε χοροισιν εφεστηκε τρυγικοις ὁ διδασ-καλος ἡμων, &c.

Τρυγωδια seems always to mean comedy here. See above, v. 498 and 499. Is this *Parabasis* to be understood of Aristophanes himself, or of Callistratus the actor, in whose name he seems to have exhibited all his dramas, before the Equites? Some of the Scholia take it of the latter (see v. 654); they also rightly understand in a ridiculous light what is here said of the Persian king, which the writer of the Poet's life, and Mad. Dacier also, seriously report as a fact.

703. Is this the Thucydides, son of Melesias, who underwent the ostracism, or, as Idomeneus says (see Schol. ad Vespas, v. 941), perpetual banishment, and that he fled into Persia, Ol. 83, 4, nineteen years before this? Cephisodemus seems to have been his accuser.

875. Νασσας, Κολοιους, &c. Is Κολοιος the jay, or the jackdaw, or the magpye? It was, as it appears, an eatable bird. It appears also, that the Greeks eat hedge-hogs, foxes, locusts, moles, otters, and cats. (see Athenæus, L. 17, p. 300.) The Megareans brought

salt, swine, garlick, &c., to sell at the Athenian markets, and bought corn there, &c. The Bœotians (see Irene v. 1003 and 4.) sold them water-fowl and wild-fowl of various sorts, manufactures of rushwork, as mats, wicks for lamps, &c., and fish from their lakes, particularly excellent eels.

883. The 'Οπλων Κρισις of Æschylus is here parodied.

1000. It is certain that this comedy was played during the Lenæa, and many parts of it seem a representation of the festival itself, as v. 238, where Dicæopolis and his family perform sacrifice to Bacchus, and here is the Certamen Bibendi, used in the Χοαι: but we are not told that this ceremony was used except on the second day of the Anthesteria. Hence it seems probable, that it was used alike in the Lenæa.

1029. Ου δημοσιευων τυγχανω. The publick elected and gave a salary to certain physicians (see Aves, v. 585, and Plutus, v. 408) who took no fees from particular people.

It appears from some of the scenes in this comedy, that the Prytanes were present in the publick assemblies, seated in the place of honour; that they kept order there, and commanded the archers to apprehend any one who made a disturbance; and that they produced ambassadors to the people, and dismissed the assembly. Ambassadors were entertained in the Prytaneum at the invitation of the senate.

EQUITES.

Olymp. 88. 4. In Lenæis, Mense Posideone.

v. 9. Olympus, the scholar of Marsyas, invented the symphony of flutes. 19. Alludes to Euripides. 61. Αδει δε χρησμους. Alluding to the Sibyll's oracles.

123. Alluding to the oracles of Bacis. The Scholiast says there were three of that name.

282. It seems, that Cleon, for his success at Sphacteria, had a publick maintenance allowed him in the Prytaneum.

399. The sottishness of Cratinus.—Morsimus, the son of Philocles, wrote Tragedy. 404. The Τεθριπποι of Simonides cited.

504. This was the first drama which Aristophanes brought upon the stage in his own name, (see Vespæ, v. 1013.) and he himself played the character of Cleon in it.

517. Ειδως α 'παθεν Μαγνης αμα ταις πολιαις κατιοισαις, &c.

Magnes, the comick poet, had great success in his plays, named, Βαρβιτιδες, Ορνιθες, Ψηνες, Βατραχοι, Λυδοι, but was hissed off the stage in his decline.

523. Κρατινου μεμνημενος. Cratinus—his ancient glory is declared; but he afterwards grew negligent, drunken, and despised in his old age. Connas, the tibicen, lost his former reputation.

524. The passage cited from the Pytine of Cratinus in the Scholia must either not be in that drama, or the poet must allude here to some other similar passage ; as the Pytine was not played till the following year, and (as the Scholia say afterwards) written upon the provocation here given by Aristophanes.

534. Crates ; his various success. Aristophanes assigns his reasons for not before exhibiting any drama in his own name.

586. The comick chorus (as the Scholiast informs us, and see also Aves, v. 298) consisted of twenty-four persons, the tragick chorus but of fifteen. They were (sometimes) composed of men, women, and children, mixed, as in the Vespæ, &c. Casaubon, in his notes to v. 495, gives an account of the Parabasis and of its seven parts, namely, the Κομματιον, Παραβασις (propriè dicta), Μακρον or Πνιγος, Στροφη, Επιρρημα, Αντιστροφη, και Αντεπιρρημα.

596. The humour of these lines, and of the naval expedition of the horses, is hardly intelligible at present.

701. Προεδρια was an honour conferred on principal citizens for their services : every one was obliged to give them place in the assembly, the senate, the theatre, &c. Cleon had this honour after his success at Sphacteria.

782. Την εν Σαλαμῖνι. It is plain what part he means : but why does he call it so ?

790. Ετος ογδοον. Must be understood of the eighth year only beginning.

810. Ω πολις Αργους. The sharpness of this parody of Euripides consists in this : Cleon, under a pretence of an embassy to Argos, was suspected of carrying on a

private correspondence with the Spartans, on the subject of restoring the prisoners he had made at Sphacteria.
(See v. 463.)

851. Here is a good account of the ostracism, in the
Scholia, but with some errours. It is said to be in use
with the Argives, Megareans and Milesians ; but Phæax
in his oration on the subject, spoken probably not many
years after this, affirms the contrary ; Μονοι γαρ αυτου
των Ἑλληνων χρωμεθα, και ουδεμια των αλλων πολιων
εθελει μιμησασθαι; and it is not likely, that those
cities should have adopted it, after it ceased to be in
use at Athens, which took place Olymp. 91. 1.   In
enumerating several great men exostracised, he mentions
Alcibiades, who never was so.

908. The ships were delivered to the Trierarchs, by
the Στρατηγοι (who seem to have appointed them) and
belonged to the publick ; but the Trierarch, at his own
expense, repaired and furnished them with all necessaries.   The Εισφοραι were paid by the richer citizens,
a catalogue of whom seems to have been drawn by the
Στρατηγοι.

947. The custom of the steward, or head-servant,
keeping his master's seal.

950. Θριον εξωπτημενον.   There are three receipts,
in the Scholia, of Greek cookery, to make a Θριον.   The
1st was in this manner : they boiled rice, or fine flour
in grains (called Χονδρος) till it was tender ; then they
kneaded it up with new cheese, and eggs, wrapped up
the whole in a fig-leaf, and boiled it in a soup of broth
of meat ; then fried it brown in honey, and served it
up to table with the honey in the dish.   2. A second

sort was made of flour, lard, or the fat of a kid, milk,
and yolks of eggs, boiled in a fig-leaf. 3. The third
sort was, the brains of any animal with garum (the
pickle of fish) and cheese; the whole put in a fig-leaf,
and baked over the fire.

959. Μολγον—μυρρινου—Σμικνθην και Κυριον—
obscure passages. The Scholia assist us very little here.

1046. Πεντεσυριγγον ξυλον. This wooden machine
had five holes in it to receive the hands, feet, and neck
of the prisoners, serving at once for the pillory and for
the stocks.

1300. It is false to say, that the Athenians had no
connection with, or thoughts of, Carthage, (see Isocrates
de Pace, 177.) whatever the commentators may say;
their ambition extended itself in proportion to their
conquests, and if their Sicilian expedition had succeeded,
they had actually thoughts of attacking that great
republick: Thucydides at least tells us, that this was
Alcibiades's view. L. 6. c. 15.

1375. Συνερκτικος γαρ εστι, &c. This imitates the
turn of phrase then in use among the young gentlemen
of Athens, who had deserted the country, and the more
manly exercises of agriculture, hunting, &c., and divided
their time between the effeminate pleasures of the city
and the publick assemblies, in which they valued themselves upon their eloquence, and the new art of speaking, then, perhaps, taught by the sophists. The terms
they use (as the Scholiast observes) bear a double meaning; and he rightly explains the sense of καταδακτυλιζειν.
There is no doubt, but that this line is spoken by the
chorus to Demus, who represents the people.

VESPÆ.

v. 139. Ιπνος is not the kitchen (as the Scholiast
would have it) but the stove for heating the bath.
Πυελος is the labrum, or bathing-tub. Τρημα, the hole
in it at the bottom to let out the water. Καπνη, the
funnel, or vent for the smoke. Τηλια, a cap or cover
to close the vent.

157. Read, Δικασοντα με.

158. 'Ο γαρ Θεος, &c. It seems to be the old man
who says this, not his son ; and Bdelycleon answers ;
Απολλον αποτροπαιε, &c.

240. Ως εσται Λαχητι νυνι (i.e. δικη.) &c.   Laches,
who had been recalled from his command in Sicily two
years before this, Ol. 88. 3 (Thucyd. L. 3. c. 115.) seems
to have been accused this year by Cleon and his party.

287. Ανηρ παχυς ηκει των προδοντων Ταπι Θρακης,
&c. Without doubt this relates to Thucydides, who
was Στρατηγος in Thrace, and condemned to banishment this very year, for his treachery or neglect in the
loss of Amphipolis.

322. Αλλ' ω Ζευ, &c. This is undoubtedly a parody
of some tragick chorus, perhaps of Æschylus or of
Euripides, though the Scholiast is silent.

388. Ω Λυκε, &c. The fane of Lycus adjoining to

all courts of justice, fenced in, and covered at the top with mats.

415. Ταυτα δητ' ου δεινα, &c. This should be spoken by the chorus.

576. When boys underwent the Δοκιμασια, their puberty was publickly examined (as it seems) in the court of Heliæa.

598. Τάμβαδι ἡμων περικωνει. The manner of blacking shoes (as it seems) was with a sponge and tar.

606. The custom of washing and anointing their feet, as soon as they came home, which was in poorer families the office of the daughters.

655. The publick revenue of Athens comprehending the contributions of the allied cities (which may be set at six hundred talents yearly, as Thucydides observes, L. 2. c. 13.); the tolls and customs from the markets, and ports, and mines; the Prytanea, or sums deposited by such as had suits in any court (v. Nubes, v. 1134, and 1193, and Kuster ad v. 1182.); and the confiscations, &c., here computed at two thousand talents per annum (£387,500), out of which one hundred and fifty talents were expended on the six thousand Δικασται kept in pay (see Isocrates de Pace, 185.) at three oboli a-day, which in ten months (for the rest of the year consisted in holidays, during which the courts did not sit) amounted to that sum. Qu. what are the Εκατοσται, and Μισθοι mentioned as branches of the revenue here? (v. Xenoph. de Athen. Republ. 404.)

688. Το σημειον, the sign given to enter the court, and take their places (v. Thesmoph. v. 285.); mentioned

also by Andocides de Mysteriis ; το σημειον καθελη,
p. 6.—The Συνηγοροι, or orators, received a drachma in
each cause (as it seems) from the publick.

700. Ωσπερ αλειρον. The metaphor seems to be
taken from some weakly young animal brought up by
the hand, by distilling milk or pap into its mouth,
gradually through a lock of wool. The Scholiast on
v. 700 comes nearer the true meaning, than on v. 699.

705. A thousand cities paid tribute to the Athenians
at this time. Genuine citizens were now above twenty
thousand.

716. In the Schol. on this verse for Ἱππαρχου read
Ισαρχου : but I do not find any revolt in Eubœa till
eleven years afterwards ; nor can there be any allusion
here to the distribution of corn under Lysimachides,
which took place twenty-three years before.

787. The obolus, a silver coin. Custom of putting
money in the mouth. (Aves, 503.)

800. Ωσπερ Ἑκαταιον. A little chapel or tabernacle
of Hecate was erected before every man's door. (Ranæ,
369.)

840. Χοιροκομειον Ἑστιας. Libations and prayers
were always begun to Vesta. (v. Aves, v. 865, and
Plato's Cratylus, p. 401.)

870. Apollo Αγνιευς was represented by a small
obelisk before the doors of houses. (v. Thesmoph. 485.)

909. It is Bdelycleon who sustains the part of the
Thesmothetes. The servant speaks for the accuser.
From Ὁ βδελυρος ουτος ου μετεδωκ' αιτουντι μοι, are
his words in the character of the Cydathenæan dog,
who represents a sycophant informer, who prosecutes

Labes (the dog defendant) because he would not give
him a share of the Sicilian cheese which he had stolen.
Τω κοινω γέμοι, I suppose means, the dog of the
publick; or this last line may be spoken by the judge
himself, who represents the people, and is angry, that
he had no part in the spoil. In the Scholia, for Χαρητα
read Λαχητα.

930. Αυτος καθελου—as far as ουδεπω, v. 934, is
said by Bdelycleon; and Philocleon adds, (as the Scholiast also reads) Τουτον δε γ' οιμ' εγω, &c., meaning the
defendant.

954. Εγω δ' εβουλομην αν, &c., seems obscure, nor
do I perceive who says this. Ακουσον ω δαιμονιε, v.
956. belongs to Bdelycleon, who from Thesmothetes
turns advocate for Labes.

981. Τηνδι λαβων, &c. The account in the Scholiast of the manner of voting, is to me unintelligible;
and Florens Christianus (who does little more than
translate the Scholia) is as much so. It seems that
the calculi put into the υστερος καδισκος acquitted the
prisoner. The matter is better explained in the Schol.
on v. 985.

1014. Eurycles, an εγγαστριμυθος or ventriloquist,
and prophet at Athens. Εις αλλοτριας γαστερας, I
imagine, means fetching his voice out of another person's belly; for persons, who have this faculty, often
seem to do so.

1025. Aristophanes—how he demolished Cleon in
his Equites: his Nubes, written against the school of
Socrates, exploded: he reckons it his best piece: ancient
Scholia, sung after meals, on Harmodius: the beginning

of another by Alcæus : Αδμητου λογος : the Parœria of
Praxilla : Æsophic and Sybaritic tales.

1037. The office of the Polemarch.   See the Schol.
on this verse.

1052. The custom of putting apples (qu. whether
the citron fruit?) among chests of clothes.

1221. This is the beginning of the Scholion on Harmodius and Aristogeïton, to which Philocleon answers,
as continuing the song, Ουκ ουτω πανουργος, &c., meaning Cleon, whom Bdelycleon personates.   Observe the
way of singing successively (see Nubes, v. 1367), and
continuing the same Scholion, giving a myrtle branch
from one to another.

1275. Εισι τινες οι, &c.   This obscure antistrophe
relates to some transaction between Cleon and the
poet, of which we know little.

1300. Didymus and others take these lines for
nonsense.

1408. I know not why this character is called Euripides : it seems a mistake.

1418. Example of a Sybaritic tale.

1481. Besides Phrynichus, son of Melanthus the
tragick poet, (who must have been dead fifty years at
least before this) and Phrynichus, the comick son of
Polyphradmon (or Eunomides, see Ranæ, v. 13.) and
contemporary with Aristophanes, there was a third
Phrynichus, a famed actor of tragedy mentioned here
in the Scholion on v. 1293, and by Andocides de
Mysteriis, p. 7, as a relation of his own. (See also Aves,
Schol. on 750.)

1491. Carcinus, the son of Thorycias, had three

sons, all players, Xenotimus, Demotimus, and the youngest Xenocles, a tragick poet.

1507. The chorus here give way to the three sons of Carcinus, or to such as imitated them, who dance a vaulting dance.

1524. For ἡμας read ὑμας. The chorus came on, but never went off, dancing.

NUBES.

OL 89. 1. In Dionysiis τοις κατ' αστυ, Mens. Elaphebol. after the Vespæ.

The Nubes was played Ol. 89. 1. and damned; it was altered and repeated Ol. 89. 2, but still with ill success. It was again altered, and published two or three years after, but never played again.

v. 10. Σισυρα, a kind of frieze (Ecclesiaz: 347) or thick woollen garment, used as a great coat, and also to cover beds, as here, like a blanket.

37. Δημαρχος, an officer presiding over each Δημος, instituted (as Aristotle says) by Clisthenes ; for before that time they were called Ναυκλαροι. They had a register of all the debts of their Δημοται, and obliged them to give their creditors security, when demanded.

178. Διαβητην. The Scholiast here exactly describes a pair of compasses. (Vid. Platon. Philebus, p. 567.)

180. Thales the Milesian.

256. The sacrifice of Athamas, in a tragedy of Sophocles.

267. Κυνῆ, a leather cap, or calotte, with which they covered their head against the rain

335. Bombast expressions of dithyrambick writers, Cinesias, Philoxenus, and Cleomenes, as the Scholiast says.

3/   C

503. Chærephon ; his leanness and paleness.

524. The *first* Nubes exploded : Aristophanes regarded it as his best work. His Δαιταλεις, the first
comedy of his brought upon the stage, but under another
person's name, Philonides or Callistratus ; its success.

534. The Choephori of Æschylus.

549. His abuse of Cleon in the Equites. Eupolis's
Maricas, a bad imitation of the Equites. Phrynichus,
the comick writer. Hermippus, his drama against
Hyperbolus. The simile of the eel-catchers in the
Equites was famous.

586. It is not necessary that we should understand
this of Cleon's expedition to Thrace, where he was killed
and the Athenians defeated, as the Scholia and Spanheim would have us understand it ; it is meant of his
Στρατηγια, in the year he took Σφακτηρια, which, however successful in that particular, is always represented
by the poet, here and elsewhere, as the misfortune and
errour of the publick, on account of the signal depravity
of manners, rapacity, and mad conduct of Cleon. It
appears, even from v. 591, that Cleon was actually alive
at the time when this was written. Hyperbolus was
chosen Hieromnemon in this year, to go to Thermopylæ
and Delphi. Mad. Dacier's explanation of v. 625, is
the best we can find.

765. A remarkable description of a burning-glass.
The Scholia here tells us, that at this time they called
rock-crystal 'Υαλος, which may possibly be, as he here
calls it, Λιθος. Not that artificial glass, from Egypt
and the east, was unknown to them : Herodotus mentions it in his account of the Ethiopians, &c.; however

it appears, that they did not put it to this use of collect-
ing the sunbeams, till they had heated it first, and rubbed
it with oil : it seems to have been then newly invented.
Spanhemius, at v. 619 and 626, does not imagine this
confusion of the year to be owing to the irregularities
before the invention of Meto's cycle, (which was not
received into publick use), but to some attempt, perhaps of the magistracy, at this time to introduce that
cycle, which, however, did not obtain : the months still
continuing of thirty, and the year of three hundred and
sixty, days.

919. The Telephus of Euripides.

961. The Greek children from ten years old to
thirteen were sent to the Γραμματιστης, who taught
them to read and write, then to the Κιθαριστης, and
next to the Παιδοτριβης.

964. The odes of Lamprocles son of Midon an
Athenian, and of Cydides of Hermione.

967. Phrynis, the musician of Mitylene, scholar of
Aristoclitus, corrupted and softened the ancient musick.

981. Schol. Cecides, was an ancient dithyrambick.

1047. All natural warm baths were sacred to
Hercules.

1264. Carcinus introduced in his tragedies, certain
deities deploring and lamenting themselves. A parody
of two lines in the Licymnius of Xenocles.

1359. Scholia of Simonides. Speeches from Æschylus and Euripides were sung at entertainments.

PAX.

Acted in the Dionysia τα κατ' αστυ, Ol. 90. 2. Archonte Archiâ.
. Bentley and Malalam.

v. 81. This whole whim of making Trygæus fly to heaven, mounted on the back of a monstrous beetle, is a ridiculous imitation of the Bellerophon of Euripides, who is introduced in like sort taming Pegasus for the same purpose, and seating himself on his back. This Ἡσυχος, ἡσυχος, ηρεμα, κανθων, is a parody of that scene which begun, Αγ' ω φιλον μοι Πηγασου πτερον : and so, from the elevated expression, I imagine the rest to be, as far as v. 155. The reason why he himself chooses to go to heaven on a beetle, he himself gives us out of Æsop's fables ;

Εν τοισιν Αισωπου λογοις εξηυρεθη
Μονος πετεινων εις Θεους αφιγμενος·

and he adds another, which shews his œconomy and prudence ; for he says, that had he used any other vehicle, he must have carried twice the provision, whereas this animal will feed on what he himself had digested.

146. The Bellerophon of Euripides introduced lame after his fall.

218. Ην εχωμεν την Πυλον. This seems to allude

to the Athenians refusing to restore Pylus after the
ratification of the truce, Ol. 89. 4. See Thucyd. L.
5. 35.

236. Τας γναθους αλγησετε, i.e. In eating the
Μυττωτος which he is cooking for them.

342. The best account of the Κοτταβισμος is in the
Scholia, and at v. 1241.

363. Prisoners condemned to death were executed
one only in a day, and drew lots who should die first.

373. Those who would be initiated at Eleusis sacri-
ficed a pig, which cost three drachmæ. (See also Plat.
Rep. L. 2. 378.)

413. The eclipse of the sun, Ol. 88. 4, mentioned by
Thucydides; and in the Nubes, v. 584.

449. Κει τις στρατηγειν, &c. This (as the Scholiast
says) is a reflection perhaps on Alcibiades, but undoubtedly on Lamachus, who was always strenuous for
continuing the war.

456. Mars and Enyalius were two different divinities.
(See Sophocles, Ajax, v. 179.)

465. The Bœotians refused to come into the truce
with Athens. See Thucyd. L. 5. 17.

530. The musick of Sophocles praised. Euripides's
little sentences and short replies.

642. 'Αττ' αν διαβαλοι, &c. This alludes to sick
stomachs, which are most inclined to eat what is most
prejudicial to them.

697. Simonides and Sophocles, now an old man;
their avarice.

699. This is not to be literally understood; for
Cratinus was alive seven years after the invasion of

Attica by the Spartans, but he had given himself up to drinking, and declined in his parts and reputation.

712. The senate seemed to have named the Θεωροι, that is, the Areopagus, as I imagine.

728. The chorus here (as in Acharnens. v. 626.) pull off their ἱματια, or mantles, or upper garments, that they may dance the Parabasis, or the anapæstick digression, with more ease.

735. Aristophanes banished (as he says) low ribaldry from the stage, and made comedy an art; he attacked without fear the most powerful men, particularly Cleon. Carcinus and his sons, Morsimus and Melanthius, tragick poets, satirized. Ion of Chius, his hymn on the morning star: now lately dead. See the account of him in the Scholia.

756. These verses are repeated from the Nubes, which proves that drama to have been exploded.

884. Ariphrades: his strange lust.

951. Chæris, the tibicen. Morychus and Melanthius; their gluttony. Parody from the Medea of the latter. Stilbides and Hierocles of Oreus, professed prophets. Bacis; three of that name (Schol.), a Bœotian, an Athenian, and an Arcadian. Sibylla, her prophecies.

966. Ceremonies in sacrificing: extinguishing a lighted torch in the water, with which they washed; carrying the vessel with barley, a garland, and knife in it, round the altar to the right; throwing whole barley among the people, &c. It appears (see Thesmoph. v. 402. and Aves, 795) that women were present in the theatres, which is amazing, when one considers the extreme indecency, not of words alone, but of actions,

in these spectacles. The preceding scene at v. 881, is a more than common instance of it. See also Lysistrata, v. 1095.

Possibly the chorus, not the audience, might be in part composed of women, for it is they who are called οἱ Θεωμενοι. The sacrificer asked before the libation, Τις τηδε; and the standers-by replied Πολλοι κᾳγαθοι: then they sprinkled them with the holy water, and begun the prayer; after which they cut the victim's throat: (1018. he calls it τον οιν. Is this a general name for all victims, or should one read το θῦμα? it appears to be a sheep, not a hog: the Schol. at verse 1019 sacrifice to Peace without any victim in the festival called Συνοικεσια.) Then having dressed the victim and piled wood on the altar, they offered up the two, sprinkling them with wine and oil and barley flour (τα θυλημματα). The Μαντεις wore laurel-crowns.

1056. Αγε νυν απαρχου, &c. The Απαργμα seems to be the first cut, due to the Μαντις. After the offering they dressed the inward parts and the tongue, made their libation, and then eat them.

1240. A cuirass was worth ten minæ; a trumpet, sixty drachmæ; a helmet, one mina.

1253. Συρμαια, an Egyptian purge. See Thesmoph. 864. In this play one would imagine, that the scene must change at v. 179, (where Trygæus arrives at the gates of heaven mounted on his winged steed), and from thence to v. 829, it lies in heaven: but how the chorus get thither I cannot imagine, as they have no hippo-canthari (or horse-beetles) to carry them to that place.

24   NOTES ON ARISTOPHANES.

OBSERVATION.

Bentley dates the time of the action of this play as
above, Ol. 90. 2. Palmerius dates it a year sooner, Ol. 90.
1.; Sam. Petitus two years earlier, Ol. 89. 3. Archonte
Alcæo; and I cannot but think the last to be in the right.
What the two former chiefly go upon, are these lines :

Οἱ σου τρυχομεθ᾽ ηδη

Τρια και δεκ᾽ ετη—

This, I think, Petitus has answered by saying, that the
poet himself, v. 605, places the beginning of the war
three years higher than the common account, that is,
from the declaration against Megara, Ol. 86. 2. Archonte
Antilochida, which was the first cause of the Peloponnesian war. So that this drama appeared during the
Dionysia, which immediately preceded the truce, (mentioned by Thucydides, L. 5. c. 20) when it was on the
point of being concluded, and before the Spartan
prisoners, taken at Sphacteria, were restored, as the
following lines seem to intimate ;

Αρ᾽ οισθ᾽, ὁσοι γ᾽ αυτων εχονται του ξυλου

Μονοι προθυμοῦντ᾽· αλλ᾽ ὁ χαλκευς ουκ εᾷ :

which the Scholiast rightly explains of these captives,
though Palmerius makes light of their interpretation,
and tries to give the passage quite another sense, understanding the words, εχονται του ξυλου, of the Γεωργοι,
and ὁ χαλκευς of the armourer, who lived by the war ;
not reflecting that the words undoubtedly relate to the
Lacedæmonians, among whom these arts belonged only
to slaves, whose inclinations could have no influence in
determining the state either to war or to peace.   And
besides in the lines 270 and 280, and 311, (Ευλαβεισθ᾽

εκεινον τον Κερβερον, &c.), there could be no manner of humour, if we imagine Brasidas and Cleon to have been dead three years. Whereas Ol. 89. 3. in spring-time, it was but a few months from the battle of Amphipolis, which happened at the end of the summer before. As to that line, 294, Πριν ετερον αυ δοιδυκα, &c. it may as well be understood of Lamachus, Hyperbolus, or any other favourer of the war, as of Alcibiades; or if it be applied to him, what occasion is there to think it is meant of his Στρατηγια in Peloponnesus (Ol. 90. 1)? What is said of the Argives at v. 474, and 492, is only a reproach for the neutrality which they had observed during the war; or their inclinations might well be suspected even at this time, before they had actually formed a new confederacy against Sparta, as it after-wards happened. For what could be more natural, than that a powerful state, which by long peace had been for many years acquiring new strength, while their ancient enemies had been continually weakening themselves by war, should (at a time when their truce with Sparta was on the point of expiring) attempt to form a league by drawing their discontented allies from them, and setting themselves at the head of a new confederacy, which necessarily must kindle a new war in Greece. As to the aversion the Bœotians and Megarensians had to peace (mentioned v. 465 and 480) see Thucydides, L. 5. 17. As to v. 210. Εκεινον πολλακις σπονδας ποιουν-των, it alludes to the Spartan offer of a truce, Ol. 88. 4, which was rejected; and the suspension of arms agreed upon Ol. 89. 1, and ill-observed, the Lacedæmonians continuing their conquests in Thrace.

AVES.

This Comedy was acted Ol. 91. 2. Archonte Chabria in Dionysiis
τοις κατ' αστυ. It was judged the second best; the Com-
astæ of Ameipsias being the first.

THE PLAN [1] OF THE AVES.

Euelpides and Pisthetærus, two ancient Athenians,
thoroughly weary of the folly, injustice, and litigious
temper of their countrymen, determine to leave Attica
for good and all; and having heard much of the fame
of Epops, king of the birds, who was once a man under
the name of Tereus, and had married an Athenian lady,
they pack up a few necessary utensils, and set out for
the court of that prince under the conduct of a jay and
a raven, birds of great distinction in augury, without
whose direction the Greeks never undertook any thing
of consequence.   Their errand is to enquire of the birds,
who are the greatest travellers of any nation, where
they may meet with a quiet easy settlement, far from
all prosecutions, law-suits, and sycophant informers,
to pass the remainder of their lives in peace and
liberty.

[1] Perhaps the reader may be inclined to think with the editor,
that the plan, or detailed argument, of the Aves is drawn up
with such peculiar vivacity, pointed humour, and originality of
manner, as to be a model of its kind.—[MATHIAS.]

Act 1. Sc. 1.

The scene is a wild unfrequented country, which terminates in mountains : there the old men are seen, accompanied by two slaves who carry their little baggage, fatigued and fretting at the carelessness of their guides, who, though they cost them a matter of a groat in the market, are good for nothing but to bite them by the fingers, and lead them out of the way. They travel on however, till they come to the foot of the rocks, which stop up their passage, and put them to their wit's end. Here the raven croaks, and the jay chatters, and looks up into the air, as much as to say, that this is the place : upon which they knock with a stone, and with their heels, (as though it were against a door,) against the side of the mountain.

Act 1. Scene 2.

Trochilus, a bird that waits upon Epops, appears above ; he is frighted at the sight of two men, and they are much more so at the length of his beak and the fierceness of his aspect. He takes them for fowlers ; and they insist upon it, that they are not men, but birds. In their confusion, their guides, whom they held in a string, escape and fly away. Epops, during this, within is asleep, after having dined upon a dish of beetles and berries : their noise wakens him, and he comes out of the grove.

Scene 3.

At the strangeness of his figure they are divided between fear and laughing. They tell him their errand,

and he gives them the choice of several cities fit for
their purpose, one particularly on the coast of the Red
Sea, all which they refuse for many comical reasons.
He tells them the happiness of living among the birds;
they are much pleased with the liberty and simplicity
of it; and Pisthetærus, a shrewd old fellow, proposes a
scheme to improve it, and make them a far more powerful and considerable nation.

Scene 4.

Epops is struck with the project, and calls up his
consort, the nightingale, to summon all his people
together with her voice. They sing a fine ode: the
birds come flying down, at first one by one, and perch
here and there about the scene; and at last the chorus
in a whole body, come hopping, and fluttering, and
twittering in.

Scene 5.

At the sight of the two men, they are in great
tumult, and think that their king has betrayed them
to the enemy. They determine to tear the two old men
to pieces, draw themselves up in battle-array, and are
giving the word to fall on. Euelpides and Pisthetærus,
in all the terrours of death, after upbraiding each the
other for bringing him into such distress, and trying in
vain to escape, assume courage from mere despair, seize
upon the kitchen-furniture which they had brought with
them, and armed with pipkins for helmets, and with
spits for lances, they present a resolute front to the
enemy's phalanx.

Act 1. Scene 6.

On the point of battle Epops interposes, pleads hard
for his two guests, who are, he says, his wife's relations,
and people of wonderful abilities, and well-affected to
their commonwealth. His eloquence has its effect ; the
birds grow less violent, they enter into a truce with the
old men, and both sides lay down their arms. Pistho-
tærus, upon the authority of Æsop's fables, proves to
them the great antiquity of their nation ; that they
were born before the creation of the earth, and before
the gods, and once reigned over all countries, as he
shows from several testimonies and monuments of
different nations : that, the cock wears his tiara erect,
like the Persian king, and that all mankind start out of
their beds at his command ; that, when the kite makes
his first appearance in the spring, every one prostrate
themselves on the ground before it ; that, the Egyptians
and Phœnicians set about their harvest, as soon as the
cuckoo is heard ; that, all kings bear an eagle on their
sceptre, and many of the gods carry a bird on their
head ; that, many great men swear by the goose, &c. &c.
When he has revived in them the memory of their ancient
empire, he laments their present despicable condition,
and the affronts put upon them by mankind. They are
convinced of what he says, applaud his oration, and
desire his advice.

Act 1. Scene 7.

He proposes that they shall unite, and build a city
in the mid-air, whereby all commerce will effectually be
stopped, between heaven and earth : the gods will no
longer be able to visit at ease their Semeles and Alc-

mænas below, nor feast on the fume of sacrifices daily
sent up to them, nor men enjoy the benefit of the
seasons, nor the fruits of the earth, without permission
from those winged deities of the middle region. He
shows how mankind will lose nothing by this change of
government; that the birds may be worshipped at a
far less expense, nothing more than a few berries or a
handful of corn; that they will need no sumptuous
temples; that by their great knowledge of futurity they
will direct their good votaries in all their expeditions,
so as they can never fail of success; that the ravens,
. famed for the length of their lives, may make a present
of a century or two to their worshippers; and besides
the birds will ever be within call, when invoked, and
not sit pouting in the clouds, and keeping their state
so many miles off. The scheme is highly admired, and
the two old men are to be made free of the city, and
each of them is to be adorned with a pair of wings at
the publick charge. Epops invites them to his nest-
royal, and entertains them nobly. The nightingale in
the mean time joins the chorus without, and the Parabasis begins. They sing their own nobility and ancient
grandeur, their prophetick skill, the benefits they do
mankind already, and all the good which they design
them; they descant upon the power of musick, in which
they are such great masters, and intermix many strokes
of satire; they shew the advantages of flying, and apply
it to several whimsical cases; and they invite all such,
as would be free from the heavy tyranny of human
laws, to live among them, where it is no sin to beat
one's father, or to lie with one's mother, &c. &c.

Act 2. Scene 1.

The old men now become birds, and magnificently fledged, after laughing a while at the new and awkward figure they make, consult about the name which they shall give to their rising city, and fix upon that of Nephelococcygia : and while one goes to superintend the workmen, the other prepares to sacrifice for the prosperity of the city, which is growing apace.

Scene 2.

They begin a solemn prayer to all the birds of Olympus, putting the swan in the place of Apollo, the cock in that of Mars, and the ostrich in that of the great mother Cybele, &c.

Scene 3.

A miserable poet, having already heard of the new settlement, comes with some lyrick poetry which he has composed on this great occasion. Pisthetærus knows his errand from his looks, and makes them give him an old coat ; but not contented with that, he begs to have the waistcoat to it, in the elevated style of Pindar ; they comply, and get rid of him.

Scene 4.

The sacrifice is again interrupted by a begging prophet, who brings a cargo of oracles, partly relating to the prosperity of the city of Nephelococcygia, and partly to a new pair of shoes, of which he is in extreme want. Pisthetærus loses patience, and cuffs him and his religious trumpery off the stage.

Scene 5.

Meto, the famous geometrician, comes next and offers a plan, which he has drawn, for the new buildings, with much importance and impertinence: he meets with as bad a reception as the prophet.

Act 2. Scene 6 and 7.

An ambassador, or licensed spy from Athens, arrives, and a legislator with a body of new laws. They are used with abundance of indignity, and go off threatening every body with a prosecution. The sacred rites being so often interrupted, they are forced to remove their altar, and finish them behind the scenes. The chorus rejoice in their own increasing power; and (as about the time of the Dionysia it was usual to make proclamation against the enemies of the republick) they set a price upon the head of a famous poulterer, who has exercised infinite cruelties upon their friends and brethren: then they turn themselves to the judges and spectators, and promise, if this drama obtain the victory, how propitious they will be to them.

Act 3. Scene 1.

Pisthetærus returns, and reports, that the sacrifice appears auspicious to their undertaking: a messenger then enters with an account how quick the works advance, and whimsically describes the employments allotted to the several birds, in different parts of the building.

Scene 2.

Another messenger arrives in a violent hurry, to tell

how somebody from heaven has deceived the vigilance
of the jack-daws, who were upon guard, and passed
through the gates down into the lower air ; but that a
whole squadron of light-winged forces were in pursuit
of this insolent person, and hoped to fetch him back
again. The birds are in great perturbation, and all in
a flutter about it.

Scene 3.

This person proves to be Iris, who in her return is
stopped short, and seized by order of Pisthetærus. He
examines her, where is her passport ? Whether she
had leave from the watch ? What is her business ?
Who she is ? in short, he treats her with great authority.
She tells her name, and that she was sent by Jove with
orders to mankind, that they should keep holiday, and
perform a grand sacrifice : she wonders at their sauci-
ness and madness, and threatens them with all her
father's thunder. The governour of Nephelococcygia
returns it with higher menaces, and with language very
indecent indeed for a goddess and a maid to hear :
however, with much-ado, she carries off her virginity
safe, but in a terrible passion.

Act 3. Scene 4.

The herald, who had been dispatched to the lower
world, returns with an account that all Athens was
gone bird-mad ; that it was grown a fashion to imitate
them in their names and manners ; and that shortly
they might expect to see a whole convoy arrive, in
order to settle among them. The chorus run to fetch

a vast cargo of feathers and wings to equip their new citizens, when they come.

Scene 5.

The first, who appears, is a profligate young fellow, who hopes to enjoy a liberty, which he could not enjoy so well at home, the liberty of beating his father. Pisthetærus allows it indeed to be the custom of his people ; but at the same time informs him of an ancient law preserved among the storks, that they shall maintain their parents in their old age.   This is not at all agreeable to the youth : however in consideration of his affection for the Nephelococcygians, Pisthetærus furnishes him with a feather for his helmet, and a cock's spur for a weapon, and advises him, as he seems to be of a very military turn, to go into the army in Thrace.

Scene 6.

The next is Cinesias, the dithyrambick writer, who is delighted with the thought of living among the clouds, amidst those airy regions, whence all his poetical flights are derived ; but Pisthetærus will have no such animal among his birds : he drives him back to Athens with great contempt.

Act 3. Scene 7.

He then drives away also (but not without a severe whipping) an informer, who, for the better dispatch of business, and to avoid highwaymen and bad roads, comes to beg a pair of wings to carry him round the islands and cities subject to Athens, whose inhabitants he is used to swear against for an honest livelihood, as did, he says, his fathers before him. The birds, in the ensuing chorus, relate their travels, and describe the strange things and strange men they have seen in them.

Act 4. Scene 1.

A person in disguise, with all the appearance of caution and fear, comes to enquire for Pisthetærus, to whom he discovers himself to be Prometheus, and tells him (but first he makes them hold a large umbrella over his head for fear Jupiter should spy him) that the gods are all in a starving miserable condition : and, what is worse, that the barbarian gods (who live no one knows where, in a part of heaven far beyond the gods of Greece) threaten to make war upon them, unless they will open the ports, and renew the intercourse between mankind and them, as of old. He advises Pisthetærus to make the most of this intelligence, and to reject all offers boldly, which Jupiter may make him, unless he will consent to restore to the birds their ancient power, and give him in marriage his favourite attendant, Basilêa.[1] This said, he slips back again to heaven, as he came. The chorus continue an account of their travels.

Act 4. Scene 2.

An embassy arrives from heaven consisting of Hercules, Neptune, and a certain Triballian god. As they approach the city walls, Neptune is dressing and scold-

---

[1] *i.e.* Sovereignty.

ing at the outlandish divinity, and teaching him how
to carry himself a little decently. They find Pisthetærus busy in giving orders about a dish of wild
fowl (i.e. of birds which had been guilty of high mis-
demeanours, and condemned to die by the publick)
which are dressing for his dinner. Hercules, who before
was for wringing off the head of this audacious mortal
without farther conference, finds himself insensibly
relent, as he snuffs the savoury steam. He salutes
Pisthetærus, who receives them very coldly, and is
more attentive to his kitchen than to their compliment;
Neptune opens his commission; owns that his nation
(the gods) are not the better for this war, and on
reasonable terms would be glad of a peace. Pisthetærus, according to the advice of Prometheus, proposes
(as if to try them) the first condition, namely, that of
Jupiter's restoring to the birds their ancient power;
and, if this should be agreed to, he says, that he hopes
to entertain my lords the ambassadors at dinner. Hercules, pleased with this last compliment, so agreeable
to his appetite, comes readily into all he asks; but is
severely reproved by Neptune for his gluttony. Pisthetærus argues the point, and shews how much it would
be for the mutual interests of both nations; and
Neptune is hungry enough to be glad of some reasonable pretence to give the thing up. The Triballian
god is asked his opinion for form: he mutters somewhat, which nobody understands, and so it passes for
his consent. Here they are going in to dinner, and all is
well; when Pisthetærus bethinks himself of the match
with Basilèa. This makes Neptune fly out again: he

will not hear of it ; he will return home instantly ; but
Hercules cannot think of leaving a good meal so ; he
is ready to acquiesce in any conditions. His colleague
attempts to shew him that he is giving up his patrimony for a dinner ; and what will become of him after
Jupiter's death, if the birds are to have everything
during his life-time. Pisthetærus clearly proves to Hercules that this is a mere imposition ; that by the laws
of Solon a bastard has no inheritance ; that if Jove
died without legitimate issue, his brothers would succeed to his estate, and that Neptuno speaks only out
of interest. Now the Triballian god is again to determine the matter ; they interpret his jargon as favourable to them ; so Neptune is forced to give up the
point, and Pisthetærus goes with him and the barbarian
to heaven to fetch his bride, while Hercules stays
behind to take care that the roast meat is not spoiled.

Act 5. Scene the first and last.

A messenger returns with the news of the approach
of Pisthetærus and his bride ; and accordingly they
appear in the air in a splendid machine, he with Jove's
thunderbolt in his hand, and by his side Basilèa magnificently adorned : the birds break out into loud songs of
exultation as they descend, and conclude the drama with
their Hymenæal.

The end of the Plan of the Aves.

NOTES ON THE AVES.

103. The birds of the drama had only the head, wings, and beak of the fowl which they represented.

115. Why is Tereus said to have been in debt?

126. This is the Aristocrates, who afterwards was one of the four hundred, mentioned by Thucydides, L. 8. 89, and by Lysias in his oration against Eratosthenes.

v. 31. Acestor, called Sacas, a tragick poet, pretended to be a citizen of Athens.

151. Melanthius, the poet, had a leprosy.

180. Πολος. This word was used at this time for the whole heavens. Χαος, the void space of air. (v. 1218.)

223. Αυλει τις. These words are not in the drama, but are a Παρεπιγραφη, a direction written on the side to signify, that an air is played on the flute, in imitation of the nightingale.

276. The second Tyro of Sophocles. Philocles called Halmion, the son of Philopeithes, and a sister of Æschylus, wrote comedy. Philocles, the tragick poet, was the son of Astydamus, the son of Morsimus, the son of the former Philocles. Another of the same name and profession, his contemporary.

285. Callias, his luxury and poverty noted. Palmerius here gives a genealogy of the family.

293. Schol. The Διαυλος was to run twice the length of the Stadium ; the Δολιχος, seven times.

298. Here the twenty-four persons, who form the comick chorus, are all enumerated, as they enter under the form of as many birds. They are, as follow: a partridge, a godwit, a guinea-hen, a male and female halcyon, an owl, a woodpecker, a turtle, a tit-lark, a pigeon, a hawk, a stock-dove, a cuckow, a dive-dapper, and ten more, of which I know not the English names ; an Ελεας, an Ὑποθυμις, a Νερτος, an Ερυθροπους, a Κεβληπυρις, a Φηνη, an Αμπελις, a Πορφυρις, a Δριοψ, and Κερχνῆς. There are also several mute personages, perched here and there to adorn the scene ; a flamingo, a Median bird, (perhaps a kind of pheasant), though it appears that this bird, under the name of Φασιανικος from v. 68, was known at that time, a hoopee, a Κατωφαγας.

437. Schol. The Andromache and the Phœnissæ of Euripides were not acted till after the Aves.

471. Silly fable of Æsop. 485. The cock, called the Persian bird.

494. The festival was on the tenth day after the child's birth, at which time they named it. See v. 924.

501. The custom of rolling on the ground, when they first saw a kite in the spring-time. In Egypt, and in Phœnicia, they began their harvest as soon as the cuckow is heard.

510. The figure of a bird was placed on the top of royal sceptres (Schol. on v. 1354.) the Scholiasts say, an eagle. The statues of Minerva were with an owl,

those of Jupiter with an eagle, of Apollo with a hawk on their heads, &c.

519. In sacrifices they first laid the inwards of the victim upon the hands of the deity, and then eat them.

521. The Nemesis of Cratinus was written long after this play.

653. The fable of Archilochus, attributed, like all other such fables, to Æsop.

670. Progne (for it was she, not Philomel, according to our poet, who was transformed to a nightingale) was represented by some famous Αυλητρις of those times, who accompanied the chorus with her flute.

716. Χλαινα, a winter garment. Ληδος or Ληδαριον, one for the summer. .

750. Phrynichus, the tragick poet, was said to borrow his musick from the nightingale.

760. They used artificial spurs for fighting-cocks, as now, called Πληκτρα. (Schol. on v. 1365.)

780. Hence I should imagine that these spectacles were exhibited in the forenoon. There was a place in the theatre assigned to the senate, called Το Βουλευτικον, and another to the youth under age, named Εφηβικον.

800. The myrmidons of Æschylus. 808. The eagle and arrow from Æschylus, who calls it a Lybian fable.

843. Schol. The Palamedes of Euripides was acted a little before this, which joined to Ælian's testimony, Var. Hist. Lib. 2. 8, proves the falseness of that story concerning the application of some lines in that drama to the death of Socrates, which did not happen till sixteen years after. This passage in the Scholiast

AVES.   41

supports Ælian, and makes the emendation of S. Petitus
(ad Thesmophoruzas) of no account.

880. Alludes to the custom at Athens of praying
jointly for their own state and that of Chios.

920. The style of the dithyrambick poets, Simonides
and Pindar, &c., laughed at.

934. Σπολας, an upper garment made of skins.

942. In the fragment of Pindar, for Στρατων, read
Στρατος ; after ακλεης εβα, something is wanting.

967. Ουδεν οιον εστι, means here, nothing hinders.

995. Meto, the geometrician, ridiculed.

1023. Επισκοποι, a sort of deputies sent from Athens
to inspect the allied cities, like the Spartan Ἁρμοσται,
as the Scholiast says.

1025. Φαυλον βιβλιον Τελεου. The Scholiast says
nothing upon this, nor any one else. Teleas, a bad
author.

1036. Εαν ὁ Νεφελοκοκκυγιεις, &c. This is the
beginning of a new law made on the occasion.

1073. I should imagine that the proclamation against
Diagoras was made this very year during the Dionysia.
(See Andocides de Mysteriis, p. 13), or that perhaps
might be the time, when such proclamations against the
publick enemies were made during these assemblies.

1114. Μηνισκοι. These were plates of brass with
which they shaded the heads of statues to guard them
from the weather and the birds.

1149. Ὑπαγωγευς. The name of a trowel, or some
such instrument, but of a forked form, I imagine, like
a swallow's tail. Ὡσπερ παιδια alludes to some children's
play.

1157. I read, Πελεκωντων, instead of Πελεκαντων.

1200. The part of Iris, played by some courtezan, which is not, as in the Irene and others, a mute personage.

1282. Εσωκρατουν. It seems, that it was now a sort of fashion in Athens, to imitate Socrates in his dress and manner, and to talk philosophy.

1294. This cannot relate (as Palmerius, deceived by the pseudo-Plutarch who wrote the life of Lycurgus, imagines) to that orator, who probably was not born at the time when this comedy was written. 1296. Chœrepho, called Νυκτερις.

1338. A parody of the Œnomaus of Sophocles.
1374. Cynesias, a bad dithyrambick writer, called Φιλυρινος, and why: he was lame. Parody of Alcæus and Simonides.

1485-93. Schol. The heroes who are supposed to walk in the night, and strike with blindness, or with some other mischief, any who met them. The persons, who past by their fanes, always kept silence.

1493. Τα επιδεξια. The nobler parts, the head and the eyes.

1508. Σκιαδιον, an umbrella, used by the Κανηφοροι, to keep off the sun in processions.

1655. The law by which a father could not give his natural son by will more than five minæ.

1675. Disputes between plenipotentiaries, determined by the majority.

1728. Alludes to the Troades of Euripides.

1762. The hymn of Archilochus to Herculcs Callinicus.

THESMOPHORIAZUSÆ.

Acted Ol. 92. 1. Archon: Callia. V. Palmerium. What
Petitus says here, is all wrong.

3. Τον σπλῆνα κομιδῆ μ' ἐκβαλειν, I imagine he
means with coughing; for it is a cold winter's
morning.

109. It cannot be the Chorus who accompany Agatho
in his hymn here; if it were, they must hear all the
distress of Euripides, and see Mnesilochus dressed up
to deceive themselves. Therefore, it must be some of
Agatho's admirers, like himself, dressed up in female
habits; or it may be a chorus whom he is instructing
to perform in some tragedy of his own; or perhaps, the
Muses who (as the servant says, v. 40) are come to make
a visit to his master.

Agatho, the tragick poet, is derided for his effeminacy
and affectation. Euripides, his abuse of women.

142. The Lycurgïa of Æschylus parodied.

175. Philocles, Xenocles, Theognis, the dramatick
poets, ridiculed.

201. The Alcestis of Euripides parodied. He is *said*
to have preached up atheism in his tragedies.

260. Κροκωτος, a woman's vest, or under-garment,
which they girt with the Στροφιον under their breast.
(So in Catullus, "et tereti *Strophio* luctantes vincta

papillas.") On their head they wore the Κεκρυφαλος,
bound about with a Μιτρα or broad fillet. On some
occasions they used a Κεφαλη περιθετος, or Φενακη, (see
Plutus, Schol. on v. 271.) like a *tower* (tot compagibus
altum œdificat caput, Juv. Sat. 6. v. 501.) or a peruke
with the head-dress fastened on it. Over their vest
they threw the Εγκυκλος, a broad flowing robe. In v.
270, Χαλαρα γουν χαιρεις φορων; is said by Mnesilochus:
Agatho answers in the next line; Συ τουτο, &c.

554. The Melanippe and Hippolytus of Euripides:
his Palamedes represented as writing on the fragments
of oars, and throwing them into the sea.

654. Ισθμον τιν' εχεις. Kusterus is mistaken here:
there are instances, in Thucydides and elsewhere, of
ships drawn by land over the isthmus of Corinth.

811. Ναυσιμαχης μεν—and 815. Αλλ' Ευβουλης.
The explanation which Palmerius gives of these two
passages from history is very good and ingenious.
Aristomache and Stratonice are, as I fancy, the names
of two famous courtezans.

818. Ζευγει ες πολιν—ελθοι. To whom does this
relate? The Cleophon (V. Isocrat. de Pace, 174.) here
mentioned, and in the Ranæ, was put to death Ol. 93.
4. during the siege of Athens by the party who had a
mind to settle an oligarchy there. See his history in
Lysias, Orat. in Agoratum, p. 234. and Orat. in Nico-
machum, p. 476.

847. Lamachus was slain in Sicily about two years
before this, and Hyperbolus was murdered at Samos in
this very year.

855. That tragedy bad and insipid. Parody of the

Helena, and of the Andromeda.   Echo introduced into
it answering to the lamentations of Andromeda.

883. Proteas, the son of Epicles, is twice mentioned
by Thucydides, as Στρατηγος commanding at sea,
particularly Ol. 87. 2. : and he died, as it appears here,
about Ol. 89. 3.

1069. The Andromeda of Euripides was played the
year before this.

LYSISTRATA.

v. 2. The feasts of Pan, of Venus Colias, and of Genetyllis, celebrated by the women with tympana, &c., like the Bacchanalian ceremonies.

58. Ουδε Παραλων, ουδ' εκ Σαλαμῖνος. This alludes to the two ships so called, which were the fleetest sailors of all the Athenian navy.

64. Τα 'κατιον. qu. Τούκατειον? i.e. το 'Εκατειον. The statue of Hecate, which was consulted by some persons about the success of any undertaking.

109. Ολισβος.   A Milesian manufacture of leather.

150. Linen tunicks of Amorgos, transparent.

174. The thousand talents in the Acropolis, called το Λβυσσον.

229. Τα Περσικα.   Persian slippers, worn by the Athenian women.

The double chorus in this play is remarkable, one of old men, the other of women.

598. Αλλ' οστις εστι, &c. ˙ There seems to be something wanting here.

633. Και φορησω το ξιφος.   This alludes to the Scolion of Harmodius and Aristogeiton.   Εν μυρτου κλαδι το ξιφος φορησω, &c., preserved by Athenæus, L. 15. p. 695.   .

643. ʹΗρριφορουν. A double meaning, quasi dixisset, αρρενοφόρειν. ʹΑλετρις also.

678. ʹΙππικωτατον γαρ, &c. This alludes to what they called Κελητιζειν.

736. Αμοργις, ἡ λινοκαλαμη, a fine kind of flax, ὑπερ την βισσον, η την καρπασον. σχ.

760. Οφις οικουρος, The serpent which lived in Minerva's temple. Owls also roosted there.

801. Την λοχμην. It appears that men wore no drawers or breeches under their tunick.

981. Conisalus, a deity of Athens, like Priapus.

1043. It is remarkable, that no one is abused by name here, except a very few infamous and low people. Pisander indeed is mentioned ; so that this drama must have been either before or after the oligarchy of the Four Hundred.

1150. Αφατος και καλος. Perhaps this should be, Αφατον, ὡς καλος : I do not understand this, as Palmerius does. They excuse themselves upon the great beauty of Attica, which would tempt any man to enjoy it. The next verse, ʹΥμας δʹ αφησειν, &c., no body explains.

1171. Τον Εχινουντα, και τον Μηλιᾶ κολπον. These places are named for the sake of the double meaning. The Scholiasts ad Vespas tell us, that Εχῖνος is used for the belly of an ox : Μῆλον for any round protuberance, like the breasts, or hinder parts of a woman.

1191. All this is very obscure, like the chorus, 1042, and upon the same subject. During this short interval the Spartans and Athenian plenipotentiaries have been entertained by Lysistrata. It is the chorus of women, and not she, who say all this from v. 1191 to 1218. Who the servant is chasing away, I do not perceive, unless it be the crowd of people who come to receive corn at the door.

The chorus in the end, and in several scenes of the play, are remarkable examples of the true Spartan Dorick.

RANÆ.

Ol. 93. 3. In Lenæis, Mense Posidæone.   Archonte Callia
post Antigenem.

Spanheim, in his introduction to his notes, has
shewn, contrary to what Palmerius, Petitus, and others
imagined, that there were comedies, as well as tragedies,
performed four times in the year in the Panathenæa,
the Lenæa, the Dionysia κατ' αστυ, and the Anthesteria : that during this last festival they were exhibited
in the Piræcus, in the theatre built there ; and that the
Lenæa were kept as well in the city, as in the country,
in a place called the Lenæum.

v. 14. Phrynichus, Ameipsias, and Lycis, comick
writers, are here satirized for their low and common-
place jokes.

48. Clisthenes, the son of Symbirtius, if not Στρατηγος, as the Scholiasts say, at Arginusæ, was at least
a Trierarch.

53. The Andromeda of Euripides.   That poet was
lately dead.

73. Iophon, the son of Sophocles and Nicostrata,
wrote tragedy with applause in his father's life-time ;
he was suspected of exhibiting his father's dramas
in his own name.   The Œneus of Euripides parodied.
Sophocles was dead not long since.   The simplicity

VOL. IV.   E

and easiness of his nature opposed to the cunning of
Euripides. Agatho was now at the court of Archelaus.

79. It is plain, that Sophocles was just dead, and
that Iophon, his son, had not yet published anything
since his death.

86. Xenocles, the son of Carcinus, and Pythangelus,
tragick writers, are mentioned with contempt. That
kind of poets were then very numerous at Athens.
The Alcmena of Euripides, and his Alexandra, and
Hippolytus, also the Melanippe of Sophocles are
alluded to.

104. Read ὡς καὶ μοι δοκει, instead of σοι.

126. This is the usual effect of the cicuta, as Plato
describes it in his Phædo.

131. The three Λαμπαδηδρομιαι celebrated in the
Ceramicus, to Minerva, to Vulcan, and to Prometheus.

141. It is sure from the Vespæ, and from other
plays, that in Cleon's time the Μισθος δικαστικος was
three oboli: probably after his death, or when the
republick began to decline, it might be again reduced
to two oboli.

193. Περι των κρεῶν. The Scholia and the Commentators make out nothing here to one's satisfaction.

233. Schol. The strings of the lyre were made of
the sinews of animals, and more anciently, as now, of
their intestines; whence they were called Χορδαι.

235. Ὑπολυριον. The bridge or some part of the
lyre, made of a reed, afterwards of horn, as it seems.
It is remarkable that the chorus of frogs does not
appear, but is heard only, and that in a single scene,
though the play takes its name from them. The true

chorus of the drama consists of the ghosts of the initiated, the Μυσται, and enters not before v. 319.

295. A description of the phantom, called Empusa.

305. Hegelochus was an actor in the Orestes of
Euripides. From this story of him, it should seem,
that in pronouncing words joined by a synalæpha, they
did not use totally to drop the vowel in the end of the
first, but liquefied it, as it were, into the following.
Otherwise, I do not conceive what difference there
could be between the sound of γαληνʹ ὁρῶ, and γαλῆν
ὁρῶ.

323. The profanation of the mysteries by Diagoras.

369. Alluding to Cynesias, the dithyrambick writer.

370. Η τους μισθους των ποιητων, &c. seems to mean
some attempt made by an orator (the Schol. on v. 103.
of the Ecclesiasuzæ, say Archinus) to reduce the expense
of the Choregi by limiting the sum they gave to their
poets : and the two distinct persons (as Aristotle says
in the Schol. 406.) under this Archon, were ordered to
furnish the tragick and the comick chorus, which before
were at the expense of one. This drama then was
played a little before that order ; and as the publick
had suffered greatly by the war the chorusses were but
poorly furnished out. From v. 412, it appears that
the chorus consisted of both sexes.

431. The Callias, who was now Archon, could not
be the son of Hipponicus, as he is here ridiculed by
name ; unless the change of his father's name into
Hippobinus might save the poet from the law. (See
also v. 504.)

475. Alludes to the Theseus of Euripides.

478. Ταρτησια, παρ ὑπονοιαν for Ταρταρια. Μυραινα is to be understood, as some dæmon very dismal, derived from Μυρεσθαι; at the same time to raise laughter; the obvious meaning being nothing, but lampreys caught and salted on the Spanish coast, and imported by the Phœnicians perhaps into Greece.

490. These two uses of a sponge are easily comprehended from the Scholia.

504. The temple of Hercules Αλεξικακος at Melite, a Δημος of Attica. Initiated there in the lesser mysteries—founded during the plague. Statue by Ageladas the Argive, the scholar of Phidias. Callias had a house at Melite.

511. A manner of civilly refusing a thing : Επαινω. καλλιστα. πανυ καλως.

546. See the history of Theramenes. Schol.

631. The horrid manner of torturing slaves, viz. Εν κλιμακι δησας, binding them down with their back on a pair of stairs, as it seems, or on a ladder; hanging them up by the arms; scourging them with the ὑστριξ, a whip made of leather with the bristles on it; stretching them on the wheel; pouring vinegar up the nostrils; pressing, by laying a weight of bricks on them, &c. &c. ! ! !

674. The iambicks of Ananias. The Laocoon of Sophocles. The Antæus of Phrynichus.

700. The poet's advice, given in this place, was actually followed the year after this, when, upon the battle of Ægos-Potami, and the siege of Athens, a decree was made upon the motion of Patroclides (still preserved in the oration of Andocides de Mysteriis), to

restore the Ατιμοι to all the privileges from which they had been degraded. It seems from what he says, v. 701, that when the government of the Four Hundred was destroyed, many had been thus degraded for having a hand in those transactions.

730. The Athenian gold coin had been debased the year before this. Copper was first coined this very year, and again cried down thirteen years afterwards.

775. This may probably enough be borrowed from the Athenian customs, namely, that the principal artist in each kind, should have a maintenance in the Prytanèum, and be seated εν Θρονω, in a chair of distinction on some occasions.

800. The modesty and candour of Sophocles, and the envious and contentious nature of Euripides.

803. Νυνι δ' εμελλεν, I take to be a solecism, used by Clidemides, or some bad orator or poet.

913. The Scholia here seem to say, that there were dramas played during the celebration of the Eleusinea; and above, v. 357, they tell us, that the scene of this play lay at Eleusis. (v. 395.) Quære, Whether any rites in honour of Ceres were joined with those of Bacchus during the Lenæa?

961. The Median hangings were wrought with grotesque and monstrous animals.

1079. 'Ως τε γε καυτον σε κατ' συνεβαλε. It should seem that love was the cause of the death of Euripides, and one would think, from the expression and from the Scholia, that his wife had not only been false to him, but that she destroyed him.

1106. Τω θαλαμακι. This seems to prove, that the

three orders of rowers were placed directly over one
another.

1100 and 1145. Reading and the arts of speaking
were more universal among all orders of people than in
these times; which the poet satirizes, as corrupting
and enervating the minds of men, and especially of the
younger sort; and he attributes it to the philosophers,
to the sophists, and to the tragick writers, particularly
Euripides.

1209. Στοιβη, a botch-word inserted only to fill up:
literally, the stuffing of a mattrass.

1231. Ληκυθιον. I have no clear idea of this
Ληκυθιον, on which so much of this scene turns; nor
of the Ιηκοπον ου πελαθεις επ᾽ αρωγαν which answers
to it, or the Φλαττοθρατ, which two last seem to relate
to the musick and the rhythm introduced by Æschylus
in his chorusses, and not to the sense of the verses.

1349. Ει—ει—ειλισσετε. This shews that in the
ancient musick they dwelt not on words alone, and
repeated them, as we do, but also on syllables; or,
does it only express the lengthening out of the vowels?

1580. It is here said, from Aristotle, that Cleophon,
after the battle of Arginusæ, in the archonship of
Callias, came into the assembly drunk and in armour,
and rejected the peace, then offered by Lacedæmon.
But Lysias (in his oration contra Agoratum) tells us
that this happened not till the following year after
the battle of Ægos-Potami, when the siege of Athens
was actually formed. I cannot but believe the latter,
as a contemporary author.

ECCLESIAZUSÆ.

See Palmerius.

v. 2. Καλλιστ' εν ευσκοποιισιν εξειρημενον. So I should read, rather than εξητημενον, of which I do not see the sense, and understand with the Scholiasts, "Thou noblest invention of wise artists." For though this expression be somewhat obscure, it is far prefer-able to Tanaquil Faber's emendation, εν ειυκοτοισιν εξητημενον, which is neither sense nor Greek.

14. Στοα, all repositories of corn were so called.

22. Ἀς Σφυρομαχος ποτ' ειπεν, &c. The allusion in these lines is too obscure at this distance of time. The Scholiasts say that it relates to a decree assigning the courtezans and the women of reputation a different place at some public spectacles (qu. whether in the theatre, as Faber says?); but the verses do not express any such matter.

63. It was the custom of the men to anoint the whole body with oil, and dry it in before the sun, and of the women to shave themselves all over.

v. 74. Λακωνικαι, was the name for the usual chaus-sure of the men, and Περσικαι, that of the women.

102. Agyrrius, the Στρατηγος, at Lemnos, re-trenched the expense of the Choregi to their poets, and appointed the sum to be given to the people at

their assemblies.   (v. 184, 284, 292, 302, 380, and Plutus, v. 330.)

128. Γαλῆ, a weasel, carried round the place of publick assemblies, ὡς καθαρσιον τι.   They came to their Εκκλησιαι with a staff (Βακτηρια) in their hands.

156. The oath peculiar to women, Μα τω Θεω, i.e. Ceres and Proserpina.

193. Το συμμαχικον.   Petitus from this passage and from a necessary emendation he makes in the Scholia here, seems to fix rightly the time of this drama to Ol. 96. 4. Archonte Demostrato.

203. What particular fact is here meant, one cannot say at present; but Faber is mistaken in thinking that it cannot be the famous Thrasybulus, for it appears (from Lysias's Apology for Mantheus, p. 307), that he was living, and present in the action before Corinth this very year; his death did not happen till three years after.   In spite of all his invaluable services to the publick, the orators and comick writers of those times did not cease to make very free with his character.   (See v. 356 of this drama.)   There is a remarkable passage of this kind in the oration of Lysias in Ergoclem, p. 456 and 7, which I take to relate to this very Thrasybulus, and to be spoken a little while after his death.

256. Ὑποκρονειν, I imagine, signifies, to stamp with their feet, a noise made in great assemblies to express their dislike.   See Acharnens. v. 38.   Sometimes it was done merely for the purpose of interrupting.   See v. 592 of this play.

318. The Ἡμιδιπλοιδιον and Κροκωτος seem to be

both the same, namely, a woman's vest, or under-garment of a light red colour. Κοθορνος and Περσικη are the same, a woman's proper chaussure.

531. Here the Κροκωτος is called by the name of ἱματιον.

534. Επιθεισα ληκυθον. On a dead body.

568. If this scheme be meant as a satire on Plato's Republick, that work must have been written when the philosopher was not thirty-six years of age.

974. Alludes to the manner of introducing causes into the courts of justice, according to the age of the plaintiffs; first those (as I imagine) above sixty years of age, and so downwards. After which, if there were several, they cast lots whose should be heard first.

1017. A woman could not deal, of her own authority, with any person for more than the value of a medimnus of corn.

1023. The manner of laying out the dead.

1081. The decree of Cannonus is mentioned by Xenophon in his Greek History, L. 1. as ascertaining the punishment of persons accused of crimes against the publick, and allowing the means of making their defence. It is probable that, in some paragraph of that *psephisma*, it was ordered that the prisoner should appear on that occasion, holden between two of the Τοξοται, or perhaps of the Ἑνδεκα.

1124. The number of citizens was now above thirty thousand.

PLUTUS.

The Plutus was first played Ol. 92. 4. and it was altered and revived Ol. 97. 4. The drama, which we now have, is compounded of both these.

Act 1. Scene 1. The prologue between Chremylus and Cario, as far as v. 58. Sc. 2. Cario goes out and returns at v. 229.

Act 2. Sc. 1. Cario returns with the chorus of old countrymen at v. 253. Sc. 2. Chremylus re-enters and salutes the chorus v. 322. Sc. 3. Conversation with Blepsidemus. Sc. 4. Poverty rushes out of Chremylus's house, and disputes with the two old men : they drive her away, and prepare to carry Plutus to the temple of Æsculapius. Here should be the Parabasis, but there is none. The chorus remain silent on the stage for a time; till

Act 3. Sc. 1. Cario returns with the news of the cure of Plutus. This interval is supposed to be a whole night. Sc. 2. Cario recounts the matter to Chremylus's wife. Sc. 3. Plutus, being now restored to sight, returns home with Chremylus. Here also is a short interval; till

Act 4. Sc. 1. Cario comes out, and describes the change which had happened on the entrance of Plutus.

Sc. 2. The honest old man comes to pay his vows to the god. Sc. 3. A sycophant comes to complain of his sudden poverty. Sc. 4. A wanton old woman enters, who has lost her love : she appears, returning from a drunken frolick. Here all, but the chorus, enter Chremylus's house.

Act 5. Sc. 1. Mercury comes begging to the gate; Cario at last takes him into his service. Sc. 2. The priest of Jupiter comes for charity. Sc. 3. The procession conducts Plutus to the Acropolis.

NOTES ON THE PLUTUS.

v. 179. Ἐρᾷ δὲ Λαΐς, &c. It is probable enough, as Athenæus shews from an oration of Lysias, L. 13. p. 586, that this should be read Ναΐς: but the Scholiast attempts to shew that the time would not permit it to be Λαΐς, as she was only seven years of age, when Chabrias was Archon; and consequently under Diocles, Ol. 92. 4, she could be but thirteen or fourteen. This I take to be the meaning of the Scholiast, though the words, as they are now read, seem to say, that from Chabrias to Diocles was a space of fourteen years, whereas it was but six in reality; and the Scholiast adds, that at this age she could not be much in vogue. If the author of this note knew, that the verse was in the Plutus, when it was first acted, he is in the right, and confirms the emendation of Athenæus; but if (see v. 303) it were only in the second Plutus, Lais was then thirty-three years old, and might be still in admiration. The Scholiast says, Epimandra, Timandra, or Damasandra, the mother of the younger Lais, as Athenæus calls her, L. 13, p. 574, supposing her to have this daughter at fourteen years of age, must be twenty-one, when Hyccara was taken by Nicias, and consequently was thirty-two, at the time of Alcibiades's death, whose mistress she was, as Plutarch and Athenæus relate. I should understand the Scholiasts here of the mother, not of the daughter, though they are confused and erroneous.

180. Timotheus was now making his appearance in the world, Conon his father being yet alive. What building of his is alluded to here, one cannot say, or whether it relate to him at all. The fact is obscure, the expression broken, and the Scholiast trifling.

253. The Scholia here explain all the marks used by the grammarians in dramas with their names.

268. Ὡ χρισον, &c. This is ironical, and not as the Scholia interpret it.

278. It suffices to know that such Athenians, as were appointed judges, drew lots (see v. 973, and Ecclesiaz. v. 677.) in which of the courts they were to sit, and that at their entrance the Κηρυξ, or crier of each court, by order of the presiding magistrate, delivered to every one a Συμβολον and, upon his carrying it to the Πρυτανις in waiting, he received his daily pay, Μισθος δικαστικος. This was done, as I imagine, every morning to prevent corruption in the judges, who did not know, till then, in what court or cause they were to give sentence. The other ceremony mentioned in the Scholia was only annual, when the tribes assembled, and each drew lots by itself for a certain number who were to sit as judges that year. There is much confusion in these Scholia, collected out of very different authors. Potter does not allow this to have been the practice in the best times, at least not in the greater courts, where the judges were fixed and certain after their first election ; in the lesser, he says, it might have

been. The passage, however, from Aristotle's polity of
Athens is to be observed.

278. Schol. The key-stone of the entrance into each
particular court was painted of a certain colour. The
judge, having received his staff, went to that court
which was distinguished by the same colour with his
staff, and marked with the same letter which was inscribed on the head of it (ὅπερ ἐν τῇ βαλάνῳ) and at
his entrance he received from the presiding magistrate
a Σύμβολον, as above. I doubt of what the Scholia
say, that there were as many courts as tribes; and that
the tribes at first drew lots, in which court each should
judge, and the tribules drew among themselves who
should be judges, and who not.

290. Philoxenus, the dithyrambick: his Galatea
parodied. The origin of that piece in the Scholia,
which appears to have been a drama.

330. The Scholia, and Kuster, and Spanheim too,
confound the Μισθός δικαστικος with the Εκκλησιασ-
τικος: the words are to be understood of the latter.

385. The picture of the Heraclidæ by Pamphilus
the painter, the master of Apelles.

408. The publick salary to physicians was no longer
in use.

596. The suppers of Hecate were distributed
monthly, every new moon, to the poor by every rich
housekeeper.

601. The Phænissæ of Euripides parodied.

663. The ceremonial of sleeping in the temple of
Æsculapius.

690. The serpents, Οφεις παρειαι, which frequented

it, as they did the temple of Minerva (Lysistr. v. 760)
and those of Bacchus (see Schol. v. 690 and 733 Plut.),
and of Trophonius. See Pausanias in Epidauro et
Lebadea.

701. Iaso and Panacea, the attendants and daughters
of Æsculapius by Lampetia.

725. Επωμοσια. The Scholia do not well explain
this, but confound it with 'Υπωμοσια, and cite a passage
from Hyperides, wherein this latter word is used.

768. Καταχυσματα, nuts, figs, almonds, dates, &c.,
which they strewed on the head of a new-bought slave,
when they had first seated him on the hearth of the
house into which he entered, and which his fellow-
servants picked up and eat.

796. Φορτος, impertinence, tiresome absurdity. The
art in use with the comick writers to win the common
people by throwing nuts and dried fruits among them.

820. Τριττυς; a sacrifice of a hog, a ram, and a he-
goat. Εντελης θυσια. See Schol.

885. Rings, worn as amulets, or preservatives from
fascination, bites of venomous creatures, &c. Δακ-
τυλιοι φαρμακιται φυσικοι

905. Merchants were exempt from the Εισφορα, or
extraordinary taxation.

984. A man's pallium (ἱματιον) cost twenty drachmæ;
his shoes, cost eight.

1127. The fourth day of every month was sacred to
Mercury, the first and seventh, to Apollo, the eighth
to Theseus. Libations to most gods were made with
pure wine; to Mercury with wine and water equally
mixed.

1195. Schol. The Ποταμοι of Stratis[1] were published before the Ecclesiazusæ or the Plutus of Aristophanes : I read the last lines here cited,

$$\text{Μη λαβοντες λαμπαδας,}$$
$$\text{Μηδ' αλλο μηδεν εχομενοι Φιλυλλιου·}$$

instead of εχομενον. Philyllius is often cited by
Athenæus, and hence he appears to have lived contemporary with Stratis.

[1] In the Scholiast we read the name uniformly written
Στρατις, and in Athenæus Στραττις.—[MATHIAS.]

NOTES ON PLATO

F

[Published by Mathias in 1814 from a MS. in Gray's handwriting, in the possession of Richard Stonehewer, and never
since reprinted.   The notes are by Gray.—ED.]

BRIEF NOTICES OF SOCRATES AND
OF HIS FRIENDS.

SOCRATES.

ALL which Socrates possessed was not worth three minæ, in which he reckons a house he had in the city.[1] Critobulus often prevailed upon him to accompany him to the comedy.[2] Xantippe, his wife, the most ill-tempered of women : he made use of her to exercise his philosophy.[3] He amused himself by dancing when he was fifty years old : his face remarkably ugly, and resembling that of the Sileni or satyrs, with large prominent eyes, a short flat nose turned up, wide nostrils, great mouth, &c. nicknamed ὁ Φροντιστής.[4] He rarely went out of the walls of Athens ;[5] was never out of Attica, but when he served in time of war, and once to the Isthmian games.[6] He was seventy years old, when he died.[7] He left three sons, the eldest a youth, the two youngest children. His intrepid and cheerful behaviour at his trial and death.[8] Compared to a torpedo.[9]

---

[1] Xenophon Œconomic.   [2] Id. Eod.
[3] Id. Sympos.   [4] Eod.
[5] Plato, Phædrus, p. 230.   [6] Id. Crito.   [7] Ibid.
[8] Plato, Apolog. and Phædo ; Xenophon, Memorabil.
[9] Plato, Menon. p. 80.

Called Prodicus, the sophist, his master.[1] Learns, at near fifty years of age, to play on the lyre of Connus, son of Metrobius.[2] His mother, Phænarete, married Chæredemus, and had by him a son named Patrocles.[3] Seldom used to bathe, and commonly went barefooted.[4] He could bear great quantities of wine without being overpowered by it, but did not choose to drink voluntarily.[5]

[1] Plato, Menon. p. 96.   [2] Id. Euthydem. p. 272.
[3] Id. Euthyd. p. 297.   [4] Plat. Sympos.
[5] Ibid. p. 214, 220.

THE COMPANIONS OF SOCRATES.

CRITOBŪLUS.

A man of fortune; his estate was worth above eight talents, which in Athens was very considerable. Had served the offices of gymnasiarch, choregus, &c. the most expensive of the city. Of an amorous disposition; negligent of œconomy; a lover of dramatick spectacles; he married a very young inexperienced woman, with whom he conversed very little :[1] he was present at the entertainment given by Callias to Autolycus, Socrates, and others, and at that time was newly married. Ol. 89. 4. He was remarkable for his beauty; his fine panegyrick on it: was passionately fond of Clinias. Crito, his father, introduced him to the acquaintance of Socrates, that he might cure him of this passion.[2]

ISCHOMACHUS.

He was called in Athens, by way of pre-eminence, ὁ καλος κ' αγαθος; he married a young maid under fifteen years of age, whom he educated and instructed himself. His first serious conversation with her, related by him to Socrates, on the duties of a mistress of a family. The order and arrangement of his house de-

---

[1] Xenophon, Œconomic.   [2] Id. Sympos.

scribed : his morning exercises, walk to his villa, and
ride from thence. He was a remarkably good horse-
man, of a vigorous constitution, and lasting health ;
was one of the richest men in Athens. His instruction
and treatment of his slaves ; his knowledge in agriculture. His father before him was a great lover of that
art.[1] He meddled not much in publick affairs :[2] was
believed, while he lived, to be worth above seventy
talents; but at his death he left not twenty, to be
divided between his two sons.[3]

CALLIAS.

His genealogy :.....Phænippus

Callias [4] ὁ Δαδοῦχος.

Hipponicus [5]

Callias [6]

Hipponicus [7]

Callias—Hipparete—Alcibiades.

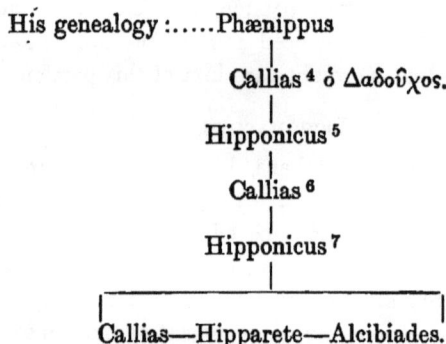

[1] Xenophon, Œconomicus.   [2] Id. Eod.
[3] Lysias, Orat. de bonis Aristophanis, p. 348.
[4] Dictus ὁ Λακκόπλουτος. Herod. 5. Plutarch in Aristide.
Scol. in Demosthen. p. 393. Victor Celeto Ol. 54.
[5] Dictus Ammon. Athenæus, L. 12. Plutarch de Malign.
Herodoti.
[6] ὁ Λακκόπλουτος, uti et avus. Plut. in Aristide. Herodot. 7.
Demosth. de Fals. Legat.
[7] Qui ad Delium occubuit, Ol. 89. 1. Thucyd.—Plut. Alcib.
Andocides in Alcibiadem.

Callias was in love with Autolycus, the son of Lyco, who gained the victory (while yet a boy) in the Pancratium during the greater Panathcnæa, Ol. 89. 4, upon which occasion Callias gave an entertainment to his friends[1] at his house in the Piræeus. He had been scholar to the sophists Protagoras, Gorgias, and Prodicus; was very wealthy; and had learned the art of memory from Hippias of Elis, at the recommendation of Antisthenes. He was Πρόξενος of the Lacedæmonians who came to Athens; was hereditary priest of the Eleusinian deities, ὁ Δαδοῦχος; was remarkable for his nobility and the gracefulness of his person;[2] he had two sons, who were instructed by Evenus, the Parian sophist;[3] he entertained Protagoras, Prodicus, and Hippias, and other sophists, their companions, in his house, Ol. 90. 1.[4]

NICERATUS.

He was son to the famous Nicias; was present at the symposium of Callias, Ol. 89. 4, and then newly married. He could repeat by heart the whole Iliad and Odyssee, and had been scholar to Stesimbrotus and Anaximander. He was very wealthy and somewhat covetous; was fond of his wife, and beloved by her;[5] was scholar to Damon, the famous musician, who had been recommended to his father by Socrates;[6] and finally, he was put to death by order of the Thirty, with his uncle Eucrates.[7]

---

[1] Xenophon, Symposium ; Athenæus, L. 5, p. 216.
[2] Ibid.   [3] Plato, Apolog.   [4] Plato, Protagoras.
[5] Xenophon, Sympos.   [6] Plato in Lachete.
[7] Xenophon, Gr. Hist. L. 2.   Andocides de Mysteriis.

ANTISTHENES.

He was extremely poor, but with a contempt of
wealth; was present in the symposium of Callias,
where he proved that riches and poverty are in the
mind alone, and not in externals. His way of life
was easy and contented: he passed whole days in the
company of Socrates, who taught him (he says) to be
mentally rich. He was much beloved in the city, and
his scholars were esteemed by the publick. He recommended Prodicus and Hippias the Elean to Callias;[1]
bore great affection to Socrates, and was present at
his death.[2]

CHÆREPHON.

A man of warmth and eagerness of temper;[3] he was
a friend to the liberties of the people; he fled to and
returned with Thrasybulus; he died before Socrates's
trial; for he is mentioned in Socrates's Apology, as
then dead, and in the Gorgias, as then living: his
death must therefore have happened between Ol. 93. 4.
and Ol. 95. 1. He consulted the Delphian oracle to
know if any man were wiser than Socrates. His
brother, Chærecrates, survived him.[4]

EPIGENES.

He was the son of Antipho of Cephisia:[5] and was
present at the death of Socrates.[6]

[1] Xenophon, Sympos.
[2] Plato, Phæd.
[3] Vid. Charmidem, p. 153.
[4] Apol. Socrat.
[5] Plato, Apol.
[6] Phædo.

APOLLODORUS.

He was brother to Aiantodorus:[1] was a man of small abilities, but of an excellent heart, and remarkable for the affection he bore to Socrates;[2] he was present in the prison at the time of his death.[3] He lived at Phalerus, of which Δημος he was;[4] was but a boy when Socrates was fifty-three years old, and must therefore have been under thirty-seven, at the time of Socrates's death. He was called Μανικος from the warmth of his temper.

PHÆDO.

He was an Elean. See his account of Socrates's last moments.[5]

SIMMIAS.

He was a Theban, and a young man at the time of Socrates's death (as was Cebes), at which they were both present. He had received some tincture of the Pythagorean doctrines from Philolaus of Crotona; and was inquisitive and curious in the search of truth, far above all prejudice and credulity.[6]

CEBES.

He was a Theban. (Vid. Simmiam.)

HERMOGENES.

He was a man of piety, and believed in divination. He was present in Callias's symposium; was a person

---

[1] Apol. Socrat. [2] Phædo. [3] Id.
[4] Plato, Sympos. [5] Plato, Phædo. [6] Plato, Phædo.

of great honesty, mild, affable, and soberly cheerful:[1] not rich, and a man of few words;[2] was son to Hipponicus and brother to Callias.[3] He was present at the death of Socrates.[4]

CHARMIDES.

He had a considerable estate in lands before the Peloponnesian war, which he thence entirely lost, and was reduced to great poverty. He was present at the symposium of Callias, where he discoursed on the advantages and pleasures of being poor. He ran at the stadium, at Nemea, contrary to Socrates's advice.[5] He was of extreme beauty when a youth.[6]

ÆSCHYLUS.

He was of Phlius, and was introduced by Antisthenes to Socrates.

CRITO.

He was father to Critobūlus; was of Alopecæ, and about the same age with Socrates.[7] He made the proposal to contrive the escape of Socrates out of prison, and to send him into Thessaly;[8] he attended him daily in his confinement, and at the time of his death; he received his last orders: he closed his eyes, and took care of his funeral.[9]

[1] Xenoph. Sympos.   [2] Ibid. p. 391 and 408.
[3] Plato, Cratylus.   [4] Plato, Phædo.   [5] Plato, Theages.
[6] Plato, Charmid.   [7] Plato, Apolog.   [8] Id. Crito.
[9] Id. Phædo.

PLATO.

PHÆDRUS.

Η, ΠΕΡΙ ΚΑΛΟΥ.

THIS is supposed to be the first Dialogue which Plato
wrote; εχει γαρ (says Laertius [1]) μειρακιωδες τι το
προβλημα· Δικαιαρχος δε και τον τροπον της γραφης
ὁλον επιμεμφεται, ὡς φορτικον. Dionysius Halicarnassensis [2] calls it one of his most celebrated discourses;
and from it he produces examples both of the beauty
and of the blemishes of Plato's style, of the χαρακτηρ
ισχνος και αφελης, which is all purity, all grace and
perspicuity; and of the ὑψηλος, wherein he sometimes

[1] Diog. Laert. L. 3, c. 38. (c. 25 edit. Kraus. Lipsiæ, 1759).
[2] Περι της Δημοσθενους δεινοτητος. p. 270. V. 2, ed. Hudsoni.
He attributes the first to Plato's education in the company of
Socrates; the latter to his imitation of Gorgias and Thucydides.
Vid. et Epist. ad Cn. Pompeium, p. 202.

NOTES ON THE GREEK TEXT.

Platonis Opera, Edit. Serrani II. Steph. 1578, Vol. 3.

Vol. 3. p. 227. Ακουμενω.] Acumenus was father to Eryxi-
machus, both of them physicians of note, and friends of Socrates.

Ib. Εν ταις δρομοις.] Places in the Gymnasia, where people
exercised themselves by walking a great pace, or by running.
See Plato's Euthydemus, p. 273. Περιεπατειτην εν τω καταστεγω
Δρομω, &c.

rises to a true sublimity, and sometimes falls into an
ungraceful redundancy of words and of ill-suited figures
ungraceful and obscure.

There is a good analysis of the Phædrus by Mr.
Abbé Sallier,[1] wherein he shews its true subject and
intention. It is upon eloquence and is designed to
demonstrate, that no writer, whether legislator, orator,
historian, or poet, can do any thing excellent without a

[1] Mémoires de l'Académie des Inscriptions, &c. V. 9, p. 49.
See also another analysis by Mr. Hardion in his tenth Dissertation on the eloquence of Greece. Ib. V. 16, p. 378, des Mémoires.

NOTES.

P. 227. Του Ολυμπιου.] The vast temple of Jupiter, begun
by Pisistratus, but never finished till the time of the emperor
Hadrian.

Ib. Προσηκουσα γε σοι.] Socrates professed the art of love.
See Xenoph. Sympos.

Ib. Πρεσβυτερω.] He was then threescore and upwards.

Ib. Κατα 'Ηροδικον.] Herodicus of Selymbria, ὁ παιδοτριβης.
See Plat. Protagoras, p. 316. There was also Herodicus, the
Leontine, a physician, and brother to the famous Gorgias (See
Plat. Gorg. 448 and 456.): the first was also a physician, and the
first who regulated the exercises of youth by the rules of medi-
cine. See de Republicâ, L. 3, p. 406, fusè.

228. Εθρυπτετο.] He played the coquet ; he denied, only to
be courted to do what he wished.

Ib. Αυτου δεηθητι, ὁπερ ταχα παντως ποιησει.] Read, ποιηση,
and make no other correction : i.e. "Be now intreated to do,
what you will do presently without any intreaty at all."

229. Της Αγραιας.] The district, or δημος, was called Αγραι,
in which stood the temple of Diana Αγροτερα. Pausanias, Attic.
L. 1, p. 45. ed. Kuhnii.

Ib. Συν Φαρμακεια.] Orithyia and Procris were the daughters
of Erectheus. Who Pharmacéa was, I do not find.

Ib. Λιαν δε δεινον.] Such disquisitions were the common
employments of the sophists and grammarians.

foundation of philosophy. The title prefixed to it, Περι
Καλοῦ, cannot be genuine; it has no other relation to
it, than that beauty is accidentally the theme of Socrates's
second little oration, which is contained in this dialogue ;
not that it is, directly, even the subject of that, for the
tendency of it is to prove, Ὡς εραστῇ μαλλον, η τω μη
ερῶντι δει χαριζεσθαι, as the two preceding orations were
to shew the contrary. These are what Laertius calls

P. 230. Typhon or Typhœus, the youngest son of Earth and
Tartarus. Hesiod, Theogon. v. 821. has given a fine description
of this portentous form.

Ib. Αχελωου.] The Achelöus was looked upon in Greece as
the principal of all rivers, and his name was used for all fresh
water in general : he was usually worshipped in common with
Pan and the Nymphs, as here.

Ib. Καρπον προσιοντες.] Read προσειοντες, shaking it before
them.

231. Ων δεομαι.] What he desired, will appear but too plainly
in the course of these little orations, and must appear a most
strange subject of conversation for Socrates, to all who are unacquainted with the manners of Greece. The President de
Montesquieu has observed, but too justly, on the nature of their
love and gallantry. Esprit des Loix, V. 1. See also Xenoph.
Œconomic. and Symposium ; and the Symposium of Plato ; see
also de Legib. L. 1. p. 636.

Ib. Τον νομον.] There were, indeed, laws of great severity
in Athens against this vice ; but who should put them in force
in such general and shocking depravity ?

234. This praise he cannot help bestowing on Lysias's composition, namely, Ὁτι σαφη, και στρογγυλα, και ακριβως ἑκαστα
των ονοματων αποτετορνευται.

235. Ὡσπερ δι εννεα.] The Archons took an oath to do this,
if they were guilty of corruption, before they took their seats in
the Στοα Βασιλειος. See Jul. Pollux, L. 8, c. 13. Plutarch in
Solon ; and Heraclides in Politiis.

Προβληματα μειρακιωδη, though he may mean it of the
whole dialogue, which is something juvenile and full of
vanity.　Dionysius very justly says, Ην γαρ εν μεν τη
Πλατωνος φυσει, πολλας αρετας εχουση, το φιλοτιμον,
and before, Πλατων το φορτικωτατον και επαχ θεστατον
των εργων προελομενος, αυτον επαινειν κατα την δυναμιν
των λογων, &c.

The Socratick Dialogues are a kind of dramas,
wherein the time, the place, and the characters are

NOTES.

P. 235. Παρα γε εμαιτου ουδεν.] It is observable, that
Socrates, whenever he would discourse affirmatively on any
subject, or when he thought proper to raise and adorn his style,
does it not in his own person, but assumes the character of
another.　Thus, for instance, he relates the beautiful fable
between Virtue and Pleasure after Prodicus; he treats of the
miseries of human life in the words of the same sophist; he
describes the state of souls after death from the information of
Gobryas, one of the Magi; he makes a panegyrick on wine in
the style of Gorgias; and here he does not venture to display
his eloquence, till the.Nymphs and the Muses have inspired
him.　This is consistent with that character of simplicity and
of humility which he assumed.

236. Κυψελιδων.] See Pausanias, L. 5, p. 378.

Ib. Ομοιας λαβας.] A metaphor taken from wrestling: you
give me a good hold of you.　So in Lib. de Republ. 8, p. 544.
Παλιν τοινυν, ωσπερ παλαιστης, την αυτην λαβην παρεχε.

Ib. Των Κωμωδων.] The repetition of a person's words by
way of reproach.

Ib. Ποιητην.] Used for one who composes any thing, whether
prose or verse.　So above, p. 234. Ωs τα δεοντα ειρηκοτος του
Ποιητου.—Ομνυμι γαρ σοι: what follows should be written thus,
Τινα μεντοι; τινα θεων; ει βουλει, την πλατανην ταυτηνι.

237. Αγετε δη, ω Μουσαι.] Thus far, says Dionysius, παντα
χαριτων μεστα: hence begins a style more turbid and obscure,
and disagreeably poetical.

almost as exactly marked as in a true theatrical representation. Phædrus here is a young man particularly
sensible [1] to eloquence and to fine writing, and thence
a follower and an admirer of the famous Lysias, whose

[1] V. p. 242, et passim. He was an Athenian, son to Pytho-
cles, of the district of Myrrhinus, and tribe Pandionis. V. the
Sympos. p. 176.

P. 237. Κρατουσης τω κρατει, σωφροσυνη ονομα.] Write thus,
Κρατουσης, τω κρατει σωφροσυνη ονομα, which answers to και
αρξασης εν ημιν, τη αρχη υβρις επωνομασθη.

238. Παθος πεπονθεναι.] The word, which Serranus would
insert here, (θειον) παθος, is not in Dionysius.

Ib. Ευροια.] An easy fluency and volubility of expression.
So Diogenes Laertius in Timone Phliasio, Lib. 9, c. 114. Αλλα
και ευρους, ὡς μηδε αρισταν συγχωρειν : i.e. he wrote with that
ease and fluency, that he could not find time to dine ; that is,
he found no interval, no interruption in the course of his writing, to bestow on the necessities of nature : though, perhaps,
the true reading is, ὡς μηδε αριστοις, so as to vie with the best.

I mention this passage, because Meric Casaubon was *wise
enough* to understand ευρους of a looseness, to which Timon was
subject, and distinguishes very accurately between ευροια and
διαῤῥοια. D. Laert. L. 9, c. 114.

241. Οστρακου μεταπεσοντος.] A proverb, taken from a
play in use among children, called Οστρακινδα, described by
Jul. Pollux, L. 9, c. 154, ed. Jungermanni, and by Eustathius.
They were divided into two parties, which fled or pursued each
other alternately, as the chance of a piece of broken potsherd,
thrown up into the air, determined it : the boy who threw it
cried out Νυξ ἠ 'Ημερα ; if the black (or pitched) side came
uppermost, his party ran away, and the other gave them chase ;
if the white one, the others ran, and they pursued them.
Hence Οστρακου Περιστροφη was used to describe a total reverse
of fortune. Erasmus, in his Adagia, has not explained it well.
See Plato de Republ. L. 7, p. 521.

reputation was then at its height in Athens. He has
sat the greatest part of the morning at the house of
Epicrates, near the Olympium, to hear Lysias recite a
discourse; and, having procured a copy of it, is medi-
tating upon it with pleasure, as he walks without the
city walls, where Socrates meets him. To avoid the
heat of the day they retire to the shade of an ancient
plane-tree, that overshadows a fane of Achelòus and
the nymphs on the banks of a rivulet, which discharges

NOTES.

242. Σιμμιαν Θηβαῖον.] See Diog. Laertius, L. 2, c. 124.
He is mentioned in the thirteenth Epistle, and is an interlocutor
in the Phædo.

Ib. Ου πολεμον γε αγγελλεις.] These words belong to
Phædrus, as H. Stephens observes. It is a proverb: you are
the messenger of no bad news. See De Legibus, L. 3, p. 702.

Ib. Εδυσωπουμην.] A fragment of Ibycus: Μη τι παρο
Θεοις αμπλακων, τιμαν προς ανθρωπων αμειψω.

243. The beginning of a Palinodia of Stesichorus on Helen.
Ουκ εστ' ετυμος ὁ λογος οὑτος, Ουδ' εβας εν νηυσιν εὐσσελμοις, Ουδ'
ικεο Περγαμα Τροιας, which is alluded to at the end of the third
Epistle, την παλινωδιαν αιτου μιμησαμενος. Plat. V. 3, p. 319.

244. Δια τε ορνιθων ποιουμενην, and afterwards ποριζομενην,
as H. Steph. corrects it.

Ib. Οιονοστικην.] He derives it from οιος and νοῦς, as
attained by human experience alone. A very bad etymology.

Ib. Εξαντη.] Serranus translates, indemnem, incolumem,
i.e. placed aloft, as it were, out of the reach of danger and envy.
See Constantini Lexicon.

246. Ἡ ψυχη πασα.] This is, indeed, an example of those
Αλληγοριαι μακραι, ουτε μετρον εχουσαι, ουτε καιρον, of which
Dionysius Halicarnassensis complains in Plato; (Dion. Halic.
Vol. 2, p. 272, ed. Oxon.); and which, indeed, Plato himself
calls in this very Dialogue (p. 265) a μυθικος ὑμνος.

Ib. Αθανατον τι ζωον.] He defines God so, εχον μεν ψυχην,
εχον δε σωμα.

itself at a little distance into the Ilyssus. The spot
lay less than a quarter of a mile above the bridge,
which led over the river to the temple of Diana Agræa.

P. 246. Κεκοινωνηκε δε πη.] I imagine he means, that the
soul of man approaches in perfection to the corporeal part of the
Gods. The translation has no affinity to the text here ; ἡ
αχρωματος και ασχηματιστος και αναφης ουσια, the true substance
and essence of things, of which the properties are only the consequences ; this is the το οντως ον of Plato.

Ib. 'Ο μεν αυτῳ καλος.] The rational and intellectual faculties
of the soul.

Ib. 'Ο δε εξ εναντιων.] The appetites and passions.

250. Μυουμενοι τε και εποπτευοντες.] An allusion to the
Attick mysteries of Ceres. See Meursius and Potter. So in
the seventh Epistle, p. 333.

251. Καυλος υπο παν.] Perhaps we should read επι.

253. 'Ωσπερ αι Βακχαι.] What Bacchanalian ceremony is
here alluded to ? See the Ion : 'Ωσπερ αι Βακχαι αρυττονται εκ
των ποταμων μελι και γαλα κατεχομεναι, &c.

256. Φιλοσοφιαν.] Polemarchus, the elder brother of Lysias,
was a friend of Socrates, and a philosopher : so Plutarch calls
him, "De esu Carnium." Polemarchus had another brother,
called Euthydemus. Polemarchus was murdered by the Thirty
Tyrants, Ol. 94. 1. See Lysias in Eratosthenem, p. 196.

257. Γλυκυς αγκων.] Erasmus explains it in his Adagia,
(Ευφημα φωνει) as though in a part of a river, where there was
a long and dangerous winding, the sailors used this piece of
flattery by way of propitiating the Nile : but this does not fully
clear up the passage here. That this proverb was so used may
appear from these words of Athenæus, L. 12, p. 516. Τον τοπον
καλουσι Γυναικων αγωνα, γλυκυν αγκωνα : which last may mean,
a specious term to cover their ignominy ; Casaubon does not
explain it : here it seems applied to such as speak one thing,
and mean another.

258. Εδοξε του.] He alludes to the form of a Psephisma,
Εδοξε τω δημω· Τισαμενος ειπε, &c. as H. Stephanus observes.

Here they pursue their conversation during the hours
of noon, till the sun grows lower and the heat becomes
more mild.

P. 258. Δαρειου δυναμιν.] See Epist. 7, p. 332.

Ib. Ερωτᾱς, ει δεομεθα; τινος μεν ουν, &c.] I do not see the
transition, and I imagine that some words are wanting here;
and also, after κεκληνται.

259. Νυσταζοντας.] The Greeks usually slept at noon in
summer, as it is still the custom in Italy and Spain, and in
other hot countries. Xenoph. Græc. Hist. L. 5. p. 557.

Ib. Ασιτον και αποτον.] The cicada is an animal with
wings, the size of a man's thumb, of a dark brown colour,
which sits on the trees and sings, that is, makes a noise like a
cricket; but much more shrill, and without any intervals,
which grows louder as the sun grows hotter. Some supposed
it to live on the air, others on dew only. Vid. Melcagrum,
Niciam, et alios in Anthologiâ, L. 3. p. 265, ed. H. Steph. and
Plin. Nat. Hist. L. 28, c. 26.

'Ο θεσπεσιος οξυμελης αχετας
Θαλπεσι μεσημβρινοις ὑφ' ἡλιω μανεις βοᾷ.

Aristophan. Aves, v. 1095.

It does in reality live on the exsudations of plants, having a
proboscis, like flies, to feed with; but is capable of living a long
time, like many of the insect race, without any nourishment at
all. The tettigometra, which is this creature in its inter-
mediate state between a worm and a fly, was esteemed a delicacy
to eat by the Greeks. See Aldrovand. de Insectis, and Reaumur,
Hist. des Insectes, V. 5, Dissert. 4.

Ib. Πρεσβυτατη.] Hesiod names the Muses in the same
order in which their names are inscribed on the books of Herodotus; and says, that Calliope was ἁπασεων προφερεστατη.
Theogon, v. 75. See also Ciceronem in Bruto, and Quintilian,
L. 3. c. 1.

260. Φησιν ὁ Λακων.] Perhaps Alcman; though the words
do not seem to be poetry.

261. Gorgias came to Athens on an embassy from the

We may nearly fix the year when this conversation is supposed to have happened. Lysias was now at Athens; he arrived there from Thurii in Italy in the

---

NOTES.

Leontines, Ol. 88. 2. (See Diod. Sic. L. 12, p. 313.) when Socrates was about forty-three years old. (V. Ciceronem in Bruto, et Quintil. L. 3. c. 1.) Tisias and Corax of Syracuse, and Gorgias the Leontine, first composed treatises on the art of speaking.

P. 261. Ουκ αρα μονον.] "Socrates apud Platonem in Phædro palam, non in judiciis modo et concionibus, sed in rebus privatis etiam et domesticis, rhetoricen esse demonstrat." (Quintil. L. 2, c. 21.) Plato here makes knowledge, that is, the perception of truth, the foundation of eloquence. Περι παντα τα λεγομενα μια τις τεχνη, ειπερ εστιν, αυτη αν ειη, ητις δια τ᾽ εσται, παν παντι ὁμοιουν των δυνατων, και ὁις δυνατον· και, αλλου ὁμοιουντος και αποκρυπτομενου, εις φως αγειν. This has some resemblance to Locke's definition of knowledge : "It is (says he) the perception of the connection and agreement, or of the disagreement and repugnancy, of any of our ideas." Locke's Essay, B. 4. ch. 1.

261. Ελεατικον Παλαμηδην.] Quintilian informs us, that the person here meant is Alcidamas of Elea. Laertius takes it to be meant of Zeno Eleates, who is looked upon as the inventor of disputation (ἡ διαλεκτικη) and of logick, and who was at Athens when Socrates was not above eight years old, that is, above fifty years earlier than the time of this dialogue ; but his contemporary Empedocles was the first who cultivated rhetorick as an art, and taught it to Gorgias who published a book on that subject.

N.B. Athenæus (L. 13. p. 592.) mentions Alcidamas, ὁ Λαϊτης, (read ὁ Ελεατης, not Ελαϊτης, as Casaubon corrects it from Suidas) ; he says, that Alcidamas was scholar to Gorgias, and had written Encomia on Lagis and Naïs, two famous courtezans from Athens ; whence, it seems, that he must have flourished about this time, and perhaps near twenty years after. There is the right read-ing of it in Athenæus, L. 9. p. 397, Ὁ Ελεατικος Παλαμηδης ονοματολογος εφη, &c. which is a name he bestows on Ulpian of Tyre, an indefatigable hunter after words. Casau-

forty-seventh year of his age, Ol. 92. 1. Euripides is
also mentioned as still in the city : he left it to go into
Macedonia, Ol. 92. 4, and, consequently, it must have

NOTES.

bon has not explained this. See also Laertius in Protagoras,
L. 9. 54. We have still an oration of Alcidamas in the person
of Ulysses against Palamedes. It may be also observed, that
Laertius (L. 9. c. 25.) when he mentions Zeno Eleates, cites
by mistake the Sophistes, instead of the Phædrus of Plato.
Isocrates, in his oration on Helena, indeed says, that Zeno in
his disputations would shew the same things to be possible
and impossible.

P. 262. Εστιν ουν όπως τεχνικος κτλ.] Read μεταβιβαζων—
απαγειν—to answer to διαφευγειν.

264. Χαλκῆ.] Epitaph on Midas, by some attributed to
Homer and by others to Cleobulus of Lindias. See Vit. Homeri,
Herodoti ut dicitur, (V. Herodot. Edit. Gronov. 1715, p. 559.)
and D. Laertius in Cleobulo, L. 1, c. 89.

265. Definition of a general complex idéa, Εκ πολλων ιων
αισθησεων εις έν λογισμω ξυναιρουμενον.—Εις μιαν τε ιδεαν συνο-
ρῶντα αγειν τα πολλαχη διεσπαρμενα.

266. Almost all these persons are mentioned by Quintilian
L. 3, 1., as having written arts of rhetorick, and were all now
flourishing, Ol. 92, except Tisias of Syracuse, Evenus of Paros,
Protagoras of Abdera, and Licymnius.

Ib. See Quintilian, L. 4. c. 1. 2. 3. and L. 5. c. 1. 4. and
L. 8. c. 5. for an explanation of the terms, Προοιμιον, Διηγησιν,
Μαρτυριας, Τεκμηρια, Πιστωσιν, Ελεγκος, Διπλασιολογια, Γνωμο-
λογια, Εικονολογια, Ενεπεια, Επανοδος or Ανακεφαλαιωσις.

267. Οικτρογοων επι γηρας και πενιαν έλκομενων.] An allusion
to some poet : he means that Thrasymachus had gained great
wealth by his art.

268. Διεστηκος το ητριον.] A metaphor from an unequal and
ill-woven texture.

269. Μελιγηρυν Αδραστον.] An allusion to Tyrtæus :

Ουδ' ει Τανταλιδεω Πελοπος βασιλευτερος ειη,
Γλωσσαν δ' Αδρηστου μειλιχογηρυν εχοι.

happened in some year of that Olympiad, probably the
2d or 3d, and Plato must have written it in less than
ten years afterwards, for his Lysis was written before

NOTES.

so that perhaps we should read in this place μειλιχογηριν for
μελιγηριν.

P. 270. Νοῦ τε και ανοιας.] He (i.e. Anaxagoras) attributed
the disposition of the universe to an intelligent cause, or mind,
whence he himself was called Νοῦς. He was nearly of the same
age with Pericles, and came to Athens Ol. 75. 1, where he
passed about thirty years.

Ib. 'Ιπποκρατει.] That famous physician was then about
fifty years of age; and his works were universally read.

272. Αλλα του πιθανου.] See the allusion to this passage in
Quintilian, L. 2, c. 15.

273. Η αλλος οστις δη ποτ' ων τυγχανει, και οποθεν χαιρει
ονομαζομενος.] The art, which bore the name of Tisias, was not
certainly known to be genuine. He says this in allusion to the
custom of invoking the gods by several names. See Callim.
Hymn. ad Jovem. Hor. Od. Sæcul. &c. &c. See also Plato in
Protagoras, p. 358. and in Cratylus, p. 400. and in Euthydemus,
p. 288.

274. Θεῦθ.] The Egyptian deity, Mercury, to whom the
bird Ibis was sacred. Vid. Platon. Philebum, Edit. Serrani,
vol. 2. p. 18. Επειδη φωνην απειρον, &c.

275. This discourse of Thamus (or Jupiter Ammon) on the
uses and inconveniences of letters is excellent; he gives a lively
image of a great scholar, that is, of one who searches for wisdom
in books alone : Τουτο των μαθοντων ληθην μεν εν ψυχαις παρεξει
μνημης αμελητησια, ατε δια πιστιν γραφης εξωθεν υπ' αλλοτριων
τυπων, ουκ ενδοθεν αυτους υφ' αυτων, αναμιμνησκομενους· ουκουν
μνημης, αλλ' υπομνησεως, φαρμακον ευρες· σοφιας δε τοις μαθηταις
δοξαν, ουκ αληθειαν, πορίζεις. πολυηκοοι γαρ σοι γενομενοι ανευ
διδαχης, πολυγνωμονες ειναι δοξωσι, αγνωμονες, ως επι το πληθος,
οντες και χαλεποι ξυνειναι· δοξοσοφοι γεγονοτες αντι σοφων.

Ib. Δρυος και πετρας.] An allusion to that saying, Απο δρυος,
η απο πετρης. Hom. Il. v. 126.

the death of Socrates, which was Ol. 95. 1, but the
Phædrus was still earlier, being his first composition ; so
he was between twenty and twenty-nine years of age.

NOTES.

P. 276. Αδωνιδος κηποι.] Corn and seeds of various kinds, sown
in shallow earth to spring up soon, which were carried in the
procession on the feast of Adonis. Theocritus, Idyll. 15. v. 113.

Παρ δ' απαλοι κᾶποι πεφυλαγμενοι εν ταλαρισκοις
Αργυρεοις·

and the Schol. on the passage : see also the Emperor Julian in
his Cæsares : "Κηποι, οὗς ἁι γυναικες τω της Αφροδιτης ανδρι
φυτευουσιν οστρακιοις επαμησαμενοι γην λαχανιαν· χλωρησαντα
δε ταυτα προς ολιγον αυτικα απομαραινεται. Julian. Op. Edit.
Lipsiæ, 1696, pag. 329.

Ib. Αντι τουτων ὁις λεγων.] Do not, with Serranus, correct
it to ἐν τι ; yet read οια λεγω.

278. Νυμφῶν νᾶμα και Μουσων.] The Ilyssus was consecrated
to the Muses, who had an altar on its banks under the title of
Μουσαι Ειλισσιαδες, possibly near the scene of this dialogue.

Ib. Ισοκρατην τον καλον.] Isocrates was now about twenty-
five years of age, and had a share in the friendship both of
Socrates and of Plato. Laertius, L. 3. c. 8.

279. Πλεον η παιδων.] Subauditur, ὁι αλλοι ανδρες ; the same
ellipsis is used in Plato's 4th Epist.

LYSIS.

II, ΠΕΡΙ ΦΙΛΙΑΣ.

THERE is no circumstance in this dialogue to inform one at what time it is supposed to have happened ; but it is certain that Plato wrote it when he was yet a young man, before Ol. 95. 1, for Socrates heard it read. The scene of it is in a Palæstra, then newly built, a little without the walls of Athens near the fountain of Panops, between the Academia and the Lycæum. The interlocutors are Socrates, Hippothales, and Ctesippus,[1]

---

[1] Νεανισκος τις Παιανιευς, μαλα καλος τε κᾳγαθος, την φυσιν ὁσον μεν, ὑβριστης δε, δια το νεος ειναι. In Euthydemo, Plat. Op. V. 1. p. 273. Both Ctesippus and Menexenus were present at Socrates's death. (In Phædone.)

NOTES ON THE GREEK TEXT.
Platon. Op. Serrani, Vol. 2. p. 203.

From 204 to 211.] Thus far the dialogue is very easy and elegant, particularly the short conversation with Lysis, which is an example how children of fortune and family ought to be treated, in order to correct that arrogance which those advantages are apt to inspire, and to win them gradually to reflection and good sense.

P. 204, Μικκος.] Perhaps the same person who is mentioned by Suidas, as a Mytilenean, who settled at Athens, and father to Alcæus the comick poet, who flourished Ol. 97. 4. V. Schol. ad Plutum Aristophan. in Argumento. We see the sophists

88 NOTES ON PLATO.

two young men of Athens; Lysis, a boy of noble birth and fortune, beloved by Hippothales, and Menexenus,[1] also a boy, and cousin to Ctesippus, and friend to Lysis. The characters are, as usual, elegantly drawn; but what is the end or meaning of the whole dialogue, I do not pretend to say. It turns upon the nature and definition of friendship. Socrates starts a hundred notions about it, and confutes them all himself; no-

[1] The discourse with Menexenus is intended to correct a boy of a bolder and more forward nature than Lysis, by shewing him that he knows nothing; and leaves him in the opinion of his own ignorance. The second title of the dialogue is a false or an incorrect one, for friendship is only by accident a part of it; the intent of the whole seems to be, to shew in what manner we should converse with young people according to their different dispositions.

NOTES.

frequented the Palæstræ, as the publick resort of the youth, and taught their art there.

P. 204. Παραταθησεται.] Enecabitur, conficietur.

Ib. Ωs'Ερμαια αγουσιν αναμεμιγμενοι, εν ταυτω εισιν δι νεανισκοι και δι παιδες.] A festival celebrated in all the places of education for boys. We see here how little the severe laws of Solon on this head were observed, which particularly forbade grown persons to be admitted on that occasion. Æschin. Orat. in Timarchum in principio.

Ib. Παιδοτριβης.] The master of the Palæstra, who taught them their exercise.

207. Επηλυγασαμενος προεστη, read προσεστη, as in p. 210, ανεμνησθην ότι και προσεστως, &c.

208. Παιδαγωγος.] Commonly some old slave who waited on them to the schools and to the Palæstræ.

211. Ορτυγα.] The passion of the Athenians for fighting quails and game-cocks is well known. See Plutarch in Alcibiade.

213. Either leave out ουκ in that passage, ότε ηκροᾶτο ουκ ούτως εχειν, or read perhaps, ουκ ήσυχως.

thing is determined, the dialogue is interrupted, and there is an end. Perhaps a second dialogue was designed on the same subject, and never executed. As to all the mysteries which Serranus has discovered in it, they are mere dreams of his own.

The first part of this dialogue is of that kind called Μαιευτικος, and the second part, Πειραστικος.

NOTES.

P. 214. Των σοφωτατων.] Empedocles, perhaps, who ascribed the first formation of things to this friendship : Αλλοτε μεν φιλοτητι συνερχομεν εις εν απαντα, &c. D. Laert. L. 8. c. 76. or Anaxagoras, who taught εκ των ομοιομερων μικρων σωματων το παν συγκεκρασθαι. Laert. L. 2. c. 8.

219. Κωνειον πεπωκοτα.] A quantity of wine, drunk after the cicuta, was believed to prevent its mortal effects.

223. Ην οψε.] It was a law of Solon, τα διδασκαλεια κλειετωσαν προ ηλιου δινοντος. (Æschines.)

ALCIBIADES I.

Η, ΠΕΡΙ ΦΥΣΕΩΣ ΑΝΘΡΩΠΟΥ.

THE title expressing the subject of this dialogue (like that of Lysis) is wrong. Dacier rightly observes, that the titles are commonly nothing to the purpose; but he is strangely mistaken in saying, they are of modern invention, and that Diogenes Laertius makes no mention

---

NOTES ON THE GREEK TEXT.

Platon. Op. Edit. Serrani, Vol. 2. p. 103.

P. 104. Μεγακλεα επιτροπον.] Megacles (the father of Dinomache, the mother of Alcibiades), and Agariste, the mother of Pericles, were brother and sister. Alcibiades was not above three years old, and his brother Clinias was still younger, when they lost their father at the battle of Coronea, Ol. 83. 1.

106. Ιεναι επι το βημα.] Boys when they had undergone the Δοκιμασια before the Thesmothetæ who presided in the court of Heliæa, (V. Lysiam in Diogeiton. p. 508 and 515., Aristophan. in Vespis, v. 576., and Antiphont. de cæde Choreutæ, p. 143, ed. H. Steph. fol.), and were enrolled among the men, though they were for a year excused from all Λειτουργιαι, seem to have been at liberty (at *this* time of the republick) to vote and speak in the assembly of the people. Therefore, Potter (Archæolog. L. 1, c. 17.) is not correct when he affirms that they could not speak there, who were under thirty years of age. They could not indeed be chosen into the senate, &c. till that age.

Ib. Γραμματα και κιθαριζειν.] The usual education of the Athenian children from seven years old to fifteen. See Æschines de Axioco, p. 94, ed. Le Clerc, and Aristoph. in Nubibus, v. 961.

of them. That author actually mentions them all, and from his account they appear to be more ancient than Thrasyllus, who lived probably under Augustus and Tiberius, and who seemingly took them to be all of Plato's own hand.

NOTES.

P. 113. Σου ταδε κινδυνευεις.] These are the words of Phædra in the Hippolytus of Euripides, v. 352. Σου ταδ' ουκ εμου κλυεις, which was played full three years after the time of this dialogue ; but this is only a slight anachronism, and I wish that Plato had never been guilty of any greater.

Ib. Σκευαριω ν.] It is here used for clothes.

118. Πυθοκλειδη.] He was a musician of great note, as well as Damon. See Aristotle, cited by Plutarch in his life of Pericles. Some attribute to Pythoclides the invention of the Mixo-Lydian harmony, used in tragedy ; but Aristoxenus ascribes it to Sappho. See Plutarch de Musicâ, and Burette's notes in the Mémoires de L'Acad. des Inscriptions, &c. vol. 13. p. 234.

Ib. Ηλιθιω εγενεσθην.] He speaks of Xanthippus and Paralus, as already dead, though in reality they were living two years after the time of this dialogue.

119. Pythodorus, son of Isolochus and scholar to Zeno of Elea. Qu ?—Whether he were the same who was Archon Ol. 94. 1. ?

120. Μειδιαν.] He is mentioned by Aristophanes in Avibus.

Ib. Ανδραποδωδη τριχα.] This is explained by Potter, L. 1. c. 10.

121. 'Ων αι γυναικες.] One office of the Ephori was, to watch over the chastity of the queen.

122. Ουδενι μελει. Of old the court of Areopagus were inspectors of the education of youth. The members of it divided that care among them, and each of them in his province took note of such fathers as gave not their children an education suitable to their fortune and way of life, as Isocrates shews at large in his beautiful Areopagitick oration. At what time their vigilance on this head began to decline, I cannot fix ; but it was probably towards the beginning of the administration of Pericles,

The true subject certainly is, to demonstrate the
necessity of knowing one's self, and that, without this
foundation, all other acquisitions in science are not only
useless, but pernicious.

NOTES.

when the authority of that venerable body was lessened and
restrained by Ephialtes, that is, before Ol. 80. 1 ; yet I find the
form of the thing still continued, though not the force of it : for
Æschines speaking of the discipline young men were subject to,
from about the age of eighteen to twenty, has these words ; Πας
ὁ του μειρακισκου χρονος εστιν ὑπο Σωφρονιστας, και την επι τους
νεους ἁιρεσιν της εξ Αρειου παγου βουλης. (Æschin. in Axiocho,
p. 96.) The Sophronistæ here mentioned, are distinct from the
Areopagites, being the name of a magistracy thus described
in Etymolog. Magn. Σωφρονισται, αρχοντες τινες χειροτονητοι,
δεκα τον αριθμον ἑκαστης φυλης, επεμελοῦντο δε της των εφηβων
σωφροσυνης.

P. 122. Πολλας γαρ ηδη γενεας.] We are not told, I believe, by
any other writer, that the use of money was so early introduced
into Lacedæmon ; but the following passage of Posidonius in
Athenæus, may help to explain it ; Λακεδαιμονιοι ὑπο των εθων
κωλυομενοι εισφερειν εις την Σπαρτην, (ὡς ὁ αυτος Ιστορει Ποσειδωνιος),
και κτᾶσθαι χρυσον και αργυρον, εκτῶντο μεν ουδεν ἡττον, παρα-
κατετιθετο δε τοις ὁμοροις Αρκασιν, ειτα πολεμους αυτους εσχον αντι
φιλων, ὁπως ανυπευθυνον το απιστον δια την εχθραν γενηται· τω
μεν ουν εν Δελφοις Απολλωνι τον προτερον εν τη Λακεδαιμονι χρυσον
και αργυρον Ιστορουσιν ανατεθηναι. κτλ. Athen. L. 6. p. 233, and
we may consult also Plato's Hip. Maj. p. 283, and De Republicâ,
L. 8, p. 548. Plutarch says, that money was not even allowed
for the uses of the publick, till after the siege of Athens and its
surrendering to Lysander, when that point was carried after a
great struggle ; though, at the same time, it was made capital
to apply it to private occasions. This happened twenty seven
years after the date of this dialogue.

Ib. Γενεθλια.] The birthday of the Persian king was yearly
observed by all Asia.

Ib. Και Μεσσηνης.] Messenia was a country far surpassing

The time of this dialogue is towards the end of
Alcibiades's nineteenth year, which (as Dodwell reckons)
is Ol. 87. 1.   Socratc∶ was then about thirty-nine years
old.

NOTES.

Laconia in fertility, and equal to the best in Greece : Euripides
describes them both.   See ap. Strabonem, L. 8, p. 367, and
Pausanias, L. 4, p. 285.

P. 122. Των τε αλλων και των 'Ειλωτικων.] The Spartans, therefore, made use of other slaves besides the Heilotæ.

123. Δεινομαχης.] The value of an Athenian matron's ward-
robe and ornaments was about fifty minæ, (£161. 9s. 2d.)

Ib. Γης πλεθρα Ερχιασιν.] Three hundred Πλεθρα of land
was a great estate for an Athenian : a plethrum is one hundred
feet square.   Observe, that the lands of Alcibiades did not lie
in that Δημος to which he belonged, for he was of Scambonidæ.

Ib. Βασιλικος φορος.] Herodotus, L. 6, enumerates the
privileges and prerogatives of the Spartan kings, but makes no
mention of this revenue, which was probably instituted after
his time.

124. Observe that Agis did not come to the crown till five
years after this conversation.

ALCIBIADES II.

Η, ΠΕΡΙ ΠΡΟΣΕΤΧΗΣ.

THIS is a continuation of the same subject; for what is said on prayer is rather accidental, and only introductory to the main purpose of the dialogue. It is nothing inferior in elegance to the former. Some have attributed it to Xenophon, but it is undoubtedly Plato's, and designed as a second part to the former.

I could be glad if it were as easy to fix the time of it, as Dacier would persuade us, who boldly fixes it Ol. 93. 1, but there are facts alluded to in it, that will

---

NOTES ON THE GREEK TEXT.

Plat. Op. Serrani, Vol. 2. p. 138.

Vol. 2. p. 138. Χαλκω διελεσθαι.] See Æschylus Sept. cont. Theb.

141. Τα παιδικα.] Craterus conspired with Hellenocrates and Decamnichus to murder that prince, (Archelaus of Macedonia) as he was hunting. Aristotle calls him Cratæus, and gives a fuller account of this conspiracy than any other author. Aristot. Politic. L. 5. c. 10. Archelaus had promised him one of his daughters in marriage, for he had two, but gave one to the king of 'Elimea and the other to his own son Amyntas. Hellenocrates was a Larissæan who had likewise been subservient to the king's pleasures.

143. Αυτικα μαλα παρασται—ειπειν—βουλομενον, &c.] All words importing the present time, and not to be in any way interpreted of the past, as Dacier pretends.

neither be reconciled to that date, nor indeed to one
another; and besides, it is better to allow Plato to be
guilty of these inaccuracies in chronology, than of those
improprieties of character which must be the consequences of Dacier's supposition. It is plain, that
Socrates continues, as in the preceding discourse, to
treat Alcibiades with a certain gentle superiority of
understanding, and that he prescribes to (and instructs)
him in a manner extremely proper to form the mind

P. 144. What Plato would prove in this place is excellent,
namely; Το των αλλων επιστημων κτημα, εαν τις ανευ του βελτιστου
κεκτημενος η, ολιγακις μεν ωφελειν, βλαπτειν δε τα πλειω τον εχοντα
αυτα. See also de Repub. L. 6. p. 506. and de Legibus, L. 2.
p. 661.

145. Αυτη δ' ην.] This relates to what he had proved in the
former dialogue, (Alcibiad. 1. p. 116.) which would be absurd if
that conversation had passed twenty years before.

147. A line from Homer's Margites; Πολλ' ηπιστατο εργα,
κακως δ' ηπιστατο παντα.

148. A Spartan prayer : τα καλα διδοναι επι τοις αγαθοις.

Ib. Οἱ πλειστας μεν θυσιας.] The Athenians were remarkably
sumptuous in their temples and publick worship, beyond any
other people : two months in the year were taken up entirely
in these solemnities. See Aristophan. in Vespis, Schol. ad v.
655, and Xenoph. de Republ. Athen. p. 699.

149. Ευφημια.] Proclamation was always made in the beginning of sacrifices in this form : Ευφημειτε, ευφημειτε, and
then followed a solemn prayer.

Ib. Κακον τοκιστην.] Perhaps we should read, Δικαστην.

150. Οὑτος ἐστιν ὡ μελει περι σου.] Socrates may either mean
the Divinity here, as in the former dialogue, Alcibiad. 1. p.
135. Εαν βουλῃ συ. Σωκ: Ου καλως λεγεις. Αλκιβ : Αλλα πως
χρη λεγειν ; Σωκ: 'Οτι εαν Θεος εθελῃ : for it was the character
of Socrates to assume nothing to himself : he ascribes all to the

of a youth just entering into the world, but ill-bred
and impertinent to a man of forty years of age, who
had passed through the highest dignities of the state
and through the most extraordinary reverses of fortune.
Plato himself may convince us of this, by what he
makes Socrates say in the first Alcibiades; p. 127.
Ἀλλα χρη θαρρεῖν· ει μεν γαρ αυτο ἠσθου πεπονθως
πεντηκονταετης, χαλεπον ην αν σοι επιμεληθηναι σαυτοῦ·
νυν δε, ἠν εχεις ἡλικιαν, αὐτη εστιν εν ἡ δει αυτο
αισθανεσθαι.

The principal difficulties are, that he speaks of
Pericles as yet living, who died Ol. 87. 4, and of the

---

dæmon who directed him, whom he calls his Επιτροπος: or
Socrates may here mean himself, as I rather think. Some
Christian writers would give a very extraordinary turn to this
part of the dialogue, as though Plato meant to prove the
necessity of a Revelation : but I spy no such mysteries in it.
Socrates has proved that we are neither fit to deal with mankind, till we know them by knowing ourselves ; nor to address
ourselves to the Divine Power, till we know enough of his
nature to know what we owe him : what that nature is, he
defers examining till another opportunity, which is done to
raise the curiosity and impatience of the young Alcibiades, and
to avoid that prolixity, into which a disquisition so important
would have naturally led him.

P. 151. Στεφανον.] Alcibiades, as going to perform sacrifice,
had a chaplet of flowers on his head, which was the custom for
all present at such solemnities.

Ib. ὁ Κρεων.] From the Phœnissæ of Euripides, v. 886.

Οιωνον εθεμην καλλινικα σοι στεφη·
Εν γαρ κλυδωνι κειμεθ', ὡσπερ οισθα συ.

Ib. Των σων εραστων.] He here continues the same style to
Alcibiades, which would be absurd to a man of forty years of age.

murder of Archelaus king of Macedon as a fact then recent, which did not happen[1] till Ol. 95. 1, the same year with Socrates's death, and near five years after that of Alcibiades.

[1] According to Diodorus Siculus, L. 16. p. 266. who, though he may have rightly fixed the period of the reign of Archelaus, contradicts himself as to the duration of it. He says, that he reigned seven years, yet mentions him as king of Macedon (L. 13. p. 175.) ten years before his death. Ol. 92. 3. According to the Marmor Parium, he must have reigned still longer, for there he is said to have come to the throne, Ol. 90. 1. ; but that date is certainly false, as Thucydides speaks of his father Perdiccas, yet living four years afterwards. But let Diodorus be mistaken or not, it is sure, from this passage of Thucydides, that Archelaus came not to the crown till at least thirteen years after the death of Pericles. See also Athenæus, L. 5. p. 217.

THEAGES.

Η, ΠΕΡΙ ΣΟΦΙΑΣ.

DEMODOCUS of Anagyrus, an old Athenian who had
passed with reputation through the highest offices of
the state, and now, after the manner of his ancestors,
lived chiefly on his lands in the country, (Euthydem.
p. 291.) employed in agriculture and rustick amusements, brings with him to Athens his son [1] Theages, a
youth impatient to improve himself in the arts then in
vogue, and to shine among his companions who studied

[1] He actually became a friend and disciple of Socrates, and
is mentioned by him as such, together with a brother of his
called Paralus, in his Apology, p. 33. Theages was probably
dead at the time of the condemnation of Socrates ; he is mentioned as of a weak and unhealthy constitution. See De Republ.
L. 6. p. 496.

NOTES ON THE GREEK TEXT.
Plat. Op. Serrani, Vol. 1. p. 121.

P. 124. Τον νεωστι Αρχοντα.] Archelaus was then just come
to the throne, and consequently this year, in which Diodorus
first mentions him, was, it is probable, the first of his reign.
(V. Alcibiad. II.) Bacis, a prophet, often cited by Herodotus.
The Scholiast on Aristophan. Equites, v. 123, says, there were
three of the name. (Clemens Alexandr. Strom. L. 1, p. 398.)

Ib. Αμφιλυτον.] The name of this Athenian prophet I do
not elsewhere meet with.

THEAGES.
99

eloquence,[1] and practised politicks, as soon as ever their
age would permit them to appear in the popular
assemblies.

Socrates, at the father's desire, enters into conversation with the young man, and decoys him by little and
little into a confession that he wanted to be a great
man, and to govern his fellow citizens. After diverting
himself with the *naïveté* of Theages, he proposes ironically several sophists of reputation, and several famous
statesmen, who were fit to instruct him in this grand
art : but as it does not appear that the disciples of those
sophists, or even the sons of those statesmen, have been

[1] Aristophanes ridicules this turn of the age in which he
lived, in many places, particularly in Equitib. v. 1375. Reading, and the knowledge of the Belles Lettres, having more
generally diffused itself through the body of the people, than it
had done hitherto, had an ill effect on the manners of a nation
naturally vain and lively. Every one had a smattering of eloquence and of reasoning, and every one would make a figure
and govern ; but no one would be governed : the authority of
age and of virtue was lost and overborne, and wit and a fluency
of words supplied the place of experience and of common sense.
See the character of Hippocrates in the Protagoras, p. 312: and
Plato himself gives this as the characteristick of the Athenians
in his time, Ἡ παντων εις παντα σοφιας δοξα, και παρανομια.
See de Legib. L. 3, p. 701.

NOTES.

P. 125. Εις διδασκαλον.] Perhaps Διδασκαλειον.—This poem of
Anacreon on Callicrete, the daughter of Cyane, is now lost.
Dacier seriously imagines that she was a female politician, like
Aspasia ; but it is more agreeable to Anacreon's gallantry, that
we should suppose the seat of tyranny was only in her face.

128. Δαιμονιον.] See Mr. Foster's note on the Euthyphro,
ad p. 22, and Fraguier's Discourse on Socrates, Mém. de l'Acad.
des Inscript. V. 6.

much the better for their lessons, both Demodocus and
Theages intreat and insist that Socrates himself would
admit him to his company, and favour him with his
instructions.   The philosopher very gravely tells them
stories of his demon, without whose permission he
undertakes nothing, and upon whom it entirely depends,
whether his conversation shall be of any use, or not,
to his friends ; but at last he acquiesces, if Theages
cares to make the experiment.

The scene of the dialogue is in the portico (described
by Pausanias, L. 1. c. 3.) of Jupiter the Deliverer, in
the Ceramicus, the principal street of Athens ; and the
time Ol. 92. 3-4, during the expedition of Thrasyllus,
in which he was defeated at Ephesus by the Persians,
and other allies of Sparta.   Socrates was then sixty
years old.

NOTES.

P. 129. Κλειτομαχον ερεσθαι.] This assassination of Nicias, the
son of Heroscamander, by Philemon and Timarchus, and the
condemnation of the latter with Euathlus, who had given him
shelter, is not recounted in any other author.

130. Θουκυδιδην.] Thucydides, the son of Melesias, was at
the head of the Athenian nobility and of the party which opposed Pericles and Ephialtes : he was a near relation to Cymon,
and banished by Ostracism about Ol. 83. 4, when Socrates was
twenty-six years old.   He had two sons, Melesias and Stephanus,
the eldest of which was father to the Thucydides here mentioned.

130. Aristides, the son of Lysimachus, surnamed the Just,
had a son, called after his grandfather, Lysimachus, whose
son was also called Aristides, which interchange of names was
common at Athens.

EUTHYPHRO.

Η, ΠΕΡΙ 'ΟΣΙΟΤ.

Plat. Op. Serrani, Vol. 1. p. 2.

Socrates,[1] about the time that an accusation had been preferred against him for impiety in the court of the Βασιλεύς,[2] walking in the portico, where that magistrate used to sit in judgment, meets with Euthyphro, a person deeply versed in the knowledge of religious affairs,

[1] Ol. 95. 1.

[2] Impeachments for murder were laid in the court of the Βασιλευς, but not tried till four months after in the court of Areopagus, where the Βασιλευς had himself a vote. The cause was judged in the open air, for all such as were (ὁμορρόφιοι) under the same roof with the defendant were thought to partake of his guilt. The accuser gave him immediate notice not to approach the forum, the assembly, the temples, or the publick games, (προσηγορευει ειργεσθαι των νομιμων) and in that state he continued, till he was acquitted of the crime. See Antipho, Orat. de cæde Herodis, and de cæde Choreutæ. Informations might also (as it seems) be laid in the court of Heliæa before the Thesmothetæ.

NOTE.

Mr. Foster having published and made remarks on this and some other pieces of Plato, it is unnecessary for me to dwell long upon them.

P. 2. The Βασιλειος Στοα was in the Ceramicus on the right hand, as you come from the gate which led to the Piræus.

as sacrifices, oracles, divinations, and such matters,
and full of that grave kind of arrogance which these
mysterious sciences use to inspire. His father, having
an estate in the isle of Naxus, had employed among
his own slaves a poor Athenian who worked for hire.
This man, having drunk too much, had quarrelled with
and actually murdered one of the slaves. Upon which,
the father of Euthyphro apprehended and threw him
into a jail, till the Εξηγηται¹ had been consulted, in
order to know what should be done. The man, not
having been taken much care of, died in his confinement : upon which Euthyphro determines to lodge an
indictment against his own father for murder. Socrates,
surprised at the novelty of such an accusation, inquires
into the sentiments of Euthyphro with regard to piety
and the service of the gods, (by way of informing himself on that subject against the time of his trial) and
by frequent questions, intangling him in his own concessions, and forcing him to shift from one principle
and definition to another, soon lays open his ignorance, and shews that all his ideas of religion were

¹ The Εξηγηται at Athens, like the Pontifices at Rome, were
applied to, when any prodigy had happened or any violent
death, to settle the rights of expiation or to propitiate the
manes of the dead. Harpocration and Suidas have these words,
Εξηγητης, ὁ εξηγουμενος τα ιερα· εστι δε και ἁ προς τους κατ-
οιχομενους νομιζομενα εξηγουντο τοις δεομενοις. So Demosthenes
contra Everg. of a woman supposed to be murdered : Επειδη
τοινυν ετελευτησεν, ηλθον ὡς τους Εξηγητας, ἱνα ειδειην ὁ τι με χρη
ποιειν περι τουτων : and the prosecution of the murderer made
a necessary part of this expiation. See Theophrasti Charact :
περι Δεισιδαιμονιας, c. 16, and Plato de Republ. L. 4, p. 427,
where he calls the Delphian Apollo, Εξηγητης πατριος.

founded on childish fables and on arbitrary forms and institutions.

The intention of the dialogue seems to be, to expose the vulgar notions of piety, founded on traditions unworthy of tho divinity, and employed in propitiating him by puerile inventions and by the vain ceremonies of external worship, without regard to justice and to those plain duties of society, which alone can render us truly worthy of the deity.

APOLOGIA SOCRATIS.

PLATO was himself present at the trial of Socrates, being then about twenty-nine years of age; and he was one of those who offered to speak in his defence, (though the court would not suffer him to proceed), and to be bound as a surety for the payment of his fine: yet we are not to imagine, that this oration was the real defence which Socrates made. Dionysius says, that it was δικαστηριου μεν η αγορᾶς ουδε θυρας ιδων, κατ' αλλην δε τινα βουλησιν γεγραμμενος, and what that design was, he explains himself by saying, that, under

---

NOTES ON THE GREEK TEXT.
Platon. Op. Serrani, Vol. 1. p. 17.

P. 18. It is remarkable that he should mention this comedy of Aristophanes, as having made a deep impression on the people; and yet it was brought on the stage twenty years before, where it was exploded; and afterwards it was produced again, but still in vain: (Vid. Prolegom. ad Nubes, and v. 524.) though the author regarded it as his best play.

23. Qr? Whether Anytus were the same person who was colleague to the great Thrasybulus, and had a principal share in restoring the democracy, mentioned by Lysias in Agoratum, p. 260, 263, by Xenophon, Hist. Græc. L. 2, p. 468, and by Isocrates, in Exc. adv. Callimachum? Melitus, who is mentioned as a bad tragick poet in the Ranæ of Aristophanes, v. 1337, and whose person is described in the Euthyphro, was not probably the same with that Melitus, who was among the accusers

the cover of an apology, it is a delicate satire on the Athenians, a panegyrick on Socrates, and a pattern and character of the true philosopher. (Dion. Halicarnass. de vi Demosthen. p. 289, and de Art. Rhetor. p. 83. Vol. 2. edit. Huds. Oxon. 1704.) Nevertheless, it is founded on truth; it represents the true spirit and disposition of Socrates, and many of the topicks used in it are agreeable to those which we find in Xenophon,[1] and which were doubtless used by Socrates himself; as where he mentions his dæmon, and the reasons he had for preferring death to life, his account of the oracle given to Chærepho, and the remarkable allusion to Palamedes,[2] &c. the ground-work is manifestly the same, though the expressions are different. In one

[1] Xenophon was absent at the time of the trial, Ol. 95. 1, in Asia; and the account, which he gives, he had from Hermogenes, the son of Hipponicus, a great friend of Socrates: we see from him, that many persons had written narrations of the behaviour of Socrates on the occasion.

[2] This doubtless gave occasion to what Ælian and others have said, (Var. Hist. and Diog. Laert. L. 2, s. 44.) that Euripides, in some lines of his Palamedes, alluded to Socrates's death; whereas that drama was played Ol. 91. 1, and Euripides died Ol. 93. 2, seven years before Socrates.

NOTES.

of Andocides, the year before this, for Socrates speaks of him as a youth not known in the world before this accusation of his (See Euthyphr.); nor with the Melitus who was deputed by the Athenians to go to Sparta, Ol. 94. 1: these two last facts seem to belong to one and the same person.

P. 24. Πολλην αφθονιαν.] Hence it appears that, in whatever court Socrates was tried, the judges were extremely numerous.

26. Δραχμης εκ της Ορχηστρας.] The price of a seat in the theatre was at most one drachma.

106   NOTES ON PLATO.

thing only they seem directly to contradict each other :
Xenophon says, he neither offered himself any thing in
mitigation of his punishment, nor would suffer his friends
to do so, looking upon this as an acknowledgment of ·
some guilt : ουτε αυτον ὑπετιμησατο, ουτε τους φιλους
ειασεν· αλλα και ελεγεν, ὁτι το ὑποτιμᾶσθαι ὁμολογοῦντος
ειη αδικειν. If the word ὑποτιμᾶσθαι means that he
would not submit to ask for a change of his sentence

NOTES.

P. 32. Εβουλευσα δε.] Socrates was in the senate of Five
Hundred, Ol. 93. 3, being then sixty-five years of age. The
Prytanes presided in the assemblies of the people, were seated
in the place of honour, and attended by the Τοξοται, who, by
their orders, seized any persons who made a disturbance ; they
introduced ambassadours, gave liberty of speaking to the orators,
and of voting to the people ; and (as it appears) any one of
them could put a negative on their proceedings, since Socrates
alone, at the trial of the Στρατηγοι, insisted, that the question
was contrary to law, and would not suffer it to be put to the
assembly.

Ib. Θολος.] A building in the Ceramicus near the Βουλευτηριον
των Πεντακοσιων, where the Prytanes assembled to perform
sacrifice and to banquet. (Pausanias, L. 1, p. 12, and Jul.
Pollux in fin. L. 8.) Who were Nicostratus and Theodotus,
the sons of Theodotides ?

34. Εις μεν, μειρακιον ηδη· δυω δε, Παιδια.] Socrates had three
sons, (D. Laert. L. 2, s. 26.) Lamprocles, Sophroniscus, and
Menexenus, the first by Xanthippe, the two others (as it is said)
by Myrto, grand-daughter to the famous Aristides. Some say,
he married the latter first; but that is impossible, because he
had Lamprocles, his eldest son, by Xanthippe ; and she certainly
survived him ; therefore, if Myrto were his wife, he must have
had two wives together. This is indeed affirmed in a treatise
on nobility ascribed to Aristotle, and by Aristoxenus and Callis-
thenes his scholars, as well as by Demetrius Phalereus, and
others. It is a very extraordinary thing, that such men should

into banishment, or perpetual imprisonment, so far it is
agreeable to Plato, p. 37. but if it means, that he would
not suffer any mulct himself, nor permit his friends to
mention it, we see the contrary, p. 38, where he fines
himself one mina (all he was worth), and where his
friends Crito, Critobūlus, Plato, and Apollodorus, offer
thirty minæ (£96. 17s. 6d.) which was, I suppose, all
they could raise, to save him. Now this being a fact,

be deceived in a fact which happened so near their own time ;
yet Panætius, in his life of Socrates, expressly refuted this
story ; and it is sure, that neither Xenophon, nor Plato, nor
any other of his contemporaries, mentions any wife but Xanthippe.

P. 35. Αριστα ειναι και ὑμιν.] Here is an interval; and we see
that Melitus, Anytus, and Lyco, having gone through their
accusations, and Socrates having made his defence, and some
of his friends, perhaps, having also supported it, the judges
proceeded to vote guilty, or not guilty. The former suffrages
exceeded the latter by three, by thirty, or by thirty and three,
for the MSS. differ in the number. Justus of Tiberias (Laert.
L. 2. s. 41.) says by 281, which is doubtless false ; and he adds
that 361 condemned him to death.—I imagine, from what occurs
afterwards, that Melitus and Anytus spoke a second time, after
Socrates had finished his defence, before the court had voted.
Xenophon tells us, that some of Socrates's friends actually pleaded
for him. Ερρηθη πλειονα ὑπ' αυτου, και των συναγορευοντων φιλων
αυτου. Xenoph. Apolog. Sect. 22.

36. Καν ωφλε χιλιας.] I do not see how Socrates should know
this, unless a small number of the judges, immediately after his
defence, had risen to give their vote against him, and the rest
deferred voting, till after Lyco and Anytus had spoken a second
time in support of Melitus. In all publick accusations (some
sorts of Εισαγγελιαι excepted) this was the case, if the accuser
did not get a fifth of the votes. The next question regards the
Τιμημα, which the court had it in their power to mitigate, if

at that time easily proved or disproved, I am of opinion
that Plato never would have inserted into his discourse
a manifest falsity, and, therefore, we are to take Xenophon's words in that restrained sense which I have
mentioned.

Potter says, that from the nature of the crime
(Ἀσεβεῖα), it is evident that the trial was before the
court of Areopagus : but I take the contrary to be

NOTES.

they were persuaded or moved by the plea of the criminal. See
Lysias in Epicratem, p. 454.

P. 37. Μη μιαν μονον.] Here we see that capital causes were
decided in a single day.

38. Αξιοχρεω.] Here follows a second interval, during which .
the court voted, and condemned him to die.

39. Τιμωριαν.] Do not imagine with Dacier, in this place,
that he is threatening them with plagues and divine judgments :
he only means that for one Socrates a hundred shall spring up
to tell the Athenians their faults, which was very true; as the
Socratick school was continually increasing.

N.B. It may be observed, that Socrates was one of the
senate of Five Hundred, and was one of the Prytanes on the
trial of the Στρατηγοι : this is certain, both from Plato, in this
piece, and from Xenophon, Hist. Græc. L. 1. p. 449, and from
Æschines in Axiocho, p. 101. This last writer tells us, that the
matter was carried the next day by the choice of certain Προεδροι
εγκαταθετοι, to take the votes ; whence it should seem that it
was not, at that time of the republick, the constant custom to
elect Προεδροι for this purpose, as it afterwards was out of the
nine tribes, which were not Prytanes ; (See Potter, L. 1. 17.)
but that the Prytanes alone, or some chosen from among them,
exercised this office. Xenophon, in his Apomnemon, L. 4. c.
4, seems to speak of the same trial, and says, that Socrates was
Επιστατης in the assembly : if so, it was his particular province
to give the people liberty of voting ; but it is certain that he
was not an Επιστατης chosen out of the Προεδροι, as was usual

evident from the style both here and in Xenophon. He always addresses his judges by the name of Ανδρες, or Ανδρες Αθηναιοι, whereas the form of speaking either to the [1] Areopagites or to the senate [2] of Five Hundred, was constantly ω Βουλη : and in the courts [3] of justice, Ανδρες Δικασται, or sometimes Ανδρες Αθηναιοι, or Ανδρες alone : he therefore was judged in some of these courts.

[1] See Lysias's Apolog. in Simonem, and his Oration, Pro sacrâ Olivâ.

[2] See Lysias in Philonem, pro Mantitheo, &c.

[3] Ib. in Epicratem in principio et sub fin. : et pro Euphileto, et passim.

NOTE.

in the time of Demosthenes : he might indeed be Επιστατης of the Prytanes, an honour which continued but one day. See also Xenophon in Apomnem: L. 1. c. 1, where a clearer account is given of the same fact, where he is called Βουλευτης and Επιστατης εν τω Δημω. See also Plato's Gorgias, p. 473, and Corsinus Fast. Attic. v. 1. Diss. 6. de Προεδρων και Επιστατων Electione.

CRITO.

Π, ΠΕΡΙ ΠΡΑΚΤΟΥ.

or (as the second Basil edition more justly entitles it)

ΠΕΡΙ ΔΟΞΗΣ ΑΛΗΘΟΥΣ ΚΑΙ ΔΙΚΑΙΟΥ.

Ol. 95. 1.

Plat. Op. Serrani, Vol. 1. p. 43.

THIS beautiful dialogue (besides Dacier's translation and Foster's notes) has been translated and illustrated by the Abbé Sallier, keeper of the printed books in the French king's library; see Vol. 14. Mém. de l'Acad. des Inscriptions et Belles Lettres, p. 38.

PHÆDO.

II, ΠΕΡΙ ΨΤΧΗΣ.

Plat. Op. Serrani, Vol. 1. p. 57.

THIS famous dialogue was supposed by Panætius[1] the stoick, a great admirer of Plato, not to be genuine, or at least interpolated, rather, as it seems, from his own persuasion[2] of the soul's mortality, than from any thing in the piece itself unlike the manner or the tenets of the philosopher, to whom it has always been ascribed. The whole course of antiquity has regarded it as one of his principal works; and (what seems decisive) Aristotle[3] himself cites it, as a work of his master.

The historical part of it is admirable, and, though written and disposed with all the art and management of the best tragick writer, (for the slightest circumstance in it wants not its force and meaning) it exhibits nothing to the eye but the noble simplicity of nature.

[1] Anthologia, L. 1. 44.   [2] Cicero, Tusc. Quæst. L. 1. 32.
[3] Meteorolog. L. 2. 2.

NOTES ON THE GREEK TEXT.

P. 58. Κατ' ενιαυτον.] This annual solemnity should be distinguished from the great Delian festival described by Thucydides, (See Taylor's Comment on the Marmor Sandvicense,) which returned only once in four years, and which, after a long intermission, was revived Ol. 88. 3.

Every intelligent reader will feel what those who were
eye-witnesses are said to have felt, namely, *αηθη τινα
κρᾱσιν, απο τε της ἡδονης συγκεκραμενην ὁμου και της
λυπης.* The innocence, the humanity, the cheerfulness,
and the unaffected intrepidity of Socrates, will draw some
tears from him (as it did many from them) as for the
loss of a father; and will, at the same time, better than
any arguments, shew him a soul, which, if it were not
so, at least deserved to be immortal.

The reasoning part is far inferior, sometimes weak,
sometimes false, too obscure, too abstracted, to convince
us of any thing; yet with a mixture of good sense and
with many fine observations. The fabulous account of
a future state is too particular and too fantastick an
invention for Socrates to dwell upon at such a time, and
has less decorum and propriety in it than the other
parts of the dialogue.

Socrates attempts in this dialogue to prove, that true
philosophy is but a continual preparation for death; its
daily study and practice being to wean and separate the
body from the soul, whose pursuit of truth is perpetu-
ally stopped and impeded by the numerous avocations,
the little pleasures, pains, and necessities of its companion. *That*, as death is but a transition from its
opposite,[1] life (in the same manner as heat is from cold,

---

[1] This was an idea of Pythagoras. *Εν βιῳ αρχη τελευτης· εν
ζωῃ δε γενεσις φθορᾱς.* Diog. Laert. L. 8. s. 22.

NOTE.

P. 61. *Φιλολαου.*] We see that Philolaus of Crotona had been
at Thebes, and that Simmias and Cebes had both received from
him some tincture of the Pythagorean doctrines.

weakness from strength, and all things, both in the natural and in the moral world, from their contraries) so life is only a transition from death ; whence he would infer the probability of a metempsychosis. *That*, such propositions,[1] as every one assents to at first, being self-evident, and no one giving any account how such parts of knowledge, on which the rest are founded, were originally conveyed to our mind, there must have been a pre-existent state, in which the soul was acquainted with these truths, which she recollects and assents to on their recurring to her in this life. *That*, as truth is eternal and immutable, and not visible to our senses but to the soul alone ; and as the empire, which she exercises over the body, bears a resemblance to the power of the Divinity, it is probable that she, like her object, is everlasting and unchangeable, and, like the office she bears, something divine. *That*, it cannot be, as some have thought, merely a harmony resulting from a disposition of parts in the body, since it directs, commands, and restrains the functions of that very body. *That*,

---

[1] Socrates has explained the same doctrine in the Meno, p. 81, &c. but rather as conjectural than demonstrable, for he adds, in the conclusion, p. 86. Τα μεν γε αλλα ουκ αν πανυ υπερ του λογου διϊσχυρισαιμην, &c.

NOTES.

P. 97. Hence it is clear that Socrates never was the scholar of Anaxagoras, (whatever Laertius and others have said) though he had read his works with application.

* See who Echecrates was, in Plato's 9th Epistle, Op. Vol. 3. p. 358. The Phliasians were ever the faithful allies of Sparta, and (though the Peloponnesian war was now at an end) it is no wonder if they had not any great intercourse with Athens.

tho soul, being the cause of life to the body, can never itself be susceptible of death ; and *that*, there will be a state of rewards and punishments, the scene of which he takes pains in describing, though he concludes, that no man can tell exactly where or what it shall be.

Dacier's superstition and folly are so great in his notes on the Phædo, that they are not worth dwelling upon.

ERASTÆ.

ΕΡΑΣΤΑΙ seu ΑΝΤΕΡΑΣΤΑΙ :

ΠΕΡΙ ΦΙΛΟΣΟΦΙΑΣ.

THE scene lies in the school of Dionysius the gram-
marian,[1] who was Plato's own master. The design is
to shew, that philosophy consists not in ostentation,
nor in that insight (which the sophists affected) into
a variety of the inferior parts of science, but in the
knowledge of one's self, and in a sagacity in discover-
ing the characters and dispositions of mankind, and of
correcting and of modelling their minds to their own
advantage.

The dialogue is excellent, but too short for such a
subject. The interlocutors are not named, nor is there
any mark of the time when it happened.

[1] Γραμματιστης, of whom children learned to read and write.
Vid. Charmidem. p. 161.

NOTE ON THE GREEK TEXT.

Platon. Op. Serrani, Vol. 1. p. 132.

P. 135. The price of a slave skilled in carpenter's work, was
five or six minæ, about £19. 7s. 6d. ; of an architect, 10,000
drachmæ, i.e. above £322. 17s. 0d.

LACHES.

II, ΠΕΡΙ ΑΝΔΡΕΙΑΣ.

THE persons in this dialogue are men of distinguished rank and figure in the state of Athens.

1. Lysimachus,[1] son to the famous Aristides, surnamed, The Just.

2. Melesias, son to that Thucydides who was the great rival of Pericles in the administration.

[1] Vid. Menonei. p. 93. 94. Both he and Melesias were persons little esteemed, except on their father's account.

NOTES ON THE GREEK TEXT.

Platon. Op. Serrani, Vol. 2. p. 178.

P. 178. Τον Ανδρα.] Stesilaus, as it afterwards appears, an Athenian.

179. Παππω οντε.] Perhaps we should read, Παππου και ουτος ονομ᾽ εχων, τούμου πατρος.

180. Οντα δημοτην.] Both Socrates and Lysimachus were of Alopecæ.

Ib. Δαμωνα.] Damon the sophist and musician, scholar to Agathocles (see the Protagoras, p. 316.) who excelled in the same professions, had been banished by the faction opposite to Pericles, on account of his intimacy with that great man, in whose education Plutarch (in Vit. Pericl.) would make one imagine he had a principal share ; but, in reality, their intimacy did not begin till Pericles was an old man, as Plato (in Alcib. I. p. 118.) expressly tells us ; and accordingly we find here, that Laches had as yet never seen Damon, who probably, after the ten years of his ostracism were expired, was returned to Athens, while Laches commanded in Sicily.

3. Nicias,[1] so often the general in the Peloponnesian war, celebrated for his goodness, for his conduct, and for his success, till the fatal expedition to Syracuse in which he perished.

4. Laches, son of Melanopus of the district Æxone, and tribe Cecropis,[2] commander of the fleet sent to the assistance of the Leontines in Sicily, Ol. 88. 2, in which expedition he defeated the Locrians, reduced Messene, Mylæ, and other places, and after his recall, seems to have been [3] prosecuted by Cleon for corruption in this very year; whence it appears, that he was in the battle of Delium.[4]

[1] Thucydides passim. — Plutarch: in Vitâ Niciæ — Lysias contra Poliuchum, p. 318.

[2] Thucydides in multis locis. Laches was also among the commanders of the troops sent into Peloponnesus to assist the Argives. Ol. 90. 3. (See Diodorus, L. 12. p. 126. edit. Rhodomanni, 1604.

[3] Aristophanes in Vespis, et Scholia; which drama was played Ol. 89. 2; see verse 890, where he is called Λαβης ὁ Αιξωνευς, as Cleon is called, Κυων ὁ Κυδαθηναιευς.

[4] He was one of the generals of the Athenians in the battle near Mantinea, Ol. 90. 3, and was slain in that action. See Thucydides, L. 5. p. 334, and Androtion in Schol. ad Aves Aristophanis, v. 13.

NOTES.

P. 180. Πατρικος φιλος.] Sophroniscus, therefore, though in low circumstances, was a man of good character, and known to the principal citizens.

182. Οὐ γαρ αγῶνος.] The war with Sparta. It is plain, that this was not one among the usual exercises of their gymnasia, and the teachers of it were but lately introduced in Athens.

183. Τραγωδιας ποιητης.] A satire on the Athenians who were devoted to these entertainments. See de Republ. L. 2. p. 376, L. 3. p. 390, and L. 8. p. 568.

5. Thucydides, son to Melesias.[1] } Two youths under twenty years of age.
6. Aristides, son to Lysimachus. }

7. Socrates, then in his forty-seventh year.

The two first of these persons, being then very ancient, and probably about seventy years of age, and sensible of that defect in their own education, which had caused them to lead their lives in an obscurity unworthy the sons of such renowned fathers, were the more solicitous on account of their own sons, who were now almost of an age to enter into the world. They

[1] Vid. Menonem, p. 94. et Theagem, p. 130. et Theætetum, p. 151.

NOTES.

P. 183. Αβατον ιερον.] Like the temples and groves of the Σεμναι Θεαι, the Furies, Χωρος—αθικτος ουδ᾽ οικητος, &c. Soph. Œd. Col. v. 39.

Ib. Ετερωθι.] In the Sicilian expedition.

Ib. Δορυδρεπανον.] A long halbard, whose head was fashioned like a scythe or broad sickle. They were used to cut the rigging of ships down, and in sieges to pull down the battlements of walls, such as Livy, L. 38, calls, "Asseres falcati ad detergendas pinnas." Vid. Fragm. Polybii, v. 2. ed. Gronov. p. 1546.

184. Επιφανεστερος γενοιτο, η οιος ην.] Perhaps we should read οιος ην, and omit the η.

185. Αλλ᾽ ου περι του, ου ενεκα αλλο εζητει.] Perhaps we should read, ο ενεκα αλλου εζητει.

188. Δωριστι, αλλ᾽ ουκ Ιαστι.] A satire on the Athenians, and a compliment to Sparta (V. de Republ. L. 3. p. 398.) which Plato seldom omits, when he finds an opportunity. (Vid. Hippiam Major, p. 283 and 4.—Protogoram, p. 342.—Symposium, p. 209, where he calls the laws of Lycurgus, Σωτηρας της Ελλαδος.

therefore invite Nicias and Laches, men of distinguished
abilities and bravery, but some years younger than
themselves, to a conference on that subject; and after
having been spectators together of the feats of arms
exhibited by Stesilaus, a professed master in the exercise of all weapons, they enter into conversation.
Socrates, who happened to be present, is introduced by
Laches to Lysimachus, as a person worthy to bear a
part in their consultation. The first question is occa-
sioned by the spectacle which they had just beheld,
namely, " whether the management of arms be an exercise fit to be learned by young men of quality ? "
Nicias is desired first to deliver his opinion, which is,
that it may give grace and agility to their persons,
and courage and confidence to their minds; that it
may make them more terrible to their enemies in
battle, and more useful to their friends; and at the
same time may inspire them with a laudable ambition
to attain the higher and more noble parts of military

NOTES.

P. 189. Ει δε νεωτερος, &c.] Socrates does not seem to have
attained a great reputation and esteem till about this time of
his life, when Aristophanes also first introduced him on the
stage, Ol. 89. 1, in his Νεφελαι.

194. Των δεινων και θαρραλεων.] Which he afterwards defines, Δεινα μεν, ά και δεος παρεχει. θαρραλεα δε, ά και μη δεος
παρεχει.

195. Ποτερον όμολογεῖς μαντις ειναι.] Dacier explains well
this piece of raillery on the supposed timidity and superstition
of Nicias's character : but when he carries it still farther, and
supposes it a part of Nicias's religion to believe in the bravery
of the Crommyonian wild-sow (p. 196.), he grows insipid, and
interprets the meaning of Socrates quite wrong.

120 NOTES ON PLATO.

knowledge. Laches has a direct contrary opinion of it : he argues from his own experience, that he never knew a man, who valued himself upon this art, that had distinguished himself in the war ; that, the Lacedemonians, who valued and cultivated military discipline beyond all others, gave no encouragement to these masters of defence ; that, to excel in it, only served to make a coward more assuming and impudent, and to expose a brave man to envy and calumny, by making any little failing or oversight more conspicuous in him.

Socrates is then prevailed upon to decide the difference, who artfully turns the question of much greater importance for a young man of spirit to know, namely, "what is valour, and how it is distinguished from a brutal and unmeaning fierceness." By interrogating Laches and Nicias, he shews, that such as had the highest reputation for courage in practice, were often very deficient in the theory ; and yet none can communicate a virtue he possesses, without he has himself a clear idea of it. He proves, that valour must have

NOTES.

P. 197. Λαμαχον.] See his character in Plutarch in Nicias's life, and in Thucydides, and in Aristophanes in Acharnens : he was remarkable for his bravery and his poverty ; he went to Sicily with Nicias and Alcibiades, as their colleague, Ol. 91. 1, and died there.

Ib. Καλλιστα τα τοιαντα ονοματα διαιρειν.] Prodicus is accordingly introduced in the Protagoras, p. 337, accurately distinguishing the sense of words, and defining all the terms he uses ; and again in the Protagoras, p. 358, and in the Meno, p. 75, and in the Charmides, p. 163. See also the Euthydemus, p. 277, and this seems to have been the subject of his Επιδειξις πεντηκονταδραχμος. Vid. Cratylum, p. 384.

good sense for its basis; that it consists in the knowledge of what is, and what is not, to be feared; and
that, consequently, we must first distinguish between
real good and evil; and that it is closely connected
with the other virtues, namely, justice, temperance,
and piety, nor can it ever subsist without them. The
scope of this fine dialogue is to shew, that philosophy
is the school of true bravery.

The time of this dialogue is not long after the
defeat of the Athenians at Delium, Ol. 89. 1, in which
action Socrates had behaved with great spirit, and
thence recommended himself to the friendship of
Laches.

NOTES.

P. 197. Αληθως Αιξωνεα.] Βλασφημον scilicet. Vid. Harpocration in Αιξωνας.

201. Αιδως.] The verse is in the Odyssey, P. v. 347 :

Αιδως ουκ αγαθη κεχρημενω ανδρι πρoικτη.

Plato here reads—ανδρι παρειναι. And so again in the Charmides, p. 161.

Ib. Ηξω παρα σε.] Accordingly Aristides and Thucydides
were actually under the care of Socrates from this time ; (see
the Theages sub fin.) but they soon left him.

HIPPARCHUS.

Η, ΦΙΛΟΚΕΡΔΗΣ.

THE intention of the dialogue is to shew, that all mankind in their actions equally tend to some imagined
good, but are commonly mistaken in the nature of it;

NOTES ON THE GREEK TEXT.

Platon. Op. Edit. Serrani, Vol. 2. p. 225.

P. 225. Ἵνα τι και ἡμεις των σοφων ῥηματων.] Ισοκωλα και
ὁμοιοτελευτα.

228. Πολιτη τω εμω.] Thucydides affirms the express contrary to Plato, that Hipparchus never reigned at all. Ουκ
Ἱππαρχος, ὡσπερ ὁι πολλοι οιονται, αλλ᾽ Ἱππιας, πρεσβυτατος ων,
εσχε την αρχην. Thucyd. L. 6. Sect. 54. p. 379. Ed. Huds.
Oxon : but he agrees with Plato that the government of the
Pisistratidæ was mild and popular, till the murder of Hipparchus. Hipparchus first brought the works of Homer to Athens;
he was intimate with Simonides, and sent a galley to bring
Anacreon to Athens, as I imagine, from Samos, after the death
of Polycrates, which happened in the fourth year of Hippias's,
(or according to Plato) of Hipparchus's reign.—The custom of
the Rhapsodi successively repeating all Homer's poems during
the Panathenœa.—Hermæ were erected by Hipparchus in the
middle of Athens, and of every Δημος in Attica, with inscriptions in verse, containing some moral precept, written by himself.

229. Της αδελφης ατιμιαν της κανηφοριας.] Perhaps, της
ΑΡΜΟΔΙΟΥ αδελφης—της Κανηφορου, or εν τη κανηφορια, unless
χαριν or ἑνεκα be understood.

and that nothing can properly be called gain which, when attained, is not a real good.

The time of the dialogue is no where marked.

NOTE.

P. 231. Αντι δωδεκαστασιου.] Gold was therefore to silver at that time, as twelve to one.

PHILEBUS.

Η, ΠΕΡΙ 'ΗΔΟΝΗΣ.

Platon. Op. Serrani, Vol. 2. p. 11.

THIS dialogue is too remarkable to be passed over slightly : we shall therefore annex the principal heads of it. The question is, Τι των ανθρωπινων κτηματων αριστον; "What is the supreme good of mankind?" and, "whether pleasure[1] or wisdom have the better pretension to it?"

The persons are, Protarchus, the son of Callias, who supports the cause of pleasure, and Socrates, who opposes it : Philebus, who had begun the ·dispute but was grown weary of it, and many others of the Athenian youth, are present at the conversation. The time of it is no where marked. The end of the dialogue is supposed to be lost.

P. 12. The name of pleasure, variously applied, to the joys of intemperance and folly, and to the satisfaction arising from wisdom, and from the command of our passions.

Though of unlike, and even of opposite natures, they agree so far, as they are all pleasures alike ; as black and white, though contrary the one to the other, are comprehended under the general head of colours.

[1] V. de Republ. L. 6. p. 505.

Though included under one name, if some are contrary and of opposite natures to others, they cannot both be *good* alike.

P. 14. Vulgar enquiry, how it is possible for many [1] to be one, and one, many, laid aside by consent as childish.

Obscure question on our abstracted idea of unity. The vanity and disputatious humours of a young man, who has newly tasted of philosophy and has got hold of a puzzling question, are well described.

Every subject of our conversation has in it a mixture of the infinite and of the finite.

P. 16. The true logician will (as the ancients prescribed,) first discover some single and general idea, and then proceed to two or three subordinate to it, which he will again subdivide into their several classes, which will form, as it were, a medium beneath finite and infinite.

Example in the alphabet. The human voice is one idea, but susceptible of a variety of modulations, and to be diversified even to infinity: to know that it is *one*, and to know that it is infinite, are neither of them knowledge; but there can be no knowledge without them.

When we first attain to the *unity* of things, we must descend from number to infinity, if we would know any thing: and when we first perceive their infinity, we must ascend through number to unity. Thus the first inventor [2] of letters remarking the endless variety of

<hr/>

[1] V. Phædon. p. 96.
[2] V. Phædrum. p. 274. V. et Politicum. p. 285. Δεον, όταν την των πολλων τις προτερον αισθηται κοινωνιαν, μη προαφιστασθαι,

126   NOTES ON PLATO.

sounds discovered a certain number of vowels, distinguished others of a different power, called consonants, some of which were mutes, and others liquids, and to the whole combination of elements he gave the form and name of an alphabet.

P. 20. The good, which constitutes happiness, must be in itself sufficient and perfect, the aim and end of all human creatures.

A life of mere pleasure considered by itself, which, (if pleasure only be that good) must need no mixture nor addition.

If we had no memory nor reflection, we could have no enjoyment of past pleasure, nor hope of future, and scarcely any perception of the present, which would be much like the life of an oyster : on the other hand, a life of thought and reflection, without any sense of pleasure or of pain, seems no desirable state. Neither contemplation, therefore, nor pleasure, are the good we seek after, but probably a life composed of both.

P. 22. Whether the happiness of this mixed state is the result of pleasure, or rather of wisdom, and which contributes most to it?

P. 23. Division of all existence into the infinite, the limited,[1] the mixed, which is composed of the two former, and the supreme cause of all.

πριν αν εν αυτη τας διαφορας ειδη πασας οποσαι περ εν ειδεσι κεινται· τας δε αυ παντοδαπας ανομοιοτητας, οταν εν πληθεσιν οφθωσι, μη δινατον ειναι δυσωπουμενον παυεσθαι, πριν αν συμπαντα οικεια εντος μιας ομοιοτητος ερξας, γενους τινος ουσια περιβαλη.

[1] Or rather, that which limits and gives bounds (το περας) such as figure, which gives bounds to extension ; as time, which limits duration, &c.

Example of the first; all that admits of increase or decrease, greater or less, hotter or colder, &c. i.e. all undetermined quantity.

Of the second; all that determines quantity, as equality, duplicity, and whatever relation number bears to number, and measure to measure.

Of the third, or mixed; all created things, in which the infinity of matter is, by number and measure, reduced to proportion.

P. 27. Pleasure and pain, having no bounds [1] in themselves, are of the nature of the infinite.

P. 28. The supreme power and wisdom of the Deity asserted.

But a small portion of the several elements is visible in our frame. Our soul is a small portion of the spirit of the universe, or fourth kind mentioned above.

P. 31. Pain is a consequence of a [2] dissolution of that symmetry and harmony in our fabrick, which is the cause of health, strength, &c. as pleasure results

---

[1] Happiness and misery, says Mr. Locke, are the names of two extremes, the utmost bounds whereof we know not ; but of some degrees of them we have very lively ideas. (Chapt. of Power, 1. 41.)

[2] This is an idea of Timæus, the Locrian : 'Οκοσαι μεν ων (των Κινασεων) εξιστᾱντι ταν φυσιν, αλγειναι εντι· ὁκοσαι δε αποκαθισ-τᾱντι ες αυταν, ἀδοναι ονομαινονται. And Mr. Locke makes much the same observation. Excess of cold (says he) as well as heat, pains us ; because it is equally destructive of that temper, which is necessary to the preservation, and the exercise of the several functions of the body, and which consists in a moderate degree of warmth, or, if you please, a motion of the insensible parts of our bodies confined within certain bounds. Essay on H. U. Ch. 7. §. 4.

from the return and restoration of the parts to their just proportions.

Thus hunger and thirst are uneasinesses proceeding from emptiness; eating and drinking produce pleasure by restoring a proper degree of repletion. Excess of cold is attended with a sensation of pain, and warmth brings with it an equal pleasure.

Pleasures and pains of the soul alone arise from the[1] expectation of pleasure or pain of the body : these are hopes and fears, and depend upon the memory.

A state of indifference is without pleasure or pain, which is consistent with a life of thought and contemplation.

P. 33. Sensation is conveyed to the soul through the organs of the body; the body [2] may receive many motions and alterations unperceived by the mind.

Memory is the preserver of our sensations.

Recollection, an act of the mind alone, restores to us ideas imprinted in the memory, after an intermission.

Desire, in the mind alone, by which it supplies the wants of the body : it depends on memory.

In the appetites, pleasure and pain go together, a

[1] "Hope is that pleasure in the mind, which every one finds upon the thought of a profitable future enjoyment of a thing which is apt to delight him. Fear is an uneasiness upon the thought of future evil, likely to befall us." Locke II.U. Ch. 20. Φοβος ἡ προ λυπης ελπις· θαρρος δε, ἡ προ του εναντιου. L. 1. Legum. p. 644.

[2] This is also from Timæus. Κινασιων δε των απο των εκτος τας μεν αναδιδομενας εις τον φρονεοντα τοπον, αισθησιας ειμεν, τας δε ὑπ' αντιλαψιν μη πιπτοισας, ανεπαισθητως, η τω τα πασχοντα σωματα γεωδεστερα ειμεν, η τω τας κινασιας αμενηνοτερας γιγνεσθαι. De Animâ Mundi. p. 100.

proportionable satisfaction succeeding as the uneasiness abates.

Memory [1] of a past pleasing sensation inspires hope of a future one, and thereby abates an uneasiness actually present; as the absence of hope doubles a present pain.

Whether truth and falsehood belong to pleasures and pains?

They do: as these are founded on our opinions [2] of things preconceived, which may, undoubtedly, be either true or false.

Our opinions are founded on our sensations, and the memory of them. Thus we see a figure at a distance beyond a certain rock, or under a certain tree, and we say to ourselves, it is a man; but on advancing up to it, we find a rude image of wood carved by the shepherd.

The senses, the memory, and the passions, which attend on them, write on our souls, or rather delineate, a variety of conceptions and representations of which, when justly drawn, we form true opinions and propositions; but when falsely, we form false ones.

On these our hopes and fears are built, and consequently are capable of truth and falsehood, as well as the opinions on which they are founded.

[1] What Plato calls by the name of Μνημη, and Αναμνησις, are by Locke distinguished under the names of contemplation and memory, L. 1. Ch. 10. being the different powers of retention. (See De Legib. L. 5. p. 732.)

[2] All this head is finely explained by Locke. (Ch. of Power, § 61, 62, 63, 64, 65, &c.) which is the best comment on this part of Plato.

P. 40. The good abound in just and true hopes, fears, and desires; the bad in false and delusive ones.

P. 41. As pleasures[1] and pains are infinite, we can only measure them by comparison, one with the other.

Our hopes and fears are no less liable to be deceived by the prospect of distant objects, than our eyes. As we are always comparing those, which are far off, with others less remote or very near, it is no wonder that we are often mistaken; especially as a pleasure, when set next a pain, does naturally appear greater than its true magnitude, and a pain less.

So much then of our pains and pleasures as exceeds or falls short of its archetype, is false.

A state of indolence, or of apathy, is supposed by the school of Heraclitus to be impossible, on account of the perpetual motion of all things.

Motions and alterations[2] proved to happen continually in our body, of which the soul has no perception.

P. 43. Therefore, (though we should allow the perpetual motion of things,) there are times when the soul feels neither pleasure nor pain; so that this is a possible state.

Pleasure, and its contrary, are not the consequences of *any* changes in our constituent parts, but of *such* changes as are considerable and violent.

[1] "If we will rightly estimate what we call good and evil, we shall find it lies much in comparison." (Locke, C. of Power. § 42.)

[2] Whatever alterations are made in the body, if they reach not the mind,—whatever impressions are made on the outward parts, if they are not taken notice of within,—there is no perception. Locke, Ch. 9.

The sect of philosophers, who affirm [1] that there is no pleasure but the absence of pain, is in the wrong, but from a noble principle.[2]

To know the nature of pleasure, we should consider such as are strongest : bodily pleasures are such.

Pleasure is in proportion to our desires. The desires and longings of sick persons are the most violent : the mad and thoughtless feel the strongest [3] degree of pleasure and of pain ; so that both the one and the other increase with the disorder and depravity of our body and mind.

Pleasures of lust have a mixture of pain, as the pain of the itch [4] has a mixture of pleasure, and both subsist at the same instant.

Anger, grief, love, envy, are pains of the soul, but with a mixture [5] of pleasure. Exemplified in the exercise of our compassion and terror at a [6] tragick spectacle, and of our envy at a comick one. The pleasure of ridicule arises from vanity and from the ignorance of ourselves. We laugh at the follies [7] of the weak, and hate those of the powerful.

[1] " Pleasure," says Mr. Selden, " is nothing but the intermission of pain, the enjoyment of something I am in great trouble for, till I have it."

[2] Δυσχερεια τινι φυσεως ουκ αγεννους λιαν μεμισηκοτων την της ήδονης δυναμιν, και νενομικοτων ουδεν ὑγιες.

[3] V. Plat. in Republ. L. 3. p. 403.

[4] Vid. Gorgiam. p. 494.

[5] V. Aristot. Rhetor. L. 2. c. 2.

[6] Μη τοις δραμασι μονον, αλλα και τη του βιου ξυμπαση τραγωδια και κωμωδια, p. 50.

[7] Γελοία μεν, όποσα ασθενη· μισητα δε, όποσα ή ερρωμενα.

Pure and unmixed pleasures [1] proved to exist : those of the senses resulting from regularity of figure, beautiful colours, melodious sounds, odours of fragrance, &c. and all whose absence is not necessarily [2] accompanied with any uneasiness. Again : satisfactions of the mind resulting from knowledge, the absence or loss of which is not naturally attended with any pain.

A small portion of pure and uncorrupted pleasure is preferable to a larger one of that which is mixed and impure.

The opinion of some philosophers, that pleasure is continually generating, but is never produced, i.e. it has no real existence, seems true with regard to mere bodily pleasures.

Enquiry into knowledge. The nature of the arts : such of them, as approach the nearest to real knowledge, are the most [3] considerable, being founded on number, weight, and [4] measure, and capable of demonstration.

Secondly, those attainable only by use and frequent trial, being founded on conjecture and experiment, such as musick, medicine, agriculture, natural philosophy, &c.

P. 60. Recapitulation.

P. 61. Happiness resides [5] in the just mixture of wisdom and pleasure; particularly when we join the

---

[1] Vid. de Republ. L. 9. p. 584.

[2] Ουτι φυσειγε, αλλ' εν τισι λογισμοις. p. 52.

[3] Vid. de Republ. L. 10. p. 602.

[4] And above all, logick, to which we owe all the evidence and certainty we find in the rest. Ὡσπερ θριγκος, τοις μαθημασιν ἡ Διαλεκτικη ἡμιν επανω κειται, &c. De Republ. L. 7. p. 534.

[5] Vid. de Republ. L. 9. p. 582. and de Leg. L. 5. p. 733.

purest pleasures with the clearer and more certain sciences.

P. 63. Prosopopœia of the pleasures and sciences, consulted on the proposal made for uniting them.

P. 64. No mixture is either useful or durable, without proportion. The supreme good of man consists in beauty, in symmetry, and in truth, which are the causes of all the happiness to be found in the above-mentioned union.

MENO.

THE subject of the dialogue is this: That virtue is knowledge, and that true philosophy alone can give us that knowledge.

I see nothing in this dialogue to make one think that Plato intended to raise the character of Meno. He is introduced as a young man who seems to value

---

NOTES ON THE GREEK TEXT.
Plat. Op. Serrani, Vol. 2. p. 70.

P. 70. Εφ' ἱππικη τε και πλουτω.] The breed of Thessalian horses was the most celebrated in Greece; and when the cities of Thessaly were united among themselves, they could raise a body of six thousand, equal to any cavalry in the world. (Xenophon Hellenic. L. 6. p. 339 Pausan. L. 10. p. 799. Plato in Hipp. Maj. p. 284.) They were of great service to Alexander in his expeditions. The country was very rich in pasture and in corn, and, as their government was generally remiss and ill-regulated, their wealth naturally introduced a corruption (Athenæus, L. 14. p. 663.) of manners, which made them first slaves themselves, and then the instruments of slavery to other people. It was they who invited the Persian (Herod. L. 7. and L. 9.) into Greece; and afterwards gave rise to the power of the Macedonians.

Isocrates (Orat. de Pace, p. 183.) produces them as an example of a strong and wealthy people, reduced by their own bad management to a low and distressed condition.

himself on his parts, and on the proficiency he has made under Gorgias the Leontine, (whose notions are here exposed) and the compliments Socrates makes him on his beauty, wealth, family, and other distinctions, are only little politenesses ordinarily used by that philosopher to put persons into good humour, and draw them into conversation with him.

The time of the dialogue seems to be not long before the expedition of the ten thousand into Asia, for Meno was even then a very young man, (ετι ωραιος, αγενειος) as he is represented here; and the menaces of Anytus (p. 94) shew, that it was not long before the accusa-

---

NOTES.

P. 70. Αριστιππου του Λαρισσαιου.] Aristippus of Larissa, one of the potent house of the Aleuadæ, descendants of Hercules, from which the Thessalians had so often elected their Ταγοι, or captains-general. There had been a friendship kept up between them and the royal family of Persia, ever since the invasion of Greece by Xerxes, in which they were of great use to him. This Aristippus had particular connections with the younger Cyrus (Xenoph. Anab. L. 1. p. 145. and 2. 173.) who lent him a body of four thousand mercenaries, which he made use of to subdue the faction which opposed him in Thessaly, and seems to have established a sort of tyranny there. Meno (also of Larissa) son of Alexidemus, led a body of fifteen hundred men to the assistance of Cyrus in his expedition against his brother, Artaxerxes, Ol. 94. 4, and (after the death of Cyrus) betrayed the Greek commanders into the hands of the Persian, who cut off their heads. He himself survived not above a year, but was destroyed by the Persians. His character is admirably drawn by Xenophon, (Anab. L. 2. p. 173.) and many have looked on this as a mark of the enmity between Plato and Xenophon. See Athenæus, L. 11. p. 505 and 506. Diog. Laert. L. 2. Sect. 57, and L. 3. s. 34, and Aul. Gellius, L. 14. s. 3.

tion of Socrates : so that we may place it Ol. 94. 4, if
Plato may be trusted in these small matters of chronology which, we know, he sometimes neglected. Gorgias
was yet at Athens, Ol. 93. 4, and it is probable, that
the approaching siege of that city might drive him
thence into Thessaly, and he returned not till after
Socrates's death.

Socrates here distinguishes (p. 75.) the true [1] method
of disputation from the false, Το Διαλεκτικον απο του
Εριστικου και Αγωνιστικου.

Χαιρειν τε καλουσι και δυνᾶσθαι : (p. 77.) this is
Meno's first definition of virtue, that it consists in
desiring good, and in being able to attain it. Socrates
proves that all men desire good, and consequently all
men are so far equally virtuous (which is an absurdity);
it must therefore consist in the ability to attain it ;
which is true in Socrates's sense of the word good,

---

[1] An art which Socrates allowed to none, but to the true
philosopher, τω καθαρως τε και δικαιως φιλοσοφουντι. V. Sophist.
p. 253.

NOTES.

P. 76. Definition of figure, Σχημα, στερεου περας, the limit or
outline of a solid : but this seems imperfect to me, except we
read Στερεου (η επιπεδου) περας. Lucretius calls it Filum, or
Circumcæsura.

Ib. Απορροας, κατ' Εμπεδοκλεα.] See Lucretius, L. 2, v. 381.
et sequent. and L. 4. v. 217.

Ib. definition of colour, in the manner of Gorgias, Χροα
απορροη σχηματων οψει συμμετρος και αισθητος (perhaps we should
read σωματων) ; that eflux, or those eflluvia, of figured bodies,
which are proportioned to our sense of seeing. This is true,
if understood of the particles of light reflected from bodies ;
and not otherwise. But Empedocles, and after him Epicurus,

(which makes him say, ισως αν ευ λεγοις): but it is
necessary to know if men's ideas of it are the same.
Upon enquiry, Meno's meaning appears to be health,
honour, riches, power, &c.; but, being pressed by
Socrates, he is forced to own, that the attainment of
these is so far from virtue, that it is vice, unless accompanied with temperance, with justice, and with piety;
as then the virtue of such an attainment consists in
such adjuncts, and not in the thing attained; and as
these are confessedly parts of virtue only, subordinate

138   NOTES ON PLATO.

to some more general idea, they are no nearer dis-
covering what virtue in the abstract is, than they were
at first.

Though the doctrine of reminiscence, repeated by
Plato in several places, be chimerical enough; yet this,
which follows it, (p. 84.) is worth attending to, where
Socrates shews how useful it is to be sensible of our
own ignorance. While we know nothing, we doubt of
nothing; this is a state of great confidence and security.
From the first distrust we entertain of our own understanding springs an uneasiness and a curiosity, which
will not be satisfied till it attains to knowledge.

NOTES.

P. 89. Εν Ακροπολει.] Where the sacred treasure was kept.
It consisted of one thousand talents never to be touched, unless
the city were to be attacked by a naval force; in any other case
it was made capital to propose it.   Χιλια ταλαντα απο των εν τη
Ακροπολει χρηματων εδοξεν αυτοις, εξαιρετα ποιησαμενοις, χωρις
θεσθαι, και μη αναλουν, αλλ' απο των αλλων πολεμειν· ην δε τις
ειπη η επιψηφιση κινειν τα χρηματα ταυτα ες αλλο τι, ην μη οι
πολεμιοι νηΐτη στρατω επιπλεωσι τη πολει, και δεη αμυνεσθαι,
θανατον ζημιαν επεθεντο.   Thucyd. Hist. L. 2. Sect. 24.   They
called this treasure Το Αβυσσον. Aristophan. Lysistrata, v. 174.
It was thus set apart the first year of the Peloponnesian war.

90. Τη αυτου σοφια.] Probably by the leather-trade, which
Anytus also carried on, as the famous Cleon, and other principal
Athenians, had done.   See Aristophanes in the Equites.
Ismenias, the Theban, had a principal hand in raising the Theban
or Corinthian war, (as it was called) against the Lacedæmonians,
being bribed by Timocrates the Rhodian, who was also bribed
by the Persians, with money for that purpose; but as this
happened five or six years after the death of Socrates, we can
hardly suppose that Plato here alluded to it. Yet I think it
very possible that he might have written this dialogue about

Whoever reads the dialogue (attributed to Æschines the Socratick) intitled Περι Αρετης, ει διδακτον; will see so great a resemblance to this of Plato, and at the same time find so great a difference in several respects, that he will believe both one and the other to be sketches of a real conversation, which passed between Socrates and some other person, noted down both by Æschines and by Plato at the time : the former left his notes in that unfinished condition, but the latter supplied them as he thought fit, and worked them up at his leisure into this dialogue.

---

that time, when the name of Ismenias was in every one's mouth, Ol. 96. 2, or perhaps not till Ol. 99. 3, when his condemnation and death must doubtless have been the general subject of conversation : Plato was then just returned to Athens, after his first voyage to Sicily. I do not find what Polycrates is here meant. Xenoph. Hellenic. L. 3. p. 294, and L. 5. p. 325, 326.

90. Anytus, the son of Anthemio. See Xenoph. Apol. Socrat. sub fin.: and Diog. Laert. L. 2. s. 38, 39, 43.

91. Αποθανειν εγγυς.] Protagoras was cast away on his voyage to Sicily, Ol. 92. 3 ; he began therefore to teach, Ol. 82. 3, being then thirty years of age.

93. Cleophantus, the youngest of the three sons of Themistocles, by Archippe. See Plutarch in his life.

94. See the Laches, where Melesias and Lysimachus are introduced in the dialogue. For the character of this Thucydides, see Plutarch in Pericle, Aristophan. in Acharn. v. 703, and Schol. ad Vespas, v. 941 : he underwent the sentence of ostracism, Ol. 83. 4.

95. Nine lines from the 'Ελεγεια of Theognis.

GORGIAS.

ON THE ABUSES OF ELOQUENCE.

Plat. Op. Serrani, Vol. 1. p. 447.

NOTES ON THE GREEK TEXT.

P. 448. Κατα τεχνην — κατα τυχην — αλλοι αλλων αλλως.] Observe the jingle of words introduced by Gorgias, and affected by his imitators in rhetorick : see Isocrates Orat. ad Philippum, p. 87. Aristotle tells us, that Isocrates was a disciple of Gorgias (Quintil. L. 3. c. 1.) ; and he too in the former part of his life, dealt in these Παρισα, Ὁμοιοτελευτα, &c. which, as frivolous as they may seem, yet they often add to the beauty of a period, when managed by skilful hands ; that is, when they are "velut oblata, non captata ; atque innata videntur esse, non accersita." Quintil. L. 9. c. 3. See also Aulus Gellius, L. 18. 8.

Ib. Ηροδικος.] The Leontine, a physician, and brother to Gorgias. There was another Herodicus about this time of Selymbria, a famous Παιδοτριβης and a sophist. See Protag. p. 316.—Aristophon and his brother, Polygnotus, were both painters, the sons of Aglaophon. Ion. p. 532.

P. 451. Σκολιον.] These Scolia were a kind of lyrick compositions, sung either in concert, or successively, by all the guests after a banquet : the subjects

of them were either the praises of some divinity, or
moral precepts, or reflections on life, or gay exhortations
to mirth, to wine, or to love. There were some Scolia
of great antiquity; the most esteemed were those of
Alcæus, of Praxilla, and of Anacreon.

P. 451. What Plato alludes to here runs in this
manner : Ὑγιαινειν μεν αριστον ανδρι θνητῳ, δευτερον
δε, καλοφυᾶ γενεσθαι, το τριτον δε, πλουτειν αδολως, και
το τεταρτον, συνηβᾶν μετα των φιλων. On this subject,
see Athenæus, L. 15. p. 694, where he alludes to this
passage of Plato ; Aristophan. Vesp : v. 1221, et Nubes,
v. 1367, and Burette on Plutarch, de Musicâ: and
Mémoires de l'Acad. des Inscript. vol. 15. p. 315.

P. 453. The first definition of rhetorick by Gorgias :
Ὅτι Πειθοῦς δημιουργος εστι.

P. 454. His second and fuller definition is, Ὅτι
δημιουργος εστι της πειθοῦς της εν τοις δικαστηριοις, και
εν τοις αλλοις οχλοις, και περι τουτων ἁ εστι δικαια τε
και αδικα.

P. 455. Περι Ιατρων ἁιρεσεως.] There were publick
physicians elected in most of the Greek cities, who
received a salary from the commonwealth, and seem to
have taken no fees of particular people. Those physicians
who exercised this office, were said δημοσιευειν. See
Aristophan. in Avibus, v. 585, and Acharnens. v. 1029.
Plutus, v. 508; but this custom seems to have been laid
aside before Ol. 97. 4, in Athens : Aristophan. Plutus,
v. 407. Gorgias, p. 514, and the Politicus, p. 259.

Ib. The third definition of rhetorick, to which
Socrates reduces Gorgias, is this ; Ὅτι πειθοῦς εστι
δημιουργος πιστευτικης, αλλ' ου διδασκαλικης.

P. 455. Περι του δια μεσου τειχους.] The Μακρα
Τειχη, which joined Athens to the Piræeus were begun
on the motion of Pericles, Ol. 80. 3. (Vid. Thucyd. L. 1.
s. 107.) Socrates at that time was about twelve years
old. See Plutarch in the lives of Pericles and Cimon.
Harpocration tells us, that of the two walls which extended
from the city to the Piræeus, the southern only, or the
innermost, was called Το δια μεσου, as lying between
the outermost, Το βορειον, and the Το Φαληρικον, which
was a third wall, drawn from Athens to the port
Phalerus; and he cites this very passage.

P. 563. Socrates's own ludicrous definitions of eloquence to mortify the professors of it, as an art, are
these : Εμπειρια τις χαριτος και ηδονης απεργασιας·
επιτηδευμα τι, τεχνικον μεν ου, ψυχης δε στοχαστικης,
και ανδρειας, και φυσει δεινης προσομιλειν τοις ανθρωποις.
Πολιτικης μοριου ειδωλον, το κεφαλαιον δε αυτου,
κολακεια· αντιστροφον οψοποιϊας εν ψυχη, ως εκεινο μεν
εν σωματι. There is much good sense in this part of
the dialogue; he distinguishes the arts, which form and
improve the body, into the gymnastick, which regulates
its motions and maintains its proper habit, and the
medical, which corrects its ill habits and cures its distempers : those of the [1] soul, which answer to the former,
are the legislative, which prescribes rules for its conduct

---

[1] Η Νομοθετικη, και η Δικαστικη, for we should so read it, as
Ficinus and H. Stephanus seem to have found it in some MSS.
though Quintilian, and Aristides also, in Orat. 1. contra
Platonem pro Rhetoricâ, p. 7. edit. Jebb. Vol. 2. doubtless
followed the common reading, η Δικαιοσυνη ; the sense is the
same, but the former reading seems more elegant. Plato com-
prehends both these arts under the general name, η Πολιτικη.

and preserves its uprightness, and the judicative, which
amends and redresses its deviation from those rules.
Flattery, ever applying herself to the passions of men,
without regarding any principle or proposing any
rational end, has watched her opportunity, and assuming the form of these several arts, has introduced four
counterfeits [1] in their room, viz. 1. Cookery, which, while
it tickles the palate, pretends to maintain the body in
health and vigour ; 2. Cosmeticks, which conceal our
defects and diseases under a borrowed beauty ; 3.
Sophistry, which, by the false lights it throws upon
every thing, misleads our reason and palliates our vices ;
and 4. Rhetorick, which saves us from the chastisement
we deserve and eludes the salutary rigour of justice.

As Quintilian has given the sense of this in Latin,
and has also hit the true scope of the dialogue better
than any one, I shall transcribe the whole passage, L.
2. § 15. "Plerique [2] autem, dum pauca ex Gorgiâ
Platonis a prioribus imperitè excerpta legere contenti,
neque hoc totum, neque alia ejus volumina evolvunt,
in maximum errorem inciderunt ; creduntque eum in
hâc esse opinione, ut rhetoricen non artem, sed peritiam
quandam gratiæ ac voluptatis, existimet, et alio loco,

---

[1] Ἡ Ὀψοποιητικη, ἡ Κομμωτικη, ἡ Σοφιστικη, και ἡ Ῥητορικη :
these deserve not the name of arts (τεχναι) ; for art (he says) εχει
λογον τινα, ᾡ προσφερει ἁ προσφερει, ὁποια αττα την φυσιν εστιν·
ᾡστε την αιτιαν ἑκαστου εχειν ειπειν : whereas these are only
Εμπειριαι, τριβαι, επιτηδευσεις (i.e. knacks, practices, businesses)
ἁι του ἡδεος στοχαζονται ανευ του βελτιστου.   See Gorgias, p. 501.
[2] Cicero himself seems to fall under this censure, L. 1. de
Oratore, where he mistakes the great end and aim of this dialogue.

civilitatis particulæ simulachrum, et quartam partem
adulationis : quod duas partes civilitatis corpori assig-
net, medicinam, et quam interpretantur, exercitatricem ;
duas animo, legalem atque justitiam. Adulationem
autem medicinæ vocet coquorum artificium et exercita-
tricis mangonum, qui colorem fuco et verum robur
inani saginâ mentiantur, legalis, cavillatricem, justitiæ,
rhetoricen.   Quæ omnia sunt quidem scripta in hoc
libro, dictaque a Socrate, cujus personâ videtur Plato
significare, quid sentiat.   Sed alii sunt ejus sermones,
ad coarguendos qui contra disputant, compositi, quos
ελεγκτικους vocant; alii ad præcipiendum qui δογματικοι
appellantur.   Socrates autem, seu Plato, eam quidem,
quæ tum exercebatur, rhetoricen talem putavit, nam et
˙dicit his verbis, τουτον τον τροπον ὁν ὑμεις πολιτευεσθε ;
non autem vera et honesta intelligit.   Itaque disputa-
tionem illam contra Gorgiam ita claudit, ουκουν αναγκη
τον ῥητορικον δικαιον ειναι, τονδε δικαιον βουλεσθαι
δικαια και πραττειν.   Ad quod ille quidem conticescit,
sed sermonem suscipit Polus juvenili calore inconsi-
deratior, contra quem illa de simulachro et adulatione
dicuntur.   Tum Callicles adhuc concitatior, qui tamen ad
hanc ducitur clausulam, τον μελλοντα ορθως ῥητορικον
εσεσθαι δικαιον αρα δειν ειναι, και επιστημονα των δικαιων:
ut appareat Platoni non rhetoricen videri malum, sed
eam veram nisi justo et bono non contingere," &c.

P. 465. Λειοτητι και αισθησει.] Read Εσθητι, as
in Aristides, Orat. 1. cont. Plat. Ed. Jebb. Vol. 2.
p. 8.

Ib. Το του Αναξαγορου.] An allusion to the first
words of Anaxagoras's philosophy, Παντα χρηματα ην

ὁμου, ειτα Νοῦς ελθων αυτα διεκοσμησε. Diog. Laert.
L. 2. Sect. 6.

P. 467. Ω λῶστε Πῶλε, ἱνα προσειπω σε κατα σε.] A
jingle of sounds, such as Polus had prescribed in his
Art of Rhetorick. So in the Symposium : Παυσανιου
δε παισαμενου (διδασκοῦσι με γαρ ισα λεγειν ὁι Σοφοι)
p. 185. and in the Hipparchus, p. 225. Και χωρᾳ και
ὡρα, &c.

Ib. Ου τουτο βουλεται ὁ πραττει, αλλ' εκεινο οὐ
ενεκα πραττει.] He is here proving that fundamental [1]
principle of his doctrine, namely, that the wicked man
is doing he knows not what, and sins only through
ignorance : and that the end of his actions, like that of
all other men, is good, but he mistakes the nature of
it, and uses wrong means to attain it.

P. 468. Το αγαθον αρα διωκοντες.] See Locke on
Hum. Und. B. 2. Ch. 21. sect. 41, 42. on Power.

P. 470. Εχθες και πρωην.] As the time of this
dialogue plainly appears (from that passage in p. 473.
και περιστι βουλευων λαχων, &c. which is taken notice
of by Athenæus, L. 5. p. 217.) to be Ol. 93. 4. the year
after the sea-fight at Arginusæ, these words must be
taken in a larger sense, as we say of a thing long since
past, "It happened but the other day," when we would

---

[1] Vid. Protagoram, p. 357. et sequent. et Epist. ad Dionis
Famil. p. 336. Meno, p. 77, 78. Philebus, p. 22. Sophist.
p. 228. This was a real maxim of Socrates ; Ουδενα γαρ ὑπε-
λαμβανε πραττειν παρα το βελτιστον, αλλα δι' αγνοιαν. Aristot.
Ethic. ad Nicom. L. 7. c. 2. Ουδεις γαρ αν εκων εθελοι πειθεσθαι
πραττειν τοιτο, ὁτω μη το χαιρειν του λυπεισθαι μαλλον ἑπεται·
σκοτοδινιᾶν δε το πορρωθεν ὁρωμενον πᾶσιν, ὡς επος ειπειν, παρεχει.
Plato de Legibus. L. 2. p. 663.

compare it with more ancient times; for Archelaus
had now reigned at least nine years, and continued on
the throne about six years longer. So in p. 503, in
those words, Περικλεα τουτονι τον νεωστι τετελευτη-
κοτα, we must understand Νεωστι in the same manner,
for Pericles had been dead 23 years, but the time
is there compared with that of Cymon, Themistocles,
and Miltiades, who died many years before. Socrates
indeed might have seen and remembered Cymon, the
other two he could not. These particulars of Archelaus's
history are curious and not to be met with elsewhere:
viz. That he was the bastard son of Perdiccas by a
female slave belonging to his brother Alcetas; that he
caused his uncle and master Alcetas, together with
Alexander his son, to be murdered after a banquet, to
which he had invited them; that he caused his own
brother, a child of seven years old (the true heir to the
crown and the son of Perdiccas by his wife Cleopatra)
to be drowned in a well. Athenæus (L. 11. p. 506.) is
absurd enough to question the truth of these particulars, or, supposing them true, he says, that they are
instances of Plato's ingratitude, who was much in favour
with Archelaus. The passage, which he cites immediately after from Carystius of Pergamus, disproves all
this, for it shews Plato's connexion to have been with
Perdiccas, *the Third*, who began to reign thirty-five
years after Archelaus's death, and was elder brother to
the famous Philip of Macedon. We have an epistle of
Plato to that prince still remaining. At the time of
Archelaus's death, Plato was under thirty years of age.

P. 471. Ευδαιμων γενεσθαι.] This is the true reading, and is meant of Archelaus. The other reading, which Ficinus followed, is very insipid, Εὐδαίμονα γενεσθαι.

P. 472. Νικιας.] The famous Nicias. He is produced here as an example, on account of his great wealth, whence Socrates supposed him to have placed the chief happiness of man in affluence of fortune. The tripods, mentioned here as dedicated in the temple of Bacchus, must be the prizes which he and his family must have gained in their frequent Χορηγιαι. Nicias was remarkable for his piety and innocency of life. See Thucydides and Plutarch. The brother of Nicias was named Eucrates : he outlived his brother, and was this very year Trierarch at Ægos-Potami ; (Lysias. Orat. contr. Poliuchum, p. 320.) and soon after was put to death with Niceratus, his nephew, by order of the thirty tyrants, in the number of which he had refused to be.

Ib. Αριστοκρατης ὁ Σκελλιου.] A principal man in the oligarchy of Four hundred (Ol. 92. 1.) and of the same party with Theramenes. Οὐ αν εστιν εν Πυθιου τουτο το καλον αναθημα. (See Thucyd. L. 8. p. 516. and Lysias Orat. cont. Eratosthenem, p. 215. Ed. Taylori. Aristophan. in Avibus, v. 125. et Schol. D. Heraclides of Pontus, speaking of the seditions at Miletus, says, Οἱ πλοισιοι κρατησαντες ἁπαντας, ὡν κυριοι κατεστησαν, μετα των τεκνων κατεπιττωσαν. (Ap. Athenæum L. 12. p. 524.)

P. 473. Καταπιττωθη.] Covered with pitch, and burned alive.

P. 480. Τουναντιον γε αυ μεταβαλοντα.] This is a conclusion so extravagant, that it seems to be only a

way of triumphing over Polus, after his defeat, or
perhaps in order to irritate Callicles, who heard with
great impatience the concessions which Polus had been
forced to make, and now breaks out with warmth, and
enters into the dispute. Or, perhaps, this may be
meant of that justice, which Socrates practised on himself and on all who conversed with him, (which made
him many enemies) in exposing their ignorance and
their vices, and in laying them open to their own
correction : and from p. 509. Τινα αν βοηθειαν μη
δυναμενος, &c. I judge this to be the true sense of it.
See also p. 521. Κρινουμαι γαρ, ὡς εν παιδιοις ιατρος,
&c. See also De Republica, L. 9. p. 591.

P. 481. Τον τε Αθηναιων Δημον, και του Πυριλαμπους.]
The son of Pyrilampes was called Demus, and Plato
here alludes to his name. It is possible too, that there
may be a secret allusion to the Equites of Aristophanes,
where the Athenian people is introduced as a person,
under the name of Demus, an old man grown childish,
over whom the demagogues try to gain an ascendant
by paying their court to his ridiculous humours. The
drama of the Equites was played about twenty years
before the time of this dialogue. Demus was much in
the friendship of Pericles, and remarkable for being
the first man who brought peacocks to Athens, and
bred them in his volaries. (Plutarch in Pericle and
Athenæus, L. 9. p. 397.) Demus is mentioned as a
Trierarch in the expedition to Cyprus (as I imagine)
about Ol. 98. 1. under Chabrias. (Lysias de Bonis
Aristophanis, p. 340.) He was, when a youth, famous
for his beauty :

Καινη Δι', αν ιδη γε που γεγραμμενον,
Τον Πυριλαμπους εν θυρα Δημον καλον, &c.

Aristophan. in Vespis, v. 98, and Scholia. The play
of the Vespæ was played eighteen years before the time
of this dialogue.

P. 482. 'Ο Κλεινιειος.] Alcibiades had now left
Athens, and taken refuge in Thrace, and the year after
he was murdered.

P. 484. Νομος, ὁ παντων βασιλευς.] A fragment
of Pindar.

Ib. Φιλοσοφια γαρ τοι.] Aulus Gellius, L. 10, c.
22, having transcribed this passage at large, ending at
the words και αλλα πολλα αγαθα, (in p. 486.) makes
several reflections upon it. "Plato veritatis homo
amicissimus, ejusque omnibus exhibendæ promptissi-
mus, quæ omnino dici possunt in desides istos igna-
vosque qui, obtento philosophiæ nomine, inutile otium
et linguæ vitæque tenebras sequuntur, ex personâ
quidem non gravi neque idoneâ, verò tamen ingenué-
que, dixit. Nam etsi Callicles, quem dicere hæc facit,
veræ philosophiæ ignarus inhonesta et indigna in phil-
osophos confert; proinde tamen accipienda sunt quæ
dicuntur, ut nos sensim moveri intelligamus, ne ipsi
quoque culpationes hujusmodi mercamur, neve inerti
atque inani desidiâ, cultum et studium philosophiæ
mentiamur," &c. though Gellius is certainly mistaken
in this, justly incurring the same censure, as those
whom Quintilian mentions, L. 2. 16, yet thus far he
is right in saying, that Plato often put much truth and
good sense into the mouth of characters which he did
not approve. The Protagoras is a remarkable instance

of this, where Socrates is introduced in the beginning,
arguing against the very doctrine which naturally follows from those principles which he himself lays down
in the end, and of which he obliges the sophist to con-
fess the truth. Dacier, in his notes, has run into a
thousand mistakes, by imagining all which is advanced
by the characters opposed to Socrates in the disputation, to be absurd and ridiculous.

The character, which Callicles here pretends to
expose, is doubtless such as Plato thought worthy of
a true philosopher, *των κορυφαιων τινος, και ου φαυλως
διατριβοντος εν φιλοσοφια.* (Vid. Theætetum, p. 173.)

P. 484. Το του Ευριπιδου.] From that famous
scene in the Antiope (a drama now lost) between
Zethus and Amphion, Joshua Barnes reads,

> Εν τουτω γαρ
> Λαμπρος θ' εκαστος, καπι ταυτ' επειγεται.

To this scene Horace alludes Lib. 1. Epist. 18. to
Lollius "Gratia sic fratrum geminorum Amphionis
atque Zethi dissiluit," &c.

P. 485. Και τας αγορας.] What passage of Homer
is here alluded to? or is it Hesiod in his Theogonia,
v. 90. Μετα δε πρεπει αγρομενοισι.

Ib. Προς τον αδελφον.] Alluding to the fragment
of Antiope : Eurip. Edit. Barnes. p. 453.

> Ψυχης ωδε γενναιαν φυσιν
> Γυναικομιμω διαπρεπεις μορφωματι.
> Ουτ' εν δικης βουλαισιν ορθον αν ποτε
> Λογον προθει, η πιθανον· ουτ' αλλων υπερ
> Νεανικον βουλευμα βουλευσαιο τι.

P. 486. Αποθανοις αν.] From this, and from many other strokes against the people of Athens, which seem to carry a strong air of indignation and concern in them, it looks as if this dialogue had been written not long after the death of Socrates, perhaps while Plato was at Megara.

Ib. Επι κορῥης.] The Ατιμοι might be struck by a citizen, without being able to call him to an account for it.

Ib. Αλλ' ω 'γαθε.] Another fragment of the Antiope:

Αλλ' εμοι πιθου,
Παυσαι δ' αοιδων, πραγματων δ' ευμουσιαν
Ασκει· τοιαυτ' αειδε, και δοξεις φρονειν·—
Αλλοις τα κομψα ταυτ' αφεις σοφισματα,
Εξ ων κενοῖσιν εγκατοικησεις δομοις.

Ib. The several kinds of Ατιμια are enumerated in the oration of Andocides Περι Μυστηριων, p. 10.

P. 487. Tisander of Aphidnæ; who seems to be the same mentioned by Socrates a year after this; (Xenoph. Aponemon. L. 2. sect. 7.) Nausicydes of Cholargi, Andro, the son of Androtion.

P. 488. First proof against Callicles (who had advanced that by the law of nature the stronger had a right to govern the weaker) that the many are stronger than the few, and consequently ought to govern them : so that the positive law of the commonwealth is the result of the law of nature.

P. 492. Τις δ' οιδεν, ει το ζῆν.] Euripides in Polycido, Fragm. p. 490. edit. Barnesii. The same sentiment is repeated again in other words in the Phryxus, ibid. p. 503.

152 NOTES ON PLATO.

P. 493. Ηκουσα των σοφων.] In Cratylo, p. 400. Σημα τινες φασιν αυτο ειναι της ψυχης, &c.

Ib. Κομψος ανηρ, ισως Σικελος τις η Ιταλικος.] This idea (whosesoever it be) is imitated by Lucretius, L. 3. v. 949 and 1022 :

Omnia, pertusum congesta quasi in vas,
Commoda perfluxere, atque ingrata interiere.

I take this to be meant of Empedocles.

P. 500. Τεχνικος.] The philosopher. Vid. Protagoram, p. 357, and p. 509, 517, and 521 of this dialogue.

P. 501. Cinesias, the son of Meles, was a dithyrambick poet in some sort of vogue among the people at this time. He was still a worse man than a writer, and the depravity of his character made even his misfortunes ridiculous ; so that his poverty, his deformities, and his distempers, were not only produced on the stage, but frequently alluded to by the orators, and exposed to the scorn of the multitude. Vid. Aristophan. in Avibus, v. 1374, et Schol. in locum ; et in Lysistrata, in Ranis, v. 369. In Fragment. Gerytadis ap. Athenæum, L. 12. p. 551.) The comick poet, Strattis, who lived at this time, made Cinesias the subject of an entire drama. See Lysias Απολογια Δωροδοκιας, p. 381. Fragm. Orat. contra Phanium ap. Athenæum ut supra, and in Taylor's edition, p. 640. Harpocration in voce *Cinesias.* Plutarch de gloria Atheniens. Pherecrates apud Plutarchum de Musicâ. See also the notes of Mr. Burette on that treatise, in the Mém. de l'Acad. des Inscript. vol. 15. p. 340, and Suidas in voce Cinesias.

P. 503. The bold attack, made in this place on some of the greatest characters of antiquity, has drawn much censure on Plato; but we are to consider that he is here proving his favourite point, (which seems to me the grand aim and intention of this dialogue) that philosophy alone is the parent of virtue, the discoverer of those fixed and unerring principles, on which the truly great and good man builds his whole scheme of life, and by which he directs all his actions; and that he, who practises this noblest art, and makes it his whole endeavour to inspire his fellow citizens with a love for true knowledge, (and this was the constant view and the employment of Socrates) has infinitely the superiority not only over the masters of those arts, which the publick most admires, as musick, poetry, and eloquence, but over the most celebrated names in history, as heroes and statesmen; as the first have generally applied their talents to flatter the ear, to humour the prejudices, and to inflame the passions of mankind; and the latter to soothe their vanity, to irritate their ambition, and to cheat them with an apparent, not a real, greatness.

P. 506. Του Αμφιονος.] Of which tragedy some few verses are still preserved to us; see Euripid. Fragm. ed. Barnesii, p. 454 :

Εγω μεν ουν αδοιμι, και λεγοιμι τι
Σοφον, ταρασσων μηδεν, ων πολις νοσει, &c.

P. 508. Τω αδικουντι και κακιον.] This was not the principle only, but the practice, of Socrates. See Diog. Laert. L. 2. sect. 21.

P. 510. Ὁπου τυραννος εστιν αρχων αγριος.] A severe reflection on the Athenian people.

P. 511. The price of a pilot from Ægina to Attica was two oboli (about two-pence halfpenny); from Attica to Pontus or to Egypt two drachmæ (fifteen-pence halfpenny).

P. 514. Εν τω πιθω την κεραμειαν μανθανειν.] Proverb. To begin with a jar before we have made, a gallipot. Hor. Art. Poet.

Amphora cœpit
Institui, currente rotâ cur urceus exit?

P. 515. Εις μισθοφοραν.] The administration of Pericles was the ruin of the Athenian constitution. By abridging the power of the Areopagus, and by impairing their authority, who were the superintendents of education and the censors of publick manners, he sapped the foundations of virtue among them; by distributing the publick revenue among the courts of justice, he made them mercenary and avaricious, negligent of their private affairs, and ever meddling in those of their neighbours; by the frequency and magnificence of the publick spectacles, he inured them to luxury and to idleness; and by engaging them in the Peloponnesian war, he exposed them to be deserted by all their allies, and left to the mercy of the braver and more virtuous Lacedæmonians. Isocrates [1] looked upon the first of these alterations only, as the ruin of his country. (Orat. Areopagit. p. 147, &c.)

[1] Though he had no prejudice to the person of Pericles, and does justice to his disinterestedness and honesty in the management of the publick money. (See Isocrat. Orat. de Pace, p. 184.)

P. 515. Εις μισθοφοραν.] The Μισθος Δικαστικος here spoken of by Socrates was three oboli a day paid to 6000 citizens (for so many sat in the courts of justice), which was to the state a yearly expense of one hundred and fifty talents ; i.e. reckoning ten months to the year, for two months were spent in holidays, when the courts did not meet. A Μισθος (appointed by Agyrrius about Ol. 96. 4, see Aristophan. Εκκλησιαζουσαι, v. 102, 185, 284, 292, 302, 380, and also his Plutus, v. 330, which last passage is wrongly interpreted by the Scholiast, by Spanheim, and by Kuster ;) a Μισθος (I say) was given by every Athenian citizen who came to the Εκκλησια, or assembly of the people. The ill effect which this had upon their manners is painted by Aristophanes with much humour in several of his dramas, and particularly in the Vespæ.

Ib. Των τα ωτα κατεαγοτων.] From such as affected to imitate the manners of the Lacedæmonians, and constantly practised the roughest exercises of the Palæstra, particularly boxing, the bruises and scars of which were visible about their temples and ears : so in the Protagoras, p. 342. Οἱ μεν ωτα τε καταγνυνται μιμουμενοι αυτους (τους Λακεδαιμονιους) &c.

P. 516. Επι τελευτη του βιου.] See Plutarch in Pericles, towards the end.

Ib. Οἱ γε δικαιοι ἡμεροι.] Hom. Odys. Ὁσοι χαλεποιτε, και αγριοι, ουδε δικαιοι. O. v. 575.

Ib. Εις το βαραθρον.] This is not related either by Herodotus, or by Cornelius Nepos, or by Justin.

P. 517. Ουτε τη αληθινη, ουτε τη κολακικη.] This

shews that Plato meant only to distinguish between
the use of eloquence and its abuse; nor is he in earnest
when he says, Ουδενα ἡμεις ισμεν ανδρα αγαθον γεγονοτα
τα πολιτικα, (for he afterwards himself names Aristides,
as a man of uncommon probity) but only to shew that
he had puzzled Callicles, who could not produce one
example of a statesman who had abilities, or art, sufficient to preserve him from the fury of the people.

P. 517. Ονδ' εγω ψεγω.] Hence it appears that he
only means to shew how much superiour the character
of a real philosopher is to that of a statesman.

P. 518. Thearion, a famous baker, mentioned by
Aristophanes (ap. Athenæum L. 3. p. 112. see also
Casaubon. in locum) in Gerytade et Æolosicone, and
by Antiphanes, another comick poet, (who lived fifty or
sixty years afterwards) in his Omphale. We should
read here Αρτοκοπος, not Αρτοποιος. The Οψαρτυτικα
of Mithæcus is a work often cited by Athenæus, L. 12.
p. 516. The Sicilian and the Italian Greeks were
noted for the luxury of the table. See Plato Epist. 7.
p. 326 and 336.

P. 519. Σου δε ισως επιληψονται.] I do not find
what became of Callicles; but Alcibiades had already
fled from his country, for fear of falling into the hands
of the people.

P. 521. Ει σοι Μυσον.] Perhaps, Ονκ· ει σοι Μυσον
ἡδιον καλεισθαι, ως ει μη, &c. i.e. Not; if you would
choose to fall into that helpless condition, (before described by Callicles, p. 486,) which you must do, unless
you practise the art which I recommend. The Mysians
were proverbial, as objects of contempt. Μυσων Λεια

was said of any poor-spirited people, who tamely submitted to every injury.   Aristot. Rhetor. L. 1.

P. 525. Προσηκει δε παντι] See Aulus Gellius, L.
6. 14. on this passage.

P. 526. Εις δε και πανυ.] Plutarch takes notice
that Aristides[1] was a favourite character with Plato.
Mr. Hardion,[2] who has written a life of Gorgias (collected with a good deal of industry from a variety of
authors) and has given us a sketch of this dialogue of
Plato, has yet been guilty of some mistakes, as where
he fixes[3] the time of it to Ol. 95. 1, which is at least
five years too late ; and where he seems to say that
Gorgias took Thessaly in his way to Olympia, which
is a strange error in geography, &c. yet his performance,
and particularly the analysis, is well worth reading.

[1] In Vitâ Aristid. towards the end.
[2] Dissertations sur l'origine et les progrès de la Rhétoriquo
dans la Grèce : Mémoires de l'Academie des Inscriptions, &c.
V. 15. p. 167, and 176.
[3] Ib. p. 175.

MINOS.

Tнɪs dialogue takes its name, (as also does the Hipparchus,) not from either of the persons introduced in it, but from the Cretan Minos, whose character and laws are mentioned pretty much at large. Socrates, and another Athenian nearly of the same age (who is not named), are considering the nature of laws in it;

NOTES ON THE GREEK TEXT.

Plat. Op. Serrani, Vol. 2. p. 313.

P. 315. Human sacrifice, and particularly of their children, to Saturn was in use among the Carthaginians: the sacrifices of the Lycians and of the descendants of Athamas, though people of Greek origin, were barbarous ; the ancient Attick custom is mentioned of sacrificing victims near the bodies of dead persons, before they were carried out to burial, and hiring Εγχυτριστριαι, (Schol. ad Arist. Vesp. v. 288.) and the still more ancient one of interring them in the houses where they died : both long since disused.

318. Εκ Κρητης.] V. Herodot. and Plut. in Lycurgo, and Strabo. L. 10. p. 477.

Ib. Λυκουργον.] The time of this dialogue is no where marked : but we see from p. 321 that Socrates was now advanced in years ; supposing him then to be only sixty, it is three hundred and sixty-seven years from the first Olympiad of Corœbus ; but most criticks agree that Lycurgus lived one

and the intention of Plato is to shew, that there is a law of nature and of truth, common to all men, to which all truly legal institutions must be conformable, and which is the real foundation of them all.

Unfortunately the dialogue remains imperfect : it is indeed probable that it was never finished.

NOTES.

hundred and eight years before that time, and Eratosthenes, with the most accurate chronologers, affirms, that he was still more ancient. Plato therefore places him half a century later than any one else has done. The computation of Thucydides, who reckons it something more than 400 years to the end of the Peloponnesian war, αφ' ου Λακεδαιμονιοι τη αυτη πολιτεια χρωνται, that is from the institution of Lycurgus's laws, comes nearest to that of Plato. The war ended Ol. 94. 1. so that, according to Thucydides, Lycurgus settled the constitution about 27 years before the first Olympiad of Corœbus.

P. 320. 'Ησιοδος.] Probably in his Heroick Genealogies, a work now lost.

CHARMIDES.

Η, ΠΕΡΙ ΣΩΦΡΟΣΥΝΗΣ.

Ol. 87. 2 or 3.

NOTES ON THE GREEK TEXT.

Platon. Op. Serrani, Vol. 1. p. 153.

THE subject of this dialogue is Ἡ Σωφροσυνη : and what was Plato's real opinion of that virtue, may be seen, De Republ. L. 4. p. 430. and De Legibus, L. 3. p. 696.

The dramatick part of it is very elegant.

P. 153. Του της βασιλικης ἱερου.] It seems to be the temple of Apollo in the Στοα βασιλειος. See Pausanias in Attic. p. 8.

Ib. Μανικος ων.] Of a warm eager temper; see the Symposium in the beginning of it.

Ib. Κριτιαν.] It is extraordinary that Plato from a partiality to his own family should so often introduce into his writings the character of Critias, his cousin, whose very name (one should imagine) must be held in detestation at Athens even to remotest times, he being a monster of injustice and cruelty. Plato seems to have been not a little. proud of his family. Vid. De Republic: L. 2. p. 368.

Ib. Μαχη εγεγονει.] I take the particular action

here mentioned to be the attack made on the city, soon
after the arrival of Agno and Cleopompus with fresh
troops. Thucyd. L. 2. p. 116. If we consider the
purport of the narration, we shall find that these words,
Φορμιων δε και οι εξακοσιοι και χιλιοι ουκετι ησαν περι
Χαλκιδεας, mean, that Phormio and his troops (among
which were Socrates and Alcibiades,) were returned
from their expedition into Chalcidice (mentioned
p. 36.) and had joined the army newly arrived from
Potidea.

P. 154. Λευκη σταθμη.] The line used by carpenters
and masons to mark out their dimensions with, after it
had been tinged with minium, or with some other
colour: it is used proverbially for a mind susceptible
of any impression which may be given to it. So
Philippus in Anthol. L. 6. cap. ult.

Μιλτοφυρῆτε
Σχοινον, ὑπ᾽ ακρονυχω ψαλλομενην κανονι.

P. 155. Δοκει αλλοις τε και εαυτω.] Perhaps εμαυτω,
or εμοι, for Critias was an excellent poet. Athenæus
has preserved several fine fragments of his writings.

Ib. Σολωνος.] Solon's poetry is well known. From
the birth of Solon to that of Plato was 210 years,
which takes in five generations of that family. Diogenes Laertius reckons six generations, making Glauco
(as it seems) the brother, and not the uncle of Critias.
Proclus, in his comment on the Timæus, observes that
Theon the Platonick had been guilty of the same
mistake, and corrects it on the authority of this very
dialogue.

P. 155. Ευλαβεισθαι.] This seems part of an hexameter, and an iambick.

Ib. Την Επωδην.] Horace alludes to these incantations, and perhaps to this very passage, Lib. 1. Epist. 1.

P. 156. Απαθανατιζειν.] Zamolxis, (Herodot. L. 4. c. 94.) (by some said to have been a slave of Pythagoras, but affirmed by Herodotus to have been of much greater antiquity) the king and prophet of the Getes, who were at first only a clan of the Thracians, but afterwards, having passed the Danube, became a great and powerful nation. It is very remarkable, that they had a succession of these high priests, (Strabo, L. 7. p. 297.) who lived sequestered from mankind in a grotto, and had communication only with the king, in whose power they had a great share from Zamolxis down to the time of Augustus, and possibly long after.

P. 157. The family of Dropides, celebrated by Anacreon.

P. 158. Pyrilampes, the great-uncle of Plato, ambassador in Persia, and elsewhere, admired as the tallest and handsomest man of his time: he was a great friend of Pericles, and father to Demus, a youth remarkable for his beauty.

P. 173. Δια κερατων.] See Hom. Odyss. T. 565. The only reason of this fable, which has puzzled so many people, seems to be a similitude of sounds between Ελεφας and ελεφαιρεσθαι (to delude) and Κερας and κραινειν (to perform or accomplish), as one of the Scholiasts has observed.

P. 167. Το τριτον τω Σωτηρι.] A proverbial expression frequent with Plato, as in the Philebus, p, 66.

Ιθι δε το τριτον τω Σωτηρι, &c. and in Epist. 7, speaking of his third voyage to Sicily, Ελθων δ' ουν το τριτον, &c. I imagine it alludes to the Athenian custom (see Athenæus from Philochorus, L. 2. p. 38.) which was to serve round after supper a little pure wine, with these words, Αγαθω Δαιμονι, and afterwards as much wine and water as every one called for, with the form of Διι Σωτηρι. See Erasmi Adag. Servatori, and Plato de Republ. L. 9. p. 583.

CRATYLUS.

ΠΕΡΙ ΟΝΟΜΑΤΩΝ ΟΡΘΟΤΗΤΟΣ.

THIS long dialogue on the origin of words was probably
a performance of Plato when he was very young, and
is the least considerable of all his works.

Cratylus,[1] a disciple of Heraclitus, is said to have

[1] Diog. Laert. in Platone, and Aristot. Metaphys. L. 1. p.
338. Εκ νεου τε γαρ συγγενομενος πρωτον Κρατυλω, και ταις
Ηρακλειτειοις δοξαις, κτλ.

NOTES ON THE GREEK TEXT.

Platon. Op. Serrani, Vol. 1. p. 383.

P. 398. Ancient Attick words, δαημων, ειρειν : and p. 401,
εσια ; 410, Οραι ; 418, 'Ιμερα, vel 'Εμερα. He remarks that the
ancient Attick abounded in the I and Δ, which in his time had
been often changed to the H or E and the Z, and that the
women preserved much of the old language among them.

399. Accents used in Plato's time, as now, Διϊ φιλος, changed
into Δι φιλος.

401. Προ παντων Θεων τη 'Εστια.] See Aristophan. Aves, v.
865, and Vespæ, v. 840.

405. The Thessalians in their dialect called Apollo, 'Απλος.

407. Οισι Ευθυφρονος Ιπποι.] An allusion to Homer.

409. Much of the Greek language derived from the Barbarians : Υδωρ, Πυρ, Κυων, borrowed from the Phrygians.

425. The Barbarians acknowledged to be more ancient than
the Greeks.

been the master of Plato after Socrates's death; but the latter part of the dialogue is plainly written against the opinions of that sect, and of Cratylus in particular.

NOTES.

P. 427. The powers of the several Greek letters, and the manner of their formation: viz. the P expressive of motion, being formed by a tremulous motion of the tongue; the I of smallness and tenuity; the Φ. Ψ. Σ. Z. of all noises made by the air; the Δ and T of a cessation of motion; the Λ of slipperiness and gliding, the same with a Γ prefixed, of the adherence and tenacity of fluids; the N of any thing internal; the A of largeness; the O of roundness; and the Π expressive of length.

428. Eν Λιταις.] The ancients called the ninth book of the Iliad, Λιται. See v. 640.

429. Cratylus seems to have been the son of Smicrio.

434. The Eretrians for σκληροτης used σκληροτηρ.

SYMPOSIUM.

Platon. Op. Serrani. Vol. 3. p. 172.

As to the time of this dialogue, Athenæus (L. 5. p. 217.) tells us, that Agatho first gained the prize when Euphemus was Archon, which was Ol. 90. 4. What he adds, namely, that. Plato was then only 14 years old, and consequently could not be at this entertainment, is very true, but nothing to the purpose; for it is not Plato who uses those words which he cites, but Apollodorus, who recounts the particulars of this banquet, as he had them from Aristodemus, who was present at it ten or twelve years before.

Among the ancients, Cicero, Dionysius of Halicarnassus, Hermogenes, Athenæus, Gellius, and Ausonius, and among the moderns, Jos. Scaliger, Petavius, Ger. Vossius, Fraguier, Freret, and La Mothe le Vayer, believed the Cyropædia of Xenophon to be a romance: on the other side, are Usher, Marsham, Le Clerc, Prideaux, Bossuet, Tournemine, Banier, Lenglet, Rollin, Guyon.

NOTES ON THE GREEK TEXT.

P. 172. Ω Γλαυκων.] Glauco was younger brother to Plato. See Xenoph. Memorabil. L. 3. c. 6.

P. 172. Πολλων ετων Αγαθων.] He was in Macedonia at the court of Archelaus.

P. 173. Aristodemus, of Cydathenæ, called the
Little, mentioned by Xenophon as inclined to atheism.
(Memorabil. L. 1. c. 4.)

P. 175. The audience in the Athenian theatre consisted of above 30,000 persons.

P. 177. Ουκ εμος ο μυθος, αλλ' εμης μητρος παρα.]
Euripid. ap Dion. Halicarnass. Περι σχηματων, L. 2.

Ib. Αλλοις μεν τισι των Θεων.] No hymns, nor
temples, nor religious rites were offered to Love in
Greece. (See Sympos. p. 189.)

Ib. Καταλογαδην.] The discourse by Prodicus in
honour of Hercules, of which the beautiful fable in
Xenophon's Memorabil. L. 2. c. 1. made a part.

Ib. Βιβλιω ανδρος σοφου.] Mentioned also by Isocrates in Encom. Helenæ, p. 210, Των μεν γαρ τοις
βομβυλιους, και τοις άλας, και τα τοιαυτα βουληθεντων
επαινειν, &c. and to this, and such like discourses, he
alludes in Panathenaic, p. 260. Εγκωμια(οισι τα φαι-
λοτατα των οντων, η τοις παραιγομωτατοις των οντων.

P. 178. Στρατοπεδον εραστων.] It is plain, that
Socrates, in Xenophon's Symposium, p. 898, is employed in refuting this very sentiment, which he attributes to Pausanias, the lover of Agatho, and not to
Phædrus, in whose mouth it is here put: it seems
to me a stroke of Xenophon's enmity to Plato, and a
remarkable one, though it has not been taken notice of.[1]

[1] See Athenæus, L. 5. p. 216., who conjectures that Xenophon might have seen some copy of Plato's Symposium, where
these words were spoken by Pausanias. Casaubon tries to con-
fute him, but with weak arguments.

Parmenides and Acusilaus quoted in the genealogy of
the gods : and again in p. 195.

P. 180. So Hesiod describes the birth of Venus,
daughter of Cœlus without a mother, v. 191. Τῃ δ'
Ερος ὡμαρτησε, &c. but he mentions nothing of the
second Venus, daughter of Jove and Dione, which is
the Venus of Homer. See also Tully de Naturâ
Deorum, L. 3.

P. 182. Εν Ηλιδι και εν Βοιωτοις.] This (which is
really spoken by Pausanias) convinces me that Xenophon wrote his Symposium after that of Plato, and
meant to throw some reflections on this part of it.

P. 187. Το γαρ ἑν.] An expression of Heraclitus
cited and censured.

P. 190. Κυβιστωσι.] An action of the tumblers
described in Xenophon's Sympos. p. 876.

P. 191. Αἱ 'Εταιριστριαι.] Αἱ Τριβαδες. See de
Legib. L. 1. p. 636.

P. 193. Καθαπερ Αρκαδες.] See an instance of this
Lacedæmonian policy on the taking of Mantinea, Ol.
98. 3, in Xenoph. Græc. Hist. L. 5. 552 and 553.

P. 194. Εγω δε δη βουλομαι.] As the comick invention and expression of Aristophanes are perfectly well
supported throughout his discourse, and the character
of the man well painted in several little peculiarities,
which Plato (who had himself undoubtedly a genius
for dramatick poetry) is never at a loss to choose ; so
the speech of Agatho is a just copy[1] of his kind of
eloquence, full of antitheses, concise, and musical even

---

[1] Χλευαξει τε τα ισοκωλα του Αγαθωνος και αντιθετα. Athen-
ræus, L. 5. p. 187.

to affectation, in the manner of Gorgias, whose pupil
he seems to have been.

P. 198. Γοργειου.] Alluding to Hom. Odyss. Λ. v. 634.
P. 199. Η γλωττα ουν.] An allusion to the Hippolytus of Euripides.

P. 201. Μαντικης.] It is plain from what follows,
that this is as good a reading as Μαντινικης.

P. 202. Diotimia of Mantinea, a prophetess.

Ib. The middle nature of dæmons, which mediate
between gods and men.

P. 203. Πορος.] The god, not of riches, but of
expedients and of contrivances.

P. 207. The following verses are attributed to Plato,
in the Anthologia, L. 1. c. 90 :

Αιων παντα φερει· δολιχος χρονος οιδεν αμειβειν
Ουνομα, και μορφην, και γενος, ηδε τυχην·

which sentiment is finely explained here.

P. 213. Ψυκτηρα.] See Athenæus, L. 11, p. 502, on
this kind of vessel.

P. 215. The figures of the Sileni in the shops of the
sculptors (εν τοις ἑρμογλυφειοις) made hollow, which
opened and discovered within the statues of the gods.

Ib. 'Α γαρ Ολυμπος.] Such as were initiated
became *possessed*, as soon as they heard these airs.

P. 216. Τα δ' Αθηναιων πραττω.] Alcibiades was
now very powerful in the state, in the thirty-fifth year
of his age.

P. 219. Η σιδηρω ὁ Αιας.] It should rather seem to
be Achilles.

Ib. Στρατεια.] They went thither with the supplies

under the command of Phormio, Ol. 87. 1. Alcibiades
being then twenty years of age, and Socrates thirty-
nine. (See Thucyd. L. 1. s. 64.) The folly of Athenæus,
who would prove, against the authority of Plato and of
Antisthenes, that Socrates was not in any of these
actions, is justly exposed by Casaubon: Annot. ad
Athenæum, L. 5. c. 15. We may add, that if the
silence of Thucydides could prove anything with regard
to Socrates, it would prove, at least as strongly, that
Alcibiades was not at Potidæa neither; but the contrary is certain from that very oration of Isocrates, to
which Athenæus refers, namely, that Περι Ζευγους,
p. 352, where he is said to have gained the Αριστεια
(which were a crown and a complete suit of armour)
before that city; and if the orator had not totally suppressed the name of Socrates, it would have been highly
injudicious in a discourse pronounced by the son of
Alcibiades, where he was to exalt the character of his
father, and by no means to lessen the merit of any of
his actions. He left that to his enemies, who (it is
likely) did not forget the generosity of Socrates on this
occasion. It is clear from the many oversights of
Athenæus here, that he either trusted to his memory,
or only quoted from his own excerpta, and not from
the originals. Plato mentions no second Αριστεια
gained at Delium, and only speaks of the coolness and
presence of mind shewn by Socrates in his retreat; as
he has done also in the Laches. Athenæus affirms,
that Alcibiades was not in the battle of Delium, but
he assigns no reasons. If he concludes it from the
silence of Thucydides, as before, this is nothing, as

that historian mentions none but the commanders in
chief on any of these occasions, and often only one or
two of the principal of these : but probably Alcibiades
and Laches might then only serve as private men.
P. 221. Βρενθυομενος.] Alluding to the Nubes of
Aristophanes.

Ib. 'Οι λογοι αυτου.] Every one who would read the
Socratick dialogues of Plato, Xenophon, &c. should first
consider this passage : it is put below in a note.[1]

P. 222. Ευθυδημος.] Probably the same youth whom
Xenophon calls Ευθυδημος ὁ καλος (Memorabil. L. 4.
c. 1.), a different person from Euthydemus, the Chian.

This dialogue (particularly the end of it), the Protagoras, the Gorgias, the Euthydemus, &c. are strong
instances of Plato's genius for dramatick poetry in the
comick kind. Κωμωδειν γαρ ηθελε Πλατων, says
Athenæus, L. 5. p. 187, speaking of the character of
Aristophanes in this place. See also Olympiodor. in
Vitâ Platonis. The Phædo is an instance of Plato's
power in the tragick kind.

---

[1] Οι λογοι αυτου ὁμοιοτατοι εισι τοις Σειληνοις (see note above
on p. 215.) τοις διοιγομενοις. Ει γαρ εθελει τις των Σωκρατους
ακουειν λογων, φανειεν αν πανυ γελοιοι το πρωτον· τοιαυτα και
ονοματα και ρηματα εξωθεν περιαμπεχονται Σατυρου αν τινα
ὑβριστου δοραν. Ονους γαρ κανθηλιους λεγει, και χαλκεας τινας, και
σκυτοτομους, και βυρσοδεψας, και αει δια των αυτων τα αυτα φαινεται λεγειν· ὡστε απειρος και ανοητος ανθρωπος πας αν των λογων
καταγελασειε· διοιγομενοις δε ιδων αν τις, και εντος αυτων γιγνο-
μενος, πρωτον μεν νουν εχοντας ενδον μονοις ευρησει των λογων,
επειτα θειοτατους, και πλειστα αγαλματα αρετης εν αυτοις εχοντας,
και επι πλειστον τεινοντας, μαλλον δε επι παν οσον προσηκει σκοπειν
τω μελλοντι καλω κἀγαθω γενεσθαι. Ταυτ' εστιν, ἁ εγω Σωκρατους επαινω. Sympos. p. 221.

EUTHYDEMUS.

About Ol. 89. 4.

Platon. Op. Serrani, Vol. 1. p. 271.

THERE is a good deal of humour, and even of the vis comica, in this dialogue. Its end is to expose the vanity and weakness of two famous sophists, and to shew, by way of contrast, the art of Socrates in leading youth into the paths of virtue and of right reason.

NOTES ON THE GREEK TEXT.

P. 271. Ου πολυ τι την ηλικιαν.] See the Symposium of Xenophon; Ουκ ὁρᾷς οτι τουτω παρα τα ωτα αρτι ιουλος καθερπει· Κλεινιᾳ δε προς το οπισθεν ηδη αναβαινει; p. 515. From whence it appears, that the time of this dialogue cannot be long after Ol. 89. 4.

Ib. Εντευθεν ποθεν εκ Χιου.] The Chians being an Ionian colony from Athens.

P. 272. Κοννω, τω Μητροβιου.] Whether the same with the Tibicen mentioned in the Equites of Aristophanes, v. 531, called Connas, who lived at this time?

P. 273. Κτησιππος.] See the Lysis of Plato.

P. 275. Alcibiades, the elder, had two sons, Clinias and Axiochus: the first (who was slain at the battle of

Artemisium, Ol. 75. 1.) left behind him two sons, the
famous Alcibiades, and Cleinias, his brother. The
latter had a son, also called Cleinias, who is the youth
here mentioned.

P. 277. Ὅπερ ὁι ἐν τη τελετῇ.] The ceremony of
seating in a chair, and dancing round, a person who is
to be initiated in the mysteries of the Corybantes, called
Θρονωσις.

P. 278. Αρα γε παντες ανθρωποι.] This example of
a Λογος προτρεπτικος, or exhortation to philosophy, is
as noble as the moral it would convey, a truth which
Plato had always at heart. Των μεν αλλων ουδεν
ειναι ουτε αγαθον ουτε κακον· τουτοιν δε δυοιν οντοιν, ἡ
μεν Σοφια αγαθον, ἡ δε Αμαθια κακον.

P. 285. Εις ασκον.] The skin of Marsyas was said to
be preserved in the castle of Celænæ (in the greater
Phrygia) even in Xenophon's time, Ol. 94. 4, (Cyri
Anab. L. 1. p. 146.) and hung there in a grotto, whence
the rivulet Marsyas took its rise. It was said to put
itself in motion at the sound of a flute.

Ib. Ὡς οντος του αντιλεγειν.] See Diog. Laert. L. 9.
s. 53, de Protagora. We see here that this sophism
was older than Protagoras.

P. 287. Ουτως ει Κρονος.] Αρχαιοτροπος, simple
and old-fashioned. It is scarcely possible to see with
patience Plato seriously confuting [1] these childish
subtleties, as low as any logical quibbles, used by our

_____
[1] Plato himself shews, p. 278, that he perfectly understood
the just value of them. Παιδιαν δε λεγω δια ταυτα, οτι ει και
πολλα τις, η και παντα τα τοιαυτα, μαθοι, τα μεν πραγματα ουδεν
αν μαλλον ειδειη, πη εχει, προσπαιζειν δε ὁιος τ' αν ειη τοις ανθρωποις, δια την ονοματων διαφοραν ὑποσκελιζων και ανατρεπων.

174 NOTES ON PLATO.

scholastick divines in the days of monkery and of deep ignorance. But he best knew the manners of his own age, and doubtless saw these things in a graver light than they of themselves deserve, by reflecting on the bad effects which they had on the understandings and on the morals of his countrymen, who not only spent their wit and their time in playing with words, when they might have employed them in inquiring into things; but, by rendering every principle doubtful and dark alike, must necessarily induce men to leave themselves to the guidance of chance and of the passions, unassisted by reason. Whereas if, in reality, there be no certain truth attainable by human knowledge, both the means and the end of disputation are absolutely taken away, and it becomes the most absurd and the most childish of all occupations.

P. 299. Euthydemus appears to have had a colossal statue erected to him at Delphi.

P. 302. The Athenians, and their colonies, worshipped not Jupiter under the name of Πατρῷος in their houses (as all other Greeks did), but Apollo. To Jupiter they gave the name of Ἑρκειος and Φρατριος, and to Minerva of Φρατρια: and these three divinities were the household gods of every Ionian. How then could Dionysidorus, a Chian, be ignorant of this?

P. 305. Μεθορια φιλοσοφον.] This seems to be aimed at Lysias or at Antipho.

HIPPIAS MAJOR.

WE learn from this dialogue in how poor a condition the art of reasoning on moral and abstracted subjects was, before the time of Socrates; for it is impossible that Plato should introduce[1] a sophist of the first reputation for eloquence and knowledge in several kinds, talking in a manner below the absurdity and weakness of a child; unless he had really drawn after the life. No less than twenty-four pages are here spent in vain, only to force it into the head of Hippias, that

[1] He always appeared at the Olympick games, and in the temple of Jupiter discoursed on all subjects, and answered all questions proposed to him. (V. Hipp. Min. p. 363.)

NOTES ON THE GREEK TEXT.

Platon. Op. Edit. Serrani, Vol. 3. p. 281.

P. 281. Πιττακου τε και Βιαντος.] This is very extraordinary, as Pittacus was continually busied in publick affairs, and both Bias and Thales occasionally.

Ib. It was acknowledged therefore, that the sculptors, painters, and architects of latter times, had far surpassed the ancients.

P. 286. Επειδη ή Τροια.] The beginning of an oration, pronounced at Sparta, by Hippias, in the character of Nestor, addressed to the young Neoptolemus. It is remarkable, what is here said of the Lacedæmonians, that the generality of them did not even know common arithmetick.

there is such a thing as a general idea ; and that, before
we can dispute on any subject, we should give a definition of it.

˙ The time of the conversation seems to be after Ol.
89. 2, for the war had permitted no intercourse between
Athens and Elis before that year, and we see in the
Protagoras that Hippias was actually at Athens Ol. 90.
1, so that it seems to fall naturally between these two
years.

NOTES.

P. 289. Passages of Heraclitus : Πιθηκων ὁ καλλιστος αισχρος
αλλω γενει συμβαλειν.—Ανθρωπων ὁ σοφωτατος προς Θεον πιθηκος
φανειται. This latter passage is undoubtedly the original of
that famous thought in Pope's Essay on Man, B. 2 ;

"And shewed a Newton, as we shew an ape,"

which some persons have imagined that he borrowed from one
Palingenius,* an obscure author, who wrote a poem called
"Zodiacus Vitæ."

290. Της Αθηνᾶς.] The colossal figure of Minerva in the
Acropolis at Athens, described by Plutarch in his life of
Pericles.

[* Pope, who was versed in the modern Latin poets, might have taken
it from Palingenius, and Palingenius from Plato.—MATHIAS.]

HIPPIAS MINOR.

Platon. Op. Serrani, Vol. 1. p. 363.

THE time of this dialogue is after the Hippias Major, with which it may be ranked.

P. 363. Εὐδικος.] Mentioned in the Hippias Major, p. 256, as an admirer of this sophist.

P. 368. Hippias appeared at Olympia in a dress of his own weaving, buskins of his own cutting out and sewing, with a ring on his finger, and a seal engraved by himself, and a beautiful zone of his own embroidery. He brought with him epick poems, dithyrambicks, tragedies, and orations, all of his own composition.

Ib. Την ζωνην.] The Greeks therefore girt their under-garment (Χιτωνισκος) with a cincture.

PROTAGORAS.

Η, ΣΟΦΙΣΤΑΙ.

Plat. Op. Serrani, Vol. 1. p. 309.

OBSERVATIONS ON THE DATE OF THIS DIALOGUE.

PLATO, in this dialogue, one of the noblest he ever wrote, has fallen, through negligence, into some anachronisms, as Athenæus has remarked, (L. 5. p. 218.) though some things in reality are only mistakes of his own, and others he has omitted, which are real faults. Dacier undertakes wholly to justify Plato. We shall shew that neither of them are quite in the right.

There are two marks which fix the time of this conversation, as it is generally thought, and as Athenæus has shewn. The one, that Callias is mentioned in it, as then master of himself, and in possession of his father Hipponicus's estate:[1] now Hipponicus was slain in the battle of Deli, Ol. 89. 1, so that it must be after that year.

Secondly, the Αγριοι, a comedy of Pherecrates, is said to have been played the year before; but that play was brought upon the stage in the magistracy of

---

[1] Εν οικηματι τινι, ω προτου μεν ως ταμιειω εχρητο Ιππονικος, νυν, υπο του πληθους των καταλυοντων, ο Καλλιας και τουτο εκκενωσας ξενοις καταλυσιν πεποιηκη. Protag. p. 315.

Aristion, Ol. 89. 4, consequently this must happen Ol. 90. 1.

There is yet a third circumstance which may ascertain the time of the dialogue. Athenæus produces it as an instance of Plato's negligence, but has only discovered his own by it. Hippias the Elean (he says) and others of his countrymen are (Protag. p. 315.) introduced, as then present at Athens, whereas it is impossible they could be there during the Peloponnesian war, while the Eleans were confederates with Sparta against the Athenians; for though a truce was agreed upon for one year, under Isarchus, (Ol. 89. 1,) yet it was broken through presently, and no cessation of arms ensued. But in reality Hippias might be at [1] Athens any year after Isarchus's magistracy, since though the war broke out afresh afterwards with Sparta, yet the Allies of Sparta entered not into it, as at first, but either continued neuter, or joined the Athenians, and Elis particularly entered into a defensive league with them this very year, (see Thucyd. L. 5. sect. 47) so that when Athenæus says, μὴ τῆς ἐχεχειριας αυτης μενοισης, it is plain that he did not know but that Sparta entered the war again with all the confederates which she had at first, and consequently had read [2] Thucy-

[1] Dacier, while he vindicates Plato on this head, has only considered Athens with regard to Sparta: but the question turns solely upon Elis, of which he takes no notice.

[2] What is no less strange, Casaubon neither attempts to justify Plato in this matter, nor did he know, that the Ενιαυσιαι Σπονδαι under Isarchus were mentioned, very much at large, by Thucydides, L. 4. sect. 117. See Casaubon's Annotations ad Athenæum, L. 5. c. 18.

dides very negligently. This very thing then may fix
it to Ol. 90. 1, at least it will prove that it could not
be earlier than Ol. 89. 1.

Athenæus further remarks, that Eupolis in his
Κολακες, which was played Ol. 89. 3, speaks of Protagoras as then present at Athens, and that Ameipsias
in his Κοννος, acted two years before, has not introduced him into his chorus of Φροντισται, or philosophers; so that it is probable that he arrived at Athens
in the interval between the representation of these two
dramas, which is three or four years earlier than the
dialogue, in which Plato nevertheless says that he had
not been three days come; and that after many years'
absence. Dacier attempts to answer this, but makes
little of it; and indeed it was impossible to do better,
since both the comedies are lost, and we do not know
to what parts of them Athenæus alludes, as he cites
nothing.

But in truth there are other circumstances inconsistent with the date of the dialogue, of which neither
Athenæus nor Dacier have taken any notice. 1. Alcibiades is represented as just on the confines of youth
and manhood, whereas in Ol. 90. 1, he was turned of
thirty. 2dly. Criso of Himera, celebrated for gaining
three victories successively in the course at Olympia
(the first of which was [1] Ol. 83.) is here spoken of
(p. 335.) as in the height of his vigour. Now it is
scarcely possible, that one, who was a man grown at
the time I have mentioned, should continue in full
strength and agility twenty-nine years afterwards: but

[1] Pausanias, L. 5. c. 23, and Diodorus.

this I do not much insist upon. 3dly. Pericles is
spoken of [1] as yet living, though he died nine years
before; and what is worse, his two sons Xanthippus
and Paralus are both represented as present at this
conversation, though they certainly died [2] during the
plague sometime before their father.

ANALYSIS OF THE DIALOGUE.

Socrates is wakened before day-break with a hasty
knocking at his door : it is Hippocrates, a young man,
who comes eagerly to acquaint him with the arrival of
Protagoras, the celebrated sophist, at Athens, and to
entreat him to go immediately and present him to that
great man ; for he is determined to spare no pains nor
expense, so he may be but admitted to his conversation.
Socrates moderates his impatience a little, and while
they take a turn about the hall together, waiting for
sun-rise, inquires into his notions of a sophist, and what
he expected from him ; and finding his ideas not very

[1] Protag. p. 320. 'Α δε αυτος σοφος εστι, ουτε αυτος παιδευει,
ουτε τω αλλω παραδιδωσι· and again, p. 329, which Dacier
tries, but in vain, to elude.
[2] Plutarch in Vit. Periclis.—Athenæus has taken notice of
this, L. 11. p. 505, and Macrobius, who seems to copy the
other, Saturnal. L. 1. c. 1.

NOTES ON THE GREEK TEXT.

P. 309. Il. Ω. v. 347.
Κουρω αισιητηρι εοικως,
Πρωτον υπηνητη, τουπερ χαριεστατη ἥβη.
Ib. Βοηθων εμοι.] Vid. infra, p. 336 and 347.
310. Του σκιμποδος.] A low bedstead, or couch, on which
Socrates lay, for he was not yet risen.

clear upon that head, shews him the folly of putting
his soul into the hands of he knew not whom, to do
with it he knew not what.   If his body had been
indisposed, and he had needed a physician, he would
certainly have taken the advice and recommendation of
his family and friends; but here, where his mind, a
thing of much greater importance, was concerned, he
· was on the point of trusting it, unadvisedly and at
random, to the care of a person whom he had never
seen, nor spoken to.   That a sophist was a kind of
merchant or rather a retailer of food for the soul, and,
like other shopkeepers, would exert his eloquence to
recommend his own goods.   The misfortune was, we
could not carry them off, like corporeal viands, set
them by a while, and consider them at leisure, whether
they were wholesome or not, before we tasted them ;
that in this case we have no vessel, but the soul, to
receive them in, which will necessarily retain a tincture,
and perhaps much to its prejudice, of all which is

NOTES.

P. 310. Εξ Οινοης.]   There were two Δημοι of Attica so called,
the one near Marathon, the other near Eleutheræ on the confines of Bœotia, which I take to be here meant.   See Meursius
and Pausan. L. 1. c. 33 and c. 38.

Ib. Πτοιησις.]   An eager desire of a thing, proceeding from
admiration.

Ib. Νεωτερος ειμι.]   He was upwards of twenty-four years of
age ; for he was a child when Protagoras first came to Athens,
which was Ol. 84. 1.

311. Τον Κωον.]   Hippocrates, the Coan, was now about
forty years old.

Ib. Φειδια.]   Phidias was not now living.   He died Ol.
87. 1.   Polycletus was younger, and might be still alive.

PROTAGORAS.   183

instilled into it. However, by way of trial only, they
agree to wait upon Protagoras, and accordingly they go
to the house of Callias, where both he and two other
principal sophists, Prodicus and Hippias, with all their
train of followers, were lodged and entertained.
The porter, an eunuch, wearied and pestered with
the crowd of sophists who resorted to the house, mis-
taking them for such, gives them a short answer, and
shuts the door in their face. At last they are admitted,
and find Protagoras with Callias, and more company,
walking in the porticos. The motions of Protagoras's
followers are described with much humour; how at
every turn they divided and cast off, as in a dance, still
falling in, and moving in due subordination behind the
principal performer. Hippias is sitting in a great chair,

NOTES.

P. 312. Ἐρυθριασας.] For the bad morals of the professors, (see
the Gorgias, p. 520, Σν δε δι' αγνοιαν, &c. and the Meno, p. 91,
Ἡρακλεῖς, ευφημει, &c.) had brought the name into general dis-
repute ; though it was once an honourable appellation, and
given afterwards to all such as called themselves Φιλοσοφοι.
Solon was the person who first bore the name of ὁ Σοφιστης.
(See Isocrat. Περι Αντιδοσεως, p. 344.) Socrates defines a sophist,
such as the character was in his time, Εμπορος τις, η καπηλος
των αγωγιμων, αφ' ὧν ἡ ψυχη τρεφεται. Protag. p. 313.

314. Ου σχολη αυτω.] i.e. "My Lord is not at leisure to be
spoken with."

Ib. Εν τω Προστοω.] Προστωον (which is also written Προσ-
τοος) is rendered by the lexicographers Vestibulum Porticûs,
that is, as I imagine, the Cavædium or open court, surrounded
with a peristyle or portico, opening upon the rooms of entertainment ; for all these rooms together composed the Ανδρων,
as Vitruvius describes it.

184   NOTES ON PLATO.

on the opposite side of the court, discoursing on points
of natural philosophy to a circle, who are seated on
forms round him; while Prodicus, in a large inner
apartment, in bed and wrapped up in abundance of
warm clothes, lies discoursing with another company of
admirers. Socrates approaches Protagoras, and presents
the young Hippocrates to him. The sophist, having
premised something to give an idea of his own profession, its use and dignity, the rest of the company, being
summoned together from all quarters, seat themselves
about him; and Socrates begins by entreating Protagoras to inform him, what was the tendency and usual
effect of his lessons, that Hippocrates might know what
he was to expect from him. His answers shew, that he
professed to accomplish men for publick and private

NOTES.

P. 314. Ἀδελφὸς ὁμομήτριος.] The widow of Hipponicus, and
mother to Callias, took to her second husband, Pericles, and
brought him a son called Paralus: they afterwards parted by
consent, and both married again. See Plutarch in his life of
Pericles, who says that she brought him two sons, Xanthippus
and Paralus; but it seems to be a mistake, as he had Xanthippus
by a former marriage. This lady was related to Pericles by blood.

Ib. Ἀδειμάντω.] The son of Cepis and of Leucolophides.
This Adimantus was Στρατηγὸς with Alcibiades, against Andros,
Ol. 93. 2. See Xenoph. Hist. Græc. L. 1.

315. Χαρμίδης.] Plato's uncle.—Φιλιππίδης.] Son of Philo-
melus.—Ἀντίμοιρος.] Of Mende.—Ἐρυξίμαχος.] A physician.

Ib. Ἀνδρων.] The son of Androtion; probably the same
person, who was afterwards one of the Four Hundred, and
brought in the decree against Antipho, the Rhamnusian: (see
Harpocration) he is mentioned in the Gorgias (p. 487) as a
friend of Callicles, and a lover of eloquence rather than of true
philosophy.

life, to make them good and useful members of the state, and of a family. Socrates admires the beauty of his art, if indeed there be such an art, which, he confesses, he has often doubted; for if virtue is a thing which may be taught, what can his countrymen the Athenians mean, who in their publick assemblies, if the question turn on repairing the publick edifices, consult the architect, and if on their fleet, the ship-builder, and laughed at such as on pretence of their wit, of their wealth, or of their nobility, should interfere in debates which concern a kind of knowledge, in which they have neither skill nor experience; but if the point to be considered relate to the laws, to the magistracy, to the administration of peace and war, and to such subjects, every merchant, every little tradesman and mechanick,

---

NOTES.

P. 315. Εφη 'Ομηρος.] An allusion to the Odyss. of Homer, Λ. v. 600, as Dacier well observes.

Ib. Παυσανιας.] A lover of Agatho, the tragick poet, who was now (he says) very young; he gained his first prize on the stage Ol. 90. 4, four years after this. See Plato, Sympos. p. 193, and Athenæus, L. 5. p. 216.

316. Ικκος.] of Tarentum.—Ηροδικος.] Of Selymbria, a sophist and Παιδοτριβης. See the Phædrus, p. 227.

316. Πυθοκλειδης.] Of Ceos; he taught Pericles musick. See Alcib. 1. p. 118. and Plutarch in Pericles.

Ib. Αγαθοκλης.] The Athenian musician and sophist; he instructed the famous Damon. See Laches, p. 80.

317. Πολλα γε ετη.] He (Pythoclides, who taught musick) was now about sixty-one years of age, and had taught it near thirty-one years: but how he can call himself old enough to be father to any one in the company, I do not see; for Socrates was near fifty years of age.

the poor as well as the rich, the mean as well as the
noble, deliver their opinion with confidence, and are
heard with attention. Besides, those greatest statesmen, who have been esteemed the brightest examples
of political virtue, though they have given their children
every accomplishment of the body which education
could bestow, do not at all appear to have improved
their minds with those qualities for which they themselves were so eminent, and in which consequently they
were best able to instruct them, if instruction could
convey these virtues to the soul at all.

Protagoras answers by reciting a fable delivered in
very beautiful language; the substance of it is this:
Prometheus and Epimetheus, when the gods had formed
all kinds of animals within the bowels of the earth, and
the destined day approached for producing them into
light, were commissioned to distribute among them the
powers and qualifications which were allotted to them.
The younger brother prevailed upon the elder to let

NOTES.

P. 318. Ζευξιππος.] Of Heraclea. I do not find this painter
mentioned any where else; perhaps it should be read, Zeuxis,
who was of Heraclea, and now a young man.

Ib. Ορθαγορας.] The Theban, who taught Epaminondas on
the flute. See Aristoxenus, ap. Athenæum, L. 4. p. 184.

319. Οἱ Τοξοται—κελευοντων των Πρυτανεων.] See Aristophanes in Acharnens. v. 239.

Ib. Αριφρονος.] Ariphron was the brother of Pericles; they
were both (by their mother Agariste) first cousins to Dinomache,
the mother of Alcibiades, and Clinias, to whom they were
guardians: Clinias was mad. (See Alcibiad. 1. p. 118.)—
Prometheus and Epimetheus (Foresight and Aftersight) were
the sons of Iapetus, the Titan, and Clymene.

him perform this work, and Prometheus consented to
review afterwards and correct his disposition of things.
Epimetheus then began, and directed his care to the
preservation of the several species, that none might ever
be totally lost. To some he gave extreme swiftness,
but they were deficient in strength ; and the strong he
made not equally swift : the little found their security
in the lightness of their bodies, in their airy wings, and
in their subterraneous retreats ; while those of vast
magnitude had the superiority of their bulk for a defence. Such as were formed to prey on others, he made
to produce but few young ones ; while those, who were
to serve as their prey, brought forth a numerous progeny.
He armed them against the seasons with hoofs of horn
and callous feet, with hides of proof and soft warm furs,
their native bed and clothing all in one. But when
Prometheus came to review his brother's work, he found
that he had lavished all his art and all his materials
upon the brute creation, while mankind, whose turn it

NOTES.

P. 320. Αφετοι.] Every divinity had some such animals, which
fed at liberty within the sacred enclosures and pastures. Such
were the oxen of the Sun, (in Homer, Od. M.) the owls of Minerva
in the Acropolis at Athens, (Aristophan. Lysistrat.) the peacocks
of Juno at Samos, (Athenæus, L. 14. p. 655. ex Antiphane et
Menodoto Samio) the tame serpents of Æsculapius, at Epidaurus,
(Pausan. L. 2. c. 28. and at Athens, Aristoph. Plut. v. 733.) the
fishes of the Syrian goddess, &c. (Xenoph. Cyri Anabas. L. 1.
p. 254.)

321. Τυλοις.] This seems to be a gloss only, as an explanation of Δερμασι στερεοις και αναιμοις, to which it is synonymous.
Insert in the end of the sentence, Ταρσους επεστερεωσεν, for a
verb is wanting, equivalent to εκοσμησε.

NOTES ON PLATO.

was next to be produced to light, was left a naked helpless animal, exposed to the rigour of the seasons and to
the violence of every other creature round him. In
compassion therefore to his wants, Prometheus purloined
the arts of Pallas and of Vulcan, and with them fire,
(without which they were impracticable and useless)
and bestowed them on this new race, to compensate
their natural defects. Men then, as allied to the divinity
and endowed with reason, were the only part of the
creation which acknowledged the being and the providence of the gods. They began to erect altars and
statues; they formed articulate sounds, and invented
language; they built habitations, covered themselves

NOTES.

P. 321. Ολιγονιαν.] This is remarked by Herodotus, and by
Aristotle, and seems to be very true with regard to the larger
size of animals ; but it does not appear in the lesser part of the
creation, as in spiders, and in other insects, which live on their
kind, the smaller rapacious fishes, snakes, &c. probably because
they themselves were to serve as food to larger creatures.

Ib. Ου πανυ τοι σοφος.] Hesiod calls him, 'Αμαρτινοον τ'
Επιμηθεα. Theogon. v. 511.

Ib. Ευπορια μεν του βιου.] See the Prometheus of Æschylus.

325. Something is understood or lost after the words, εκων
πειθηται, as, ευ εχει, or καλως.

327. Ευρυβατω και Φρινωνδα.] Phrynondas is mentioned by
Isocrates, as a name grown proverbial for a villain. Παραγρα-
φικος προς Καλλιμαχον, p. 382. And Æschines in Ctesiphont :
Αλλ' οιμαι ουτε Φρινωνδας, ουτε Ευρυβατος, ουτ' αλλος πωποτε των
παλαι πονηρων, τοσουτος μαγος και γοης εγενετο. p. 73. See also
Aristophanes, Θεσμοφορ. Eurybatus was an Ephesian, who
being trusted by Croesus with a great sum to raise auxiliaries,
betrayed him, and went into the service of Cyrus. See Ephorus
ap. Harpocrat. and Diodorus, Excerpt. de Virt. et Vitiis, p. 240.

with clothing, and cultivated the ground. But still they were lonely creatures, scattered here and there, for Prometheus did not dare to enter the citadel of Jove, where Policy, the mother and queen of social life, was kept near the throne of the god himself; otherwise he would have bestowed her too on his favourite mankind. The arts, which they possessed, just supported them, but could not defend them against the multitude and fierceness of the wild beasts: they tried to assemble and live together, but soon found that they were more dangerous and mischievous to one another than the savage creatures had been. In pity then to their condition Jove, lest the whole race should perish, sent Mer-

---

NOTES.

P. 328. *Της πραξεως του μισθου.*] It is remarkable in what general esteem and admiration Protagoras was held throughout all Greece. If any scholar of his thought the price he exacted was too high, he only obliged him to say upon his oath, what he thought the precepts he had given him were worth, and Protagoras was satisfied with that sum. Yet he got more wealth by his profession than Phidias the statuary, and any other ten the most celebrated artists of Greece, as Socrates (in Menone, p. 91, and in Hipp. Maj. p. 282) tells us. Euathlus (see Quintilian, L. 3. c. 1.) gave him 10,000 drachmæ (about £300. sterling), for his art of rhetorick in writing. He was the first sophist in Greece who professed himself a *Παιδευσεως και αρετης διδασκαλος,* and such an one as could make men better and better every time he conversed with them, p. 318 et infra, p. 349.

329. *Ει δε επανεροιτο, τινα.*] See the Phædrus, where he uses the same thought, p. 275. *Δεινον γαρ που, ω Φαιδρε,* &c.

333. *Παρατεταχθαι.*] To be set against it, that is, to have an aversion to it.

336. *Ουκ οτι παιζει.*] Perhaps we should read, *καιτοι παιζει.*

cury to earth, with Shame and Justice; and when he
doubted how he should bestow them, and whether they
should be distributed, as the arts had been, this to one,
and that to another, or equally divided among the whole
kind; Jove approved the latter, and commanded, that
if any did not receive his share of that bounty, he should
be extirpated from the face of the earth, as the pest and
destruction of his fellow-creatures.

This then, continues Protagoras, is the cause why
the Athenians, and other nations, in debates, which
turn on the several arts, attend only to the advice of
the skilful; but give ear in matters of government,
which are founded on ideas of common justice and
probity, to every citizen indifferently among them: and
that this is the common opinion of all men, may hence
appear. If a person totally ignorant of musick should
fancy himself an admirable performer, the world would
either laugh or be angry, and his friends would repri-
mand or treat him as a madman: but if a man should
have candour and plain-dealing enough to profess himself a villain and ignorant of common justice, what in
the other case would have been counted modesty, the

NOTES.

P. 339. Προς Σκοπαν.] The son of Creon and Echecratia, of
Cranon in Thessaly, a citizen of great riches and power, and a
principal patron of Simonides, who repaid him with immortality.
See also Theocritus Idyll. 16. v. 36. Πολλοι δε Σκοπαδαισιν, &c.
Here is also a large fragment of one of the odes of Simonides to
him.

340. Θεια τις ειναι παλαι.] Perhaps, Κεια τις.

341. Και ουδαμως Κειον.] Dacier corrects this to Ουδαμως
Θειον.

simple confession of truth and of his own ignorance,
would here be called impudence and madness. He that
will not dissemble here, will be by all regarded as an
idiot; for to own that one knows not what justice is,
is to own that one ought not to live among mankind.

He proceeds to shew, that no one thought our idea
of justice to be the gift of nature ; but that it is acquired by instruction and by experience : for with the
weak, the deformed, or the blind man, no one is angry ;
no reprimands, no punishments attend the unfortunate,
nor are employed to correct our natural defects ; but
they are the proper consequences of our voluntary
neglects or offences. Nor is the punishment, which
follows even these, intended to redress an evil already
past, (for that is impossible) but to prevent a future,
or at least to deter others from like offences ; which
proves, that wickedness is by all regarded as a voluntary ignorance.

Next he shews, how this knowledge is acquired ; it
is by education. Every one is interested in teaching
another the proper virtue of a man, on which alone all
his other acquisitions must be founded, and without

P. 341. Λεσ.ℓιοι.] The Lesbians then spoke a corrupt dialect ;
yet that island produced Alcæus, Sappho, Theophrastus, &c. ·

342. This is a beautiful compliment to the Cretans and
Lacedæmonians.

Ib. Ωτα τε καταγνινται.] The rougher exercises of boxing
and of the cæstus. See Diog. Laertius in Menedemo, and the
Gorgias, p. 515.

350. Πελτασπκοι.] A light-armed militia, a Thracian invention, and borrowed from that nation by the Greek colonies on

which he cannot exist among his fellow-creatures. His
parents, as soon as understanding begins to dawn in
him, are employed in prescribing what he ought to do
and what he ought not to do ; his masters, in filling his
mind with the precepts, and forming it to the example,
of the greatest men, or in fashioning his body to perform with ease and patience whatever his reason commands ; and lastly, the laws of the state lay down a
rule, by which he is necessitated to direct his actions.
If then the sons of the greatest men do not appear to
be greater proficients in virtue than the ordinary sort,
it must not be ascribed to the parent's neglect ; much
less must it be concluded, that virtue is not to be acquired by instruction : it is the fault perhaps of genius
and of nature.   Let us suppose, that to perform on a
certain instrument were a qualification required in every
man, and necessary to the existence of a city, ought we
to wonder, that the son of an admirable performer
fell infinitely short of his father in skill?   Should we
attribute this to want of care, or say, that musick were
not attainable by any art? or should we not rather
ascribe it to defect of genius and to natural inability?
Yet every member of such a state would doubtless far
surpass all persons rude and unpractised in musick.

---

their coast, whence it was afterwards introduced in Athens,
Sparta, and in the rest of Greece.   They fought on foot armed
with a crescent-like shield, bow and arrows, long javelins, and
a sword.   See Xenoph. ap. Pollucem. L. 1. c. 10.   This species
of shield was afterwards introduced by Iphicrates among the
heavy-armed foot also.   (Diodorus. L. 15. c. 44.)

In like manner, the most worthless member of a society, civilized by some sort of education and brought up under the influence of laws and of policy, will be an amiable man, if compared with a wild and uncultivated savage. It is hard indeed to say, who is our particular instructor in the social virtues ; as, for the same reason, it is hard to say, who taught us our native tongue ; yet no one will therefore deny that we learned it. The publick is in these cases our master : and all the world has a share in our instruction. Suffice it (continues the sophist) to know, that some there are among us, elevated a little above the ordinary sort, in the art of leading mankind to honour and to virtue ; and among these I have the advantage to be distinguished.

Socrates continues astonished for a time and speechless, as though dazzled with the beauty of Protagoras's discourse. At last, recovering himself, he ventures to propound a little doubt which has arisen in his mind (though perfectly satisfied, he says, with the main question), whether temperance, fortitude, justice, and the rest, which Protagoras has so often mentioned, and

---

NOTES.

P. 357. 'Ότι Αμαθια.] This is the true key and great moral of the dialogue, that knowledge alone is the source of virtue, and ignorance the source of vice : it was Plato's own principle, (see Plat. Epist. 7. p. 336. Αμαθια, εξ ης παντα κακα πασι ερριζωται και βλαστανει, και ύστερον αποτελει καρπον τοις γεννη- σασι πικροτατον. See also Sophist. p. 228 and 229. and Enthy- demus. from p. 278 to 281. and De Legib. L. 3. p. 688.) and probably it was also the principle of Socrates : the consequence of it is, that virtue may be taught, and may be acquired ; and that philosophy alone can point us out the way to it.

seemed to comprehend under the general name of
virtue, are different things, and can subsist separately
in the same person; or whether they are all the same
quality of mind, only exerted on different occasions.
Protagoras readily agrees to the first of these; but is
insensibly betrayed by Socrates into the toils of his
logick, and makes such concessions, that he finds himself forced to conclude the direct contrary of what he
had first advanced. He is sensible of his disgrace, and
tries to evade this closer kind of reasoning by taking
refuge in that more diffuse eloquence, which used to
gain him such applause. But when he finds himself
cut short by Socrates, who pleads the weakness of his
own memory, unable to attend to long continued
discourses, and who intreats him to bring down the
greatness of his talents to the level of a mind so much
inferiour, he is forced to pick a frivolous quarrel with
Socrates, and break off the conversation in the middle.
Here Callias interposes, and Alcibiades, in his insolent
way, by supporting the request of Socrates and by
piquing the vanity of Protagoras, obliges him to accommodate himself to the interrogatory method of disputation, and renews the dialogue.[1]

To save the dignity of Protagoras, and to put him
in humour again, Socrates proposes that he shall conduct the debate, and state the questions, while he himself will only answer them; provided Protagoras will

[1] The episodical characters of Prodicus and Hippias, introduced as mediating a reconciliation, are great ornaments to the
dialogue; the affectation of eloquence and of an accurate choice
of words in the former, and the stately figurative diction of the
latter, being undoubtedly drawn from the life.

in his turn afterwards condescend to do the same for
him. The sophist begins by proposing a famous ode
of Simonides, which seems to carry in it an absolute
contradiction, which he desires Socrates to reconcile.
Socrates appears at first puzzled, and after he has
played awhile with Protagoras and with the other
sophists, (that he may have time to recollect himself)
he gives an explanation of that poem, and of its pretended inconsistency, in a manner so new and so just
as to gain the applause of the whole company. He
then brings back Protagoras (in spite of his reluctance)
to his former subject, but without taking advantage of
his former concessions, and desires again his opinion on
the unity, or on the similitude, of the virtues. Protagoras now owns, that there is a near [1] affinity between
them all, except valour, which he affirms that a man
may possess, who is entirely destitute of all the rest.
Socrates proves to him, that this virtue also, like the
others, is founded on knowledge and is reducible to it;
that it is but to know what is really to be feared, and
what is not; that good and evil, or in other words,
pleasure and pain,[2] being the great and the only movers

---

[1] See Gorgias, p. 507.

[2] Plato reasons on the principles of the most rational Epi-
curean in this place, and indeed on the only principles which
can be defended. (See Gorgias, p. 467 and 499. Τελος απασων
των πραξεων το αγαθον.) As our sense of pleasure and of pain
is our earliest sentiment, and is the great instrument of self-
preservation, some philosophers have called these affections,
Τα πρωτα κατα φυσιν. See Aul. Gell. L. 12. c. 5. Ουδεμια ἡδονη
καθ᾽ ἑαυτην κακον, αλλα τα τινων ἡδονων ποιητικα πολλαπλασιους
επιφερει τας οχλησεις των ἡδονων. Epicurus in Κυριαις Δοξαις.
apud Laert. L. 10. s. 141.

of the human mind, no one can reject pleasure, but where it seems productive of a superior degree of pain, or prefer pain, unless the consequence of it be a superior pleasure. That to balance these one against the other with accuracy, to judge rightly of them at a distance, to calculate the overplus[1] of each, is that science on which our happiness depends, and which is the basis of every virtue. That, if our whole life's welfare and the interests of it were as closely connected with the judgment, which we should make on the real magnitude of objects and on their true figure, (or with our not being deceived by the appearance which they exhibit at a distance,) who doubts but that geometry and opticks would then be the means of happiness to us, and would become the rule of virtue? That there is a kind of knowledge no less necessary to us in our present state, and no less a science; and that, when we pretend to be misled by our passions, we ought to blame our ignorance, which is the true source of all our follies and vices. And now (continues Socrates) who would not laugh at our inconsistency? You set out with affirming that virtue might be taught, yet in the course of our debate you have treated it as a thing entirely distinct[2] from knowledge, and not reducible to

[1] Plato de Legib. L. 1. p. 644. and L. 2. p. 663. and L. 5. p. 733.

[2] It was the opinion of Socrates, that all the virtues were only prudence (or wisdom) exerted on different occasions. Πασας τας αρετας φρονησεις ειναι· και Σωκρατης (adds Aristotle) τῇ μεν ορθως εξητει, τηδ' ημαρτανεν· ὁτι μεν γαρ φρονησεις ωετο ειναι πασας τας αρετας ημαρτανεν· ὁτι δ' ουκ ανευ φρονησεως καλως ελεγε. Ethic. ad Nichom. L. 6. c. 13. and Plato de Legib. L. 3. p. 688. calls prudence, Συμπασης ηγεμων αρετης, φρονησις μετ' ερωτος και επιθυμιας ταυτῃ επομενης.

it : I, who advanced the contrary position, have shewn that it is a science, and consequently that it may be learned.

Protagoras, who has had no other share in the dispute than to make (without perceiving the consequence) such concessions as absolutely destroy what he set out with affirming, tries to support the dignity of his own age and reputation, by making an arrogant compliment to Socrates, commending his parts (very considerable, he says, and very promising for so young a man,) and doing him the justice to say to all his acquaintance, that he knows no one more likely, some time or other, to make an extraordinary person ; and he adds that this is not a time to enter deeper into this subject, and on any other day he shall be at his service.

IO.

Η, ΠΕΡΙ ΠΟΙΗΤΙΚΗΣ ἙΡΜΙΙΝΕΙΑΣ.

ON THE IMPERFECTION OF POETRY AND OF CRITICISM WITHOUT PHILOSOPHY.

As Serranus, and (I think) every commentator after him, has read this dialogue with a grave countenance, and understood it in a literal sense, though it is throughout a very apparent and continued irony ; it is no wonder if such persons, as trust to their accounts of it, find it a very silly and frivolous thing. Yet under that irony, doubtless, there is concealed a serious meaning, which makes a part of Plato's great design, a

---

NOTES ON THE GREEK TEXT.

Plat. Op. Serrani, Vol. 1. p. 530.

P. 530. Ασκληπιεια.] Pausanias, in his description of the temple of Æsculapius near Epidanrus, speaks of the adjoining stadium and theatre, where these games were celebrated during the festival of the deity. L. 2. p. 174.

Ib. Αλλοις Ποιηταις.] The Rhapsodi sung, in the theatres, not only the poems of Homer, but those also (V. de Legib. L. 2. p. 658.) of Hesiod, Archilochus, Mimnermus, and Phocylides, the Iambicks of Simonides, &c. (see Athenæus, L. 14. p. 620.) and even the history of Herodotus.

design which runs through all his writings. He was
persuaded that virtue[1] must be built on knowledge,
not on that counterfeit[2] knowledge, which dwells only
on the surface of things and is guided by the imagination rather than by the judgment, (for this was the
peculiar foible of his countrymen, a light and desultory
people, easily seduced by their fancy wherever it led
them), but on the knowledge which is fixed and settled
on certain great and general truths, and on principles
as ancient and as unshaken as nature itself, or rather
as the author of nature. To this knowledge, and con-

[1] See Plato's seventh Epistle to the friends of Dion ; as well
as his Protagoras, Meno, Laches, and Alcibiades.
[2] Δοξοσοφια, δοξαστικη επιστημη. (Vid. Sophist. p. 233.)

P. 530. Μαλιστα εν 'Ομηρω.] These were distinguished by
the name of Homeristæ, or Homeridæ. See Pindar Od. Nem.
2. and Plato de Republ. L. 10, p. 599.

Ib. Ει μη ξυνιη.] They were remarkable for their ignorance.
See Xenoph. Sympos. p. 513. Οισθα ουν εθνος τι ηλιθιωτερον
Ραψωδων, &c. Metrodorus of Lampsacus here is not to be
confounded with the friend of Epicurus, who was also of
Lampsacus.

Ib. The first Metrodorus (mentioned in the preceding note)
was a disciple of Anaxagoras, and seems to have written on the
moral and natural philosophy of Homer. See Diog. Laert. L.
2, s. 11. Stesimbrotus of Thasus was contemporary with
Socrates, but elder than he : he is often cited by Plutarch (in
Themistocle, in Cimone, in Pericle) having, as it seems, given
some account of these great men, with the two last of whom
he had lived : (see Athenæus, L. 13, p. 589.) he was a sophist
of reputation, and gave lessons to Niceratus the son of Nicias.
See Xenoph. Sympos. p. 513.

sequently to virtue, he thought that philosophy was
our only guide : and as to all those arts, which are
usually made merely subservient to the passions of
mankind, as politicks,[1] eloquence, and poetry, he
thought that they were no otherwise to be esteemed
than as they are grounded on philosophy, and are

[1] See the Gorgias, Meno, Phædrus, and this dialogue.

NOTES.

P. 532. Polygnotus, son of Aglaophon, the painter.

533. Dædalus was the son of Palamaon, of that branch of
the royal family, called Metionidæ, being sprung from Metion,
the son of Erectheus: (See Pausan. L. 7. p. 531. and L. 1. p.
13.) there were statues of his workmanship still preserved in
several cities of Greece, at Thebes, Lebadea, Delos, Olus, and
Gnossus, even in the time of Pausanias, above six hundred
years after this. See Pausan. L. 9, p. 793. and Plato Hippias
Maj. p. 282. Epèus, the son of Panopeus, was the inventor
of the Trojan horse ; in the temple of the Lycian Apollo at
Argos, was preserved a wooden figure of Mercury made by him.
Theodorus, the Samian, son of Telecles, first discovered the
method of casting iron, and of forming it into figures : he also
(with his countryman Rhæcus the son of Philæus) was the first
who cast statues in bronze ; he worked likewise in gold, and
graved precious stones.

Ib. Ολυμπου.] Olympus, the Phrygian, lived in the time
of Midas before the Trojan war, yet his compositions, or Νομοι,
as well the musick as the verses, were extant even in Plutarch's
days ; see Burette on the Treatise de Musicâ, Mémoires de
l'Acad. des Inscript. Vol. 10, note 30, V. 13, note 104, V. 15,
note 228. and Aristotel. Politic. L. 8. c. 5. and Plato Sympos.
p. 215. Και ετι νυνι κηλει τους ανθρωπους, ὸς αν τα εκεινου αυλῇ.
(Marsyæ scilicet, qui Olympum edocuit) see also Plato in
Minoe, p. 318. hence also it seems that they had the musick
of Orpheus, of Thamyris, and of Phemius, then in being. (See
Hom. Odyss. A. 325, and X. 330.)

directed to the ends of virtue. They, who had best
succeeded in them before his time, owed (as he thought)
their success rather to a lucky hit, to some gleam¹ of
truth, as it were providentially, breaking in upon their
minds, than to those fixed and unerring² principles
which are not to be erased from a soul, which has once

¹ Such as Plato calls Ορθη Δοξα,—Αληθης Δοξα. (This is
explained in the Meno, p. 97.) or in the language of irony,
Θεια Δυναμις, θεια μοιρα, κατακωχη. (Ibid. p. 99.) and De
Legib. L. 3. p. 682.
² To which he gives the name of Φρονησις, Επιστημη, ου
δραπετευουσα, αλλα δεδεμενη αιτιας λογισμω· διαφερει γαρ δεσμω
επιστημη ορθης δοξης· (Meno, ubi supra) and on this only he
bestows the name of Τεχνη. (Vid. Gorgiam, and in Sophista,
p. 253.) 'Η των ελευθερων επιστημη, and p. 267. Αρετης
ιστορικη μιμησις, opposed to ἡ Δοξομμητικη. Vid. et Symposium, p. 202. De Republ. L. 5. p. 477. and L. 7. p. 534.

NOTES.

P. 533. The verses of Euripides are in his Oeneus, a drama
now lost ;

Τας βροτων
Γνωμας σκοπησας, ὡστε Μαγνητις λιθος,
Την δοξαν ἑλκει και μεθιστησιν παλιν·

he gave it the name probably from the city of Magnesia ad
Sipylum, where it was found. It is remarkable, that Mr.
Chishull tells us, as they were ascending the castle-hill of this
city, a compass, which they carried with them, pointed to different quarters, as it happened to be placed on different stones,
and that at last it entirely lost its virtue ; which shews that hill
to be a mine of loadstone. Its power of attracting iron and of
communicating its virtue to that iron, we see, was a thing well-
known at that time, yet they suspected nothing of its polar
qualities.
534. Αρυττονται.] Vid. Phædrum, p. 253, and Euripides in
Bacchis, v. 142. and 703.

202   NOTES ON PLATO.

been thoroughly convinced of them. Their conduct
therefore in their actions, and in their productions, has
been wavering between good and evil, and unable to
reach perfection. The inferiour tribe have caught something of their fire, merely by imitation, and form their
judgments, not from any real skill they have in these

NOTES.

P. 534. Οἱ Ποιηται.] Such expressions are frequent in Pindar :
he calls his own poetry, Νεκταρ χυτον, Μοισᾶν δοσιν, γλυκυν
καρπον φρενος, and he says of himself, Εξαιρετον Χαριτων νεμομαι
κᾶπον, (Olymp. Od. 9) and Μελιτι εναορα πολιν βρεχω. (Olymp.
10.) &c. &c.

Ib. 'Ο δε εγκωμμα.] Of this kind are all the odes remaining
to us of Pindar, as the expressions in Olymp. Od. 4, Od. 8, 10,
and 13, and in many other places, clearly shew.

Ib. 'Υπορχηματα.] Pindar was famous for this kind of compositions, though we have lost them, as well as his dithyrambicks. Xenodemus also, Bacchylides, and Pratinas the Phliasian,
excelled in them ; Athenæus has preserved a fine fragment of
this last poet. L. 14, p. 617. These compositions were full of
description, and were sung by a chorus who danced at the same
time, and represented the words by their movements and ges-
tures. Tynnichus of Chalcis, whose pæan was famous, and
indeed the only good thing he ever wrote.

535. Επι τον ουδον.] See Hom. Odyss. X. v. 2. Αλτο δ'
επι μεγαν ουδον, &c.

Ib. Απο του βηματος.] The Rhapsodi, we find, were mounted
on a sort of suggestum, with a crown of gold (See p. 530. and
541. of this dialogue) on their heads, and dressed in robes of
various colours, and after their performance was finished, a collection seems to have been made for them among the audience.

536. 'Οι κορυβαντιῶντες.] This was a peculiar phrenzy supposed to be inspired by some divinity, and attended with violent
motions and efforts of the body, like those of the Corybantes
attendant on Cybele : (Strabo, L. 10. p. 473.) they believed
that they heard the sound of loud musick continually in their

arts, but merely from (what La Bruyere calls) a *gout de comparaison*. The general applause of men has pointed out to them what is finest; and to that, as to a principle, they refer their taste, without knowing or inquiring in what its excellence consists. Each Muse [1] (says Plato in this dialogue) inspires and holds sus-

[1] Ο δε θεος δια παντων τουτων ἑλκει την ψυχην, ὁποι αν βουληται, των ανθρωπων, ανακρεμαννυς εξ αλληλων την δυναμιν· και ὡσπερ εκ της λιθου (της Ηρακλειας) ὁρμαθος παμπολυς εξηρτηται χορειτωντε, και διδασκαλων, και ὑποδιδασκαλων εκ πλαγιου εξηρτημενων, των της Μουσης εκκρεμαμενων δακτυλιων. p. 536.

NOTES.

ears, and seem, from this passage, to have been peculiarly sensible to some certain airs, when really played, as it is reported of those who are bitten by the tarantula. As these airs were pieces of musick usually in honour of some deities, the ancients judged thence by what deity these demoniacks were possessed, whether it were by Ceres, Bacchus, the Nymphs, or by Cybele, &c. who were looked upon as the causes of madness.

P. 541. 'Η γαρ ἡμετερα πολις.] The time therefore of this dialogue must be earlier than the revolt of the Ionian cities, which happened Ol. 91. 4, and it appears from what Ion says in the beginning, that it must be later than Ol. 89. 3, since before that year the communication between Epidaurus and Athens was cut off by the war. Apollodorus of Cyzicus, Phanosthenes of Andrus, and Heraclides of Clazomenæ were elected by the Athenians into the Στρατηγιαι, and other magistracies, though they were not citizens. See Athenæus, L. 11. p. 506. It is plain that Athenæus saw the irony of this dialogue, for, if it be literally taken, there is nothing like abuse in it either on poets or on statesmen.

542. Οειον ειναι και μη τεχνικον.] Hence we see the meaning of Socrates, when he so frequently bestows the epithet of Οειος on the sophists and poets, &c. &c. See also Plato's Meno, p. 99, which is the best comment on the Io which can be read.

pended her favourite poet in immediate contact, as the
magnet docs a link of iron, and from him (through
whom the attractive virtue passes and is continued to
the rest) hangs a long chain of actors, and singers, and
criticks, and interpeters [1] of interpreters.

[1] Ἑρμηνέων ἑρμηνεῖς. p. 535.

THEÆTETUS.

Ol. 95. 1.

Platon. Op. Serrani, Vol. 1. p. 142.

TERPSION meeting Euclides at Megara, and inquiring where he has been, is informed that he has been accompanying Theætetus, who is lately come on shore from Corinth, in a weak and almost dying condition upon his return to Athens. This reminds them of the high opinion which Socrates had entertained of that young man, who was presented to him (not long before his death) by Theodorus[1] of Cyrene, the geometrician. The conversation, which then passed between them, was taken down in writing by Euclides who, at the request of Terpsion, orders his servant to read it to them.

The Abbé Sallier (Mém. de l'Academie des Inscriptions, V. 13, p. 317.) has given an elegant translation of the most shining part of this[2] dialogue; and also in vol. 16. p. 70. of the Mém. de l'Acad. des Inscript. he

[1] Theodorus was celebrated also for his skill in arithmetick, astronomy, and musick. (p. 145.) He had been a friend of Protagoras, who was dead about ten years before the time of this dialogue, and had left his writings in the hands of Callias, the son of Hipponicus.

[2] P. 172 of this dialogue. See also Gorgias, p. 484.

has translated all that part of the dialogue in which
Plato has explained the system of Protagoras, from
p. 151. to 168. The description of a true[1] philosopher
in this place, (though a little aggravated, and more in
the character of Plato than of Socrates,) has yet an
elevation in it which is admirable. The Abbé Sallier
has also given a sketch of the dialogue, which is a very
long one, and (as he rightly judges) would not be much
approved in a translation. It is of that kind called
Πειραστικος, in order to make trial of the capacity of
Theætetus, while Socrates (as he says) only plays the
midwife, and brings the conceptions of his mind to
light. The question is; what is knowledge? and the
purpose of the dialogue is rather to refute the false
definitions of it, as established by[2] Protagoras in his
writings, and resulting from the tenets of Heraclitus,[3]

[1] P. 172 of this dialogue. See also Gorgias, p. 484.

[2] His fundamental tenet was this; viz: Παντων χρηματων
μετρον Ανθρωπον ειναι· των μεν οντων, ὡς εστι· των δε μη οντων
ὡς ουκ εστι· that every man's own perceptions of things were (to
him) the measure and the test of truth and of falsehood.

[3] Viz. That motion was the principle of being, and the only
cause of all its qualities. Mr. Hardion has given us a short
view of the arguments used by Protagoras in support of these
doctrines in his seventh Dissertation on the Rise and Progress
of Eloquence in Greece. See Mémoires de l'Academie des Inscriptions, &c. V. 15. p. 152. This seems to be much the same
with the doctrine of the new Academy; "Omnes omnino res,
quæ sensus omnium movent των προς τι esse dicunt: id verbum
significat nihil esse quicquam quod ex se constet, nec quod
habeat vim propriam et naturam ; sed omnia prorsum ad aliquid
referri, taliaque videri esse, qualis sit eorum species, dum
videntur, qualiaque apud sensus nostros, quo pervenerunt,
creantur, non apud sese, unde profecta sunt." Aul. Gell. L.
11. c. 5.   Vid. Platon. Cratylum, p. 385.

of Empedocles, and of other philosophers, than to produce a better definition of his own. Yet there are
many fine and remarkable passages in it, such as the
observations of Theodorus on the faults of temper,
which usually attend on brighter parts, and on the
defects of genius often found in minds of a more sedate
and solid turn ; Socrates's illustration of his own art by
the whimsical comparison between that and midwifery ;
his opinion, that admiration [1] is the parent of philosophy ; the active and passive powers [2] of matter, arising from the perpetual flux and motion of all things,
(being the doctrine of Heraclitus and others,) explained ; the reflections on philosophical leisure, and
on a liberal turn of mind opposed to the little cunning
and narrow thoughts of mere men of business ; the
description of Heraclitus's followers, then very numerous in Ionia, particularly at Ephesus ; the account of
the tenets of Parmenides and of [3] Melissus, directly

---

[1] Δια το θαυμαζειν δι ανθρωποι, και νυν και πρωτον, ηρξαντο
φιλοσοφειν, &c. Aristot. Metaphys. L. 1. p. 335. Ed. Sylburg.

[2] There is a near affinity between this, and Mr. Locke's account in the beginning of his chapter on Power, L. 2. c. 21.
and in his reflections on our ideas of secondary qualities. B. 2.
c. 8. See also Cudworth's Intellectual System, B. 1. c. 1.
sect. 7.

[3] They maintained, ως εν τα παντα εστι, και εστηκεν αυτο εν
αυτω, ουκ εχον χωραν, εν ω κινειται.

Socrates speaks with respect of these two philosophers, particularly of Parmenides : Παρμενιδης δε μοι φαινεται (κατα το του
'Ομηρου) αιδοιος τε μοι ειναι αμα δεινος τε· συμπροσεμιξα γαρ τω
ανδρι πανυ νεος πανυ πρεσβυτη, και μοι εφανη βαθος τι εχειν
πανταπασι γενναιον. (p. 183.) and in the Sophist, p. 217. Οιον
ποτε και Παρμενιδη χρωμενω, &c. and ib. p. 237. Παρμενιδης δε
ὁ μεγας, &c.

contrary to those of the former ; the distinction between our senses, the instruments through which the mind perceives external objects, and the mind itself, which judges of their existence, their likeness and their difference, and founds[1] its knowledge on the ideas which it abstracts from them ; to which we may add, the comparison of ideas fixed in the memory[2] to impressions made in wax, and the dwelling on this similitude in order to shew the several imperfections of this faculty in different constitutions.

[1] P. 184, 5, and 6.] Compare this with Locke's Definition of Knowledge, B. 4. c. 1.

[2] P. 191 to 194.] Here also see Locke on retention, B. 2. c. 10. and C. 29. § 3. on clear and obscure ideas.

THE SOPHIST.

II, ΠΕΡΙ ΤΟΤ ΟΝΤΟΣ.

ON THE DISTINCTION BETWEEN PHILOSOPHY AND SOPHISTRY.

Platon. Op. Serrani, Vol. 1. p. 216.

I AM convinced that this is a continuation of the Theætetus, which ends with these words, Εωθεν δε, ω Θεοδωρε, δειρο παλιν απαντωμεν, as this begins, Κατα την χθες ὁμολογιαν, ω Σωκρατες, αυτοι τε κοσμιως ἡκομεν, και τονδε τινα ξενον αγομεν. The persons are the same, except the philosopher of the Eleatick school, who is here introduced, and who carries on the disputation

---

NOTES ON THE GREEK TEXT.

P. 216. Ἑτερον τε των αμφι Παρμενιδην και Ζηνωνα ἑταιρων.] Read for ἑτερον, ἑταιρον.

Ib. Οποσοι μετεχουσιν αιδοῖς.] Hom. Odyss. P. v. 485.

Ib. Καθορωντες ὑψοθεν.] Lucretius, L. 2. v. 9.

217. Δι' ερωτησεων.] We see therefore that Parmenides practised the dialectick method of reasoning, which his scholar Zeno first reduced to an art, as Aristotle tells us, and also Laertius, L. 9. § 25.

218. Σωκρατη.] The younger Socrates about the same age with Plato and Theætetus. (Vid. Plato Epist. 11.)

226. Οικετικων ονοματων.] Vulgar and trivial terms. Vide Longinum, s. 43.

210 NOTES ON PLATO.

with Theætetus while both Theodorus and Socrates
continue silent. The apparent subject of it is the
character of a sophist, which is here at large displayed
in opposition to that of a philosopher; but here too he
occasionally attacks the opinions of Protagoras, Heraclitus, Empedocles, and others, on the incertitude of all
existence and on the perpetual flux of matter.

This dialogue, in a translation, would suit the taste
of the present age still less even than the Theætetus;

NOTES.

P. 232. Τα Πρωταγορεια.] Laertius (L. 9. sect. 52.) tells us that
the works of Protagoras were publickly burnt at Athens, yet he
reckons up a number of them as still extant in his time: and
we see, both here and in the Theætetus, that they were left by
the author, at his departure from Athens, in the hands of
Callias, and were known to every one there: δεδημοσιωμενα που
καταβεβληται.

Ib. Της Αντιλογικης.] Protagoras had left a work in two
books entitled Αντιλογιαι; whence Aristoxenus (Laert. L. 3. s.
37.) accuses Plato of borrowing a great part of his work De
Republica.

234. Ὡς εγγυτατατω ανευ των παθηματων.] This is undoubtedly the true reading; ὡς εγγυτατω μαθηματων is very poor and
insipid.

235. Ουκουν ὁσοι γε των μεγαλων.] Hence the Abbé Sallier
collects (Mém. de l'Acad. des Inscriptions, Vol. 8. p. 97.) that
the Ancients were no strangers to perspective, both lineal and
aerial. See Plato de Republ. L. 10. p. 606. on poetical imitation, and Vitruvius, L. 7. c. 5. The words seem only to relate
to colossal figures, where the upper parts must be made larger,
as they are farther removed from the eye.

Ib. Της παιδειας μετεχοντων.] Read, της παιδιας.

Ib. Ουδε αλλο γενος ουδεν.] Plato seems to triumph here in
his own method of division and distinction.

particularly that part which is intended to explain the
nature of existence, and of non-existence, which to me
is obscure beyond all comprehension, partly perhaps
from our ignorance of the opinions of those philosophers, which are here refuted; and partly from the
abstracted nature of the subject, and not a little, I
doubt, from Plato's manner of treating it.

The most remarkable things in this dialogue appear
to be, his description of that disorder and want of symmetry in the soul, produced by ignorance, which puts

<hr/>

NOTES.

P. 237. Παρμενιδης δε ο μεγας.] A fragment of Parmenides's
Poem. See at large in Sextus Empiricus.

Ib. Αυτον τε καταχρησασθαι, used for χρησασθαι simply.

242. Ὡς τρια τα οντα.] Perhaps Anaxagoras, who thought
the formation of animals was εξ υγρου, και θερμου, και νεωδους.
Diog. Laert. L. 2. s. 9. See also Plutarch de Iside et Osiride.
Παντων εκ μαχης και αντιπαθειας την γενεσιν εχοντων.

Ib. Δυω δε ετερος ειπων.] See Themistius in Physica Aris-
totelis, and D. Laert. L. 9. 22 and 29.

Ib. Απο Ξενοφανους και ετι προσθεν.] Xenophanes the Colo-
phonian, was master to Parmenides. We see there was an
Eleatick school, even before Xenophanes's time.

Ib. Ενος οντος των παντων.] This was a tenet of Parmenides,
though far more ancient than he. See the Theætetus, p. 180.
Οιον ακινητον τελεθει, &c. : these Plato calls οι του Ολου στασι-
ωται, and the opposite sect he calls οι ρεοντες, the followers of
Heraclitus. (Theætetus, p. 181.) This tenet was continued
from him to his scholars, Zeno and Melissus. D. Laert. L. 9.
s. 29.

Ib. Ιαδες.] Which he calls αι σιντονωτεραι των Μουσων· I
imagine that he speaks of Heraclitus : Σικελικαι αι μαλακωτεραι·
he means Empedocles ; Αλλοτε μεν φιλοτητι, &c. ap. Plutarch.

244. Fragment of Parmenides : Παντοθεν ευκυκλου, &c. read
the last verse thus : Ουτε βεβαιοτερον πελειν χρεων εστι τη η τη.

212 NOTES ON PLATO.

it off its bias on its way to happiness, the great end
of human actions : the distinction he makes between
Αγνοια and Αμαθια ; the first of which, Αγνοια, is
simply our ignorance of a thing, the latter, Αμαθια, an
ignorance which mistakes itself for knowledge, and
which (as long as this sentiment attends it) is without
hope of remedy : the explanation of the Socratick mode
of instruction (adapted to this peculiar kind of ignorance) by drawing a person's errors gradually from his
own mouth, ranging them together, and exposing to his
own eyes their inconsistency and weakness : the comparison of that representation of things given us by the
sophists, and pieces of painting, which placed at a

NOTES.

P. 246. Γιγαντομαχια.] Between those whom he calls δι γηγενεις, the materialists, and the spiritualists, among which was
Plato himself.

Ib. Πετρας και δρυς.] An allusion to the Giants' manner of
fighting, armed with mountains and rocks ; and also to that
proverb, Απο δρυος ηδ' απο πετρης.

249. See the opinions of Heraclitus apud Sext. Empiricum,
and in Plato's Theætetus.

251. Τοις οψιμαθεσι.] Either the sophists themselves, or such
as admired their contests.

252. Εντος υποφθεγγομενον, ως τον ατοπον Ευρυκλεα.] Eurycles
was an Εγγαστριμυθος, who could fetch a voice from the belly
or the stomach, and set up for a prophet. Those who had the
same faculty were called after him Euryclitæ. See Aristophanes
Vespæ, v. 1014. et Scholia. For such as are possessed of this
faculty can manage their voice in so wonderful a manner, that
it shall seem to come from what part they please, not of themselves only, but of any other person in the company, or even
from the bottom of a well, down a chimney, from below stairs,
&c. of which I myself have been witness.

certain distance, deceive the young and inexperienced into an opinion of their reality : and the total change of ideas in young men when they come into the world, and begin to be acquainted with it by their own sensations, and not by description. All these passages are extremely good.

NOTES.

P. 265. We see here that it was the common opinion, that the creation of things was the work of blind unintelligent nature, Την Φυσιν παντα γενναν απο τινος αιτιας αυτοματης, και ανευ διανοιας φυουσης: whereas the contrary was the result of philosophical reflection and disquisition, believed by a few people only.

268. Ταυτης της γενεας.] See Hom. Il. Z et passim

POLITICUS.

Π, ΠΕΡΙ ΒΑΣΙΛΕΙΑΣ.

This dialogue is a continuation of the Sophist, as the Sophist is a continuation of the Theætetus; and they are accordingly ranged together by Thrasyllus in that order (Diog. Laert. in Platon. s. 58.); though Serranus in his edition has separated them. The persons are the same, only that here the younger Socrates is introduced, instead of Theætetus, carrying on the conversation with the stranger from Elea. The principal heads of it are the following :

P. 258. The division of the sciences into speculative and practical.

P. 259. The master, the œconomist, the politician, the king; which are taken as different names for men of the same profession.

Platon. Op. Serrani. Vol. 2. p. 257.

P. 257. Τον Αμμωνα.] Theodorus was of Cyrene.

264. Ταις εν τω Νειλω τιθασσειαις.] Probably in or near those cities of Egypt where the Lepidotus, Oxyrinchus, and other fish of the Nile were worshipped; those fish, by being unmolested and constantly fed, might be grown tame, as in the river Chalus in Syria, mentioned by Xenophon (Cyri Anab. L. 1. p. 254. ed. Leunclav.), where all fish were held sacred.

The private man, who can give lessons of government to such as publickly exercise this art, deserves the name of royal no less than they.

No difference between a great family and a small commonwealth.

The politician must command on his own judgment, and not by the suggestion of others. (αυτεπιτακτος.)[1]

P. 262. The absurdity of the Greeks, who divided all mankind into Greeks and barbarians. The folly of all distinction and division without a difference.

P. 269. The fable of the contrary revolutions in the universe at periodical times, with the alternate destruction and reproduction of all creatures.

P. 273. The disorder and the evil in the natural world, accounted for from the nature of [2] matter, while it was yet a chaos.

The former revolution, in which the Divinity himself immediately conducted every thing, is called the

---

[1] P. 261. Κᾳν διαφυλαξης το μη σπουδαζειν επι τοις ονομασι, πλουσιωτερος εις το γηρας αναφανηση φρονησεως.

[2] Plato, with the Pythagoreans, looked upon matter as co-eternal with the Deity, but receiving its order and design entirely from him. (See Timæus, the Locrian, de Animâ Mundi.)

NOTES.

P. 266. Των προς γελωτα.] An allusion perhaps to the Aves of Aristophanes, or to some other comick writer, for Plato (as well as Socrates) had often been the subject of their ridicule.

Ib. Εν τη περι τον σοφιστην.] V. Sophistam, p. 227.

268. Περι την Ατρεως.] See Euripid. Orest. v. 1001. and Electra v. 720.

269. Μητ' αυ δυω τινε θεω.] Alluding to the Persian doctrine of a good and of an evil principle.

Saturnian age ; the present revolution, when the world
goes the contrary way, being left to its own [1] conduct.
Mankind are now guided by their own free-will, and
are preserved by their own inventions.

P. 275. The nature of the monarch in this age is no
other than that of the people which he commands.

P. 276. His government must be with the consent
of the people.

Clear and certain knowledge is rare and in few
instances ; we are forced to supply this defect by comparison and by analogy. Necessity of tracing things
up to their first principles. Examples of logical
division.

Greater, or less, with respect to our actions, are not
to be considered as mere relations only depending on
one another, but are to be referred to a certain middle
term, which forms [2] the standard of morality.

P. 284. All the arts consist in measurement, and
are divided into two classes : 1st. those arts which
compare dimensions, numbers, or motions, each with
its contrary, as greater with smaller, more with less,

[1] He here too, with Timæus, considers the universe as one
vast, animated, and intelligent body. Ζωον ον, και φρονησιν
ειληχος εκ του συναρμοσαντος αυτο κατ' αρχας. p. 269. Τελειον,
εμψυχον τε και λογικον, και σφαιροειδες σωμα. Timæus, p. 94.

[2] This is the fundamental principle of Aristotle's ethicks,
L. 2. c. 7. et passim.

NOTE.

P. 272. Μυθους.] He seems to allude to the Æsopick (See
Aristot. Rhetor. L. 2. Sect. 21.) Libyan, and Sybaritick
fables. See Aristophan. Aves v. 471. 652. and 808. and Vespæ
v. 1418.

swifter with slower; and 2dly, those, which compare
them by their distances from some middle point, seated
between two extremes, in which consists what is right,
fit, and becoming.

The design of these distinctions, and of the manner
used before in tracing out the idea of a sophist and a
politician, is to form the mind to a habit of logical
division.

The necessity of illustrating our contemplations,[1]
on abstract and spiritual subjects, by sensible and
material images is stated.

P. 286. An apology[2] for his prolixity.

Principal, and concurrent,[3] or instrumental causes,
are named; the division of the latter, with their several
productions, is into *seven* classes of arts which are necessary to society : viz.

[1] See p. 286. Thus Mr. Locke, speaking of the institution
of language, observes, that "men to give names which might
make known to others any operations they felt in themselves,
or any other idea which came not under their senses, were fain
to borrow words from ordinary known ideas of sensation, by
that means to make others the more easily to conceive those
operations which they experimented in themselves, which made
no outward sensible appearances."

[2] Athenæus has preserved a large fragment of Epicrates, a
comick poet, in which Plato's divisions are made the subject of
his ridicule. L. 2. p. 59.

[3] Αιτιον και σιναιτιον. Terms also used by the Pythagoreans.
Vid. Timæum Locrum in principio.

NOTE.

P. 283. Μακροτερα του δεοντος.] It is plain, that the length of
Plato's digressions had been censured and ridiculed by some
of his contemporaries (particularly his dialogue called "the
Sophist"), and that he here makes his own apology.

1. Το πρωτογενες ειδος. That class which furnishes materials for all the rest; it includes the arts of mining, hewing, felling, &c.

2. Οργανον. The instruments employed in all manufactures, with the arts which make them.

3. Αγγειον. The vessels to contain and preserve our nutriment, and other moveables furnished by the potter, joiner, brazier, &c.

4. Οχημα. Carriages, seats, vehicles for the land and water, &c. by the coach-maker, ship and boat-builder, &c.

5. Προβλημα. Shelter, covering, and defence, as houses, clothing, tents, arms, &c. by the architect, weaver, armourer, &c.

6. Παιγνιον. Pleasure and amusement, as painting, musick, sculpture, &c.

7. Θρεμμα. Nourishment, supplied by agriculture, hunting, cookery, &c. and regulated by the gymnastick and medical arts.

NOTES.

P. 284. Το μη ον.] V. Sophist, p. 237.

290. The Egyptian kings were all of them priests, and if any of another class usurped the throne, they too were obliged to admit themselves of that order.

291. Παμφυλον τι γενος.] Vid. mox, p. 303.

299. Μετεωρολογος.] Alluding to the fate of Socrates, and to the Nubes of Aristophanes, as he frequently does. This is a remarkable passage.

302. The corruption of the best form of government is the worst and the most intolerable of all.

Ib. Γην του και λιθους.] See the ancient manner of refining gold, in Diodorus L. 2. or in the Excerpta of Agatharchides de Mari Erythræo.

303. Αδαμας.] Found in the gold-mines mixed with the ore.

P. 289. None of these arts have any pretence to, or competition with, the art[1] of governing; no more than the ὑπηρετικον και διακονικον γενος, which voluntarily exercise the employment of slaves, such as merchants, bankers, and tradesmen : the priesthood too are included under this head, as interpreters between the gods and men, not from their own judgment, but either by inspiration, or by a certain prescribed ceremonial.

P. 291. There are three kinds of government, monarchy, oligarchy, and democracy : the two first are distinguished into four, royalty, tyranny, aristocracy, and oligarchy-proper.

P. 294. The imperfection of all laws arises from the impossibility of adapting them to the continual change of circumstances, and to particular cases.

P. 296. Force may be employed by the wise and just legislator to good ends.

P. 299. The supposition of a set of rules in physick, in agriculture, or in navigation, drawn up by a majority of the citizens, and not to be transgressed under pain of death; applied to the case of laws made by the people.

P. 307. Some nations are destroyed by an excess of spirit; others by their own inoffensiveness and love of quiet.

[1] Aristotle in the same manner calls this great art, Κυριωτατη και μαλιστα αρχιτεκτονικη των επιστημων και δυναμεων· τινας γαρ ειναι χρεων εν ταις πολεσι και ποιας έκαστους μανθανειν, και μεχρι τινος, αυτη διατασσει. Όρωμεν δε τας εντιμοτατας των δυναμεων ύπο ταυτην ουσας όιον στρατηγικην, οικονομικην, ῥητορικην, &c. Aristot. Ethic. Nicom. L. 1. c. 2. See also p. 304. of this dialogue.

P. 308. The office of true policy is to temper courage with moderation, and moderation with courage. Policy presides over education.

This dialogue seems to be a very natural introduc- tion to the books *De Republicâ*, and was doubtless so intended. See particularly L. 3. p. 410. &c. and L. 4. p. 442.

DE REPUBLICA.

ΠΟΛΙΤΕΙΩΝ,

Η

ΠΕΡΙ ΔΙΚΑΙΟΥ.

Plat. Op. Serrani, Vol. 2. p. 327.

THE scene of this dialogue lies at the house of Cephalus, a rich old Syracusan, father to Lysias the orator, then residing in the Piraeus, on the day of the Bendidea, a festival, then first celebrated there with processions, races, and illuminations in honour of the Thracian[1] Diana. The persons engaged in the conversation, or present at it, are Cephalus himself, Polemarchus, Lysias and Euthydemus, his three sons; Glauco and Adimantus, sons of Aristo and brothers to Plato; Niceratus, son of Nicias; Thrasymachus the sophist of Chalcedon; Clitophon,[2] son of Aristonymus, and Charmantides of Pæania, and Socrates.

As to the time of these dialogues, it is sure that

[1] She had a temple in the Piraeus, called the Bendideum, (Xenoph. Gr. Hist. L. 2. p. 472.) founded perhaps on this occasion. See the Republ. p. 354. " Εἰστιασθω εν τοις Βενδιδειοις :" the festival was celebrated in the heat of summer, (see Strab. L. 10. p. 471. Των Βενδιδιων Πλατων μεμνηται.) on the 19th day of Thargelion, as Proclus tells us, Comment. 1. ad Timæum.

[2] An admirer and scholar of Thrasymachus, (See Clitophont. p. 406.) and friend of Lysias.

Cephalus died about Ol. 84. 1, and that his son Lysias
was born fifteen years before Ol. 80. 2, consequently
they must fall between these two years, and probably
not long before Cephalus's death, when he was seventy
years old or more; and Lysias was a boy of ten or
twelve and upwards. Therefore I should place it in
the 83d Ol. (Vid. Fastos Atticos Edit. Corsini, V. 2.
Dissert. 13. p. 312.) but I must observe that this is not
easily reconcileable with the age of Adimantus and
Glauco, who are here introduced, as men grown up,
and consequently must be at least thirty-six years older
than their brother Plato. If this can be allowed, the
action at Megara there mentioned must be that which
happened Ol. 83. 2. under Pericles; and the institution
of the Bendidea must have been Ol. 83. 3 or 4. It is
observable also that Theages is mentioned in L. 6. p.
496 of this dialogue, as advanced in the study of philosophy. He was very young, when his father Demodocus
put him under the care of Socrates, which was in Ol.
92. 3. and consequently thirty-five years after the time
which Corsini would assign to this conversation.

DE REPUBLICA.

BOOK I.

HEADS OF THE FIRST DIALOGUE.

The pleasures of old age and the advantages of wealth.

P. 335. The just man hurts no one, not even his enemies.

P. 338. The sophist's definition of justice ; namely, that it is the advantage of our superiours,[1] to which the laws of every government oblige the subjects to conform. Refuted.

P. 341. The proof, that the proper office of every art is to act for the good of its inferiors.

P. 343. The sophist's attempt to shew, that justice (πανυ γενναια ειηθεια p. 348.) is not the good of those who possess it, but of those who do not : and that injustice is only blamed in such as have not the art to carry it to its perfection. Refuted.

P. 347. In a state composed all of good men, no one would be ambitious of governing.

[1] Το του κρειττονος συμφερον—Τιθεται γε τους νομους ἑκαστη ἡ αρχη προς το αυτη συμφερον· δημοκρατια μεν δημοκρατικους, τυραννις δε τυραννικους, και αλλαι ουτω· θεμεναι δε απεφηναν τουτο—δικαιον τοις αρχομενοις ειναι το σφισι συμφερον. Vid. Plat. de Legib. L. 4. p. 714.

P. 349. The perfection of the arts consists in attaining a certain rule of proportion. The musician does not attempt to excel his fellows by straining or stopping his chords higher or lower than they; for that would produce dissonance and not harmony: the physician does not try to exceed his fellows by prescribing a larger or less quantity of nourishment, or of medicines, than conduces to health; and so of the rest. The unjust man therefore, who would surpass all the rest of his fellow-creatures in the quantity of his pleasures and powers, acts like one ignorant in the art of life, in which only the just are skilled.

NOTES ON THE GREEK TEXT.

P. 327. Κατεβην χθες.] Vid. Dionys. Halicarnass. de Colloc. Verborum.—Quintil. L. 8. c. ult. A remarkable instance of Plato's nice and scrupulous attention to the sound and numbers of his prose. "Nec aliud potest sermonem facere numerosum, quam opportuna ordinis mutatio; neque alio in ceris Platonis inventa sunt *quatuor illa verba,* (Κατεβην χθες ες Πειραια) quibus in ILLO PULCHERRIMO OPERUM in Piræeum se descendisse significat, plurimis modis scripta, quam quod eum quoque maxime facere experiretur.

Ib. Τῃ Θεω.] To Diana, and not to Minerva, as Serranus imagined. See De Republ. p. 354.

328. 'Ωσπερ τινα ὁδον.] V. Cicer. de Senect. c. 2. who here and elsewhere has closely imitated these admirable dialogues.

331. Γηροτροφος.] A fine fragment of Pindar, and another of Simonides. Tully (Epist. ad Attic. L. 4. E. 16.) has observed the propriety of Cephalus leaving the company, as it was not decent for a man of great age and character to enter into dispute with boys and sophists on such a subject, nor to have continued silent without any share in the conversation. Tully himself had imitated the conduct of Plato, in his books de Republicâ: the interlocutors were Scipio Æmilianus, Lælius, Scævola, Philus,

P. 351. The greatest and most signal injustices, which one state and society can commit against another, cannot be perpetrated without a strict adher· ence to justice, among the particular members of such a state and society: so that there is no force nor strength without a degree of justice.

P. 352. Injustice even in one single mind must set it at perpetual variance with itself, (De Republ. L. 8. p. 554.) as well as with all others.

P. 353. Virtue is the proper office, the wisdom, the strength, and the happiness of the human soul.

NOTES.

Manilius, and others. Philus there supported the cause of in-justice, as Thrasymachus does here; and the whole concluded with a discourse on the Soul's immortality, and the Dream of Scipio, as this does with the Vision of Er, the Pamphylian. Vid. Cicer. de Amicitiâ, C. 5 and 7. and Macrob. in Somn. Scip. L. 1. c. 1.

P. 336. Περδικκου.] The second of the name, often mentioned by Thucydides.

Ib. Ισμηνιου.] This must probably be some ancestor of that Ismenias, who betrayed Thebes to the Spartans about eighteen years after the death of Socrates.

338. Polydamas a celebrated pancratiast, whose statue at Olympia was looked upon as miraculous in after-ages, and was believed to cure fevers. (Lucian. in Concil. Deor. Vol. 2. p. 714.)

DE REPUBLICA.

BOOK II.

HEADS OF THE SECOND DIALOGUE.

P. 357. Good is of three kinds: the *First* we embrace for[1] itself, without regard to its consequences; such are all innocent delights and amusements.

. The *Second*, both for itself and for its consequences, as health, strength, sense, &c.

The *Third*, for its consequences only, as labour, medicine, &c. The second of these is the most perfect: the justice of this class. Objection: To consider it

[1] De Legib. L. 2. p. 667.

NOTES.

P. 358. 'Ωσπερ οφις.] An allusion to the manner of charming serpents, both by the power of certain plants and stones, and by incantations, still practised, and pretended to be valid, in the east, and described by many travellers.

360. Επαινοιεν αν αυτον.] See Locke on the Human Understanding, C. 3. s. 6.

362. Ανασχινδιλευθησεται.] Hesychius explains it, ανασκολοπισθηναι, ανασταυρωθηναι.

363. Ακρας μεν τε φερειν.] Hesiod Εργ. και Ημερ. v. 233.

Ib. Παιδας γαρ παιδων.] The Oracle given to Glaucus. Vid. Herodot. Erato, c. 86. see also the description of the Elysian fields: καλλιστος αρετης μισθος, μεθη αιωνιος. Musæus was of

rightly we must separate it from honour and from reward, and view it simply as it is in itself, viz :

P. 358. Injustice is a real good to its possessor, and justice is an evil : but as men feel more pain in suffering than inflicting injury, and as the greater part are more exposed to suffer it than capable of inflicting it, they have by compact agreed neither to do nor to suffer injustice ; which is a medium calculated for the general benefit, between that which is best of all, namely, to do injustice without fear of punishment, and that which is worst, to suffer it without a possibility of revenge. This is the origin of what we call justice.

Such as practise the rules of justice do it from their inability to do otherwise, and consequently against their will. Story of [1] Gyges's ring, by which he could

[1] V. Cic. de Offic. L. 3. c. 9. where he attributes to Gyges himself what Plato relates of one of his ancestors.

NOTES.

Eleusis, and scholar to Orpheus ; he addressed a poem which bore the title of 'Ὑποθηκαι, to his son Eumolpus : they were of Thracian origin :

Ὀρφευς μεν γαρ τελετας θ' ἡμῖν κατεδειξε, φονων τ' απεχεσθαι·
Μουσαιος, δ' εξακεσεις τε νοσων, και χρησμους. Aristophan.
Ranæ. v. 1064 ;

where the Scholiast adds, speaking of Musæus ; Παιδα Σεληνης και Ευμολπου Φιλοχορος φησιν· παραλυσεις, και τελετας και καθαρμους συντεθεικεν. Suidas makes him the son of Antiphemus και Ἑλενης (read Σεληνης) γυναικος. But it is apparent, that in Plato's time he was understood to be the son, not of a woman, but of the moon ; and so the inscription on his tomb at Phalerus represents him, which is cited by the Scholiast before-mentioned, and in the Anthologia.

228   NOTES ON PLATO.

make himself invisible at pleasure. No person, who
possessed such a ring, but would do wrong.

P. 360. Life of the perfectly unjust man, who con-
ceals his true character from the world, and that of
the perfectly just man who seems the contrary in the
eye of the world, are compared : the happiness of the
former is contrasted with the misery of the latter.

P. 362. The advantages of probity are not therefore (according to this representation) in itself, but in
things exterior to it, in honours and rewards, and they
attend not on being, but on seeming, honest.

P. 363. Accordingly the praises bestowed on justice,
and the reproaches on injustice, by our parents and
governours, are employed not on the thing itself, but
on its consequences. The Elysian fields and the
punishments of Tartarus are painted in the strongest
colours by the poets ; while they represent the practice
of virtue as difficult and laborious, and that of vice, as
easy and delightful. They add, that the gods often

NOTES.

P. 363. Εις πηλον.] See the Ranæ of Aristophanes.
Ib. Επαγωγαι και καταδεσμοι των Θεων.] Incantations and
magical rites, to hurt one's enemies, were practised in Greece
and taught by vagabond priests and prophets : a number of
books ascribed to Musæus and Orpheus were carried about
by such people, prescribing various expiatory ceremonies and
mysterious rites : so the chorus of Satyrs in the Cyclops of
Euripides ;

Αλλ' οιδ' επωδην Ορφεως αγαθην πανυ,
'Ωs αυτοματον τον δαλον εις το κρανιον
Στειχονθ' υφαπτειν τον μονωπα παιδα γης.
V. 642. Cycl. Eurip.

bestow misery on the former, and prosperity and success on the latter; and, at the same time, they teach
us how to expiate our crimes, and even how to hurt our
enemies, by prayers, by sacrifices, and by incantations.
P. 366. The consequence is, (by this mode of argument) that to dissemble well with the world is the way
to happiness in *this* life; and for what is to come, we
may buy the favour of the gods at a trifling expense.
P. 369. The nature of political justice. The image
of a society in its first formation: it is founded on our
natural imbecility, and on the mutual occasion we have
for each other's assistance. Our first and most pressing necessity, is that of food; the second, of habitation; the third, of clothing. The first and most necessary society must therefore consist of a ploughman, a
builder, a shoemaker, and a weaver: but, as they will
want instruments, a carpenter and a smith will be
requisite; and as cattle will be wanted, as well for their
skins and wool, as for tillage and carriage, they must

NOTES.

P. 364. Fragment of Pindar; Ποτερον δικας τειχος ὑψιον, &c.
and of Archilochus, Αλωπεκα ἐλκτεον, &c. All the ideas which
the Greeks had of the gods, were borrowed from the poets.

366. Οἱ λυσιοι θεοι.] These divinities were probably enumerated in the Παραλυσεις of Musæus: there were mysterious rites
celebrated to Bacchus under the name of Λυσιοι τελεται. See
Suidas.

368. Την Μεγαροι μαχην.] This must, as I imagine, be the
action particularly described by Thucydides, L. 4. p. 255. which
happened Ol. 89. 1, and if so, both Glauco and Adimantus must
have been many years older than their brother Plato, who was
then but five years old.

take in shepherds and the herdsmen. As one country produces not everything, they will have occasion for some imported commodities, which cannot be procured without exportations in return, so that a commerce must be carried on by merchants; and if it be performed by sea, there will be an occasion for mariners and pilots. Further; as the employment of the shepherds, agricultors, mechanics, merchants, and such persons will not permit them to attend the markets, there must be retailers and tradesmen, and money to purchase with; and there must be servants to assist all these, that is, persons who let out their strength for hire. Such an establishment will not be long without a degree of luxury, which will increase the city with a vast variety of artificers, and require a greater extent of territory to support them: they will then encroach on their neighbours. Hence the origin of war. A militia will be required: but as this is an art, which will engross the whole man, and

---

NOTES.

P. 368. Ω παιδες εκεινου του ανδρος.] So Socrates in the Philebus, speaking of Callias.

372. Ερεβινθων καὶ κναμων.] This was a common dessert among the Greeks, both eaten raw, when green and tender, or when dry, parched in the fire. See Athenæus, L. 2. p. 54. So Xenophanes of Colophon in Parodis:

Χειμωνος εν ὡρῃ
Πινοντα γλυκιν οινον, ὑποτρωγοντ' ερεβινθους.

And Theocritus, in describing a rustick entertainment, .

Οινον απο κρατηρος αφυξω
Παρ πυρι κεκλιμενος· κυαμον δε τις εν πυρι φρυξεῖ,
Χὰ στιβας εσσεῖται πεπυκασμενα εστ' επι πᾶχυν.
Κνυσạ τ', ασφοδελω τε, πολυγναμπτωτε σελινω.

Theocr. Idyll. 7. v. 65.

take up all his time, to acquire and exercise it, a distinct body will be formed of chosen men for the defence of the state.

P. 374. The nature of a soldier : he must have quickness of sense, agility, and strength, invincible spirit tempered with gentleness and goodness of heart, and an understanding apprehensive and desirous of knowledge.

P. 376. The education of such a person. Errors and dangerous prejudices are instilled into young minds by the Greek poets. The scandalous fables of Homer and of Hesiod, who attribute injustice, enmity, anger and deceit to the gods, are reprobated : and the immutable goodness, truth, justice, mercy, and other attributes of the Divinity are nobly asserted.

P. 372. Τῶν πολιν.] So Crobylus (ap. Athenæum p. 54.) calls this kind of eatables, Πιθηκου τραγηματα, the monkey's dessert.

373. Συβωται.] So he calls the οψοποιοι και μαγειροι, alluding to what Glauco had said before of the ὑων πολις : or perhaps, because the flesh of hogs was more generally eaten and esteemed than any other in Greece, he mentions them principally.

DE REPUBLICA.

BOOK III.

HEADS OF THE THIRD DIALOGUE.

P. 386. Wrong notions of a future state are instilled into youth by the poets, whence arises an unmanly fear of death.

P. 388. Excessive sorrow and excessive[1] laughter are equally unbecoming a man of worth.

P. 389. Falsehood and[2] fiction are not permitted, but where they are for the good of mankind; and con-

[1] V. Plato. de Legib. L. 5. p. 732.

[2] Plato himself has given the example of such inventions in his Phædo, in his Phædrus, in the De Republ. L. 10 : and in the Gorgias he follows the opinion of Timæus and of the Pythagoreans. Vid. de Animâ Mundi, p. 104. Vid. et de Legib. L. 2. p. 663. Νομοθετης δε ὁυ τι και σμικρον οφελος, &c.

NOTES.

P. 378. Ου χοιρον.] The usual sacrifice before the Eleusinian mysteries. See Aristoph. in Pace,

Ες χοιριδιον μοι νυν δανεισον τρεις δραχμας,
Δει γαρ μυηθηναι με. v. 373.

381. Περιερχονται νυκτωρ.] The heroes were supposed to walk in the night, (see Lucian de morte Peregrini, p. 579. Ed. Grævii.) and to strike with blindness, or with some other mischief, any who met them : they who passed by their fanes

sequently they are not to be trusted but in skilful hands.

P. 390. Examples of impiety and of bad morality in the poets,[1] and in other ancient writers.

P. 392. Poetick eloquence is divided into narration (in the writer's own person), and imitation (in some assumed character). Dithyrambicks usually consist wholly of the former, dramatick poesy of the latter, the epick, &c. of both mixed.

P. 395. Early imitation becomes a second nature. The soldier is not permitted to imitate any thing misbecoming his own character, and consequently he is neither permitted to write, nor to play, any part which he himself would not act in life.

P. 396. Imitative expression in oratory, or in gesture, is restrained by the same principle.

Musick must be regulated. The Lydian, Syntono-Lydian, and Ionian harmonies are banished, as accommodated to the soft enervate passions; but the Dorian and the Phrygian harmonies are permitted, as manly,

[1] See also de Republ. L. 8. p. 568.

NOTES.

always kept a profound silence: see the Aves of Aristophan. v. 1485.

Ει γαρ εντυχοι τις ηρωϊ

Των βροτων νυκτωρ—κτλ. and the Schol. on the passage.

P. 387. Αυτος αυτω αυταρκης.] V. Cicer. de Amicitiâ, c. 2, who has imitated this passage.

389. Των δι δημιοεργοι εασιν.] Hom. Odys. P. v. 383.

393. Μιμεισθαι.] Tully says of himself: "Ipse mea legens, sic interdum afficior, ut Catonem, non me, loqui existimem." (De Amicit. c. 1.)

234   NOTES ON PLATO.

decent, and persuasive. All instruments of great compass and of luxuriant harmony, the lyra, the cythara, and the fistula, are allowed; and the various rhythms or movements are in like manner restrained.

P. 398. Μιξολυδιστι.] The Dorian harmony is thus described by Heraclides Ponticus ap. Athenæum, L. 14. p. 624. Ἡ μεν ουν Δωριος ἁρμονια το ανδρωδες εμφαινει και το μεγαλοπρεπες, και ου διακεχυμενον ουδ' ιλαρον, αλλα σκυθρωπον και σφοδρον, ουτε δε ποικιλον, ουτε πολυτροπον. The Syntono-Lydian and Ionian are mentioned by Pratinas; (Athenæus ib.)

Μη συντονον διωκε, μητ' ανειμενην
Ιαστι ουσαν·   Athenæus ut sup. (Platon. Lachet. p. 188.)

The Ionian was frequently used in the tragick chorus, as being accommodated to sorrow, as was also the Mixo-Lydian, invented by Sappho. See Burette on Plutarch de Musicâ, note 102. 103. Vol. 10. and 13. of the Mém. de l'Acad. des Belles-Lettres.

399. Τριγωνων.] The Τριγωνος was a triangular lyre of many strings, of Phrygian invention, used (as the Πηκτις) to accompany a chorus of voices. The latter is said to have been first used by Sappho:

Πολυς δε Φρυξ τριγωνος, αντισπαστα γε
Αυδης εφυμνει πηκτιδος συγχορδια.

Sophocles in Mysis, ap. Athenæum, L. 14. p. 635, where perhaps we should read Αυδης for Αυδης; for Pindar, cited in the same place, calls the Πηκτις a Lydian instrument, and Aristoxenus makes it the same as the Μαγαδις, which Anacreon tells us had twenty strings; afterwards, according to Apollodorus, it was called Ψαλτηριον.

400. Τρια ειδη, εξ ων αἱ βασεις πλεκονται.] Τετταρα, ὁθεν αἱ πασαι ἁρμονιαι.

Ib. Εις Δαμωνα.] (V. Lachetem, p. 180.) These opinions of Plato on the efficacy of harmony and rhythm seem borrowed from Damon: Ου κακως λεγουσι ὁι περι Δαμωνα τον Αθηναιον, ὁτι τας ωδας και τας ορχησεις αναγκη γινεσθαι κινουμενης πως της ψυχης, και ἁι μεν ελευθεριοι και καλαι ποιουσι τοιαυτας· ἁι δ' εναντιαι τας εναντιας. Athenæus, L. 14. p. 628.

P. 401. The same[1] principle is extended to painting, sculpture, architecture, and to the other arts.

P. 403. Love is permitted, but abstracted from bodily enjoyment. Diet and exercises, plain and simple meats, are prescribed.

P. 405. Many judges and physicians are a sure sign of a society ill-regulated both in mind and in body. Ancient physicians knew no medicines but for wounds, fractures, epidemical distempers, and other acute complaints. The diætetick and gymnastick method of

[1] Ἱνα μη εν κακιας εικοσι τρεφομενοι ἡμῖν ὁι φυλακες, ὡσπερ εν κακῃ βοτανῃ, πολλα ἑκαστης ἡμερας κατα σμικρον απο πολλων δρεπομενοι τε και νεμομενοι, ἐν τι ξινισταντες λανθανωσι κακον μεγα εν τῃ αυτων ψυχῃ. Αλλ' εκεινους ζητητεον τους δημουργοις, τοις ευφιως διναμενοις ιχνειειν την του καλου τε και ευσχημονος φυσιν· ἱν', ὡσπερ εν ὑγιεινω τοπω οικουντες, ὁι νεοι ωφελωνται απο παντος, ὁποθεν αν αιτοις απο των καλων εργων η προς οψιν η προς ακοην τι προσβαλῃ, ὡσπερ αυρα φεροισα απο χρηστων τοπων ὑγιειαν, και ευθις εκ παιδων λανθανῃ εις ὁμοιοτητα τε και φιλιαν και σιμφωνιαν τω καλω λογω αγοισα. Πολυ καλλιστα ούτω τραφεῖεν. De Republ. 3. p. 400.

P. 404. Ὑπνωδης αυτη.] Euripides describes them as great eaters; Γναθου τε δουλος νηδυος θ' ἡσσημενος. Fragment. Autolyci (Dramatis Satyrici) ap. Athenæum, L. 10. p. 413, where Athenæus gives many instances of extreme voracity in the most famous athletæ, and adds, παντες γαρ ὁι αθληται μετα των γιμνασματων και εσθιειν πολλα διδασκονται.

Ib. Συρακουσιων τραπεζαν.] Vid. Plat. Epist. 7. p. 326. 327. and 336.

405. Φειγων και διωκων.] The image of the talents and turn of the Athenians at that time.

437. Πιλιδια.] Sick people went abroad in a cap, or little hat.

cure, or rather of protracting diseases, was not known before Herodicus introduced it.

P. 409. The temper and disposition of an old man of probity, fit to judge of the crimes of others, is described.

P. 410. The temper [1] of men, practised in the exercises of the body, but unacquainted with musick and with letters, is apt to run into an obstinate and brutal fierceness; and that of the contrary sort, into indolence and effeminacy. The gradual neglect of this, in both cases, is here finely painted.

P. 412. Choice of such of the soldiery, as are to rise to the magistracy; namely, of those, who through their life, have been proof to pleasure and to pain.

P. 414. An example of a beneficial fiction. It is difficult to fix in the minds of men a belief in fables, originally; but it is very easy to deliver it down to posterity, when once established.

P. 416. The habitation of the soldiery: all luxury in building to be absolutely forbidden them: they are to have no patrimony, nor possessions, but to be supported and furnished with necessaries from year to year by the citizens; they are to live and eat in common, and to use no plate, nor jewels, nor money.

[1] Vid. Platon. Politicum, p. 307 and 308.

NOTES.

P. 409. Ουκουν και ιατρικην.] See the Gorgias, p. 587 and 588.

414. Φοινικικον τι.] He alludes to the Theban fable of the earth-born race, which sprang from the dragon's teeth, and which, in another place, he calls Το του Σιδωνιου μυθολογημα, meaning Cadmus. See de Legibus, L. 2. p. 663.

DE REPUBLICA.

BOOK IV.

HEADS OF THE FOURTH DIALOGUE.

P. 419. Objection: that the Φυλακες (or soldiery), in whose hands the government is placed, will have less happiness and enjoyment of life than any of the meanest citizens.[1]

Answer: that it is not the intention of the legislature to bestow superiour happiness on any one class of men in the state; but that each shall enjoy such a measure of it, as is consistent with the preservation of the whole.

P. 421. Opulence and poverty are equally destructive of a state;[2] the one producing luxury, indolence, and

[1] See De. Republ. L. 5. p. 466. and L. 7. p. 519.
[2] See De Legib. L. 5. p. 729 and 743.

NOTES ON THE GREEK TEXT.

P. 420. Ανδριαντας γραφοντας.] Ανδριας seems used here for a painting, and not for a statue.

Ib. Ξυστιδας.] Ξυστις was a long variegated mantle, which swept the ground, worn by the principal characters in tragedy, and on great solemnities by the Greek women:

Βυσσοιο καλον συροισα χιτωνα,
Καμφιστειλαμενα ταν ξυστιδα ταν Κλεαριστας.
Theocrit. Id. 2. v. 73.

a spirit of innovation; the other producing meanness,
cunning, and a like spirit of innovation.

The task of the magistracy is to keep both the one
and the other out of the republick.

P. 422. Can such a state, without a superfluity of
treasure, defend itself, when attacked by a rich and
powerful neighbour?

As easily as a champion, exercised for the olympick
games, could defeat one or more rich fat men unused
to fatigue, who should fall upon him in a hot day.

The advantage of such a state, which neither needs
riches nor desires them, in forming alliances.

Every republick formed on another plan, though it
bear the name of a state, is in reality several states
included under one name; the rich making one[1] state,
the poor another, and so on; always at war among
themselves.

P. 423. A body of a thousand men bred to war, and
united by such an education and government as this, is
superiour even in number to any thing that almost any
state in Greece could produce.

P. 424. No innovation is to be ever admitted in the
original plan of education. A change of[2] musick in a
country betokens a change in their morals.

[1] See De Republ. L. 8. p. 551.
[2] This was an opinion of the famous Damon. See De Legib.
L. 2. p. 657. and L. 3. p. 700.

NOTES.

P. 420. Οστρειω.] The colour of the purple-fish used in
painting, and not only in dying; so in Plato's Cratylus: Ενιοτε
μεν οστρεον, ενιοτε δε ὁτιοῦν αλλο φαρμακον επηνεγκαν.

427. Εξηγητης.] See Plato's Euthyphro.

P. 425. Fine satire on the Athenians, and on their demagogues.

P. 428. The political wisdom of the new-formed state is seated in the magistracy.

P. 429. Its bravery is seated in the soldiery: in what it consists.

P. 430. The nature of temperance : the expression [1] of *subduing one's self*, is explained ; when reason, the superiour part of the mind, preserves its empire over the inferiour, that is, over our passions and desires. The temperance of the new republick, whose wisdom and valour (in the hands of the soldiery) exercise a just power over the inferiour people by their own consent, is described.

P. 433. Political justice distributes to every one his proper province of action, and prevents each from encroaching on the other.

P. 435. Justice in a private man : its similitude to the former is stated. The three distinct [2] faculties of

[1] See De Legib. L. 1. p. 626.   [2] De Republ. L. 9. p. 580.

P. 427. Του Ομφαλου.] See Pausan. Phocic.

429. 'Αλουργα.] Cloths dyed purple would bear washing with soap (μετα ρυμματων), without losing their bloom, το ανθος

430. Ετι καλλιον διϊμεν.] As he has done in the Laches.

433. Και ταυτη αρα ποιητου οικειου τε και εαυτου.] Perhaps we should read, του ποιειν το οικειον τε και το εαυτου, &c. i.e. ἡ οικειοπραγια, as he afterwards calls it.

435. The Scythians, the Thracians, and other northern nations (ὁι κατα τον ανω τοπον, and, as Virgil says, "Mundus ut ad *Scythiam* Riphæasque arduus arces *Assurgit*, &c.) were distinguished by their ferocity, the Greeks by their curiosity and

the soul, namely, appetite, or desire, reason, and indignation ; or the concupiscible, the rational, and the
irascible, are described.

P. 441. The first made to obey the second, and the
third to assist and to strengthen it. Fortitude is the
proper virtue of the irascible, wisdom of the rational,
and temperance of the concupiscible, preserving a sort
of harmony and consent between the three.

P. 443. Justice is the result of this union, maintain-
ing each faculty in its proper office.

P. 444. The description [1] of injustice.

P. 445. The uniformity of virtue, and the infinite
variety of vice. Four more distinguished kinds of it
are enumerated, whence arise four [2] different kinds of
bad government.

[1] V. Plat. Sophist. p. 223.   [2] Vid. Plat. Politicum, p. 291.

---

love of knowledge, and the Phœnicians and Egyptians by their
desire of gain. (See de Legibus, L. 5. p. 747.) Plato marks the
threefold distinction of men in these words ; Εισιν ανθρωπων
τριττα γενη· φιλοσοφον, φιλονεικος, φιλοκερδες. p. 581.

439. The story of Leontius the son of Aglaïon.

Ib. Ἀημειω.] The place in which the bodies of malefactors
were exposed, so called.

Ib. Το Βορειον.] See the Gorgias, p. 453.

DE REPUBLICA.

BOOK V.*

P. 451. On the education of the women. There is no natural difference between the sexes, but in point of strength; their exercises, therefore, both of body and mind, are to be alike, as are their employments in the state.

* It is probable that this (the 5th) book of the Πολιτειαι and perhaps the 3rd. were written when Plato was about thirty-five years old, for he says in his 7th Epistle, (speaking of himself before his first voyage into Sicily) Λεγειν τε ηναγκασθην, επαινων την ορθην φιλοσοφιαν, &c. p. 326 ; and Aulus Gellius says, "Quod Xenophon inclito illi operi Platonis, quod de optimo statu reipublicæ civitatisque administrandæ scriptum est, lectis ex eo duobus fere libris, qui primi in vulgus exierant, opposuit contra, scripsitque diversum regiæ administrationis genus, quod Παιδειας Κυρου inscriptum est, &c. L. 14. c. 3. I know not how ancient the division of this work into ten books may be ; but there is no reason at all for it, the whole being one continued conversation.

NOTES ON THE GREEK TEXT.

P. 450. Χρυσοχοησοντας οιει.] A proverbial expression used of such as are idly employed, or sent (as we say) on a fool's errand. See Erasmi Adagia, Aurifex.

P. 452. Custom is forced in time to submit to reason. The sight of men exercising[1] naked, was once held indecent in Greece, till the Cretans first, and then the Lacedæmonians, introduced it : it is still held scandalous by the Persians, and by other barbarians.

P. 454. When the entire sexes are compared with each other, the female is doubtless the inferior : but, in individuals, the woman has often the advantage of the man.

P. 456. Choice of the female soldiery. (αἱ Φυλακειαι.)

P. 457. Wives in common to all men of the same class. Their times of meeting to be regulated on solemn days accompanied with solemn ceremonies and sacrifices, by the magistracy, who are to contrive by lots

---

[1] Εγυμνωθησαν τε πρωτοι δι Λακεδαιμονιοι, και ες το φανερον αποδυντες, λιπα μετα του γυμναζεσθαι ηλειψαντο· το δε παλαι εν τω Ολυμπιακω αγωνι διαζωματα εχοντες περι τα αιδοια δι αθληται ηγωνιζοντο, και ου πολλα ετη επειδη πεπαυται, &c. See Thucyd. L. 1. c. 6. This change is said to have been made about the 32d Olymp. See also Etymolog. in Γυμνασιαι and Schol. ad Hom. Il. Ψ.

P. 452. Των χαριεντων σκωμματα.] Vid. Platon. Politicum. p. 266.

454. The difficulty of avoiding disputes merely about words. Ἡ γενναια δυναμις της αντιλογικης τεχνης. Δοκουσι γαρ μοι εις αυτην και ακοντες εμπιπτειν, και οιεσθαι ουκ εριζειν, αλλα διαλεγεσθαι, δια το μη δυνασθαι κατ' ειδη διαιρουμενοι το λεγομενον επισκοπειν, αλλα, κατ' αυτο το ονομα, διωκειν του λεχθεντος την εναντιωσιν, εριδι ου διαλεκτω προς αλληλους χρωμενοι.

457. Ατελη του γελοιου.] An allusion to some passage of a poet ; and also to some comick writer, perhaps Aristophanes or Epicrates, who had ridiculed this institution.

(the secret management of which is known to them
alone) that the best and bravest of the men may be
paired with women of like qualities, and that those,
who are less fit to breed, may come together very
seldom. P. 460. Neither fathers nor mothers are to know
their own children, which, when born, are to be conveyed to a separate part of the city, and there (so
many of them as the magistrate shall choose) to be
brought up by nurses appointed for that purpose.

The time of propagation to be limited, in the men
from thirty years of age to fifty-five, in the women
from twenty to forty.   No children born of parents

NOTES.

P. 458. The following is so just a description of the usual contemplations of indolent persons, especially if they have some
imagination, that I cannot but transcribe it. Εασον με εορτασαι,
ωσπερ οι αργοι την διανοιαν ειωθασιν εστιασθαι υφ' εαυτων, οταν
μονοι πορευωνται· και γαρ οι τοιουτοι που, πριν εξευρειν τινα τροπον
εσται τι ων επιθυμουσι, τουτο παρεντες, ινα μη καμνωσι βουλευομενοι
περι του δυνατου, και μη, θεντες ως υπαρχον ο βουλονται, ηδη τα
λοιπα διαταττουσι, και χαιρουσι διεξιοντες οια δρασουσι γενομενου,
αργον και αλλως ψυχην ετι αργοτεραν ποιουντες.

460. This was actually the practice of Sparta, (See Plutarch
in Lycurgo) where the old men of each tribe sate in judgment
on the new-born infants, and, if they were weakly or deformed,
ordered them to be cast into a deep cavern, near mount Tay-
getus ! ! !   Thence also are borrowed the prohibition of gold
and silver, the ξυσσιτια, or custom of eating together in publick,
the naked exercises of the women, the community of goods, the
general authority of the old men over the young, the simplicity
of musick and of diet, the exemption of the soldiery from all
other business, and most of the fundamental institutions in
Plato's republick, as Plutarch observes in his Lycurgus.

under or above this term to be brought up, but exposed, and the parents severely censured; as are all who meet without the usual solemnities, and without the license of the magistrate.

P. 461. All children, born within seven or ten months from the time any person was permitted to propagate, are to be considered as their own children : all that are born within the time, in which their parents are suffered to breed, are to regard each other as brethren. Marriage is to be prohibited between persons in these circumstances.

P. 462. Partiality and dissension among the soldiery are prevented by these appointments. A fellow-feeling of pleasures and of pains is the strongest band of union which can connect mankind.

P. 466. Children are to be carried out to war very

NOTES.

P. 473. 'Ριψαντας τα ιματια.] It was the custom of the Greeks, when they prepared themselves for sudden action, to throw off their pallium : so the chorus in Aristophanes's Irene, v. 728. Acharn. v. 626. Lysistrat. 663 and 687, and Thesmophor. v. 663, lay by their upper garment to dance the Parabasis.

474. Ερωτικω.] Vid. p. 402 and 368. L. 3 and 2.

Ib. 'Ο μεν οτι σιμος.] This is imitated by Ovid. de Arte Amandi L. 2. v. 657.

　　　Nominibus mollire licet mala ; fusca vocetur,
　　　Nigrior Illyricâ cui pice sanguis erit, &c.

and by Lucretius, L. 4. v. 1150. "Nigra, μελιχροος, est &c." Whence H. Stephanus would correct this passage, and read for μελαγχλωρους, μελιχροου, but the true reading is μελιχλωρου. So Theocritus Idyll. 10. v. 26.

　　　Συραν καλεοντι τυ παντες,
. Ισχναν, άλιοκαυστον· εγω δε μονος μελιχλωρον.

early, to see and to learn their intended profession, and wait on their parents in the field.

P. 468. A soldier, who deserts his rank, or throws away his arms, is to be reduced to the rank of a mechanick : he, who is taken prisoner alive, is never to be ransomed.—The reward of the bravest.

P. 469. It is not permitted to reduce a Greek to captivity, nor to strip the dead of any thing but of their arms, which are forbidden to be dedicated in the temples; it is not permitted to ravage the country farther than to destroy the year's crop, or to burn the buildings.

P. 472. The reason, why a state, thus instituted,

NOTES.

P. 474. Περιθεουσι τοις Διονυσιοις.] The Dionysia were celebrated three times * a year at Athens, the Ανθεστηρια in the month which took its name from them, and answers nearly to our February; the Ληναια immediately afterwards in the same month, anciently called Ληναιων; and the Διονυσια εν Αστει, (particularly so named) between the eighth and eighteenth of Elaphebolion (or March), and once in the Piræus. All these were accompanied with tragedies, comedies, and other musical entertainments. There were also Τα κατ' αγρους solemnized in the country in Posideon, or December. The Scholiast on Aristophanes, and some other authors, confound these with the Lenæa, which were undoubtedly held in the city.

Ib. Των κατα Κωμας.] We see therefore that chorusses were performed in the villages on these festivals, as well as in the city. Isocrates indeed tells us, that the city was divided into Κωμαι, and the country into Δημοι. (Areopagit.)

* See the Fasti Attici Edw. Corsini V. 2. Diss. 13. and Spanheim. ad Ranas Aristophan. in procœmio, who imagines those in the Piræus to be the same with the Anthesteria.

seems an impossibility. No people will ever be rightly governed, till kings shall be philosophers, or philosophers be kings.

P. 474. The description of a genius truly philosophick.

P. 476. The distinction of knowledge and opinion.

DE REPUBLICA.

BOOK VI.

HEADS OF THE SIXTH DIALOGUE.

PLATO is no where more admirable than in this book : the thoughts are as just as they are new, and the elocution is as beautiful as it is expressive ; it can never be read too often : but towards the end it is excessively obscure.

P. 485. The love of truth is the natural consequence of a genius truly inclined to philosophy. Such a mind will be little inclined to sensual pleasures, and consequently will be temperate, and a stranger to avarice and to illiberality.

P. 485. Της ουσιας της αει ουσης, και μη πλανωμενης υπο γενε-σεως και φθορας.] Our general abstracted ideas, as they exist in the mind independent of matter which is subject to continual changes, were regarded by Plato as the sole foundations of knowledge, and emanations, as it were, from the divinity himself.

Ib. Of ideas independent of matter. Το τω σκοτω κεκρα-μενον, το γιγνομενον τε και απολλυμενον, or το αισθητον, are put in opposition to the το νοητον, το οντως ον, η ουσια. Thus he calls pure speculative geometry, η του αει οντος γνωσις. See Mr. Locke on the reality of our knowledge with regard to mathematical truths. L. 4. c. 4. s. 6. See also De Republ. L. 9. p. 585.

P. 486. Such a mind, being accustomed to the most extensive views of things and to the sublimest contemplations, will contract an habitual greatness, and look down, as it were, with disregard on human life and on death, the end of it; and consequently will possess the truest fortitude. Justice is the result of these virtues.

Apprehension and memory are two fundamental qualities of a philosophick mind.

P. 487. Such a genius is made by nature to govern mankind.

: Objection from experience: *that*, such as have devoted themselves to the study of philosophy, and have made it the employment of their maturer age, have turned out either very bad men, or entirely useless to society.

P. 488. Their inutility, with regard to government, is allowed and accounted for. The comparison of a bad government to a ship, where the mariners have agreed to let their pilot have no hand in the steerage, but to take that task upon themselves.

NOTES.

P. 488. Μεγεθει μεν και ρωμη.] Aristotle (Rhetor. L. 3. 121.) speaking of similes, mentions this of Plato; ἡ εις τον δημον, ὁμοιος ναυκληρω, ισχυρω μεν, ὑποκωφω δε. The image seems borrowed from the Equites of Aristophanes.

Ib. Οἱ γραφεις τραγελαφους.] The figures of mixed animals, such as are seen in the grotesque ornaments of the ancients, and imitated by the modern painters, &c.

Ib. Μητε εχοντα αποδειξαι.] Vid. Menonem, et Protagoram, p. 357.

Ib. Μετεωροσκοπον.] Vid. Politicum, p. 299, and Xenoph. Œconomic. p. 494. 496.

P. 491. Those very endowments, before described as necessary to the philosophick mind, are often the ruin of it, especially when joined to the external advantages of strength, beauty, nobility, and wealth, when they light in a bad soil, and do not meet with their proper nurture, which an excellent education only can bestow.

Extraordinary virtues and extraordinary vices are equally the produce of a vigorous mind : little souls are alike incapable of one or of the other.

The corruption of young minds is falsely attributed to the sophists, who style themselves philosophers : it is the publick example which depraves them; the assemblies of the people, the courts of justice, the camp, and the theatres, inspire them with false opinions, elevate them with false applause, and fright them with false infamy. The sophists do no more than confirm the opinions of the publick, and teach how to humour its passions and to flatter its vanities.

P. 495. As few great geniuses have strength to resist the general contagion, but leave philosophy abandoned and forlorn, though it is their own peculiar pro-

P. 489. Ὁ τουτο κομψευσαμενος.] i.e. Simonides: who, when his wife asked him, Ποτερον γενεσθαι κρειττον, πλουσιον, η σοφον; answered, Πλουσιον· τους γαρ σοφους ὁραν επι ταις των πλουσιων θυραις διατριβοντας. Aristot. Rhetor. L. 2. p. 92.

490. Λ ηγοι ωδινος.] Vid. Sympos. p. 206.

493. Η Διομηδεαι.] Vid. Erasmi Adagia.

494. Εαν τις ηρεμα.] The two conversations with Alcibiades are an example of this.

495. Εκ των τεχνων.] This seems to be aimed at Protagoras, who was an ordinary countryman and a woodcutter.

vince, the sophists step into their vacant place, assume their name and air, and cheat the people into an opinion of them. They are compared to a little old slave (worth money) dressed out like a bridegroom to marry the beautiful, but poor, orphan daughter of his deceased lord.

P. 495. A description of the few of true genius who escape depravation, and devote themselves really to philosophy; which happens commonly either from some ill fortune, or from weakness of constitution. The reason why they must necessarily be excluded from publick affairs, unless in this imaginary republick.

P. 500. The application of these arguments to the proof of his former proposition, namely, that until princes shall be philosophers or philosophers shall be princes, no state can be completely happy.

P. 503. The Φυλακες, therefore, are to be real philo-

P. 496. 'Υπο φυγης.] This was the case with Pythagoras, and other great men, particularly with Dion, Plato's favourite scholar; though I rather imagine, that this part of the dialogue was written before Dion's banishment.

Ib. Θεαγει.] Theages died before Socrates, a very young man.

497. 'Οταν και απτομενοι.] This is a remarkable passage, as it shews the manner in which the Athenians usually studied philosophy, and Plato's judgment about it, which was directly opposite to the common practice.

Ib. Αποσβεννυνται πολυ μαλλον του 'Ηρακλειτειου ηλιου, οσον αυθις ουκ εξαπτονται.] P. 498. Εις εκεινον τον βιον. Does he speak of some future state?

499. 'Οταν αυτη η Μουσα.] So in the Philebus; Των εν Μουσῃ φιλοσοφω μεμαντευμενων εκαστοτε λογων. p. 67.

sophers. The great difficulty is to find the requisite qualifications of mind united in one person. Quickness of apprehension and a retentive memory, vivacity and application, gentleness and magnanimity, rarely go together.

P. 505. The idea of the supreme good is the foundation of philosophy, without which all acquisitions are useless. The cause of knowledge and of truth is compared to light; truth, to the power which bodies have of reflecting light, or of becoming visible; and the sovereign good itself is compared to the [1] sun, the lord and father of light.

P. 509. The author of being is superiour to all being.

P. 510. There are different degrees of certainty in the objects of our understanding.[2]

[1] Πατηρ και Κυριος. Vid. Plat. Epist. 6. et Epist. 2. p. 312. et Macrob. L. 1. c. 2.

[2] See Aristot. Metaphys. on these opinions of Plato, L. 1. p. 338. and L. 6. p. 365.

NOTES.

P. 499. Εν βασιλειαις οντων υιεσιν, η αυτοις.] I do not doubt, but that this was meant as a compliment and incitement to the younger Dionysius (See Plato Epist. 7. p. 327), of whom both Dion and Plato had once entertained great hopes; and I understand what follows, p. 502, Αλλα μεν εις ικανος γενομενος, &c. in the same manner. Hence it seems that this part of the dialogue was written after his first voyage to Sicily, and probably not long before his second, about Ol. 103, 1, when the elder Dionysius was just dead.

504. Τριττα ειδη ψυχης.] See Lib. 4. Πολιτ. p. 439. et sequent.

505. Ουκ εχουσι δειξαι τις φρονησις.] Vid. Platonis Philebum, passim.

DE REPUBLICA.

BOOK VII.

HEADS OF THE SEVENTH DIALOGUE.

P. 514. The state of mankind is compared to that of persons confined in a vast cavern from their birth, with their legs fettered, and with their heads so placed in a machine that they cannot turn them to the light, which shines full in at the entrance of the cave, nor can they see such bodies as are continually in motion, passing and repassing behind them, but only the shadows of them, as they fall on the sides of the grotto directly before their eyes.

If any one should set them free from this confinement, oblige them to walk, and drag them from their cavern into open day, they would hang back or move

---

NOTES ON THE GREEK TEXT.

P. 514. Εν δεσμοις.] The machine called Κυφων or Κλοιον, and the Πεντεσυριγγον ξυλον, which served at once as a pillory and a pair of stocks, confining at the same time the head, arms, and legs of the prisoner, was commonly used in Greece. See Aristophan. Equites. v. 1046.

Ib. Τα παραφραγματα.] A screen or fence of three or four feet in height, still in use round the stages of mountebanks and jugglers.

with unwillingness or pain ; their eyes would be dazzled
with the brightness of each new object, and comprehend
nothing distinctly ; they would long for their shadows
and darkness again, till, being more habituated to
light, they would first be brought to gaze on the
images of things reflected in the water, or elsewhere ;
then on the bodies themselves ; then on the skies, on
the stars and the moon, and gradually on the sun himself, whom they would learn to be the source and the
author of all these beautiful appearances.

If any thing should induce one of these persons to
descend again into his native cavern, his eyes would
not for a long time be reconciled to darkness, his old
fellow-prisoners would treat him as stupid and blind,
would say that he had spoiled his eyes in those upper
regions, and grow angry with him, if he proposed to
set them at liberty.

P. 519. An early good education is the only thing
which can turn the eyes of our mind from the darkness
and uncertainty of popular opinion to the clear light
of truth. It is the interest of the publick neither to
suffer unlettered and unphilosophick minds to meddle
with government, nor to allow men of knowledge to
give themselves up for their whole life to contemplation,
as the first will have no principle to act upon, and the
others no practice nor inclination to business.

P. 522. The use of the mathematicks,[1] in education,
is principally to abstract the mind from sensible and

---

[1] Arithmetick and geometry, to which studies astronomy,
and the mathematical musick, and lastly logick to crown the
whole, are to succeed. See also Phileb. p. 58 and 61.

material objects, and to turn it to contemplate certain
general and immutable truths whence it may aspire to
the knowledge of the supreme good, who is immutable,
and is the object only of the understanding.

The great improvement of a mind versed in these
sciences which quicken and enlarge the apprehension,
and inure us to intense application, and what are their
practical uses, particularly in military knowledge, is
eloquently described.

P. 537. The Φυλακες are to be initiated in mathematical knowledge and studies before seventeen, and
for three years more are to be confined to their continual and necessary[1] exercises of the body, that is,
till about twenty years of age; they are not to enter
upon logick till after thirty, in which they are to
continue five years.

Knowledge is not to be implanted in a free-born
mind by force and violence, but by gentleness accompanied with art and by every kind of[2] invitation.

The dangerous situation of the mind, when it is
quitting the first prejudices of education and has not

[1] When they are to be presented with a general view of the
sciences, of which they have hitherto tasted separately, and are
to compare them all together.

[2] Among which honour is the most prevailing. See p. 551.

NOTES.

P. 531. Αλαζονειας χορδων.] Terms of art used by the professed musicians.

Ib. Του προοιμιου.] A musical prelude to introduce a more regular composition, called ὁ Νομος· "Ὀιμη cantus est, et citharœdi
pauca illa, quæ, antequam legitimum carmen inchoent, emerendi
favoris gratiâ canunt, procemium vocaverunt." Quintil. L. 4.

yet discovered the true principles of action, is here
admirably described. It is compared to a youth
brought up in affluence (and surrounded by flatterers)
by persons who have passed hitherto for his parents,
but are not really so; when he has found out the
imposition, he will neglect those whom he has hitherto
obeyed and honoured, and will naturally incline to the
advice of his flatterers, till he can discover those persons to whom he owes his duty and his birth.

The levity, the heat, and the vanity of our *first*
youth make it an improper time to be trusted with
reasoning and disputation, which is only fit for a mind
grown cooler and more settled by years; as old age
on the other hand weakens the apprehension, and
renders us incapable of application.

From thirty-five to fifty years of age the Φυλακες
are to be obliged to administer the publick affairs, and
to act in the inferiour offices of the magistracy; after
fifty they are to be admitted into the highest philosophy,
the doctrine of the supreme good, and are in their turn
to submit to bear the superiour offices of the state.

NOTES.

c. 7. Vid. et de Legibus, L. 3. p. 700. Νομους δε (αυτο τοῦτο
τ' οινομα) εκαλοῦν, ωδην ὡς τινα ετεραν· επελεγον δε και κιθαρω-
δικοις. And in L. 4. p. 722. Και δη του κιθαρωδικης ωδης
λεγομενων Νομων, και πασης μουσης, προοιμια θαυμαστως εσπου-
δασμενα προκειται.

P. 540. Δεκετων.] This is undoubtedly a false reading for
ἑξηκονταετων or ἑβδομηκονταετων; so that, till some MSS.
inform us better, we must remain in the dark as to the age,
when Plato would permit his statesmen to retire wholly from
the world.

DE REPUBLICA.

BOOK VIII.

HEADS OF THE EIGHTH DIALOGUE.

PLATO here resumes the subject which he had dropped at the end of the fourth book. (p. 445.)

P. 544. Four distinct kinds of government are enumerated, which deviate from the true form, and gradually grow worse and worse : namely, 1. the timocracy, (so he calls the Lacedæmonian or Cretan constitution,) 2. the oligarchy, 3. the democracy, and 4. tyranny : they are produced by as many different corruptions of the mind and manners of the inhabitants.

P. 545. The change from the true aristocracy (or constitution of Plato's republick) to a timocracy is described. Every thing, which has had a beginning,

---

NOTES ON THE GREEK TEXT.

P. 544. Ἡ Κρητικη.] Lycurgus borrowed his constitution from that of the Cretans, as Herodotus, Strabo, Plutarch, and other writers, allow ; and it is plain, that Plato thought it the best form of government that any where existed, which seems indeed to have been the general opinion of the greatest men in Greece : ἡ ὑπο πολλων επαινουμενη.

546. Χαλεπον μεν κινηθηναι.] He here assumes a more concise and figured diction, and lays aside the familiar air of conversation.

is subject to corruption.   The introduction of property, and the division of land among the Φυλακες.   The encroachment on the liberty of the inferiour part of the commonwealth.   Secret avarice and love of pleasure are the consequence of private property.   The neglect of musick and of letters.   The preference given to the exercises of the body.   The prevalence of the irascible over the rational part of the soul.

The character of a citizen in such a state and the origin of such a character are described.

P. 550. The mutation of a timocracy into an oligarchy, where none are admitted to the honours and offices of the commonwealth, who do not possess a certain proportion of property.   The progress of avarice

---

NOTES.

P. 547. Χρυσοῦν.] Vid. L. 3. p. 414. et Hesiod. Oper. et Dies. v. 109.

1b. Περιοικοις και οικεταs.] The Lacedæmonians gave the name of Περιοικοι to their subjects, the inhabitants of Laconia, who were not Spartans.   As they were used, I imagine, hardly enough by their superiours, and had no share in the government, many authors do not distinguish them from the Heilotæ, who were absolutely slaves ; yet, in reality, they seem to have been on a distinct footing, being reckoned free men, and employed by the Spartan government to command such troops as they often sent abroad, consisting of Heilotæ, to whom they had given their liberty. The Περιοικοι likewise seem to have had the property of lands, for when Lycurgus divided the country into thirty thousand portions, and gave nine thousand of them to the Spartans, to whom did the other twenty-one thousand portions belong, unless to the Περιοικοι ? who else should people the hundred cities, besides villages, which were once in Laconia ? It is plain, also, that the Περιοικοι served in war, as ὁπλιται, or heavy-armed foot, which the Heilotæ never did : see Thucy-

258   NOTES ON PLATO.

is the cause of this alteration.   Such a state is always
divided into two (always at enmity among themselves)
the rich and the poor, which is the cause of its weakness.   The alienation of property, which is freely permitted by the wealthy for their own interest, will still
increase the disproportion of fortune among the citizens.
The ill consequences of prodigality, and of its attendant
extreme poverty, in a state.   The poor are compared
to drones in a bee-hive, some with stings and some
without.

P. 552. The gradual transition of the mind from the
love of honour to the love of money.

When a young man has seen the misfortunes which
ambition has brought upon his own family, as fines,
banishment, confiscation, and even death itself, adversity and fear will break his spirit and humble his parts,
which he will now apply to raise a fortune by securer

NOTES.

dides, L. 4. p. 238. and in the battle of Platææ, Herodotus
says, there were ten thousand Lacedæmonians, of which five
thousand were Spartans ; it follows, that the other five thousand were Περιοικοι, for he mentions the Heilotæ by themselves,
as light-armed troops in number thirty-five thousand, that is,
seven to each Spartan, (L. 9. c. 29); and Xenophon plainly
distinguishes the Ὑπομειονες (who were Spartans, but excluded
from the magistracy), the Νεοδαμωδεις (who were Heilotæ made
free), the Heilotæ, and the Περιοικοι. (Xenoph. De Lacedæmon.
Republ. 289. and Græc. Hist. L. 1. p. 256.) See also Isocrates in
Panegyr. and in Panathenaic. p. 270.   The Cretans called their
slaves, who cultivated the lands, Περιοικοι. See Plutarch. in
Lycurg. and Aristot. in Polit. L. 2. c. 10.
P. 548. Γλαυκωνος τουτου.] Something of Glauco's spirit and
ambition may be seen in Xenophon's Memorabil. L. 3. c. 6.

methods, by the slow and secret arts of gain : his rational faculties and nobler passions will be subjected to his desire of acquisition, and he will admire and emulate others only in proportion as they possess the great object of his wishes : his passion for wealth will keep down and suppress in him the love of pleasure and of extravagance, which yet, for want of philosophy and of a right education, will continue alive in his heart and exert itself, when he can find an opportunity to satisfy it by some secret injustice at the expense of others.

P. 555. The source of a democracy : namely, when the meaner sort, increasing with a number of men of spirit and abilities, reduced to poverty by extravagance and by the love of pleasure, begin to feel their own strength, and compare themselves to the few wealthy persons who compose the government, whose body and

NOTES.

P. 553. Χαμαι ενθεν.] An allusion to those statues or bas-reliefs, where some king, or conqueror, is represented with captive nations in chains sitting at his feet ; as in that erected to the honour of Justinian in the Hippodrome at Constantinople. See Antholog. L. 4. Tit. 4. Epigr. 2.

Ib. Τιαρας τε.] The usual dress of the king and nobility of Persia. So Cyrus (in Xenoph. Anab. p. 147.) presents to Syennesis king of Cilicia, ἱππον χρυσοχαλινον, και στρεπτον χρυσοῦν, και ψελλια, και ακινακην χρυσοῦν, και στολην Περσικην, δωρα ἁ νομιζεται παρα βασιλευσι τιμια. The tiara was a cap, like the Phrygian bonnet (Herodot. Polymn. c. 61.) common to all the Medes and Persians ; the royal family (Xenoph. Cyropæd. I. 8. p. 127.) alone wore a sash or diadem wreathed round it, which formed a sort of turband ; the king himself was distinguished by the top or point of his tiara which was upright, whereas all others had it bending down.

mind are weakened by their application to nothing but
to the sordid arts of lucre. The change of the constitution. The way to the magistracy laid open to all,
and decided by balloting. A lively picture of the
Athenian commonwealth.

P. 558. The distinction between our necessary and
unnecessary desires, is stated; when the latter prevail
over the former by indulgence, and by keeping bad
company, they form a democratick mind. The description of such a soul, when years have somewhat allayed
the tumult and violence of its passions; it is the sport
of humour and of caprice, inconstant in any pursuit,
and incapable of any resolution.

P. 562. When liberty degenerates into extreme
license and anarchy, the democracy begins to tend
towards tyranny. The picture of the Athenian government and manners is continued with great force and
severity : where youth assumes the authority and de-
cisiveness of age, and age mimicks the gaiety and
pleasures of youth; where women and slaves are upon
the same footing with their husbands and masters; and
where even the dogs and horses march directly onwards,
and refuse to give way to a citizen. The common
mutation of things from one extreme to another.

NOTES.

P. 563. 'Οι εωνημενοι.] Των δουλων δ'αυ και των μετοικων πλειστη
εστιν Αθηνησιν ακολασια, και ουτε παταξαι εξεστιν αυτοθι, ουτε
υπεκστησεται σοι ο δοῦλος. (Xenoph. Athen. Respubl. p. 403.)

565. 'Ως αληθως ολιγαρχικοι.] Εστι δε παση γη το βελτιστον
εναντιον τη δημοκρατια. Xenoph. ut supra.

Ib. Διος του Λυκαιου.] Pausanias speaks of this mysterious
solemnity performed on the most ancient altar in Greece.

P. 564. The division of those who bear sway in a
democracy into three kinds: 1. the busy, bold, and
active poor, who are ready to undertake and execute
any thing; 2. the idle and insignificant poor, who
follow the former, and serve to make a number and a
noise in the popular assemblies; and 3. the middling
sort who earn their bread by their labour, and have
naturally little inclination to publick affairs, nor are
easily brought together, but when allured by the hopes
of some gain, yet, when collected, are the strongest
party of all. The conversion of a demagogue into a
tyrant, from necessity and from fear, the steps which
he takes to attain the supreme power, the policy of
tyrants, and the misery of their condition, are excel-
lently described.

P. 568. The accusation of the tragick poets, as in-
spiring a love of tyranny, and patronized by tyrants;
they are encouraged also in democracies, and are little
esteemed in better governments.

NOTES.

P. 566. Τον Κροισω.] See Herodotus, L. 1. c. 55.
567. Εως αν μητε φιλων.] Compare this description with the
Hiero of Xenophon ; it is, in almost every step, a picture of the
politicks and way of life of the elder Dionysius.
568. Ουκ ετος ή τε Τραγωδια.] This is spoken ironically.
1b. Σοφοι τυραννοι.] A line from the Antigone of Euripides.
569. Μεγας μεγαλωστι.] Alluding to Homer, Odyss. Ω. v.
40. speaking of Achilles :

Συ δε στροφαλιγγι κονιης
Κεισο μεγας μεγαλωστι, λελασμενος ιπποσυναων.

DE REPUBLICA.

BOOK IX.

HEADS OF THE NINTH DIALOGUE.

P. 571. The worst and most lawless of our unnecessary desires are described, which are particularly active in sleep, when we go to our repose after drinking freely, or eating a full meal.

P. 572. The transition of the mind from a democratick to a tyrannical constitution. Debauchery and (what is called) love are the great instruments of this change. Lust and drunkenness, names for two different sorts of madness, between them produce a tyrant.

P. 573. Our desires from indulgence grow stronger and more numerous. Extravagance naturally leads to want, which will be supplied either by fraud or by violence.

P. 575. In states, in which there are but a few persons of this turn, and the body of the people are uncorrupted,

---

NOTES ON THE GREEK TEXT.

P. 571. Ὑγιεινῶς τις ἔχη.] Cicero cites and translates this whole passage, De Divinatione, L. 1. c. 30. these notions seem borrowed from the Pythagoreans.

575. Μητρίς.] A Cretan expression, meaning the country of one's mother.

they usually leave their own country, and enter into
the guards of some foreign prince, or serve him in his
wars : or, if they have not this opportunity, they stay
at home and turn informers, false evidences, highwaymen, and housebreakers, cut-purses, and such characters ; but, if they are numerous and strong, they form
a party against the laws and liberties of the people, set
at their head commonly the worst among them, and
erect a despotick government.

The behaviour of a tyrannical nature in private
life ; unacquainted with friendship, always domineering
over, or servilely flattering, his companions.

P. 577. The comparison between a state enslaved,
and the mind of a tyrant. The servitude, the poverty,
the fears, and the anguish of such a mind are described ;
and it is proved to be the most miserable of human
creatures.

P. 579. The condition of any private man of fortune,
who has fifty or more slaves. Such a man with his
effects, wife and family, supposed to be separated
from the state and his fellow-citizens (in which his
security consists), and placed in a desert country at

NOTES.

P. 577. 'Ος αν δυνηται τη διανοια.] Plato himself is doubtless
the person ; and qualified for the office by his intimate acquaintance with the younger Dionysius.

578. 'Ος αν τυραννικος ων.] Have a care of inserting any
negative particle here, as H. Stephanus would do, which would
totally destroy the sense. Plato's meaning is, that a tyrannical
mind, when it has attained to the height of power, must make
its possessor worse, and consequently more miserable, than while
he remained in a private condition.

some distance, surrounded with a people, who look
upon it as a crime to enslave one's fellow-creatures,
and are ready to favour any conspiracy of his servants
against him : how anxious and how intolerable would
be his condition ! Such, and still worse, is that of a
tyrant.

P. 581. The pleasures of knowledge and of philosophy are proved to be superiour to those which result
from honour or from gain, and from the satisfaction of
our appetites. The wise man, the ambitious man, the
man of wealth and pleasure, will each of them give the
preference to his favourite pursuit, and will undervalue
that of the others ; but experience is the only proper
judge which can decide the question, and the wise man
alone possesses that experience ; the necessity of his
nature must have acquainted him with the pleasure
which arises from satisfying our appetites. Honour
and the publick esteem will be the consequence of his
life and studies, as well as of the opulent or of the

P. 578. Ανδραποδα πεντηκοντα.] The more wealthy Greeks
had very large families of slaves. In Athens the number of slaves
was to that of citizens as 20 to 1 : the latter being about 21,000,
the former, 400,000. Mnaso of Phocis, a friend of Aristotle,
had 1000 slaves, or more, as had likewise Nicias, the famous
Athenian. In Corinth, there were reckoned 460,000 slaves : at
Ægina, above 470,000 : and many a Roman had in his own
service above 20,000 : this was a computation made Ol. 110. by
Demetrius Phalereus. See Athenæus from the Chronicle of
Ctesicles, L. 6. p. 272. and Xenophon περι Προσοδων. p. 540.

579. Λιχνω.] Implies curiosity, and an eager love of novel-
ties ; and is the same with regard to the eye, that liquorishness
is to the taste.

ambitious man; so that he is equally qualified with them to judge of their pleasures, but not they of his, which they have never experienced.   .

P. 584. Most of our sensual joys are only a cessation from uneasiness and pain, as are the eager hopes and expectations which attend them. A fine image is drawn of the ordinary life of mankind, of their sordid pursuits, and of their contemptible passions.

P. 588. The recapitulation, and conclusion, that the height of injustice and of wickedness is the height of misery.

P. 590. The intention of all education and laws is to subject the brutal part of our nature to the rational. A scheme of life, worthy of a philosophick mind, is laid down.

NOTES.

P. 583. 'Ηδονη τις εσκιαγραφημενη.] An expression borrowed perhaps from Heraclitus or Parmenides.

592. Εν ουρανω.] That is, in the idea of the divinity: see the beginning of the following (the 10th) book. Diogenes Laertius alludes to this passage in his epitaph on Plato:

Πολιν ηλυθεν, ην ποθ' ἑαυτω
Εκτισε, και δαπεδω Ζηνος ενιδρυσατο.

DE REPUBLICA.

BOOK X.

HEADS OF THE TENTH DIALOGUE.

P. 595. Plato's apology for himself. His reasons for banishing all imitative [1] poetry from his republick : 1. because it represents things not as they really are, but as they appear ; 2. the wisdom of the poets is not equal to their reputation ; 3. there is no example of a state having been better regulated, or of a war better conducted, or of an art improved, by any poet's instructions ; and 4. there is no plan of education laid down, no sect, nor school founded, even by Homer and the most considerable of the poets, as by the philosophers.

[1] V. L. 3. p. 392.

NOTES ON THE GREEK TEXT.

P. 595. Plato professes a great admiration, even from a child, for Homer, but yet is forced to exclude him from his commonwealth, ου γαρ προ γε της αληθειας τιμητεος ανηρ. The Greeks had carried their admiration for Homer to a high pitch of enthusiasm in Plato's time : it was he (they said) who first had formed Greece to knowledge and humanity ; (πεπαιδευκε την Ελλαδα, p. 606.) and that in him were contained all the arts, all morality, politicks, and divinity. p. 578.

599. Χαρωνδαν μεν.] Charondas was of Catana in Sicily, and gave his laws to that city, and to others of Chalcidick foundation in the island, and also to Rhegium in Italy ; (see Bentley on Phalaris, p. 364, &c.) these laws were calculated for an aristocracy.

P. 602. Their art concurs with the senses to deceive us and to draw off the mind from right reason, it excites and increases the empire of the passions, enervates our resolution, and seduces us by the power of ill example.

P. 604. The passions and vices are easy to imitate by reason of their variety; but the cool, uniform, and simple character of virtue is very difficult to draw, so

---

P. 600. Εἰς τεχνας.] Thales is said to have discovered the annual course of the sun in the ecliptick, and to have made several improvements in astronomy and geometry. To Anacharsis is ascribed the invention of anchors, and of the potter's wheel. See Diog. Laertius.

Ib. Πυθαγορειον.] The Pythagorean sect was in high repute in Plato's time, while Archytas, Philolaus, Lysis, Echecrates, and others, supported it; but it seems to have declined soon after, for Aristoxenus mentions these latter, whom he remembered, as the last of any note. Vid. Diog. Laert. L. 8. sect. 46.—Aristoxenus flourished about thirty years after Plato's death.

Ib. Του ονοματος.] The name signifies a lover of flesh-meat: but Callimachus (Epig. 6.) and Strabo (L. 14.) and Eustathius (ad Hom. Il. B. p. 250.) write it Creophȳlus. He was a Samian, who entertained Homer at his house; and wrote a poem, called Οιχαλιας ἁλωσις, which some attributed to Homer himself.

607. 'Η λακερυζα, &c.] Fragments of poets against philosophy.

608. Εμβλεψας μοι και θαυμασας ειπε, Μα Δι' ουκ εγωγε.] Is it possible that the immortality of the soul should be a doctrine so unusual, and so little known at Athens, as to cause this surprise in Glauco?—In the Phædo too, Cebes treats this point in the same manner: Τα δε περι της ψυχης πολλην απιστιαν παρεχει τοις ανθρωποις, μη, επειδαν απαλλαγῃ του σωματος, ουδαμου ετι ῇ· &c. Ουκ ολιγης παραμυθιας δειται και πιστεως, ὡς εστι ψυχη αποθανοντος του ανθρωπου, και τινα δυναμιν εχει και φρονησιν. p. 70.

2   NOTES ON PLATO.

as to touch or delight a theatre, or any other mixed
assembly of men.

P. 607. The power of numbers and of expression
over the soul is great, which renders poetry more particularly dangerous.

P. 608. Having shewn that virtue is most eligible
on its own account, even when destitute of all external
rewards, he now comes to explain the happiness which

NOTES.

P. 611. Ὥσπερ οἱ τον θαλαττιον Γλαυκον ὁρωντες.] He speaks
as if this divinity were sometimes actually visible to seafaring
men, all covered with sea-weed and shells.

Ib. Παντι μαλλον θηριω.] And so he is described by Ovid,
who says of Scylla,

Tuta loco, monstrumne, deusne,
Ille sit, ignorans, admiraturque colorem,
Cæsariemque humeros subjectaque terga tegentem,
Ultimaque excipiat quod tortilis inguina piscis.
Metam. L. 13. v. 913.

And he tells her;

Non ego prodigium, non sum fera bellua, Virgo,
Sum Deus, inquit, aquæ.

613. Απο των κατω.] From the place of starting at the lower
end of the stadium : τα ανω, the upper end, whence they ran
back again.

Ib. Τα ωτα επι των ωμων.] A metaphor, taken from horses,
and other animals, which let their ears drop, when they are
tired, and over-driven.

614. The story of Er, the Pamphylian, who, when he had
lain twelve days dead in appearance on the field of battle, and
was placed on the funeral pile, came to life again, and related
all he had seen in the other world. The judgment of souls,
their progress of a thousand years through the regions of bliss
or of misery, the eternal punishment of tyrants, and of others
guilty of enormous crimes, in Tartarus, the spindle of Necessity, which turns the eight spheres, and the employment of her

waits upon it in another life, as well as in the present. The immortality of the soul and a state of future rewards and of future punishments are asserted.

---

three daughters, the Fates, are all described, with the allotment and choice of lives (either in human bodies, or in those of brute animals) permitted to those spirits, who are again to appear on earth ; as of Orpheus who chooses that of a swan, Ajax of a lion, Thersites of a monkey, Ulysses that of an obscure private man, &c. their passage over the river Lethe is also mentioned. The whole fable is finely written.

Milton alludes to the spindle of Necessity in his entertainment called the *Arcades*. Virgil has also imitated many parts of the fable in his sixth Æneid, and Tully in the Somnium Scipionis. See Macrob. L. 1. c. 1.

P. 614. Του Αρμενιου.] It appears from Plutarch that the right reading is Ἁρμονιου, the son of Harmonius. Plut. Sympos. L. 9. Probl. 7.

616. Πλακατην τε και το αγκιστρον.] Vid. P. Bellonium Lat. Reddit. a C. Clusio, L. 1.'c. 46. where he describes the Greek manner of spinning, which seems to be the same exactly that it was of old. "Attractilis herba (quæ ex usu nomen habet) fusi vicem illis præbet ; ejus enim caulis rectus est et lævis, tanquam arte expolitus esset. In ejus penuriâ bacillo minimi digiti crassitiem non æquante, æqualis ubique crassitudinis, utuntur, cui ferrum hamuli piscatorii modo efformatum infigunt, ut filum comprehendat, e quo fusus dependeat. Verticillum (σφονδυλος) solummodo excogitatum est, ad fila commodius ducenda, atque ut fuso pondus addat ; dimidiato pyro in binas partes per medium secto simile est, per medium perforatum est: hoc superiori fusi parti infigunt, inferiore fusi parte deorsum propendente."

621. Περιαγειρομενοι.] Read, Περιαγομενοι.

THE END OF THE TENTH AND LAST BOOK.

DE LEGIBUS.

ΠΕΡΙ ΝΟΜΩΝ.

Plat. Op. Serrani, Vol. 2. p. 624.

THE persons of the dialogue are Clinias, a Cretan of
Gnossus, and two strangers, who are his guests, the one
a Lacedæmonian, called Megillus, the other an Athenian,
who is not named, but who appears by the character
and sentiments, to be Plato himself. (See Diog. Laert.
L. 3. sect. 52.)¹

They are, all three, men far advanced in years, and
as they walk¹ or repose themselves in the fields under
the shade of ancient cypress trees, which grew to a

¹ As Cicero had taken Plato for his model in his books de
Republicâ, so he had also in those De Legibus. "Visne igitur,
ut ille Crete cum Cliniâ et cum Lacedæmonio Megillo æstivo,
quemadmodum describit, die in cupressetis Cnossiorum et spatiis
sylvestribus crebrò insistens, interdum acquiescens, de institutis
rerum publicarum et de optumis Legibus disputat : sic nos inter
has procerissimas populos in viridi opacâque ripâ inambulantes,
tum autem residentes, quæramus iisdem de rebus aliquid uberius
quam forensis usus desiderat." L. 1. c. 5. (N. B. The Gnossians put
the cypress tree, which was a principal ornament of their country,
on the reverse of their silver coins. See Fulv. Ursinus.) Tully
also confines his discourse to the length of a summer's day, in
imitation of Plato. See De Legib. L. 2. c. 27. V. Platon. de
Legib. L. 3. p. 653. and L. 4. p. 722.

great bulk and beauty in the way, that led from the city of Gnossus to the temple and grotto of Jupiter, (where Minos was believed to have received his laws from the god himself) they enter into conversation on the policy and constitution of the Cretans.

There is no prooemium nor introduction to the dialogue, as there is to most of Plato's writings. I speak of that kind of prooemium usual with Plato, which informs us often of the occasion and of the time of the dialogue, and of the characters of the persons introduced in it. In reality the entire four first books of "the Laws" are but introductory to the main subject, as he tells us himself in the end of the fourth book. p. 722.

DE LEGIBUS.

BOOK I.

HEADS OF THE FIRST DIALOGUE.

P. 625. The institutions of Minos were principally directed to form the citizens to war. The great advantages of a people superiour in military skill over the rest of mankind are stated.[1] Every people is naturally in a state of war with its neighbours[2]; even

[1] Xenophon makes the following observation: Ελευθεριας οργανα και ευδαιμονιας την πολεμικην επιστημην και μελετην δι Θεοι τοις ανθρωποις απεδειξαν'—τοις αει εγγιτατω των όπλων ουσι, τουτοις και οικειοτατα εστιν ά αν βουλωνται. Cyropæd. L. 7. p. 549. See also Ephorus ap. Strab. L. 10. p. 480.

[2] Πασαις προς πασας τας πολεις πολεμος ακηρυκτος κατα φυσιν εστι. These are the original expressions in this place.

NOTES ON THE GREEK TEXT.

P. 625. Τα ξυσσιτια.] These assemblies were styled by the Cretans Ανδρεία (or rather Ανδρια, see Aristot. in Polit. L. 2. c. 10.) as they were also by the Lacedæmonians, who changed the name to Φιδιτια. (Strabo L. 10. p. 488). The manner of conducting them may be seen at large from Dosiadas's history of that country in Athenæus, L. 4. p. 143.

Ib. Απολλωνα.] See Plutarch. in Lycurgo.

Ib. Δι' εννατου ετους.] See the Minos of Plato, and Strabo. L. 10. p. 476. et L. 16. p. 762.

particular cities, nay private families are in a like
situation within themselves, where the better and more
rational part are always contending for that superiority,
which is their due, over the lower and the less reasonable. An internal war is maintained in the breast of
each particular man who labours to subdue himself by
establishing the empire of reason over his passions and
his desires.

P. 628. A legislator, who makes it the great end of
his constitution to form the nation to war, is shewn to
be inferiour to him who reconciles the members of it
among themselves, and prevents intestine tumults and
divisions.

P. 631. The view of the true lawgiver is to train

NOTES.

P. 625. 'Η των Θετταλων.] Vid. Menonem, p. 70. et Hero-
dotum. L. 7. p. 268.

Ib. 'Ηδε γαρ ανωμαλος.] "Quoniam adeo frequentes in Cretâ
sunt montes, rara sunt istic campestria." P. Bellonius, L. 1.
c. 5. "Quoique la Candie soit un riche païs—les deux tiers de
ce royaume ne sont que des montagnes seches, pelées, desagré-
ables, escarpées, taillées a plomb, et plus propres pour des chévres
que pour des hommes." Tournefort, Lett. 2. p. 109. vol. 1.

Ib. Των δε τοξων.] Vid. Ephorum ap. Strabonem fusè. L.
10. p. 480. "Cretenses etiam hodie (circ. A.D. 1550.) veterem
consuetudinem sequentes naturæ impulsu, Scythico arcu se
exercere solent. Quin et ipsi pueri in incunabulis si irascantur
et ejulent, ostenso illis arcu aut sagittâ in manus datâ, pla-
cantur ; propterea ipsos etiam Turcas arcus jaculatione super-
ant." Bellonius, L. 1. c. 5. Which is confirmed by Tournefort, who was there one hundred and fifty years after Belon.
See Lett. 2. p. 100. V. 1.

626. Ω Θειε.] Vid. Menonem, p. 99. et Aristot. Eth.
Nichom. L. 7. c. 1.

VOL. IV.   T

the mind and manners of his people to the virtues in
their order, that is, to wisdom, to temperance, and to
justice, and, in the fourth place, to valour.   The

P. 629. Προs τον πολεμον μαλιστα.] Yet this was Plato's
real judgment concerning the constitutions of Minos and of
Lycurgus, as may be seen by his description of a timocracy, in
the eighth book De Republ. p. 548.

Ib. Διαβαντες δε ευ.] The Spartans, when they passed
the frontier of their own state to enter into the territory of an
enemy, always performed sacrifice, which was called τα δια-
βατηρια θυειν: and if the victims proved inauspicious, they
retired, and gave over their enterprise.   This sense of the
word διαβηναι seems peculiar to that people.

Ib. Των μισθοφορων.] In Plato's time (about Ol. 106,) and
soon after, the intestine tumults in the Greek cities, joined to
a sort of fashion, which prevailed, of going to seek their fortune
in a foreign service, had so depopulated Greece, that Isocrates
tells Philip of Macedon, that he might form a better and
stronger army out of these mercenaries, than he could out of the
citizens themselves, who continued in their own country.   The
strength of the Persian king's armies was entirely composed of
these Greeks, as was that of his enemies also the kings of
Egypt, and of Cyprus, and the revolted vice-roys in Asia
Minor.   They were also employed by Athens, and by other
states of Greece, to save their own troops ; so that the Athenian
heavy-armed infantry now consisted of mercenaries, though the
citizens themselves served as rowers on board the fleet ; just
contrary to what had been the ancient practice, when the ships
were manned by the Ξενοι, and slaves, and the Athenians themselves composed the 'Οπλιται.

Ib. A fragment of Tyrtæus, Ουτ' αν μνησαιμην, &c.

630. A fragment of Theognis, Πιστοs ανηρ χρυσον, &c.

631. Ουκ εισι ματην.] Vid. Plat. de Republ. p. 544.

Ib. Επικοινωνουμενους.] There seems something defective in
the syntax in several parts of this period.

method he ought to lay down in the disposition of his laws is stated.

P. 634. The fault of the Cretan and of the Lacedæmonian laws is, that they do not fortify the soul as well against pleasure as against pain. Youth is not permitted to examine into the rectitude of those laws by which they are governed, nor to dispute about them ; this is the privilege of age, and only to be practised in private.

P. 635. The division of the citizens into companies, (called Ξυσσιτια) which daily assembled to eat together in publick, was apt to create seditions and conspiracies.

NOTES.

P. 633. Τριτον η τεταρτον.] Does Plato here allude to the order in which he has ranged the virtues, (which, however, is not very clear, except that he ranges valour in the fourth place) ? or does he allude to the heads which he has laid down for a legislator to proceed with method ? in which the laws that are to fortify the mind against pleasure and pain, and the passions which they produce, come under the third and fourth head.

Ib. Κρυπτεια τις.] Vid. Plutarch. in Lycurgo.

Ib. Γυμνοπαιδιαις.] Plutarch, ibid. Propert. L. 3. Eleg. 13. These exercises were performed during a solemn festival held in honour of Apollo, at which strangers were permitted to be present in Sparta.

635. Φυξεισθαι τους.] The translation is very deficient here : the sense is this ; "They will fly before such as have been fortified by exercise and habit against labour, pain, and terror, and will become their slaves :" and afterwards, Δουλευσουσι δε τροπον ετερον, &c. "They will become slaves in a different, but a more ignominious, manner both to those who have the power of resisting pleasure, and to those who possess all the arts of pleasing, who are often the worst of men."

276   NOTES ON PLATO.

The regular naked exercises of the youth were often
the cause of an unnatural passion among them. Crete
and Lacedæmon are blamed particularly on this account.
P. 636. Pleasure and pain are the two great sources

NOTES.

P. 636. Δηλουσι δε Μιλησιων.] The confusions at Miletus
were frequent, after that state had fallen into luxury and dis-
soluteness of manners: Heraclides Ponticus says of it; Ἡ
Μιλησιων πολις περιπεπτωκεν ατυχιαις δια τρυφην βιου και πολιτι-
κας εχθρας· οἱ το επιεικες ουκ αγαπῶντες εκ ῥιζων ανειλον τους
εχθρους: and he gives a remarkable instance of the implacable
cruelty which these parties shewed to each other. (Athenæus.
L. 12. p. 524.)
    Ib. Και δη και παλαιον.] Επιτηδευμα in this place seems
to me to be the nominative, and Νομμον the accusative: thus,
Τουτο το επιτηδευμα (τα γυμνασια) δοκει μοι διεφθαρκεναι το
παλαιον και κατα φυσιν νομμον, τας περι, &c. i.e. "This practice
(of exercising constantly naked) appears to me to have weakened
greatly that ancient and natural law, by which the pleasures of
love, not only among human creatures, but even in the brute
creation, mutually belong to the two sexes." This is a remarkable passage: and Tully judges in the same manner of these
exercises. How far the Cretans indulged their passions in the
way here mentioned, may be seen in Ephorus, (ap. Strabonem
L. 10.) The purity of manners at Sparta is strongly asserted
by Xenophon, (De Lacedæmon. Republ. p. 395.) and by Plutarch
in his life of Lycurgus; but here is a testimony on the other
side at least of equal authority.
    Ib. Δηλοῦσι δε Μιλησιων.] We learn from Polybius that
the Ξυσσιτια were in use among the Bœotians (though under
no such regulations, probably, as those of Crete and Lacedæmon), for speaking of that nation after the great victory
at Leuctra, Ol. 102. 2. he says, Κατα μικρον ανεπεσον ταις
ψυχαις, και ὁρμησαντες επ' ευωχιας και μεθας, διεθεντο και κοινωνεια
τοις φιλοις· πολλοι δε των εχοντων γενεας απεμεριζον τοις ξυσσιτιοις
το πλεον μερος της ουσιας, ὡστε πολλους ειναι Βοιωτων, ὁις ὑπηρχε
δειλινα του μηνος πλειω των εις τον μηνα διατεταγμενων ἡμερων.

of all human actions : the skill of a legislator consists
in managing and opposing one of them to the other.
P. 639. The use of wine, when under a proper
direction, in the education of youth.

(Ap. Athenæum, L. 10. p. 418. et Casaub. Annotat. in locum.)
Many instances more may bo observed in history of the intestine divisions in the cities of Bœotia, (see Xenoph. Grœc. Hist.
L. 5. p. 325.) and among the Thurians. (Thucyd. I. 7. c. 33.
and Aristot. Politic. L. 5. c. 7.)

P. 637. No assemblies for the sake of drinking were ever seen
in Lacedæmon, nor intemperate revels, nor frolicks, tho consequences of such entertainments.

Ib. 'Ωσπερ εν αμαξαις.] A sort of drunken farces performed
in the villages of Attica, during the Dionysia, which seem to
bo the origin of the ancient comedy and tragedy. Hence the
proverb, Εξ αμαξης λεγειν, and hence, too, Aristophanes gives
the name of Τραγωδια to comedy. Acharnenses, v. 498, 499,
and 627. They seem to have still continued in use in the
country.

Ib. Εν Ταραντι.] Vid. Plutarch. in Pyrrho, and Strabo, L.
6. p. 230. We see here the beginnings of those vices, which
some years afterwards were the ruin of Tarentum ; though as
yet the Pythagorean sect flourished there, and Archytas was
probably at tho head of their affairs.

Ib. Γυναικων παρ' υμιν ανεσιν.] Aristotle finds the same fault
in this part of the Lacedæmonian constitution ; he says of their
women, Ζωσι μεν ακολαστως προς απασαν ακολασιαν, και τρυφερως·
and he gives an instance of it in their behaviour, when the
Thebans invaded Laconia. Χρησιμοι μεν γαρ ουδεν ησαν, ωσπερ
εν ετεραις πολεσι· θορυβον δε παρειχον πλειω των πολεμων. (Polit.
I. 2. c. 9.)

Ib. 'Ωσπερ Σκυθαι.] Herodot. L. 6. c. 84.—Περσαι.] Xenoph.
Cyropæd. L. 8. p. 142.—Χαρχηδονιοι.] Were the Carthaginians
remarkable for drinking ?—Κελτοι.] See Posidonius ap. Athenæum, L. 4. p. 152.

278   NOTES ON PLATO.

P. 642. An apology for his own garrulity and diffuseness, which is the characteristick of an Athenian.
P. 643. The nature and intent of education.
P. 644. Mankind are compared to puppets : but whether they are formed by the gods for their diversion, or for some more serious purpose (he says) is uncertain. Their pleasures and pains, their hopes and fears, are

---

NOTES.

P. 637. Θρᾶκες.] Xenophon, describing an entertainment given by Seuthes, a Thracian king, at which he himself was present, says, Αναστας ὁ Σευθης συνεξεπιε, και συγκατεσκεδασε το μετ' αυτου το κερας.

638. Λοκροι.] The Locri Epizephyrii were governed by the laws of Zaleucus, and were an aristocracy, till the elder Dionysius marrying Doris, a Locrian lady, her relations grew powerful enough to bring that state into subjection to the Syracusans.

Ib. Πολλαι. γαρ δη φυγαι.] This may possibly allude to the unexpected defeat of the Spartans at Leuctra.

Ib. Χιους.] The wisdom of the Chian government appears from what Thucydides says of them. Χιοι μονοι μετα Λακεδαιμονιους, ὦν εγω ησθομην, ευδαιμονησαντες ἁμα και εσωφρονησαν, και ὁσω επεδιδου ἡ πολις αυτοις επι το μειζον, τοσω και εκοσμοῦντο εχυρωτερον. L. 8. c. 24. But I doubt if Κειους be not the true reading, for Chios revolted from the Athenians, Ol. 91. 4. when Plato was but seventeen years old, and Plato's Νομοι were written in the latter end of his life.

641. The character of Athens, ὡς φιλολογος εστι και πολυλογος, that of Lacedæmon and Crete, ὡς ἡ μεν βραχυλογος, ἡ δε πολυνοιαν μαλλον η πολυλογιαν ασκουσα.

642. 'Η ἑστια της πολεως ουσα ὑμων προξενος.] As each private family had its Vesta, to whom the hearth was particularly sacred, so that of the publick was seated in the Prytanèum, (Pindar. Nem. Od. 11.) where in most cities a perpetual lamp was kept burning in honour of this goddess : and as every private family of rank had their Προξενοι in several cities of Greece, with whom they were connected by the ties of hospi-

the springs which move them, and often draw contrary
ways at once. Reason is the master-spring which
ought to determine their motions; but as this draws
gently and never uses violence, some of the passions
must be called to its aid, which may give it strength
to resist the force of the others.

P. 645. The effects of wine upon the soul: it

NOTES.

tality, and in whose houses they were lodged and entertained,
so cities themselves had a like connection with each other; and
there were publick Προξενοι nominated to receive and to defray
the expenses of such as came on business from other cities in
alliance with them. The character of the Athenians is thus
drawn : Το υπο πολλων λεγομενον, ως οσοι Αθηναιων εισιν αγαθοι,
διαφεροντως εισι τοιουτοι·—μονοι γαρ ανευ αναγκης, αυτοφυως, θειᾳ
μοιρᾳ, αληθως και οιτι πλαστως εισιν αγαθοι.

P. 642. Προ των Περσικων.] Epimenides, therefore, came to
Athens, Ol. 70. 1. ten years before the battle of Marathon.
This is not reconcileable with Plutarch (in Solone), Diogenes
Laertius, or any other author, who mentions Epimenides. It
is sure that he arrived at Athens ninety-six years earlier, and
was then extremely old. Plato must therefore mean some
other person of the same name, country, and family, perhaps
descended from the old Epimenides, and practising, like him,
the art of divination.

644. Θαυμα μεν.] It is plain, that by θαυμα he means a
puppet, νευροσπαστον, and I suppose, that the θαυματοποιοι, or
jugglers, used to carry such figures about to draw the crowd
together, as the mountebanks do at Venice. To this he alludes
also, L. 7. Πολιτειων· Παρ' ην ιδε τειχιον παρωκοδομημενον, ωσπερ
τοις θαυματοποιοις των ανθρωπων προκειται τα παραφραγματα,
ὑπερ ὡν τα θαυματα δεικνυσι, &c. Puppet-shews were in such
request among the Greeks, that Pothinus, a famous man in that
way, performed before the whole Athenian people in the same
theatre (says Athenæus, L. 1. p. 19.), in which Euripides had
represented his tragedies.

heightens all our passions and diminishes our understanding, that is, in reality, it reduces us again to
childhood. As physicians, for the sake of our body,
give us certain potions, which for a time create sickness
and pain in us, and put our whole frame into disorder;
so possibly might the legislator (by a singular experiment) make wine subservient to a good purpose in
education, and, without either pain or danger, put the
prudence, the modesty, and the temper of youth to the
trial, and see how far they could resist the disorder of
the mind which is naturally produced by this liquor.

P. 646. The fear of dishonour is opposed to the fear
of pain : the first is a great instrument in the hands of
a wise legislator to suppress and to conquer the latter.

P. 647. If there were any drug or composition
known that would inspire us with fear and with dejection of spirits, for the time its influence lasted, what
need would there be of fatiguing our youth with long
laborious exercises, or of exposing them in battle to
real danger, in order to fortify the soul against the
attacks of fear and of pain ? This draught alone, properly applied, would be a sufficient trial of our valour
under the eye of the magistrate, who might confer
honour and disgrace on a youth, according to his

NOTE.

P. 647. Καλῶν αιδῶ.] This is what we call honour, that is, the
fear of shame ; and which is left to supply (as well as it can)
the place of all the virtues among us. Plato calls this sentiment in another place (p. 674. Lib. 2.) Θειος φοβος. Montesquieu
makes it the grand principle of monarchical governments,
(L'Esprit des Loix, L. 1. c. 6.) and in France its effects are
most conspicuous.

behaviour during the operation. Unluckily, there is
no such drug discovered ; but there is a potion which
exalts our spirits, and kindles in the mind insolence,
and imprudence, and lust, and every fiercer passion,
while it lays open to view our ignorance, our avarice,
and our cowardice. Why should we wait till these
vices exert themselves into real action, and produce
their several mischiefs in society ; when, by a well-
regulated use of this liquor, we might, without danger,
discover them lurking in the disposition of youth, and
suppress them even in their infancy ?

DE LEGIBUS.

BOOK II.

HEADS OF THE SECOND DIALOGUE.

P. 653. The great purpose of a right education is to fix in the mind an early habit of associating its ideas of pleasure and of desire with its ideas of virtue, and those of pain and aversion with that of vice : so that reason, when it comes to maturity, (and happy are they with whom, even in their old age, it does come to maturity!) may look back with satisfaction, and may approve the useful prejudices instilled into the soul in its infancy.

The early inclination of children to noise and motion is noticed, which, when reduced to order and symmetry, produce harmony and grace, which are two pleasures known only to human kind. The origin of musick and of the dance.

P. 655. In what kind of imitation their true beauty

NOTES ON THE GREEK TEXT.

P. 655. 'Ωσπερ δι χοροδιδασκαλοι.] I take the word ευχρους, applied to harmony, to be an affected term of art, then used by the musicians and connoisseurs, like those in the fifth book de Republ. p. 531. namely, Εξαρνησις, κατηγορια, αλαζονεια χορδων.

consists. Every sound, or movement, or attitude, which
naturally accompanies and expresses any virtue, or any
laudable endowment of mind and of body, is beautiful,
as the contrary is deformed and unpleasing. The error
of such as make pleasure the sole end of these arts.

Reasons for the diversity of men's taste and judgment in them are assigned. Some from having been
early depraved, and little accustomed to what is lovely,
come to approve and take delight in deformity : others
applaud what is noble and graceful, but feel no pleasure
from it, either because their mind has a natural depravity in it, though their education has been good, or
because their principles are right, but their habits and
practice have not been conformable to them. The
danger of this last defect is stated, when men delight
in what their judgment disapproves.

P. 657. The restraint, which ought to be laid on
poets in all well-disciplined states, is named. Musicians in Egypt[1] were confined by law, even from the
remotest antiquity, to certain simple species of melody,
and the painters and sculptors to some peculiar stand-

[1] Σκοπων δ' ευρησεις αυτοθι τα μυριοστον ετος γεγραμμενα η
τετυπωμενα, (ουκ, ως επος ειπειν, μυριοστον ετος, αλλ' οντως) των
νυν δεδημιουργημενων ουτε καλλιονα, ουτε αισχιω, την αυτην δε
τεχνην απειργασμενα. This will account for the little improvement the Egyptians ever made in the fine arts, though they
were perhaps the inventors of them : for undoubtedly the ad-
vancement and perfection of these things, as well as their corruption, are entirely owing to liberty and innovation.

P. 655. Τα μεν αρετης εχομενα.] Vid. de Republ. L. 3. The
opinion of Damon the musician.

ards for their measures and attitudes, from which they were not to deviate.

P. 658. A reflection on the usual wrong determinations of the persons appointed to judge of their musical and poetical entertainments at Athens, who (though they took an oath to decide impartially) were biassed, either through fear or from the affectation of popularity, by the opinion of the crowd; whereas they ought to have considered themselves as masters and directors of the publick taste. From this weakness arose the corruption of their theatrical entertainments. In Italy and in Sicily the victory was adjudged by the whole audience to that poet, who had the greatest number of hands held up for him.

P. 659. The manners, exhibited in a drama to the people, ought always to be better than their own.

P. 661. The morality inculcated by the poets, even in Sparta and in Crete, where all innovations were by law forbidden, was defective enough. What sentiments

NOTES.

P. 658. It is here said, that puppet-shews and jugglers' tricks are best accommodated to the taste of young children; as comedy is to that of bigger boys, tragedy to that of the young men, and of the women of the better sort, and of the bulk of the people in general, and the rhapsodi to that of the older and wiser sort.

Ib. Κινυρα τε.] The verses of Tyrtæus, here alluded to, are these:

Ουδ' ει Τιθωναιο φυην χαριεστερος ειη,
Πλουτοιη τε Μιδεω και Κινυραο πλεον.

See also Phædrum, p. 269.

661. Ὑγιαινειν.] An allusion to an ancient song. See Gorgias, p. 451.

they ought to inspire. Plato's[1] great principles are explained, namely, that happiness is inseparable from virtue and misery from wickedness, and that the latter is rather an error of the judgment than of the will.

P. 663. If these opinions were actually false, (as they are immutably founded on truth) yet a wise lawgiver would think himself obliged to inculcate them, as true, by every method possible.

It is easy to persuade men, even of the most absurd fiction; how much more of an undoubted truth?

P. 664. The institution of the three chorusses, which are to repeat in verse (accompanied with musick and with dances) these great principles of society, and to fix them in the belief of the publick: the first chorus is composed of boys under eighteen, and sacred to the Muses; the second, from that age to thirty, and sacred to Apollo; the third, to Bacchus, consisting of all from thirty to sixty years of age.

P. 666. The use of wine is forbidden to boys; it is

[1] V. Alcibiad. 2. p. 144. Aristotle looked upon this as the distinguishing part of his master Plato's doctrine, as we see from a fragment of his elegy to Eudemus, preserved in Olympiodorus's commentary on the Gorgias. See also de Legib. I. 5. p. 733 and 742.

<hr/>

NOTES.

P. 663. Το του Σιδωνιου.] This fable of Cadmus and the dragon's teeth was firmly believed at Thebes: the principal families were supposed to be descended from the five persons who survived the fight: and bore on their bodies (as it was reported) the mark of a lance, as a proof of their origin. They were called Σπαρτοι, και Γηγενεις. (See Eurip. Hercules Furens, v. 794. and Barnes ad locum.)

allowed, but very moderately, to men under thirty;
after that age, with less restraint: the good effects of
it in old age are mentioned.

P. 667. The principles and qualifications which are
required in such as are fit to judge of poetry, and of
the other imitative arts.

P. 669. Instrumental musick by itself (which serves
not to accompany the voice) is condemned, as uncertain
and indefinite in its expression.   The three arts of
poetry, of musick, and of the dance (or action), were
not made to be separated.

P. 671. The regulation of entertainments, with the
manner of presiding at them is enforced ; without which
the drinking of wine ought not to be permitted at all,
or in a very small degree.

NOTES.

P. 665. Πεφωνασκηκοτες.] The singers in these chorusses
were subjected to a course of abstinence and of physick, for a
considerable time before they put their voices to the trial.
(Vid. Antiphont. Orat. de cæde Choreutæ.)

669. An expression of Orpheus : Λαχειν ὡραν τερψιος.

672. Ὁταν αποκτεινη τις αυτο, or, ακταινωση ἑαυτο—a false
reading ; perhaps, ὁταν ανακινη τις, or ανακινη τι αυτο.

DE LEGIBUS.

BOOK III.

P. 676. The immense antiquity of the earth, and the innumerable changes it has undergone in the course of ages. Mankind are generally believed to have been often destroyed (a very small remnant excepted) by inundation and by pestilence.

The supposition of a handful of men, probably shepherds, who were feeding their cattle on the mountains, and were there preserved with their families from

---

NOTES ON THE GREEK TEXT.

P. 677. Ὁ, τι μεν γαρ μυριακις.] Perhaps we should read ουτι μεν γαρ. I imagine he means to say, as follows ; " For (taking the great antiquity of the earth for granted) without supposing some such destruction as this, how can we account for all the useful arts among mankind, invented as it were but yesterday, or at farthest, not above two thousand years old ? It is impossible that men in those times should have been utterly ignorant of all which had passed so many thousand ages, unless all records, and monuments, and remains of their improvements and discoveries, had perished."

" Quo tot facta virûm toties cecidere ? nec usquam
Æternis famæ monumentis insita florent ?"

Lucret. L. 5. v. 329.

a general deluge, which had overwhelmed all the cities and inhabitants of the country below.

P. 677. The destruction of arts and sciences, with their slow and gradual revival among this infant society, is nobly described.

P. 680. The beginnings of government : the paternal way first in use, which he calls the justest of all monarchies. Assemblies of different families agree to descend from the mountain tops, and to settle in the hill-country (εν ταις ὑπωρειαις) below them; and as each of them has a head or a prince of its own, and customs in which it has been brought up, it will be

---

NOTES.

P. 677. Χιλια δ' αφ' οὐ γεγονεν, η δις.] From Ol. 108. 1. the year of Plato's death, to the age of Marsyas (a contemporary of Midas) is usually computed about thirteen hundred years, to that of Amphion, eleven hundred, to that of Dædalus and Orpheus, not quite one thousand, and to that of Palamedes, who lived about the siege of Troy, nine hundred and sixty.

Ib. Τα δε περι Μουσικην.] Perhaps we should add, Αυλη-τικην.

Ib. χθες τε και πρωην.] See Gorgias, p. 471.

Ib. Ὁ λογω μεν Ἡσιοδος.] I know not what lines in Hesiod are here alluded to, unless it be these :

Οὑτος μεν παναριστος, ὁς αυτος παντα νοησει,
Φρασσαμενος τα κ' επειτα και ες τελος εσσετ' αμεινω.
Oper. et Dies. v. 293.

nor do I clearly see, whether this is said seriously, or by way of irony on Epimenides and on the art of divination.

680. Τοις ξενικοις ποιημασι.] Homer was but little known or read in Crete, even in Plato's time. The Cretans, as they closely adhered to their ancient customs, did so likewise to the compositions of their own countrymen.

necessary to describe certain laws in common, and to settle a kind of senate, or of aristocracy.

P. 683. The causes of the increase and declension of states, are exemplified in the history of Sparta, Messene, and Argos. The original league between the three kingdoms founded by the Heraclidæ, and the mutual engagements entered into by the several kings and by their people, are stated.

P. 684. The easiness of establishing an equality of property in a new conquest, which is so difficult for a

---

NOTES.

P. 681. Τριτον τοινυν ειπωμεν.] See what Strabo (L. 13. p. 592. 3.) says on this subject : whence I should suspect that there was something deficient here in the text of Plato concerning the third migration of mankind, at which time Ilus is supposed to have founded Ilium in the plain.

682. Την εις Λακεδαιμονα κατοικησιν.] This happened eighty years after the taking of Troy. See the history in Pausanias. Corinthiac. L. 2. p. 151. and Messeniac. p. 285.

683. Ἡ εκ θερινων.] The time of the dialogue was one of the longest days in the year, soon after the summer-solstice.

684. Γην τε αναμφισβητητως.] The equal distribution of lands is, however, by all attributed to Lycurgus, who lived at least two hundred and thirty years after the return of the Heraclidæ, nay Plato himself (in the Minos, p. 318.) brings him near four hundred years lower still. Erastosthenes and Apollodorus (ap. Plutarch. in Lycurgo) place Lycurgus a little earlier. Xenophon alone makes him a contemporary with the Heraclidæ, who first settled in Peloponnesus : (Respubl. Lacedæm. p. 399.) at least so Plutarch interprets the passage.

Ib. Βασιλειαι τρεις—ωμοσαν.] This was performed at Sparta every month. Ὁ δε ορκος εστι τω μεν βασιλεῖ, κατα τους της πολεως κειμενους νομους βασιλευσειν, τη δε πολει εμπεδορκουντος εκεινου αστυφελικτον την βασιλειαν παρεξειν. (Xenoph. Lacedæm. Respubl. p. 402.)

legislator to accomplish, who would give a better form to a government already established.

P. 688. States are destroyed, not so much for the want of valour and of conduct, as for the want of virtue, which only is true wisdom. The greatest and the most pernicious of all ignorance is, when we do not love what we approve.

P. 691. *Absolute power, unaccountable to any and uncontrolled, is not to be supported by any mortal man.*

NOTES.

P. 685. Της αρχης γαρ εκεινης ην μοριον.] This is a singular passage. The kingdom of Troy (he says) was a part of the great Assyrian empire, ην γαρ ετι της αρχης εκεινης σχημα το σωζομενον ου μικρον. According to Herodotus, the empire of Assyria had continued five hundred and twenty years in Upper Asia, when the Medes revolted from it; but this happened near five hundred years after the fall of Troy, so that Troy was taken about the twentieth year of the Assyrian dominion, and, if so, the words of Plato, τη περι Νίνον γενομενη, might be taken literally, as though Ninus were then on the throne. But, in truth, Plato (from the words cited above, Ην γαρ ετι, &c.) appears to have given the Assyrian power a much longer duration, as Ctesias has done, who makes it seven hundred and eighty-six years older than Herodotus. Diodorus, who follows the authority of Ctesias in these matters, says, that Troy depended on the Assyrians, and that Teutamus, or Tautanes, who then reigned over them, sent ten thousand men and two hundred chariots to the assistance of Priam, under the command of Memnon son to the governor of Susiana.

Ib. Το δευτερον.] Troy had been taken by Hercules and Telamon about a hundred years before its final destruction: but perhaps το δευτερον may signify, afterwards, in process of time, that is, in the reigns of Darius and of Xerxes.

689. Proverb, Μητε γραμματα, μητε νεῖν, επισ:ασθαι, for a person completely ignorant.

The aiming at this was the destruction of the Argive and Messenian monarchs. That which probably preserved the Lacedæmonian state, was the originally lodging the regal power in the hands of two; then the institution of the senate by Lycurgus, and lastly, that of the Ephori by Theopompus. Had the three kingdoms been united and governed in the Spartan manner, the Persian king would never have dared to invade Greece: his repulse was entirely due to the Athenians and Lacedæmonians, and not to the common efforts of the Greeks.

NOTES.

P. 690. Και κατα φυσιν, ὡs ὁ Θηβαιοs.] See the passage of Pindar at length, cited in the Gorgias, p. 484.

691. Τηρ κατα γηραs.] The institution of the Γεροντεs, or senate of twenty-eight, by Lycurgus.

Ib. Ισοψηφον.] The two kings sat in the senate, and had each a single vote, like the other citizens: they had only this privilege, that they could give their vote by proxy, when absent.

Ib. Διδυμον.] Euristhenes and Procles were twins. (Herod. I. 6. c. 52.)

Ib. Μισθουμενοι.] Vid. L. 1. p. 630.

692. Ο τριτοs σωτηρ.] i.e. Theopompus, who, as it is generally agreed, instituted the Ephori. I look upon this passage as one proof, that the eighth epistle of Plato is supposititious, for in that epistle this institution is expressly attributed to Lycurgus. Many sentiments in that letter seem borrowed from this book of the Laws.

Ib. Πολεμουσα αυτη.] I do not know any war in which the Spartans were engaged with the Messenians at the time of the battle of Marathon (see also p. 698.); but this doubtless is a better reason than that given by Herodotus (L. 6. c. 106.), namely, that it was not agreeable to their customs to take the field, before the moon was at the full.

P. 693. The two great forms of government, from which all the rest are derived, are monarchy and democracy : Persia is an example of the first carried to its height, and Athens an example of the latter. The best constitution is formed out of both.

P. 694. The reason of the variations observable in the Persian power is given ; the different administra-

---

NOTES.

P. 692. 'H περι το Αργος.] Their pretence for refusing was a point of honour : they insisted upon dividing the confederate army with Sparta ; but it was believed, that they had secretly promised the Persian to observe a neutrality. As to the rest of Greece, the Thessalians had called in Xerxes, the Bœotians readily received him, the Cretans pretended an oracle which obliged them to continue quiet, and the Corcyreans waited to see the event of the first battle. After the action at Thermopylæ, a great part of Peloponnesus had determined to fortify the Isthmus, and to give up all the countries which lie north of it ; and what is worse, even after the great victory at Salamis, they went on, Lacedæmonians and all, with the work, and gave up Attica a second time to the barbarians. It was with great difficulty that Themistocles could keep the fleet together at Salamis, or prevent the several squadrons which composed it from returning home ; and, in the battle of Platæœ, no one scarcely had any share, except the Lacedæmonians, the Athenians, and the Tegeætæ ; and particularly, the Mantineans and the Eleans did not arrive till after the fight.

694. Παιδειας δε ορθης.] This passage has been generally looked upon as reflecting on the Cyropædia of Xenophon, and taken for a mark of ill-will in Plato : but I do not see how the words themselves carry in them any such reflection. They are plainly meant, not of the education which Cyrus himself received, but, of the little care he took (busied as he was in great affairs all his life long) of that of his two sons. There is nothing in this at all contradictory to Xenophon who scarcely mentions these princes any farther than to say, that they were

tion of different princes, who succeeded one another,
and the cause of it is accounted for from their education. The care of Cyrus's children, while he was
abroad in the field, was trusted entirely to the women,
who bred them up in high notions of that grandeur to
which they were to succeed, and in the effeminate and
luxurious manners of the Medes. Darius, who suc-

present and heard the excellent counsels which Cyrus gave
them on his death-bed, and which they forgot immediately.
Επει μεντοι Κυρος ετελευτησεν, ευθυς μεν αυτου οι παιδες εστα-
σιαζον. —ταυτα δ' ετι το χειρον ετρεχετο. The great abilities
and virtues of Cyrus himself are represented alike in Plato and
in Xenophon.

P. 695. Διειλετο επτα μερη.] I know not whether any historian
tells us, that Darius divided the empire into seven parts, or
great provinces, over which we are to suppose that he placed
the great men who had entered into the conspiracy with him,
and made these vice-royalties hereditary in their families. It
is natural to imagine, that such an appointment could not continue many years under a succession of kings so absolute as
those of Persia ; but yet Plato says, that some faint shadow of
this division was still left even in his days.

Ib. Του Κυρου δασμον.] We see here, that the division of
the empire into twenty satrapiæ or governments, and the imposition of a regular tax or tribute, were originally designed by
Cyrus, though they were never executed till Darius came to the
throne. The Persians, according to Herodotus, attributed it to
the avarice of Darius : Δια δε ταυτην την επιταξιν του φορου και
παραπλησια ταυτη αλλα, λεγουσιν, ως Δαρειος μεν ην καπηλος·
Καμβυσης δε δεσποτης· Κυρος δε πατηρ. Ο μεν γαρ, οτε εκαπη-
λευε παντα τα πρηγματα· ο δε, οτι χαλεπος τε ην και ολιγωρος·
ο δε, οτι ηπιος ην και αγαθα σφι παντα εμηχανησατο.

Ib. Ποιμενες.] Herodotus says, that four of the Persian
tribes, the Dai, Mardi, Tropici, and Sagartii, were Νομαδες,
L. 1. p. 54. c. 125.

ceeded them, had been bred as a private soldier, and
he restored the declining empire to its former greatness.
Xerxes, his son, brought up as great princes usually
are, by his folly weakened it again, and ever since it
has been growing worse and worse.

NOTES.

P. 695. Τραχειας χωρας.] See Herodotus, L. 1. c. 71. and
L. 9. c. ult.

Ib. Του λεγομενου το τε Ευνουχου.] The account of this fact,
which Plato had received, seems different from that given us
by Herodotus, or by Ctesias. The counterfeit Smerdis and the
Magus, his brother, were Medes, but neither of them eunuchs.
He may possibly mean the eunuch Bagapates, who (according
to Ctesias) was the favourite both of Cyrus and Cambyses, was
privy to the secret murder of Tanyoxarces, and contrived after
the death of Cambyses to place the Magus, or Mede, upon the
throne, and afterwards betrayed him to the conspirators.

Ib. Των ἑπτα.] Ctesias calls them, Onophas, Idernes,
Norondabates, Mardonius, Barisses, Artaphernes, and Darius.

Ib. Βασιλεως ουκ ην ὑιος.] Hystaspes, the father of Darius,
was of the same family with Cyrus, and, at the time of his
son's coming to the empire, was governor of Persia properly
so called. Darius was brought up in that country, he served
in Egypt among the guards of Cambyses, λογου ουδενος κω
μεγαλου, says Herodotus, and came to the throne at about
twenty-eight years of age.

Ib. Διειλετο ἑπτα μερη.] Herodotus tells us, that Otanes
(who first laid the plan of the conspiracy) gave up all preten-
sions to the crown, on condition that he and his family might
enjoy a perfect liberty ; and even now (adds he) the descendants
of Otanes are the only family in Persia which can be called free,
· obeying the orders of the court no farther than they please, and
under no other restraint than that of the laws. The other six
agreed among themselves, that to whichever among them fortune should give the empire, he should engage to marry out of
no other family than theirs, and should never refuse them access
to his person, except he were in the apartment of the women.

P. 696. Honour is the proper reward of virtue only ; in what manner it ought to be distributed in a well-regulated state.

P. 697. The impossibility is stated of any government's subsisting long, where the people are enemies to the administration, which, where despotism in its full extent prevails, must always be the case.

P. 698. A picture of the reverse of this, a complete democracy, as at Athens. The constitution of that

---

NOTES.

P. 698. Πολιτεια παλαια.] See the admirable Areopagitick oration of Isocrates, p. 147. and 150. for an account of the ancient Athenian manners and education ; and the oration de Pace, p. 176. and Panathenaic. p. 260.

Ib. Εκ τιμηματων τετταρων.] See this division instituted by Solon in Plutarch's life of him. Aristides, after the victory at Platæœ, proposed a law, whereby every citizen of Athens, without regard to rank or fortune, might be a competitor for the archonship, or principal magistracy, which afterwards gave a right to a seat in the senate of Areopagus.

Ib. Δατις.] This is all agreeable to Herodotus, L. 6. c. 98. See also Plato's Menexenus, p. 240.

699. 'Ην αιδω.] Vid. L. 1. p. 647.

700. Η Μουσικη.] Vid. L. 2. p. 657 and 658. and de Republ. L. 4. p. 424. The state of the Athenian musick before the Persian invasion. Certain kinds of harmony and of movement were appropriated to distinct species of poetry : prayers and invocations to the gods formed one kind, called 'Υμνοι ; lamentations for the dead formed a second, called Θρηνοι ; the Παιανες were a third sort ; the Διθυραμβοι (the subject of which was the birth of Bacchus) a fourth ; and the Νομοι Κιθαρωδικοι, a fifth, with other kinds : these were afterwards confused and injudiciously mingled all together by the ignorance and by the bad taste of the poets and of their audience.

Ib. Ου συριγξ ην.] The Athenians used this instrument, as in modern theatres whistles and cat-calls.

state was different before the Persian invasion. The reasons for their distinguished bravery on that occasion. An account of the change introduced in their musick, and the progress of liberty, or rather of license, among them.

P. 701. The great aim of a legislator is to inspire liberty, wisdom, and concord. Clinias, being appointed with nine other citizens to superintend and to form a body of laws for a new colony they are going to settle, asks advice of the Athenian and Lacedæmonian strangers on that head.

DE LEGIBUS.

BOOK IV.

HEADS OF THE FOURTH DIALOGUE.

P. 704. The advantages and disadvantages arising from the situation of a city, and the great difficulty of preserving the constitution and the morals of a maritime and trading state, are described.

P. 704. He is speaking of the difficulty of preserving the constitution and morals of a maritime and trading state. Εμποριας γαρ και χρηματισμου δια καπηλειας εμπιπλασα εαυτην, ηθη παλιμβολα και απιστα ταις ψυχαις εντικτουσα, αυτην τε προς αυτην την πολιν απιστον και αφιλον ποιει, και προς τους αλλους ανθρωπους ωσαυτως. The great advantage of a maritime power with respect to its influence, its commerce and riches, its politeness of manners and language, and the enjoyment of every pleasure and convenience of life, are admirably explained by Xenophon (in Athen. Republ. p. 204.), who considers it in every light, in which Montesquieu and the best modern political writers would do. But Plato extended his views farther: he says, Ου το σωζεσθαι τε και ειναι, μονον ανθρωποις τιμωτατον ηγουμενοι, καθαπερ οι πολλοι, το δε ως βελτιστους γιγνεσθαι τε και ειναι, τοσουτον χρονον οσον αν ωσιν. (707. see also p. 714. and L. 5. p. 743.) Plato never regards policy as the art of preserving mankind in a certain form of society, or of securing their property or their pleasures, or of enlarging their power, unless so far as all these

P. 706. The manner of carrying on a war by sea is unworthy of a brave and free people; it impairs their valour, depends too much on the lower and more mechanick arts, and is hardly ever decisive. The battles of Artemisium and of Salamis could not have preserved Greece (as it has been commonly thought), from the Persians, had they not been defeated in the action at Plataeae.

P. 709. The difficulties, which attend new colonies, if sent out by a single city, are stated: they will more hardly submit to a new discipline, and to laws different from those of their native country: but then they concur more readily in one design, and act with more strength and uniformity among themselves. If they are collected from various states, they are weak and disjointed, but more apt to receive such forms and impressions as a legislator would give them.

The constitution of states and of their laws is owing more to nature, or to chance, or to the concurrence of

---

NOTES.

are consistent with the preservation of their virtue and of that happiness, which is the natural result of it. He had, undoubtedly, in what he says here, a view to his own country.

Isocrates (in his oration Panathenaic. p. 256.) is constrained to own, that when Athens became a great naval power, she was forced to sacrifice her good order and morals to her ambition, though he justifies her for doing so from necessity: but (in the orat. de Pace, p. 174.) he speaks his mind more freely, and he shows at large that the dominion of the sea was every way the ruin of the Athenians, and afterwards of the Lacedaemonians.

P. 704. Ἐλάτη.] We see here that the principal ship-timber of the Greeks was fir, and pine and cypress for the outside work, as the picea and plane-tree were for the inside.

various accidents, than to human foresight : yet the
wise lawgiver will not therefore despair, but will accommodate his art to the various circumstances and
opportunities of things. The mariner cannot command
the winds and the waves, yet he can watch his advantages, and make the best use possible of both, for the
expedition and security of his voyage.

P. 710. The greatest advantage which a lawgiver
can ever meet with is, when he is supported by an
arbitrary prince, young, sober, and of good understanding, generous and brave ; the second lucky opportunity
is, when he can find a limited monarch of like disposition to concur in his designs ; the third is, when he
can unite himself to the leading men in some popular
government ; and the fourth and most difficult is, in an
oligarchy.

NOTES.

P. 706. Την χωραν πληρη.] The Athenians brought their
timber chiefly from Macedonia, for Attica afforded but little
for these uses. (Xenoph. Hellenic. L. 6. p. 340.)

707. Αλλοθεν των Ελληνων.] According to Herodotus (L. 7.
c. 170.) the ill-success of the expedition of Minos against the
Sicilians, and the settlement of those troops which accompanied
him in Italy after his death, had left Crete in a manner destitute of inhabitants ; for he mentions only Præsus and Polichne,
as cities of the Eteocrétes (or original Cretans) remaining. This
happened about one hundred years before the Trojan war, and
accordingly Homer speaks of this island as peopled by various
nations, and most of them of Greek origin :

Αλλη δ' αλλων γλωσσα μεμιγμενη· εν μεν Αχαιοι,
Εν δ' Ετεοκρητες μεγαλητορες, εν δε Κυδωνες,
Δωριεες τε τριχαικες, διοι τε Πελασγοι.
                                    Odyss. T. v. 175.

P. 711. The character and manners of a whole people, in a despotick government, are easily changed by the encouragement and by the example of their prince.

P. 712. The best governments are of a mixed kind, and are not reducible to any of the common forms. Thus those of Crete and of Sparta were neither tyrannical, nor monarchical, nor aristocratical, nor democratical, but had something of all these.

P. 713. The fable of the Saturnian age is introduced, when the gods or dæmons in person reigned over mankind. No mortal nature is fit to be trusted with an *absolute* power of commanding its fellow-creatures : and therefore the law, that is, pure reason, divested of all

---

P. 710. This great opportunity was Plato's inducement to go twice into Sicily, and (when he found that nothing could be made of the younger Dionysius) to support Dion in his expedition against him. Dion was of the royal family, possessed of every qualification here required, and ready to concur with Plato in all his designs, but he was cut off in the midst of them by a base assassin, whom he had taken into his bosom and counsels.

712. This is also the opinion of Polybius (Excerpt. ex Lib. 6. p. 452. ed. Casaub.) who produces the Spartan and Roman commonwealths as instances of it.

712. Isocrates calls the Lacedæmonian constitution a democracy. Λακεδαιμονιοι δια ταυτα καλλιστα πολιτευονται, ὁτι μαλιστα δημοκρατουμενοι τυγχανουσι. (Areopag. p. 152.) and in another place he calls it a democracy mixed with an aristocracy. (Panathen. p. 265.) His reason for naming it a democracy was, doubtless, because the senate was elected by the people, as were also the Ephori, in whose hands the supreme power was lodged, which Aristotle calls λιαν μεγαλη, και ισοτυραννος, and

human passions and appetites, the part of man which
most resembles the divinity, ought alone to be implicitly
obeyed in a well-governed state.

P. 715. The first address to the citizens of the new
colony, is to inculcate the belief of providence and of
divine justice, humility, moderation, obedience to the
laws, and piety to the gods and to parents : this should
be by way of procemium to the laws ; for free men are
not to be treated like slaves ; they are to be taught and
to be persuaded, before they are threatened and punished.

P. 721. The laws of marriage, and the reasons and
inducements to observe them, are stated.

P. 722. The necessity and the nature of general and
of particular introductions are stated.

NOTES.

adds, that by these means, Δημοκρατια εξ Αριστοκρατιας σινεβαινε.
(Politic. L. 2. c. 9.)

P. 714. Το συμφερον ἑαυτω.] See de Republ. L. 1. p. 338. This
was the doctrine of Thrasymachus, and it is in appearance that
of Montesquieu in his Esprit des Loix ; but this great man did
not dare to speak his mind, in a country almost despotically
governed, without disguise. Let any one see the amiable picture which Montesquieu draws of freer governments, and, in
contrast to it, his idea of a court, and they will not be at a loss
to know his real sentiments. That constitution and policy which
is founded (as he says himself) on every virtue, must be the
only one worthy of human nature.

716. 'Ωs φασιν ανθρωπος.] He alludes to a principle of Protagoras (V. Theæt. p. 152.)

720. The method of practising physick in these times is
observable.

DE LEGIBUS.

BOOK V.

HEADS OF THE FIFTH DIALOGUE.

P. 726. After he has shewed the reason of that duty which men owe to the gods and to their parents, he comes to that duty which we owe to ourselves; and first, of the reverence due to our own[1] soul; that it consists not in flattering its vanity, nor indulging its pleasures, nor in soothing its indolence, nor in satisfying its avarice.

P. 728. The second honours are due to our body, whose perfection is not placed in excess of strength, of bulk, of swiftness, of beauty, nor even of health, but in a mediocrity of all these qualities; for a redundancy,[2] or a deficiency, in any one of them is always prejudicial to the mind.

The same holds with regard to fortune.[3] The folly

[1] Παντων των αιτου κτηματων μετα Θεους ψυχη θειοτατον, οικειοτατον ον. p. 728.

[2] Τα μεν γαρ χαυνους τας ψυχας και θρασειας ποιει, τα δε ταπεινωστε και ανελευθερους. p. 728.

[3] Ἡ μεν γαρ νεων ακολακευτος ουσια, των δε αναγκαιων μη ενδεης, αυτη πασων μουσικωτατη τε και αριστη· ξυμφωνουσα γαρ ἡμῖν και ξυναρμοττουσα εις ἁπαντα αλυπον τον βιον απεργαζεται. p. 729.

of heaping up riches for our children is exposed, as the
only valuable inheritance which we can leave them is a
respect for virtue. The reverence due to youth is inculcated. True education consists not in precept, but in
example.

The duty to relations and to friends : strict justice,
hospitality, and compassion, are due to strangers and
foreigners, but above all to suppliants.

What is that habit of the mind which best becomes
a man of honour and a good citizen. Veracity is the
prime virtue. Justice consists in this : not only to do
no injury, but to prevent others from doing any, and to
assist the magistrate in punishing those who commit
them. Temperance and wisdom : the persons who
possess these or any other virtues, deserve our praise ;
those, who impart them to others, and multiply their
influence, are worthy of double honours. The use of
emulation in a state : the hatefulness of envy and
detraction.

P. 731. Spirit and indignation are virtues, when
employed against crimes and vices, which admit of no
other cure than extreme severity :[1] yet they are not
inconsistent with lenity and tender compassion, when
we consider that[2] no man is voluntarily wicked ; and
that the fault is in his understanding, and not in his
intention. The blindness of what is called self-love.
Excessive joy and sorrow are equally condemned.

[1] Χαλετα, και δυσιατα, η και το παρατα̣ν ανιατα, αδικηματα.
(See the Goigias.)

[2] Vid. Protagoram, p. 357.—Η γαρ δι᾿ αμαθιαν, η δι᾿ ακρα-
τειαν, η δι᾿ αμφοτερα του σωφρονειν ενδεης ων, ζη ὁ πας ανθρωπινος
οχλος. p. 734.

P. 732. A life of virtue is preferable[1] to any other, even with respect to its pleasures. (This passage is admirable.)

P. 736. The method of purgation requisite in forming a society, in order to clear it of its noxious parts, either by punishments, or by sending out colonies.

P. 737. The number of citizens limited. Equal · division of lands among them. The institution of temples and sacred rites, in which nothing of novelty is to be permitted, nor the slightest alteration[2] made; but ancient opinions and traditions are to be religiously followed. Festivals and general assemblies serve to familiarise the citizens to one another, and to bring the whole people acquainted with the temper and character of each particular man.

P. 739. The recommendation of his first scheme of government laid down in the book de Republicâ, in which all things are in common; and the whole state, their possessions, their families, their passions,[3] are so united as that they may all act together, like the faculties of a single person. The present scheme comes next to it in perfection.

The number of the shares allotted to the citizens is never to be diminished nor increased. Each man is to choose one among his sons who is to succeed to his portion; the rest to be given in adoption to those who have none of their own. The supreme magistrate is to

[1] Vid. de Republica, p. 581. L. 9. Philebum, p. 61. et Protagoram.

[2] Τουτων Νομοθετῃ το σμικροτατον ἁπαντων ουδεν κινητεον.

[3] Vid. de Republ. L. 5. p. 462.

preside over this equality, and to preserve it. If the number of children exceed the number of shares, he may send out a colony; if it fall short, he may (in cases of great necessity) introduce the sons of foreigners. No alienation of lands to be permitted.

P. 741. The increase of fortune by commerce is to be prohibited, and the use of gold or silver small money, of a species not valued, nor in request with other people, only permitted for the ordinary uses of life. The common coin of Greece is to be in the hands of the publick, or employed only on occasion of an embassy, or of an expedition into foreign states. No private person may go abroad without leave of the government; and if he bring back with him any foreign money, he must deposit it in the hands of the magistrate, or he, and all who are privy to the concealment, shall forfeit twice the value, and incur disgrace.

P. 742. No securities shall be given among citizens in any case: no fortune paid on a marriage; no money lent on interest.

The folly of a legislator who thinks of making a great, a flourishing, a rich, and a happy state, without regard to the virtue [1] of the inhabitants.

P. 743. The inconsistency of great wealth [2] and of great virtue. The good men will never acquire any thing by unjust means, nor ever refuse to be at any expense on decent and honest occasions. He, therefore, who scruples [3] not to acquire by fair and by unfair

[1] Vid. L. 4. p. 707.
[2] V. de Republ. l. 4. p. 421. and L. 8. p. 552.
[3] Ἡ εκ δικαιου και αδικου κτησις πλεον η διπλασια εστι της εκ του δικαιου μονον· τα τε αναλωματα μητε καλως μητε αισχρως

means, and will be at no expense on any occasion, must
naturally be thrice as rich as the former.   A good man
will not 'lavish all he has in idle pleasures and prodigality; he will not therefore be very poor.   Business
and [1] acquisition ought to employ no more of our time,
than may be spared from the improvement of our mind
and of our body.

P. 744. A colony cannot be formed of men perfectly
equal in point of fortune; it will be therefore necessary
to divide the citizens into classes according to their
circumstances, that they may pay impositions to the
publick service in proportion to them.   The wealthier
members are also, cæteris paribus, to be preferred
before others to offices and dignities of expense; which
will bring every one's fortune gradually to a level.

Four such classes to be instituted : the first worth
the value of his land, the fourth, four times as much.
Above or below this proportion no one is to go, on pain
of forfeiture and disgrace : therefore, the substance of
every man is to be publickly enrolled, under the inspec-
tion of a magistracy.

P. 745. The division of the country.   Every man's
lot is to consist of two half-shares, the one near the
city, the other near the frontier : every one also is to
have two houses, likewise within the city, the one near
the midst of it, the other near the walls.   The country
is to be divided into twelve tribes, and the city into as

εθελοντα αναλισκεσθαι των καλων, και εις καλα εθελοντων δαπα-
νᾶσθαι διπλασιως ελαττονα. —Ουκ εισιν δι παμπλουσιοι αγαθοι, ει
δε μη αγαθοι, ουδε ευδαιμονες.

[1] Οποσα μη χρηματιζομενον αναγκασεῖεν αμελειν, ὡν ενεκα
πεφυκε τα χρηματα· ταυτα δ' εστι ψυχη και σωμα.

many regions ; and each of them to be dedicated to its several divinity.

P. 746. An apology for this scheme, which to some will seem impracticable.

P. 747. The great difference of climates and of situations, and the sensible effects which they produce not on the bodies alone, but on the souls of men, are stated.

THE END OF THE FIFTH BOOK.

* * * * *

It is matter of just but unavailing regret, that Mr. Gray proceeded no further in his analysis and annotations on the books of Plato De Legibus.—[MATHIAS.]

THE EPISTLES.

Ed. Serrani, H. Steph. 1578. Vol. 3. p. 309, &c.

· DIOGENES LAERTIUS, who lived probably about the time of Septimius Severus, in the catalogue he gives us of Plato's works, counts thirteen epistles, and enumerates their titles, by which they appear to be the same as those which we now have. Yet we are not thence to conclude them to be all genuine alike. Fictions of this kind are far more ancient than that author's time; and his judgment and accuracy were not sufficient to distinguish the true from the false, as plainly appears from those palpable forgeries, the letters of the seven sages, which yet easily passed upon him as genuine.

EPISTLE I.   To DIONYSIUS.   Ol. 103. 2.

Plat. Op. Serrani, Vol. 3. p. 309.

This letter is not from Plato, but from his favourite scholar, the famous Dion; nor is it possible that the philosopher himself could have any hand in it, he being with Dionysius at Syracuse (as he tells us himself) when Dion was forced away, and continuing there some time after.   It is sent by Baccheus, who had conducted Dion on his way, together with a sum of money which Dionysius had ordered to be given to him for his expenses, which he returns to the tyrant with much contempt. The spirit of it and the sentiments are not amiss; and yet it is not very consistent with the indignation which Dion must have felt, and with the suddenness of the occasion, to end his letter with three scraps of poetry, though never so well applied. To say the truth, I much doubt of this epistle, and the more so, as it contradicts a fact in Plutarch, who assures us, that at the same time when Dion was hurried away, his friends were permitted to load two ships with his wealth and furniture, and to transport them to him in Pelopounesus, besides which [1] his revenues were regularly remitted to him, till Plato went into Sicily for the last time, which was at least six years after.

EPISTLE II.   To Dionysius.   Ol. 105. 1.

Plat. Op. Serrani, Vol. 3. p. 310.

This epistle appears to have been written soon after Plato's return [2] from his third voyage to Syracuse, and the interview which he had with Dion at the olympick games, which he himself mentions, Epist. 7. p. 350. and in this place also. Archedemus, who brought the letter from Dionysius, and returned with this answer,

[1] Ου πολυν χρονον διαλιπων, &c. Plato, Ep. 7. p. 345.
[2] The reasons for placing the voyages of Plato so early, and Dion's banishment so different from the chronology of Diodorus, will appear in the observations on Plato's seventh epistle.

310   NOTES ON PLATO.

was a friend and follower of Archȳtas, the Pythagorean
of Tarentum (Epist. 7. p. 339.), but was himself probably a Syracusan; at least he had a house in that
city where Plato was lodged, after he had been turned
out of the citadel. (Ibid. p. 349.) He was sent on
board a ship of war (with Dionysius's letters of invitation to Plato, wherein he pressed him to come the
third time into Sicily), as a person well known and
much esteemed by the philosopher, and he is mentioned
as present in the gardens of the palace at an interview
which Plato had with Dionysius, about three weeks
before he returned home again. (Ep. 3. sub fin.)

NOTES ON THE GREEK TEXT.

P. 311. Δοξαν εχων πολυ των εν φιλοσοφια διαφε-
ρειν.] It may be observed that Plato's reputation was
at the height before he went to the court of the younger
Dionysius, that is, before he was sixty-two years of age.

P. 312. Αλλα δε εσπουδακας.] In the intervals
between Plato's two last voyages, Dionysius had been
philosophizing with Archȳtas and others, and perhaps
with Aristippus. See Ep. 7. 338.

Ib. Φραστεον δη σοι δι' αινιγμων.] We[1] see here
that Plato, as well as the Pythagoreans whom he
imitated in many respects, made a mystery of his art :
for none but adepts were to understand him. It was
by conversation only that he cared to communicate
himself on these subjects.[2] In the seventh epistle he

[1] See Theodoret, Serm. 1. ad. Græcos.
[2] And in the end of this very epistle, p. 314. Ουδ' εστι συγγραμμα Πλατωνος ουδεν, ουδ' εσται· τα δε νυν λεγομενα Σωκρατους

professes never to have written any thing on philosophy ; and all that has been published in his name he attributes to Socrates. As I am not initiated, it is no wonder if this passage is still a riddle to me, as it was designed to be. Thus much one may divine indeed ; namely, that it is a description of the Supreme Being, who is the cause and end of all things, which is an answer to Dionysius's first question ; the second seems to be concerning the origin of evil, which Plato does not explain, but refers to a conversation which they had had before.

P. 314. Φιλιστιωνι.] Philistio was a Syracusan,[1] famous for his knowledge in physick : Eudoxus of Gnidos, a person accomplished in various kinds of learning, was his scholar in this art. Diog. Laert. L. 8. c. 86.

Ib. Σπευσιππω.] Speusippus had accompanied his uncle Plato into Sicily, and continued there after him ; where (as Plutarch[2] says) he thoroughly acquainted himself with the temper and inclinations of the city, and was a principal promoter of Dion's expedition.

Ib. Τον εκ των Λατομιων.] This was some prisoner of state, as it seems, who was confined in those horrid

εστι, καλου και νεου γεγονοτος : which is a remarkable passage. This is alluded to by Theodoret, Serm. 1. Vol. 4. ed. Simondi. See Epist. 7. p. 341. Ουκουν εμον γε περι αυτων εστι συγγραμμα ουδε μηποτε γενηται, &c. See also Athenæus, L. 15. p. 702.

[1] Athenæus, who cites him L. 3. p. 115. calls him a Locrian, as does Plutarch, Sympos. L. 7. Quæst. 1. Μαρτυρων τω Πλατωνι, προσκαλουμαι Φιλιστιωνα τον Λοκρον, ευ μαλα παλαιον ανδρα, και λαμπρον απο της τεχνης ιμων γενομενον. See also Rufus Ephesius, p. 31. so that this seems the more probable.

[2] Plutarch in Dione.

caverns, the Latomiæ, which was the publick dungeon
of the Syracusans, being a vast quarry in that part of
the city, called the Epipolæ. Thucydides L. 7. and
various other [1] authors speak of this place. Tully
particularly describes it in the fifth oration against
Verres. See Cluverii Sicilia Antiqua. L. 1. p. 149.

EPISTLE III.   To Dionysius.   Ol. 105. 4.

Plat. Op. Serrani, Vol. 3. p. 315.

This epistle, like those to the friends of Dion afterwards, was apparently written to be made publick ; and
is a justification of Plato's conduct, as well as an
invective against the cruelty and falsehood of Dionysius. The beginning of the letter is a reproach, the
more keen for being somewhat disguised ; and in the
rest of it, he observes no longer any measures with the
tyrant : whence I conclude, that it was written after
that Dion's expedition against him was professedly
begun, and perhaps after his entry into Syracuse, particularly from that expression, p. 315. Νῦν δε Διωνα
διδασκοιμι δρᾶν αντα ταυτα, και τοις διανοημασι τοις
σοις την σην αρχην αφαιρουμεθα σε, κτλ.

NOTES ON THE GREEK TEXT.

P. 315. Ευ πραττειν.] This address of letters was
first used by Plato instead of Χαιρειν, the common form
of salutation.

Ib. Τας δε Ελληνιδας πολεις οικιζειν.] The Greek

---

[1] Ælian. Var. Hist. L. 12. c. 44.

cities, which had been either totally destroyed, or dis-
mantled, and miserably oppressed by the Carthaginians
and by the elder Dionysius, were Himera, Agrigentum,
Gela, Camerina, Messana, Naxus, Catana, and Leontini.
P. 315. Ὑπο Φιλιστιδου.] I doubt not but it should
be read Φιλιστου. Philistus, who had married a natural
daughter of Leptines, the king's uncle, and commanded
his fleet, was an inveterate enemy of Plato. He had
been recalled from his banishment in Italy, on purpose
to oppose Dion and his friends. (Plutarch in Dione.)

Ib. Χαιρε και ἡδομενον.] The addresses to the
Delphick Apollo, as well as his answers, were often in
verse. This of Dionysius seems to have been sent on
account of Dion's first successes in Sicily.

P. 316. Νομων προοιμια.] Syracuse had been
governed ever since Ol. 91. 4. by the laws of Diocles,
whose history and character Diodorus gives us. (L. 13.
c. 33. and 35.) Plato began to form a new body of
them, but his quarrel with Dionysius, and afterwards
the murder of Dion, and the tumults which followed,
hindered his system from being brought to any degree
of perfection. Timoleon was happier in his great
attempt; he restored Syracuse to its liberty, and,
with the advice of Cephalus the Corinthian, supplied
and amended the laws of Diocles: and afterwards, in
the reign of Hiero, they were again revised or corrected
by Polylarus. Yet these were only looked on as
Εξηγηται των Νομων; Diocles alone bore the title of
Νομοθετης, and had publick honours paid to him as to
a hero. His laws were adopted by several other cities
in the island, and continued in use down to the times

of Julius Cæsar (which is about three hundred and
sixty-eight years) when the Sicilians received the Jus
Latii.

P. 316. Εν ἡλικιᾳ δε οντος μεση και καθεστηκυια.]
Cornelius Nepos tells us that Dion was fifty-five years
old at his death, so that he must have been about forty-
one when Plato came the second time into Sicily. See
also Epist. 7. p. 328. 'Ηλικιας τε ηδη μετριως εχον.

Ib. Σφοδρα νεον.] Dionysius was, I suppose, at
least twenty years younger than Dion.

Ib. Πλευσαι μεν οικαδε εμε.] I defer examining
into the time of Plato's voyages into Sicily, and his
stay there, that I may do it all at once when I come
to the seventh epistle.

P. 317. Την θ' ἡλικιαν.] Plato was then about
sixty-seven years old.

P. 318. Ξυνεχης.] Read, ξυνεχη τω νυν γενομενιω·
this is his apology to the first accusation; he has said
in the beginning, προς δυω δη μοι διττας αναγκαιον
ποιησασθαι απολογιας.

P. 319. Ουκουν παιδευθεντα (εφησθα) γεωμετρειν;
η πως;] I do not understand the meaning of this
insult at all: it relates, however, to the advice which
Plato had ventured to give him, that he should lighten
the load of the Syracusans, and voluntarily limit his
own power.

EPISTLE IV. To Dion. Ol. 105. 4.

Plat. Op. Serrani, Vol. 3. p. 320.

This was written probably the same year with the former, or the beginning of the next, on account of those differences which Dion had with Heraclides and his uncle Theodotes, who at last drove him out of Syracuse : their history may be seen in the seventh epistle, and in Plutarch.

NOTES ON THE GREEK TEXT.

P. 320. Την εμην προθυμιαν.] Plato, after all his ill usage from Dionysius, expressed some backwardness to join in the expedition against him, as appears Ep. 7. p. 350. where he expresses some little tenderness which he retained for him, when he reflected on their former familiarity ; and that the king amidst all his anger and suspicions, had attempted on his life : however, when he saw Dion engaged, he joined in the cause with great zeal, and assisted him with all his power.

Ib. Αναιρεθεντος.] This seems to fix the time to Ol. 106. 1. for when Dionysius had sailed away to Locri, and his son Apollocrates had surrendered the citadel, it was natural to imagine that his empire was at an end.

P. 320. Ενδεεστερως του προσηκοντος θεραπευτικος.] Plutarch cites this passage in Dion's life ; and another in the same epistle.

Ib. Το δε νυν υπαρχον περι σε, &c. as above.

EPISTLE V.   To Perdiccas.   Ol. 103. 4.

Plat. Op. Serrani, Vol. 3. p. 321.

Perdiccas, the second son of Amyntas, succeeded to
the crown of Macedon, after the death of his brother
in law, Ptolemy of Alorus, Ol. 103. 4.   There seem
to have been ancient ties of hospitality and of friendship between the royal family of Macedon, from
Archelaus's time, and the principal literati of Athens.
Plato here recommends his friend and scholar, Euphræus, a native of Oreus in Eubœa, to be of Perdiccas's
council, and his secretary.   He grew into the highest
favour with Perdiccas, and was trusted with the entire
management of all his affairs.   He used his power
arbitrarily enough.   Caristius,[1] of Pergamus, gives the
following instance of it; that, he would not suffer any
one to sit at the king's table, who was ignorant of
geometry or of philosophy.   And yet to Plato and to
Euphræus did the great Philip of Macedon owe his
succession to the kingdom, (as [2] Speusippus writes
in a letter to Philip reproaching him with his
ingratitude,) for by them was his brother Perdiccas
persuaded to bestow on him some districts as an
appanage, where, after his death, Philip was enabled
to raise troops, and to recover the kingdom.   Euphræus,
upon the death of his master, having rendered himself
hateful to the principal Macedonians, was obliged, as
it seems, to retire into his own country; where, soon

[1] Ap. Athenæum, L. 11. sub fin. p. 506. and 508.
[2] Ap. Athenæum, ut supra.

after Philip was settled on the throne, Parmenio was ordered to murder him.

Ficinus and H. Stephanus, finding in the margin of some manuscripts this fifth epistle ascribed to Dion, and not to Plato, seem inclined to admit that correction, but without reason. Plato has in his other undoubted epistles spoken of himself, as he has done in this, in the third person. He is here apologising for his recommendation of a man, who was to have a share in the administration of a kingdom. Some may object (says he), "How should Plato be a competent judge, he who has never meddled in the government of his own country, nor thought himself fit to advise his own citizens?" He answers this by shewing his reasons for such a conduct; but the last sentence, Ταυτον δη οιμαι δρᾶσαι, &c. is not at all clear. The thought is the very same with that in the famous seventh epistle to Dion's friends, (Εγω τον συμβουλευοντα ανδρι καμνοντι, &c. p. 330.) but some principal word seems to be omitted; perhaps after δρᾶσαι αν should be inserted ιατρικον ανδρα, or ιατρον αγαθον.

EPISTLE VI.   To HERMEIAS, ERASTUS, AND CORISCUS.
The date not settled.
Plat. Op. Serrani, Vol. 3. p. 322.

This letter, cited by Clemens Alexandrinus (Strom. L. 5.) and by Origen (contra Celsum, L. 6.), Menage [1] tells us is no longer extant among the epistles of Plato,

[1] Ad. Diog. Laertium, L. 3. c. 57. See also Card. Quirini Decas Epistolarum Romæ 1743. 4to. p. 23.

and is supposed to be a fiction of the Christians. Bentley[1] had reason to wonder at the negligence of that critick, who did not know that the epistle was still preserved : and he adds, that there is no cause to believe the letter not to be genuine, as there are passages in the Dialogues themselves as favourable to the Christian opinions, as any thing in this epistle. The passage, which those Fathers cite, is at the end of the letter, and has indeed much the air of a forgery. I do not know any passages in the Dialogues[2] equally suspicious ; nor do I see why it might not be tacked to the end of an undoubtedly original letter : there is nothing else here but what seems genuine.

Erastus and Coriscus were followers of Plato, and born at Scepsis,[3] a city of Troas, seated on mount Ida, not far from the sources of the Scamander and of the Æsepus : they seem to have attained a principal autho-

[1] Bentley in Philelenthero Lipsiensi.

[2] Vid. de Republ. L. 6. p. 506. Εκγονος τε του Αγαθου, και ὁμοιοτατος εκεινω . . . ὁ τοκος. By which he means the idea of Himself, which the Sovereign Good has bestowed on us, and which is the cause of knowledge and of truth. The Supreme Good itself he calls 'Ο Πατηρ, and compares him to the sun, ὁ Κυριος του φωτος. Vid. et ibid. L. 7. p. 516.

[3] Vid. Strabonem, L. 13. p. 602. and 607. The Coriscus here mentioned had a son called Neleus, a follower of Aristotle and a particular friend of Theophrastus, who left his library (in which was contained all that Aristotle had ever written, in the original manuscript) to him, when he died. It continued in the possession of his family at Scepsis, about one hundred and fifty years, when Apellicon of Teos purchased and transferred it to Athens, whence, soon after, Sylla carried it to Rome. (Strabo, L. 13. p. 602. and 607 ; Plutarch in Sylla, and Diog. Laert. in Theophrasto.)

rity in their little state, and Plato recommends to them
here to cultivate the friendship of Hermias their neighbour, and sovereign of Assus and Atarneus, two strong
towns on the coast of the Sinus Adramyttenus near the
foot of Ida. Coriscus had also been scholar to Plato,[1]
though an eunuch, and slave to Eubulus, a Bythynian
and a banker. His master having found means to erect
a little principality in the places before mentioned, made
Hermias his heir. He gave his niece Pythias in marriage to Aristotle, who lived with him near three years,
till Ol. 107. 4. about which time Memnon[2] the Rhodian, general to the Persian king, by a base treachery[3]
got him into his hands, and sending him to court he
was there hanged. (Strabo, L. 13. p. 610. and Suidas.)
Aristotle wrote his epitaph,[4] and a beautiful ode[5] or
hymn in honour to his memory, which are still[6] extant.

[1] So Strabo tells us ; but Plato himself says, that he had
never conversed with him. 'Οσα μηπω ξυγγεγονοτι, &c. infra.

[2] Or Mentor, his brother, according to Diodorus, L. 16.
c. 52. which is right. See Aristot. Œconomic. ap. Leon.
Aretinum, L. 2. c. 38.

[3] Probably he had taken part in the grand rebellion of the
Satrapæ against the Persian king (which caused their indignation), and had shaken off his dependency.

[4] See Antholog. Gr. p. 526. Ed. H. Stephani. It was inscribed on a cenotaph erected to him and Eubulus jointly by
Aristotle ; for which piece of gratitude Theocritus of Chios has
abused him in a satirical epigram : Antholog. ib. p. 523.

'Ερμειου ευνουχου ηδ' Ευβουλου άμα δουλου
      Σημα κενον κενοφρων τευξεν Αριστοτελης.

[5] Vid. Athenæum, L. 15. p. 696. and Diog. Laert. L. 5. in
Aristotele.

[6] After the words, μαλιστα μεν αθροους· ει δε μη, insert κατα
δυο κοινῆ, from the Vatican MSS. (See Montfaucon Bibl.
Bibliothecarum, p. 2.)

P. 323. Ὁ εστι δικαιον.] There I take the true
epistle to end; as what follows is very extraordinary
as to the sense and the expression: Του τε ἡγεμονος
και αιτιου Πατερα Κυριον, ὁν—ειϲομεθα ϲαφως, εἰς
δυναμιν ανθρωπων ευδαιμονων.

EPISTLE VII. To the Friends and Relations of Dion.

Ol. 105. 4.

Plat. Op. Serrani, Vol. 3. p. 323.

Callippus, after the treacherous murder of Dion, was
attacked in Syracuse by the friends of that great man,
but they were worsted by him and his party; and,
being driven out, they fled to the Leontini, and he
maintained his power in the city for thirteen months,
(Diodor. Sic. L. 16. c. 36.) till [1] Hipparinus, nephew
to Dion, and half-brother to Dionysius, found means to
assemble troops; and while Callippus was engaged in
the siege of Catana, he, at the head of Dion's party,
re-entered Syracuse, and kept possession of it for two
years.   At the end of which time Hipparinus, in a
drunken debauch, was assassinated, but by whom I do
not find; and his younger brother, Nysæus, succeeded
to his power, and made the most arbitrary use of it for

[1] See Theopompus ap. Athenæum, L. 10. p. 435. and 436.
where we should correct the mistake of Athenæus, and of Ælian,
who call Apollocrates son to the elder Dionysius; for he was
(as Plutarch often repeats) the eldest son of the younger
Dionysius.

near five years; when Dionysius, returning from Locri, (see Plutarch in the life of Timoleon,) became once more master of Syracuse, and, as it seems, put Nysæus to death.

Who were the friends of Dion to whom Plato writes, is hard to enumerate: the principal were his son[1] Hipparinus, and his sister's son, likewise called Hipparinus, and his brother, Megacles, if living, though I rather imagine he had been killed in the course of the war before the death of Dion; and Hicetas, who afterwards was tyrant of the Leontines.

Plato was about forty years of age, when first he came to Syracuse. His fortieth year was Ol. 97. 4.

<hr/>

NOTES ON THE GREEK TEXT.

P. 323. Σχεδον ετη τετταρακοντα γεγονως.] Plato was about forty years of age, when he first came to Syracuse: his fortieth year was Olymp. 97. 4. Archonte Antipatro. Diodorus mentions the same fact three years later, but does not expressly say when it happened; and Dion was then in his twentieth year: consequently Hipparinus was now about twenty. But whether the son of Dion, or his nephew, be here meant, is hard to distinguish; if it could be proved to be the former, Plutarch would be convicted of a mistake. (See the next Epistle.) We must read here, συμφωνον ποιησειε, as Serranus observes.

[1] I call him by the name of Hipparinus, because Timonides the Leucadian, a principal friend of Dion, assures us of it (ap. Plutarch.), and his testimony must doubtless be preferred to that of Timæus, who gives this youth the name of Aretæus. See Plato's eighth Epistle.

P. 324. Μεταβολη γιγνεται.] This great change in
the Athenian constitution took place, when Plato was
in his twenty-fifth year.

Ib. 'Ενδεκα μεν εν Αστει, δεκα δ' εν Πειραιει.] The
'Ενδεκα were a magistracy, to whom persons condemned
to death were consigned, and who presided over the
prisons and executions. Those who bore this office
under the Thirty were their creatures, and at the head
of them was Satyrus, whom Xenophon calls, ὁ θρασυ-
τατος αυτων και αναιδεστατος. (See Xen. Hist. Græc.
L. 2. p. 470. Ed. Leunclavii. 1625.) He seems upon
some vacancy (possibly on the death of Theramenes)
to have been afterwards elected one of the Thirty.
(See Lysias in Nichomachum, p. 476. Ed. Taylori, and
Palmerius ad locum.) The Ten, who commanded in
the Piræeus, were appointed by the authority of the
Thirty, and were probably the accomplices of their
guilt, (Xenoph. Hist. Græc. L. 2. p. 474 and 478.)
being with them and the Eleven, were excepted out of
the general amnesty.

Ib. Οικειοι και γνωριμοι.] Critias, a man as remarkable for the brightness of his parts as for the
depravity of his manners and for the hardness of his
heart, was Plato's second cousin by the mother's side;
and Charmides, the son of Glauco, was his uncle,
brother to his mother, Perictione. The first was one
of the Thirty, the latter one of the Ten, and both were
slain in the same action. Plato's family were deeply
engaged in the oligarchy; for Callæschrus, (See Lysias
in Eratosthenem, p. 215.) his great-uncle, had been a
principal man in the Council of Four hundred. (Ol.

92. 1.) It is a strong proof of Plato's honesty and resolution, that his nearest relations could not seduce him to share in their power, or in their crimes at that age. (Xenoph. Apomnemon. L. 3. c. 6 and 7, and in Symposio.) His uncle, though a great friend of Socrates and of a very amiable character, had not the same strength of mind.

P. 324. Επι τινα των πολιτων.] The Thirty, during the short time of their magistracy, which was less than a year, put fifteen hundred persons to death, (Isocr. Orat. Areopagitic. Ed. A. Steph. 1593, p. 153.) most of whom were innocent, and they obliged about five thousand more to fly. The prisoner here meant was Leo, the Salaminian. (See Apolog. p. 32.)

P. 326. Λεγειν τε ηναγκασθην.] These are the sentiments which he has explained at large in his Πολιτειαι, (L. 5. p. 472, &c.) and one would thence imagine that he had written, and perhaps published that celebrated work before his first voyage to Sicily, and consequently before he was forty years old. It is certain, that there are some scenes in the Εκκλησια-ζουσαι of Aristophanes, (ver. 568 &c. Ed. Kusteri.) which seem intended to ridicule the system of Plato, and the Scholia affirm that it was written with that view. If so, he must have finished it, when he was thirty-five years of age, or earlier, for that comedy was played Ol. 96. 4.

P. 327. Εις Συρακουσας ότι ταχιστα ελθειν εμε.] Hence, and from Plutarch, it is certain that Plato was invited into Sicily immediately after the death of the elder Dionysius, which happened Ol. 103. 1. so that

we must necessarily place his second voyage to Syracuse
that very year, or the next at farthest; and it is as
sure, that, four months after his arrival, happened the
quarrel between Dionysius and Dion, and the banishment of the latter.   I cannot but observe the inaccuracy
of Diodorus, who says that this last event happened
Ol. 105. 3. which is a mistake of at least ten years.
See also Aulus Gellius, L. 17. c. 21. who is likewise
mistaken in placing this voyage of Plato after the
year 400 of Rome, and after the birth of Alexander.—
Hence we see the folly of trusting to compilers where
we might recur to original authors.

P. 328. Ουκ ἢ τινες εδοξαζον.] Plato had been
most severely reflected upon for passing his time at
the court of Dionysius.   Athenæus (a very contemptible writer, though his book is highly valuable for the
numberless fragments of excellent authors, now lost, of
which it is composed) has taken care to preserve
abundance of scandal on this head. L. 11. p. 507. and
see Laertius in his life.   This and the third Epistle
are his justification of himself, and are written with a
design to clear his character.

Ib. Ελθοι παρ' ὑμας φευγων.]   Read παρ' ἡμᾶς.

P. 330. Μετα δε τουτο απεδημησα.]   We are not
informed how long Plato staid, after Dion was sent away,
but probably many months; the preceding account of
Dionysius's treatment of him implies as much.

P. 331. Πατερα δε ουκ ὁσιον.]   Cicero alludes to
this sentiment, and to that of the same in the 5th
Epistle, in his Letter to Lentulus, L. 1. ad Familiares,
Ep. 1.   "Id enim jubet idem illo Plato, quem ego

vehementer auctorem sequor," &c., where he expresses the thought, but not the words.

P. 331. Πολιτειας μεταβολης.] Insert περι, or ένεκα.

P. 332. Αδελφων, όυς εθρεψε.] Leptines and Thearides.

Ib. Τον Μηδον και Ευνουχον.] He follows some history, in this transaction,' seemingly different from Herodotus and Ctesias. The Mede is Smerdis, one of the Magi, which was an order of men instituted in Media; and to carry on so strange a cheat as that usurpation, it is sure that the concurrence of the eunuchs of the palace must have been necessary; but what particular eunuch he means is hard to say. Ctesias says, that the counterfeit Tanyoxarces was betrayed to the conspirators by his eunuchs.

P. 333. Ὁ πατηρ αυτον φορον εταξατο φερειν τοις βαρβαροις.] The elder Dionysius being defeated by the Carthaginians at Cronium, in a great battle, Ol. 99. 2. was forced to make peace on their terms, and engaged to pay them one thousand talents. Fifteen years afterwards he engaged with them in another war, and lost one hundred and thirty of his best ships, which they surprised, and took or destroyed in the bay of Eryx or Drepanum: he died the same year, and left his son with this war upon his hands. Thus far Diodorus, L. 15, c. 17 and 73. Whether the Carthaginians had offered peace on condition of a new tribute, or had never been paid the old one, we can only guess from this expression of Plato; yet I am inclined to think, both from the third Epistle and from this, that Dionysius the father had agreed to a peace before his death, and

consented to pay a tribute to Carthage; and that his
son entered not again into the war till two or three
years afterwards, which lasted probably not three years.
We must not wonder if we find little account of this in
Diodorus, as he has said nothing at all of the eight first
years of Dionysius the younger ; only in the ninth year
(which is Ol. 105. 2.) he tells us that he made peace
with Carthage and the Lucanians : but it does not, by
the narration, appear to be a transaction of that year,
but rather makes part of a summary account of what
had passed since his father's death.   That peace was
certainly made about four years earlier than Diodorus
seems to have placed it.

P. 333. Απεδωκεν αυτος δις την πολιν.] Have a
care of correcting this passage, as Serranus has done,
who reads instead of δις, Διων. It is again repeated in
the next, or eighth Epistle, p. 355. Εγω δε απο
τυραννων νυν δις. He twice preserved Syracuse, first
by driving out Dionysius, and afterwards by beating
Nypsius, the Neapolitan. See Plutarch.

Ib. Αδελφω δυω.] They were Callippus and Philo-
crates, or (as some MSS. of Cornelius Nepos have it)
Philostratus.

P. 336. 'Αυτη παντα το δευτερον.] 'Αυτη seems to
agree with αμαθια. Either a word is lost, or the sentence
is an example of that ανακολουθια, which is not uncommon with Attick writers.

P. 338. 'Οτι γερων τε ειην.] Plato was then about
sixty-six years old.

P. 339. Τα νομιμα.] The usual salutations and
compliments at the beginning of a letter.

P. 340. Τοις των Παρακονσματων μεστοις.] This
word (Παρακονσμα) means a transitory application to
any science, sufficient to give a superficial tincture of
knowledge, but neither deep, nor lasting. Such proficients Plato calls, δοξαις επικεχρωσμενοι.

P. 342. I know not what to say to this very uncommon opinion of Plato, that no philosopher should
put either his system, or the method of attaining to
a knowledge of it, into writing. The arguments he
brings in support of it are obscure beyond my comprehension. All I conceive is, that he means to shew,
how inadequate words are to express our ideas, and
how poor a representation even our ideas are of the
essence of things. What he says, on the bad effects
which a half-strained and superficial knowledge produces in ordinary minds, is certainly very just and very
fine. See the Phædrus, p. 274 to p. 276, where he.
compares all written arts to the gardens of Adonis,
which look gay and verdant, but, having no depth of
earth, soon wither away. Lord Bacon expresses himself strongly on this head. " Homines per sermones
sociantur ; at verba ex captu vulgi imponuntur : itaque
mala et inepta verborum impositio miris modis intel-
lectum obsidet. Neque definitiones aut explicationes,
quibus homines docti se munire et vindicare in nonnullis
consueverunt, rem ullo modo restituunt, sed verba planè
vim faciunt intellectui, et omnia turbant, et homines
ad inanes et innumeras controversias deducunt." (Nov.
Organ. L. 1. aphorism 43 and 59.)

P. 342. Ονομα.] Is the name of a thing ; Λογος is
the definition, or verbal description of its properties ;

Ειδωλον, its representation by a figure to our senses ;
Επιστημη, the mental comprehension, or the complete
and just idea of it : what the το πεμπτον is, I do not
know, except it be the perfect notion of things, such
as it exists in the mind of the Divinity.

P. 343. I put a comma after και ταυτα εις αμετα-
κινητον, and read, ο τε δη πασχει· &c.

P. 344. We here learn that Dionysius had written
a treatise on philosophy.

P. 345. Αδελφιδου αυτου.] Arete, Dion's wife, was
half-sister to Dionysius, consequently, Hipparinus, her
son, was his nephew.

P. 345. Ιττω Ζευς, φησιν ο Θηβαιος.] That is
Pindar, as I imagine; though I find not the expression in any of his odes extant. It was a common
phrase with the Bœotians, Ιττω 'Ηρακλης, ιττω Ζευς.
.See Aristophan. Acharn. v. 911. the French use "Dieu
sçait," and we say, "God knows," in the same manner.

P. 346. Καρπουσθω δε Διων.] Let him receive the
rents, or interest, but let him not touch the principal.

Ib. Εις δε ωρας.] The next summer, when the
season returns for sailing.

P. 348. Theodotes was uncle to Heraclides, as
Plutarch says : and I imagine that Euribius was his
brother. See the life of Dion.

P. 349. Εις την Καρχηδονιων επικρατειαν.] Sicily
was then divided between the Carthaginians and the
Syracusans.

P. 350. Των υπηρεσιων.] Athenians that served on
board the fleet of Dionysius for hire.

Ib. Πεμπουσι τριακοντορον.] The Tarentine de-

puties were Lamiscus and Photidas. The original
letter in the Dorick dialect is preserved by Diogenes
Laertius in his life of Plato.

Ib. Εἰς Ὀλυμπίαν Δίωνα καταλαβὼν θεωροῦντα.]
Hence we may settle pretty exactly the time of Plato's
third voyage. It is plain that he landed (on his
return) in Peloponnesus, and immediately went to
Olympia, where the games were then celebrating, to
acquaint Dion with what so nearly concerned him.
This must be Ol. 105. 1. It could not be earlier,
because there is not time from the death of Dionysius
the elder for all that happened, according to Plato's
own account, in his two voyages and in the interval
between them. He went not to Syracuse at soonest
before Ol. 103. 1. and probably not till the year following : he staid there at least a year, and came back
because of the war which broke out in Sicily. When
that was over (and it could not well be determined in less
than one campaign) Dionysius invited him back again.
He hesitated a full year, and then went; and he spent
a year and upwards at Syracuse, before he returned :
all which must be, on the least computation, above five
years. Besides the improbability that Dion, after he
lost his revenues, and was deprived of his wife, should
be near seven years before he attempted to right himself. As I have placed it, he was near three years in
preparing for his design, which he executed Ol. 105. 4.
as Diodorus tells us, and which Plutarch confirms,
reckoning forty-eight years from the establishment of
Dionysius the elder's tyranny to Dion's entry into
Syracuse. He began to reign Ol. 93. 4. from which

to Ol. 105. 4. is just forty-eight years. See Xenoph.
Græc. Hist. L. 2. p. 460. and Dodwell's Annals. It
was in the beginning of the year, for Plutarch tells us
that it was the midst of summer, the Etesian winds
then blowing; and the olympick year began after the
summer solstice. · If then Plato came to Olympia,
Ol. 105. 1. he must have gone to Syracuse towards the
end of Ol. 104. 3. for, from his own account, he must
have passed a year or more there.

EPISTLE VIII.   To the Friends of Dion.   Ol. 106. 4.

From a passage in this epistle (p. 354. τον των
Εφορων δασμον.) it appears that Plato, as well as
Herodotus, makes Lycurgus the author of the institution of the *Ephori*, and not Theopompus, as late writers
do.   See Aristot. Politic. L. 5. c. 11.

NOTES ON THE GREEK TEXT.

P. 352. Πλην ειτις αυτων ανοσιουργος γεγονε.]   He
means those engaged in the murder of Dion, Callippus
and his brother, and their party.

P. 353. Κινδυνος εγενετο εσχατος.]   When they had
sacked the rich and powerful city of Agrigentum, and
demolished it.   (Diodorus, L. 13.)

Ib. Οπικων.]   The ancient inhabitants of Campania,
particularly that country which lies round the Bay of
Naples. (Aristot. Politic. L. 8. c. 10.)   In a passage
cited from Aristotle by Dionysius Halicarnassensis (L.
1. p. 57. ed. Huds. Oxon. 1704.), he seems to extend

the name to all the inhabitants of that coast to the
south of the Tuscans. Aristotle mentions the Opici as
the same people with the Ausones; but Polybius
judged them to be a distinct people. (See Strabo, L.
5. p. 242.) The Siculi probably might speak the same
tongue, having been driven out of Italy (Thucyd. L. 6.
p. 349.) by these Opici some years after the Trojan
war, and settling in a part of this Island. This name
grew into a term of reproach, which the more polished
Greeks bestowed upon the Romans, as Cato the censor
complains in Pliny, L. 29. c. 1. "Nos quoque dictant
barbaros, et spurciùs nos quam alios *Opicos* appellatione
fœdant;" and in time it became a Latin word to
signify barbarous and illiterate. (See Tullius Tyro ap.
Aul. Gell. L. 13. c. 9. "Ita ut nostri *Opici* putaverunt,
&c.)

P. 354. Τους δεκα στρατηγους κατελευσαν.] This
fact is contrary to Diodorus, who only tells us, that
the generals were deposed; (L. 13. c. 92.) and that
afterwards, Daphnæus, the chief of them, and Demar-
chus (who were both enemies to Dionysius) were put
to death (Ib. c. 96.); neither does he inform us of
what we are here told, that Hipparinus, the father of
Dion, was joined in commission with Dionysius, both
being elected Στρατηγοι αυτοκρατορες, and both called
Τυραννοι. (See Aristot. Politic. L. 5. c. 6.)

P. 355. Τον εμον υιον.] This directly contradicts
both Plutarch and Cornelius Nepos, who particularly
describe the tragical end of Hipparinus, Dion's son,
when just arrived at man's estate. All that story, and
the apparition which preceded it, must be false, if this

epistle be genuine, which I see no reason, but this, for doubting. The only way to reconcile the matter is, by supposing that Plato might here mean the infant son of Dion, who was born after his father's death; and who was not yet destroyed by Hicetas, for Plutarch intimates, that he continued to treat both the child and its mother well for a considerable time after the expulsion of Callippus. What makes against this supposition is, that in the end of this letter, p. 357. he speaks of Dion's son, as of a person fit to judge of, and to approve, the scheme of government which he has proposed to all parties.

P. 356. Ἕκων τὴν πολιν ἐλευθεροῖ.] Here we see that Hipparinus, the son of Dionysius the elder by Aristomache, had put himself at the head of Dion's party, and supported the war against his brother.

EPISTLE IX. To Aᴆcᴨʏᴛᴀs.

The date not settled.

Plat. Op. Serrani, Vol. 3. p. 317.

NOTES ON THE GREEK TEXT.

P. 357. Ου δυνασαι της περι τα κοινα ασχολιας απολυ-θηναι.] Archytas was seven times elected Στρατηγος of Tarentum, which was then a democracy.

Ib. Κᾳκεινο δει σε ενθυμεῖσθαι, ὁτι ἑκαστος ἡμων ουκ ἁυτω μονον γεγονεν, αλλα της γενεσεως ἡμων το μεν τι ἡ πατρις μεριζεται, το δε τι, ὁι γεννησαντες· το δε, ὁι λοιποι φιλοι· πολλα δε τοις καιροις διδοται τοις τον βιον ἡμων καταλαμβανουσι. κτλ.] This fine sentiment is quoted by Cicero De Officiis, L. 1. c. 7. and again, De Finibus, L. 2. so that the seventh, the fourth, and this epistle, are of an authority not to be called in question.

P. 357. Προς την πολιν.] They were to negociate something with the Athenians.

Ib. Εχεκρατους.] Echecrates, the son of Phrynio, now a youth, was born at Phlius, and instructed in the Pythagorean principles by Archytas. Aristoxenus, a disciple of Aristotle (see Diog. Laert. L. 8. c. 46.), speaks of him as of a person whom he could remember, and one of the last of that sect who were considerable. Iamblichus also mentions him, c. 35. et ultim. de Vitâ Pythagoræ; and Plato introduces him as desiring to hear the manner of Socrates's death from Phædo.

EPISTLE X. To Aristodorus,

or, as Laertius writes, To Aristodemus.

The date not settled.

Plat. Op. Serrani, Vol. 3. p. 358.

AND

EPISTLE XI. To Laodamas.

The date not settled.

Plat. Op. Serrani, Vol. 3. p. 358.

Laodamas of Thasus was a great geometrician and scholar to Plato, who first taught him the method of analytick investigation. (See Laertius, L. 3. c. 24. and Proclus in Euclidem, L. 3. Prob. 1. and L. 2. P. 19.)

He seems from this letter to have been principally concerned in founding some colony.

NOTES ON THE GREEK TEXT.

P. 358. Η Σωκρατη.] This cannot possibly be the great Socrates, for he died when Plato was in his twenty-ninth year; and we see that in this passage he excuses himself from travelling on account of his age: it must, therefore, be the younger Socrates whom Plato introduces in his Πολιτικος (and in the Theætetus, p. 147. and in Sophista, p. 218. and 268.) and who is mentioned by Aristotle in his Metaphysicks. (L. 6. p. 370. edit. Sylburgii.)

P. 358. Παντα κινδυνων.] The most considerable settlements which happened in Plato's time, were those at Messenia and at Megalopolis, Ol. 102. and we are told that he was actually applied to by this last city to form for them a body of laws; but he excused himself. Whether Laodamas had any share in that foundation, I cannot tell; if he had, it is no wonder that Plato should object the danger of his journey into the Peloponnesus that year, when every thing was in the utmost confusion.

EPISTLE XII. To ARCHYTAS.

Plat. Op. Serrani, Vol. 3. p. 359.

This fragment (for such it is) is preserved by Laertius, together with the letter from Archýtas, to which it is an answer.

P. 359. Ὑπομνήματα.] He alludes to the comment-
aries of Ocellus, the Lucanian, which Archytas had
procured from the descendants of that philosopher.
The subjects of them were Περι Νομῳ, και βασιληϊας,
και ὁσιοτατος, και τὰς τω παντος γενεσιος; the last of
which is still in being.

Ib. Μυριοι.] Read Μυραῖσι, of Myra, a city in
Lycia. Homer speaks of another Lycia between mount
Ida and the Æsepus, subject to Troy : the Lycians, on
the south coast of Asia Minor, were probably a colony
from thence. (Strabo, L. 12. p. 565. and L. 14. p.
665.) The family of Ocellus might be originally of
Myra ; but the Lucanians in general were of Italian
origin, being sprung from the Samnites, who were a
colony of the Sabines.

P. 359. Τῆς Φυλακης.] The work of Plato was
undoubtedly his Πολιτεια, of which he sent a copy to
Archytas, who, he says, was of his own opinion as to
the institution of the Φυλακες : what they were see in
the Πολιτεια itself. None of the commentators on
Laertius have understood this passage.

This epistle is marked in the first editions of Plato
as spurious : (Αντιλεγεται ὡς ου Πλατωνος. MSS.
Vatican. cod. 1460. and Serranus sees mysteries here,
where there are none ; the same is said also of the
thirteenth epistle :) but there seems no reason for it.

EPISTLE XIII. To Dionysius.   Ol. 103. 3 or 4.

Plat. Op. Serrani, Vol. 3. p. 360.

In the order of time this is the second epistle in the
collection.   It is marked in the MSS. as spurious, and,
I must own, it does little honour to Plato's memory;
yet it is sure that Plutarch esteemed it genuine.   He
cites (in Vit. Dion.) a passage from it relating to Arete,
the wife of Dion ; and in his discourse περι Δυσωπιας,
he mentions the character of Helico the Cyzicenian,
which is to be found here.   I know not what to determine ; unless we suppose some parts of it to be inserted
afterwards by some idle sophist who was an enemy to
Plato's character.   It is observable, that Plutarch in
the place last mentioned says, ειτα προσεγραψε τη Επισ-
τολη τελευτωση, Γραφω δε σοι ταυτα περι ανθρωπου,
&c. whereas the words are here not far from the beginning.   Possibly some fragments of the true epistle
might remain, which were patched together and supplied by some trifler.

Helico, the astronomer, is mentioned by Plutarch
as in the court of Dionysius, when Plato was there for
the last time ; (and this letter was written four years
before, soon after Plato's return from his first voyage
to Syracuse) but we do not find elsewhere that he had
been a disciple of Eudoxus and of Polyxenus.

NOTES ON THE GREEK TEXT.

P. 360. Ειπερ ηκει παρα σε Αρχυτης.]   Plato in his
first voyage made a league of amity between Archytas

and Dionysius ; and after his return to Athens, Archytas
came to Syracuse, as Plato himself tells us in his seventh
epistle.

P. 360. Πολυξενω, των Βριτωνος τινι εταιρων.]
Polyxenus, the sophist, is mentioned by Laertius in
the life of Aristippus, sect. 76. Bryso, his master, had
also the famous Theban cynick, Crates, for his scholar,
as Laertius says L. 6. s. 85. who calls him Bryso, the
Achæan. But Theopompus (ap. Athenæum, L. 11.
p. 509.) informs us that he was of Heracleæ, and
accuses Plato of borrowing many things of him, which
he inserted in his dialogues. There is an elegant fragment from a comedy of Ephippus, where he reflects
alike on the scholars of Plato and of this Bryso (to
whom he gives the epithet of ὁ θρασυμαχειολημψικερ-
ματων), for their sordid desire of gain, and for the
studied neatness of their dress and person.

Ib. Ελαφρος και ειηθης.] Words here used in their
best sense,[1] "easy and well-natured." Plutarch interprets them επιεικης και μετριος.

P. 361. Τοτε οτ' οντ' εγω εστεφανοημην.] What is
meant by this date, I cannot divine. His brother's, or
sister's, daughters died at the time when Dionysius
ordered him to be crowned, though he was not. However, we learn that Plato had four great nieces, the
eldest then marriageable, the second, eight years old,
the third, above three, and the fourth, not one year
old ; and that he intended to marry the eldest to

---

[1] Plato in Republicâ. L. 3. p. 400. Ειηθεια, ουκ ην ανοιαν
ουσαν υποκοριζομενοι καλουμεν ως ειηθειαν, αλλα την ως αληθως ευ
τε και καλως το ηθος κατεσκευασμενην διανοιαν.

his nephew, Speusippus; but how she could be the daughter of that Speusippus's sister, I do not comprehend; so that I take it, we must either read Αδελφου here, or αποθανοντων before.

P. 362. Πεμψας Εραστον.] Hence we see that Erastus was still with Plato, and consequently the sixth epistle was written after this time.

P. 362. Κρατινω.] Here we find that Timotheus had a brother called Cratinus. This cannot, I think, be the great Timotheus, for his father, Conon, in his will (the substance of which is preserved in Lysias's oration in de Bonis Aristophanis, p. 345.) makes no mention of any other son he had, but this one.

P. 362. Των πολυτελων των Αμοργινων.] The fine linen of Amorgos, of which they made tunicks for women, was transparent. See the Lysistrata of Aristophanes, v. 46. and 150. and 736. where the Scholia call the plant, of which the thread was made ἡ λινοκαλαμη, and say, that it was in fineness ὑπερ την βυσσον, η την καρπασον : they were dyed of a bright red colour.

APPENDIX.

WHEN the fourth of these volumes was passing through the press, I was enabled, by the courtesy of Mr. John Morris, of 13 Park Street, Grosvenor Square, to examine the very curious and valuable collection of Graiana now in his possession. Of this collection, which has never been described, I will here give a brief account. It consists of five folio volumes, based upon a copy of Mathias's quarto edition of the *Works*, printed in 1814. This copy was presented by Mathias to Dawson Turner, who divided, enlarged, and rebound it. It was further again enlarged by Mr. John Dillon, from whom it passed, in its present condition, into the hands of Mr. J. Morris.

It is not necessary to describe all the portraits, illustrations, letters from persons interested in Gray, or other curious additions which have swelled this remarkable collection to its present bulk. I will here mention only what is of original interest. In the first place, certain memoranda of Gray's family, mostly in his own handwriting, including the draft, in pencil, which is almost obliterated, of the epitaph of his mother, which runs thus :—

in the same pious confidence
beside her sister and faithful friend
sleep the remains of
DOROTHY GRAY
Widow, the careful tender Mother
of many children, of whom one
only had the misfortune to
survive her
She died March 11, 1753, aged 67.

It may be observed that this reading differs in several respects from that hitherto repeated.

Horace Walpole's copy of the *Six Poems* of 1753 has been let into the volumes. It contains notes in his handwriting, but none of any importance.

There are thirty-four autograph letters of Gray, but all of these have been published already, and are found in their proper places in the present edition. They consist mainly of the letters to Norton Nicholls. I have collated them all, and find no variations worthy of record.

The original of the *Essay to Walpole on his Lives of the Painters* appears here in Gray's handwriting. It is correctly printed in this edition (voL i. pp. 303-321) in all but the most inconsiderable particulars.

The sheets yet unprinted are copious, but rather dry and impersonal notes of the journey in France in 1739, up to the point where the journal printed here (voL i. pp. 235-246) begins. Of more general interest is an account, in Gray's handwriting, of his stay at Naples with Walpole in 1740, and of the excursions they took in various directions. Had this reached me before the completion of my work, I should have thought it my duty to print these notes, although they have little personal importance. As a specimen of their character I transcribe the following passage :—

" We made a *little journey* also on the other side of the *Bay of Naples to Portici*, where the King has a Villa about 4 Miles out of town, the way thither is ↕thro' a number of small towns, and seats of the nobility close by the Sea, for Mount Vesuvius has not ever been able to deter people from inhabiting this lovely coast, and as soon as ever an eruption is well over, tho' perhaps it has damaged or destroy'd the whole country for leagues round

it, in some months every thing resumes its former face, and
goes on in the old channel. That mountain lies a little
distance from Portici towards the left, divided into 2
Summits, that farthest from the Sea is rather the largest,
& highest, called Monte di Somma. This has hitherto
been very innocent ; the lesser one, which is properly
Vesuvius, is that so terrible for it's fires ; it is better than
3 Miles to ascend, and those extremely laborious. 'Twas
extremely quiet at the time I saw it ; some days one could
not perceive it smoke at all, others one saw it riseing like
a white Column from it, but in no great quantity. About
a mile beyond Portici we saw the Stream of combustible
Matter, which run from it in the last eruption ; within $\frac{1}{8}$
of a mile, or less, from the Sea is a small church of Our
Lady, belonging to a certain Zoccolanti, into this church
it enter'd thro' one of the side-doors without otherwise
damageing the fabrick, run cross it, and was stop'd, I
suppose, by the opposite Wall. The Fryars have dugg
away that part of it, and left it whole riseing in a great
rough mass at the door where it enter'd, as if the miraculous
power of Our Lady had forbid it to advance further : this
is well-contrived, and carries some appearance with it.
That part of the Stream which comes along thro' the
fields at a distance resembles plough'd Land, but rougher,
and in huge Clods ; they are hard and heavy, like the
dross of some metals ; the people pile the pieces up, and
make an enclosure to their fields with them. This place
is call'd Torre del Greco ; it is about 4 Years since the
Eruption happen'd. I imagine the river of fire, or Lava,
as they call it, may be 20 Yards, or more, in breadth. It
is not above a year since they discover'd under a part of
the town of Portici a little way from the Shore an ancient
and terrible example of what this mountain is capable of ;

as they were digging to lay the foundations of a house for
the Prince d'Elbœuf, they found a statue or two with
some other ancient remains which comeing to the King's
knowledge he order'd them to work on at his expence, and
continuing to do so they came to what one may call a
whole city under ground ; it is supposed, and with great
probability to be the Greek settlement call'd Herculaneum,
which in that furious Eruption, that happen'd under Titus
(the same in which the elder Pliny perish'd) was utterly
overwhelmed, and lost with several other on the same
coast. Statius, who wrote as it were on the spot, and
soon after the accident had happen'd, makes a very poetical explanation on the subject, which this discovery sets
in its full light :—

'Haec ego Chalcidicis ad te, Marcelle, sonabam,' etc.

The work is unhappily under the direction of Spaniards,
people of no taste or erudition, so that the workmen dig,
as chance directs them, wherever they find the ground
easiest to work without any certain view."

From the biographical point of view the most interesting addition to our knowledge of Gray, presented by Mr.
John Morris's collections, is a short paper of notes on a
journey in Scotland, of which no previous biographer or
editor of Gray has given any account. It has not hitherto
been known how the poet occupied his leisure between
his recovery from the severe surgical operation of July
1764, and what he called his "Lilliputian Travels" in
the south of England in October of the same year. It
now appears, from Mr. Morris's MS., that in August 1764
he went to Netherby, on the Scotch border, to visit the
Rev. Mr. Graham, the horticulturist, and from his house
set out in a tour in Scotland. His route took him by

Annan and Dumfries to the Falls of Clyde and Lanark.
At Glasgow he called on Foulis, the publisher, from whom
he afterwards received many courtesies. He admired
Foulis' academy of painting and sculpture, and lamented
that the Cathedral of Glasgow was so miserably out of
repair. He passed on to Loch Lomond, sailed on the
loch, and returned to Glasgow by Dumbarton. At Stir-
ling he enjoyed the view from the castle, and went on
by Falkirk and the coast to Edinburgh. He took excursions to Hawthornden and Roslin, and then to Melrose.
He was next at Kelso, Tweedmouth, and Norham Castle.
He made an excursion at low tide to Holy Island, and
the itinerary closes at Bamborough Castle, from which
place he went, no doubt, to his customary haunt, Dr.
Wharton's house at Old Park, in the county of Durham.
This was Gray's first visit to Scotland.

Mr. John Morris also possesses the original MS. of
Norton Nicholls's *Recollections of Gray*, and many other
papers of a minor interest. For his kindness in placing
the whole of this beautiful and valuable collection in my
hands I owe him my most sincere thanks. There is now
but a very small portion of Gray's writings remaining
of which I have not been able to examine the original
manuscript.—[ED.]

GENERAL INDEX.

Abbies, Mitred, by Willis, reference to, ii. 377.

Aberdeen, Marischal College of, desires to confer the degree of LL.D.; this Gray declines, iii. 220.

Gray proud of his connection with its University, iii. 221.

Achilles, The death of, by Bedingfield, ii. 338.

Adam Bell, reference to the old romance of, i. 338.

Adami, Patricia, Italian actress, ii. 76.

Ad Amicos, a Latin elegy, by R. West, ii. 8.

Adams, Dr., reference to, i. 138.

Addison, Joseph, his quotations from the Classics, ii. 240.

his endeavour to suppress the raillery on the clergy, i. 406.

Addison, Mr., sends a friendly admonition to C. Smart, ii. 161.

his friendship for Smart, ii. 179.

Lord Walpole, of Wolterton, and Keene, Bishop of Chester, his patrons, ii. 287.

Adversity, Hymn to, i. 23-26.

editorial note, i. 24.

Agis, a tragedy, by John Home, ii. 360.

Agrippina, a fragment of a tragedy, i. 101-111.

first published in 1775, i. 100.

editorial note, i. 101.

the argument written by Mason, i. 101-103.

Gray submits a speech in, to the criticism of West, ii. 106.

previously dramatised by May, ii. 106.

Gray lays it aside, ii. 110.

sends it to Horace Walpole, ii. 167.

Horace Walpole requested not to mention it, ii. 171.

Gray sends Walpole the first scene in, ii. 227.

Ailesbury, Lady, declaration that Gray, during a long afternoon in her company, only spoke once, iii. 42.

Aislaby, Mr., with Rev. Norton Nicholls at Studley, iii. 240.

Akenside, Dr., his erroneous conjectures in Architecture, ii. 255.

criticism of his *Pleasures of Imagination,* ii. 120-121.

Dr. Wharton asks Hurd to be lenient with, ii. 299.

erroneously criticises an expression of Gray's, ii. 331.

his contribution to Dodsley's Collection of Poems, ii. 364.

reference to, ii. 389.

Albemarle, Lord, one of Lord George Sackville's judges, iii. 31.

Alcaic Fragment, i. 176.

reference to, ii. 90.

Ode, written in the album of the Grande Chartreuse, ii. 182.

editorial note, ii. 182.

Alderson, Rev. Christopher, shows Mason's library to Mitford, ii. 299.

curate to Mason, subsequently rector of Aston, ii. 282.

invited to Old Park, iii. 348.

Alderson, Mrs., portrait of Dr. Delap in her possession, ii. 309.

Aldovrandi, Cardinal Pompeo, note on, ii. 93.

Algarotti, Count Francesco, friend of Frederick the Great, of Voltaire, and of Augustus III. of Poland, iii. 147.

distinguished as one of the best literary judges in Europe, iii. 148.

sends panegyrics to Gray and Mason, iii. 151.

his Dissertation on Painting and Music, with dedication to Pitt (Earl of Chatham), iii. 151, 150.

Gray compliments him on his literary effort, iii. 155.

Gray reads his works with increasing satisfaction, iii. 150.

worthy to be the "Arbiter Elegantiarum" of mankind, iii. 160.

Algarotti, his works, iii. 162.
Gray's opinion of his *Saggio sopra l'opera in musica*, iii. 162.
account of his *Il Congresso di Citera*, iii. 162.
Gray sees no objection to T. Howe publishing his works ; gives advice as to the preparation, iii. 165.
Gray cannot advise an English translation of, iii. 298-299.
thinks of visiting England, iii. 166.
his works, in 8 vols., swarm with errors of the press, iii. 293.
his works printed at Leghorn, iii. 307.
Gray's opinion of his merit, iii. 299.
his verse above mediocrity, iii. 300.
employed by King of Poland to buy pictures, iii. 307.
purchases a famous Holbein, "The consul Meyer and his family," iii. 307.
Allegory, Gray no friend of, iii. 166.
Allen, Ralph, of Prior Park, recommends Mr. Hurd for a sinecure, iii. 189.
Allin, Sir A., reference to his death, iii. 386.
Allin, Miss, inclined to part with the estates, iii. 383.
Alloa, triumphs and illuminations of, iii. 383.
Alps, description of a journey across the, ii. 40-42, 45.
near Lanslebourg, ii. 41.
Alren, Dr., iii. 62.
Altieri, Cardinal Giambattista, illness of, ii. 63, 84.
Altieri, Cardinals, ii. 63.
Alvis, Andrew, Fellow of St. John's, note on, candidate for the Mastership of St. John's, iii. 190.
Amatory Lines. Paraphrase of an epigram of "Ad Carolum," i. 137.
editorial note, i. 137.
Amherst, General, speech in commendation of, iii. 18.
Amusemens sur le langage des Bêtes, by Bougeant, reference to, ii. 27.
Ancaster, Duke of, at the trial of Lord Ferrers, iii. 85.
Ancient authors, Gray's Catalogue of, ii. 148-154.
chronological table of their works compiling at Cambridge, ii. 156.
Ancients, Gray's reading from the, ii. 112-113.
Ancram, Lord, to take part in a secret military expedition, ii. 320.
Andrews, Dr., gives an opinion on the Cambridge statutes, ii. 133.

Anecdotes of Painting, Walpole's, iii. 125.
Anglesey, Marquis, his disputed peerage, iii. 374.
Anguish, Mr., interested in Smart, iii. 163.
Ansel, Mr., Fellow of Trinity, his recent death, iii. 254, 255.
Anstey, Christopher, translated Gray's *Elegy* into Latin, i. 72, 227.
his *New Bath Guide*, ii. 240.
Anthologia Græca, Gray's paraphrases from, i. 195-198.
Anti-gallican, Gray an, ii. 226.
"Antiquities, Houses, etc., in England and Wales," catalogued by Gray and printed posthumously by Mason, ii. 360.
Gray pursues the study of, ii. 359-360.
Antrobus, Robert, Gray's maternal uncle, ii. 9.
Antrobus, Mrs. Mary, Gray's aunt, death of, i. 72 ; ii. 203.
Antrobus, Miss Dorothy, Gray's cousin, postmistress of Cambridge, iii. 130, 134, 283, 319.
Gray informs her of his appointment as Professor of Modern History, iii. 318.
Apothecary's, Gray calls a country, shop a terrible thing, iii. 265.
Archimage, Mr., visits Gray, iii. 191.
Archimedes, his speculum discovered by Buffon, ii. 230.
Architecture, Essay on Norman (or, according to Wren, the Saxon), i. 294-302.
better suited for military than for domestic purposes, i. 294.
its distinctive character (1) semicircular arches, examples at Ely and Peterborough, i. 296.
(2) massy piers or pillars, i. 297.
examples at Durham, Peterborough, and Ely, and in views of Old St. Paul's, i. 298.
(3) variety of the *capitals* of the piers, i. 298.
examples at Ely and Peterborough, i. 299.
(4) wider ceilings, of timber only, examples at Ely and Peterborough, i. 299.
(5) its ornaments, i. 299-300.
examples at Hereford, Peterborough, and views of Old St. Paul's, i. 300.
reference to ancient statues on Crowland Bridge, Worcester, and Gloucester, i. 300.

Architecture, remarks on the Essay, by Mr. Basil Champneys, i. 301.
Gray's opinion of the source of Gothic, ii. 255.
reason of the beauty of Gothic, iii. 110.
beauty of Gothic, began to appear in reign of Henry III., iii. 146.
rise of Gothic, iii. 146.
Gothic perfection, i. 317.
nothing finer than the nave of York, i. 317.
Lady chapel (Trinity Church, Ely), i. 317.
chapel of Bishop West at Ely, i. 317.
had introduced itself in the reign of Charles I., iii. 158.
criticisms on James Bentham's Essay, iii. 228-231.
the Saxon, had no niches or canopies, and escutcheons of arms are hardly ever seen, iii. 229.
billeted-moulding, examples of, iii. 229.
nail-head, examples of, iii. 230.
nebule, examples of, iii. 230.
rise of the pointed arch, example of, iii. 230.
spirit of Gray's time little less destructive than the civil wars, iii. 231.
Aristophanes, notes on, iv.
Aristotle, Gray's opinion of his writings, ii. 147.
Arlington Street, residence of Walpole, ii. 139.
Armstrong, Dr. John, his poem on Health, ii. 121.
his pseudonym of Lancelot Temple, ii. 372.
Arthur, King, popular superstition in Lydgate's time concerning, i. 389.
Asheton, Thomas, friend of Gray and West, ii. 71.
publishes a book against Dr. Middleton, ii. 210.
Horace Walpole's Epistle to, ii. 221, 225.
reference to, ii. 227.
Ashton, Dr., an Epistle by Horace Walpole to, ii. 90.
his prospect of marriage, ii. 141.
his marriage, iii. 87.
visits Gray at Stoke, ii. 148.
reference to, ii. 147.
preacher of Lincoln's Inn, iii. 87.
reference to, and Eton, iii. 86, 107, 111.
Askew, Dr., ii. 117.
Aston, Rev. Dr. Delap's portrait in Mason's dining-room at, ii. 309.

Athelstan, by Dr. Brown, ii. 261.
Garrick wrote the Epilogue of, ii. 261.
Atheism is a vile dish, iii. 378.
Athens, antiquities of, J. Stuart's, ii. 283.
Autumn of 1753, ii. 247-249.
Avison, Charles, his Essay on Musical Expression as his Friend, ii. 242.
reference to, ii. 250.
Avon, a poem, printed by Baskerville, ii. 372.
Axton, Mr., Fellow of Pembroke College, ii. 283.
Ayscough, Dr. Francis, candidate for Bishopric of St. David's, iii. 78.
Ayscough, Mr., instrument maker on Ludgate Hill, iii. 241.

Bach, Carlo, his lessons for the pianoforte, iii. 164.
Gray thinks them charming, though others disagree, iii. 164.
Baiardi, Ottavo Antonio, Parmesan antiquary, ii. 277.
Gray's criticism of his work on Herculaneum, ii. 277-278.
Baif, French poet, reference to, ii. 341.
Balbi, Constantino, Doge of Genoa, ii. 48.
Balguy, Dr. Thomas, of St. John's. Gray accompanies him to town, ii. 291.
Gray sends him a copy of The Odes, ii. 320.
takes his doctor's degree and preaches the commencement sermon, ii. 368, 371.
returns to his prebendary of Winchester, ii. 371.
friend of Rev. Mr. Ludham, iii. 144.
Gray visits him at Winchester, iii. 178.
his action at Winchester, iii. 178.
says Mrs. Mason is very handsome, iii. 224.
Balmerino, Lord, his trial for rebellion, ii. 141.
his last action on the scaffold, ii. 146.
Balmerino, Lady Margaret, ii. 142.
Barbarossa, A play by Dr. Brown, ii. 261.
Bard, The, i. 39-50.
editorial note, i. 40.
portion submitted to Dr. Wharton, ii. 267.
fragment of, as sent to Dr. Wharton, ii. 268-271.
no further progress of, ii. 273, 294.
no further progress of (old Caradoc), ii. 276.

Bard, The, sends a fragment to Stone-hewer, ii. 279.
further fragment sent to Mason, ii. 312.
the Moses of Parmegiano and Raphael's figure of God in the vision of Ezekiel furnished models for, ii. 313.
Gray comments on Mason's criticism, ii. 314-315.
Gray does not like notes, yet will give one or two, ii. 319.
Gray comments to H. Walpole on, ii. 318-319.
criticised by Mr. J. Butler anonymously, ii. 344-346.
references to, ii. 284-286.
Barnard, Dr., his quarrel at the Commons, iii. 68.
Barnard, Lord, reference to, ii. 238.
Barnwell, Dr., of Trompington, his daughter marries Dr. Chapman, ii. 193.
Barrett, Mr., of Lee Priory, offers Rev. N. Nicholls £100 a year as travelling companion, iii. 324.
Barrington, Lord, Secretary for War, ii. 292.
Barrington, Daines (one of the Welsh judges), Gray wishes a copy of his poems to be sent to, ii. 344.
Bartholomew Fair, reference to, iii. 77.
Baskerville, beauty of his type, iii. 165.
Bath, Lord, death of, iii. 172.
conduct of his lady during a riot, iii. 339.
Bathurst, Mr., reference to, iii. 69.
Battey-Langley manner of architecture, ii. 253.
Battle of the Summer Islands, quotation from Waller's, ii. 49.
Beadon, Richard, Bishop of Gloucester, executor of Dr. Newcome, iii. 189.
Beattie, Dr. James, note on, iii. 219.
invites Gray to Aberdeen, iii. 219.
Gray would be glad to see him at Glamis, iii. 220.
visits Glamis, iii. 220.
sends Gray two books on popular superstition, iii. 222.
Gray criticises his poetry, iii. 279.
Gray thanks him for his many friendly offers, iii. 285.
receives permission to issue a Scotch edition of Gray's poems, and to entrust its publication to Foulis of Glasgow, iii. 285-286.
criticism of his Ode on Lord Hay's birthday, iii. 287.

Beattie, Gray's reasons for the notes to his Pindaric Odes, iii. 290.
thanked for the edition of Gray's poems, iii. 325 ; its success, iii. 346.
informed of the appointment of Gray to the Chair of Modern History, and its value, iii. 326.
sends Gray in MS. the first book of the *Minstrel ;* Gray's criticism, iii. 376.
his *Essay on Truth,* iii. 377.
Gray's criticism of the *Minstrel,* with Beattie's comments, iii. 395-400.
obliged to Gray for his freedom of criticism, iii. 400.
Beauchamp, Earls of Warwick, their monuments, ii. 257.
Beauclerk, Lady Harry, receives a pension of £400 a year, iii. 78.
Beauvau, Marshall, Prince, son of Prince Craon, ii. 85.
Beckford, Alderman, reference to his manner whilst delivering a speech, iii. 13.
at the coronation banquet, iii. 116.
Bedford, Duke of, brings his son Francis to Trinity College, ii. 309.
and Duchess likely to be of the new Ministry, iii. 153.
Bedford, Mr., Fellow of Pembroke, ii. 283.
Mr. Buller of Cornwall his patron, ii. 289.
Bedingfield, †Mr., makes the acquaintance of, ii. 276.
The Death of Achilles, a poem by, ii. 338.
relates opinions expressed respecting Gray's *Odes,* ii. 340.
Mason's attitude towards, iii. 163.
references, ii. 338 ; iii. 329.
Bedlam, tragedy by Nat. Lee, ii. 106.
Beedon, Mr., reference to, iii. 97.
Bell, Mr., his taste for Gothic, iii. 20.
Belleisle, news of its surrender daily expected, iii. 105.
Sir William Williams killed at, iii. 109.
Bellers visits Maltham and engraves a view of Gordale, i. 273.
Bellingham, extinct family of, i. 269.
Benedict XIV., his election as Pope, i. 93.
Bentham, James, Prebendary of Ely, Gray returns his *Essay on Gothic Architecture* with criticisms, iii. 228-231.
Bentinck, Lady Anne, and Sir Conyers d'Arcy, i. 367.

Bentley, Mr. Richard, Stanzas to, i. 121-122.
editorial note to Stanzas, i. 121.
the Stanzas first published in 1775, i. 100.
assists in preparing the Chronological table of ancient authors, ii. 158.
his designs for Gray's Elegy, ii. 234 : their publication, ii. 237 ; a second edition, i. 227.
sale at London in 1882 of his drawings for the six poems, ii. 237.
reference to, ii. 218.
Berger, a disciple of Linnæus, iii. 88.
Bernardi, Francesco, reference to, ii. 65.
Bevis, Earl of Southampton, The Reportes of, i. 338.
his residence at Duncton, i. 338.
his sword one of the relics at Arundel Castle, i. 338.
Bibliographical statement of Gray's writings, i. ix-xiii.
Bickham, James, Fellow of Emmanuel, ii. 320.
Gray sends him a copy of The Odes, ii. 320.
laments Mason's indolence, ii. 394.
reference to, iii. 98.
Bickham, Rev. Jeremy, obtains a living, iii. 108.
Biographia, Dr. Nicholls wrote the latter articles of, ii. 244.
Birch, Dr. Thomas, his State Papers, ii. 194.
his State Papers of Sir T. Elmondes, ii. 281.
Birds, Couplet about, i. 139.
editorial note on, i. 139.
Birds in Norfolk, table of their noises being first heard during 1755, iii. 95-96.
Birkett, Rev. George, asked by Gray to pay his Italian master, ii. 44.
Blacowe, Rev. Mr., Canon of Windsor, his death, iii. 40, 63.
Blue-Coat or Man-in-Blew, an attendant on the Vice-Chancellor of Cambridge University, ii. 117.
Bonden's Life of Kemble, extract relative to Mason, ii. 242.
Boadicea, Glover's play of, ii. 134.
Boar, the silver, badge of Richard III., i. 47.
Boccaccio, introduced the Ottava Rima measure, i. 347.
his de Cassibus Illustrium Virorum, i. 391.
Bolby, Mr., reference to, ii. 187.
Bolton, Duke of, his duel with Mr. Stuart, iii. 34.

Bonfoy, Nicholas, resided at Abbot's Ripton, ii. 378.
his marriage and family, ii. 379.
visits Gray at Cambridge, ii. 320.
his belief that everything turns out for the best, ii. 321.
dines with Gray, iii. 21.
Bonfoy, Mrs. Elizabeth, references to, ii. 378 ; iii. 32.
who taught Gray to pray, is dead, iii. 152.
her fortitude, iii. 152.
Bonfoy, Mr. and Mrs., Gray sends them a copy of The Odes, ii. 320.
Bonstetten, Charles von, Baillie of Nion, Switzerland, letter to Norton Nicholls, with footnote of Gray's opinion of the writer, iii. 355-356.
proceeds to London with Gray, iii. 357.
returned to France, iii. 358.
note on, iii. 360.
Gray laments the loss of his presence, iii. 360-362, 369.
Gray's expression of warm regard, warns him against vice, iii. 371.
sends Gray views of Switzerland, iii. 389.
is disordered in his intellect, or has exasperated his friends, iii. 401.
Borneil, Girard de, his invention of the Canzone, i. 352.
Boscawen, Admiral, his victory over the French, iii. 14.
Boswell, James, tells Mitford that Gray received forty guineas for The Odes, ii. 330.
his Account of Corsica and Memoir of Paoli, iii. 310.
Gray's light estimate of his abilities, iii. 310-311.
Botanical Calendar for 1755, iii. 92-94.
Bougeant, Guillaume Hyacinthe, ii. 27.
his Langage des Bêtes, ii. 27, 96.
Epistle to, by Gresset, ii. 184.
Bourbon, Duke of, Governor of Burgundy, ii. 31.
Bourne, Mr., a friend of Mason's, ii. 349.
Bower, Archibald, his career and proposals for a History of the Pope, ii. 180.
Bowes, George, of Streatham Castle, his daughter married to the ninth Earl of Strathmore, ii. 369 ; iii. 276.
Boycot, Mr., may be of assistance to Rev. N. Nicholls, iii. 342.
Bradshaw, Mr., secretary to the Duke of Grafton, ii. 241.

Braidalbane, Lord, his Scottish domain or "policy," lii. 216.
Bramston, Rev. James, reference to his poetry, ii. 220.
Brandenburg, Frederick the Great's *Memoirs* of the House of, ii. 229.
reviewed in the *Mercure Historique*, ii. 229.
Brawn, collars of, stuck with rosemary, ii. 118.
Brian, King of Dublin, death of, i. 54.
Bridgewater, Duke of, accompanied by P. Wood through Italy, ii. 328.
Bristol Cathedral, elegiac verses to Mrs. Mason in, i. 141.
Bristol, Lord, Ambassador to Spain, iii. 116.
Britannicus, tragedy by Racine, ii. 167.
performed in Paris, ii. 27.
British Museum, a treasure, ii. 396.
its excess of expenditure over income, ii. 396 ; iii. 2.
Gray expects to see the collection offered for sale, iii. 4.
very crowded, ii. 396.
Gray's chief amusement, iii. 1.
persons attending the reading-room, iii. 2.
dissension of its officers, iii. 6.
Gray's researches in the Ledger-Book of the Signet preserved in, iii. 11.
Gray's further researches, iii. 29.
Gray's MSS. in, i. xiv. 73, 113, 140.
Brivio, Signor, singing instructor, ii. 284.
Brockett, Lawrence, Professor of Modern History, iii. 136, 140.
tutor to Sir James Lowther, iii. 137.
agent for Earl of Sandwich at Cambridge, iii. 168.
his death, and Gray's succession to his Chair, iii. 318.
manner of his death, iii. 322.
Bromwick, dealer in wall-papers, iii. 83, 118, 120.
Brook, Dr. Zachary, of St. John's, note on, iii. 189.
elected Margaret Professor, iii. 189.
candidate for the Mastership of St. John's, iii. 190.
reference to, iii. 168.
Broschi, Carlos, sopranist, ii. 22, 57 ; iii. 80.
Brown, Sir Anthony, supposed portrait in St. John's College, i. 311.
Brown, Mr. (one of the six clerks in Chancery), his house on banks of Eden, i. 250.
Brown, li., a contributor to Dodley's Miscellaneous Poems, ii. 220.

Brown, Rev. James, of Pembroke College, note on, ii. 138.
his fortitude, ii. 138.
supports the case of Tuthill, ii. 161, 188.
interests himself on behalf of C. Smart, ii. 178.
successful in his endeavour to elect Tuthill and others Fellows of Pembroke, ii. 188.
presented to the living of Tilney, ii. 189.
contributes to Dodsley's Miscellaneous Poems, ii. 221.
visits Gray at Stoke, ii. 259.
Gray canvasses on his behalf for an office in the University, ii. 287-289.
asked to distribute copies of Gray's *Odes*, ii. 320.
Gray enquires if the parcel of *Odes* have reached him, and asks that he will send any criticisms he may hear, ii. 322.
if he has paid any of Gray's Cambridge bills, Gray wishes to be informed, ii. 384.
laments Mason's indolence, ii. 394.
invited to Gray's lodgings in Southampton Row, iii. 6.
requested to prepare Gray's Cambridge apartments, iii. 61, 63.
his opinion requested of young Ponsonby, iii. 67.
favourable opinion of young Ponsonby, iii. 77.
his pictures of Ware Park, near Hertford, iii. 69.
inclined to suffer from sciatica, iii.86.
proposition that he should visit Lady Strathmore, iii. 86.
not at all well, iii. 125.
his evening prayer to the congregation, iii. 152.
called familiarly by Gray "Petit Bon," iii. 164.
preparing some grafts for Dr. Wharton, iii. 169.
invincibly attach'd to his duties, iii. 200.
deep in Quintilian and Livy, iii. 205.
visits his brother near Margate, iii. 245.
Gray has been nursing him,iii.259,262.
will he accompany Gray to Mason's? iii. 267-268.
visits Mason, iii. 272.
visits Lord Strathmore at Gibside, and accompanies him to Scotland, iii. 282.

Brown, Rev. James, and the livings of Framlingham and Oddington, iii. 328.

accompanies Gray to York, iii. 347.

receives the Mastership of Pembroke and the living of Streath-ham, Isle of Ely, iii. 388.

joint executor with Mason of Gray's will, ii. 138.

references to, ii. 155, 203, 230, 231, 287, 346; iii. 58.

Brown, Rev. John, his *Estimate of the Manners and Principles of the Times*, ii. 310.

his praise of Gray, ii. 328, 330. reference to, iii. 42.

Brown, Dr., suicide of, iii. 250, 251.

Brydges, Sir Egerton, his account of Gray's feelings on kissing hands for the Professorship, iii. 323.

Buchanan, Mrs., Gray dines with her at Penrith, i. 250.

Buffon, his *Histoire du Cabinet du Roi*, commended by Gray, ii. 199.

discovers the Speculum of Archimedes, ii. 230.

arrival in England of the 9th and 10th volumes of his history, iii. 85; 11th and 12th volumes, iii. 172; 13th volume, iii. 235; 14th volume, iii. 245.

Buller, Mr., of Cornwall, patron of Mr. Bedford, ii. 289.

Buondelmonte, Guiseppe Maria, a littérateur of Tuscany, ii. 103.

Sonnet by, with Gray's imitation, ii. 103.

Burg, Elizabeth de, Countess Clare, i. 95.

Burgundy, Dukes of, tombs of, ii. 31.

Burke, Edmund, reference to, iii. 126.

Burleigh, Lord Treasurer, Chancellor of Cambridge, i. 97.

Papers, reference to, ii. 128.

House, Lord Exeter refurnishing, iii. 11.

Burlesque account of Gray's travels in France and Italy, ii. 55-61.

Burney, Dr., and The Installation Ode, ii. 92.

his opinion of *Il Ciro Riconosciuto*, ii. 391.

Burnham Beeches, description of, ii. 9.

Burroughs, Vice-Chancellor and Master of Caius College, i. 307.

Burton, Dr. John, M.D., author of *Monasticon Eboracense*, iii. 2.

Business, the great art of life is to find oneself, iii. 32.

Bussy, setting out for France, iii. 116.

Bussy, Pitt's contempt for his proposals on behalf of France, iii. 122.

Bute, Earl of, Groom of the Stole, ii. 290.

a botanist, iii. 89.

his new system of botany, iii. 89.

his favouritism, iii. 123.

refuses an application on behalf of Gray for the Professorship of Modern History, iii. 136-137.

ill of an ague in his eye, iii. 269.

Bute, Lady, bequests from her father, Wortley Montagu, iii. 91.

her second son to take the name of Wortley, iii. 91.

Butler, Dr. Joseph, Bishop of Durham, ii. 241.

Butler, J., of Andover, criticises Gray's *Bard*, ii. 341, 346.

description of his residence, ii. 349.

Byron, Lord, kills Mr. Chaworth in a duel, iii. 203.

CADWALLADER, his device, i. 70.

Caius, Dr., an original portrait of, i. 306-307.

date of his death, i. 308.

his tomb, i. 309.

Caius College, old portrait in, believed to be Theodore Haveus of Cleves, i. 307-309.

Calas, Voltaire's good action on behalf of the family of, iii. 173.

Calendar (Botanical), of Upsal (Sw.), Stratton, and Cambridge, for 1755, iii. 92-94.

Cambis, Marquis de, *see* Velleron, ii. 27.

Cambridge, Richard Owen, purchases Mr. Zolman's library, ii. 373.

presented H. Walpole with Lord Whitworth's MS. of *Account of Russia in 1710*, ii. 373.

his powers of conversation, iii. 2.

his account of the *Life of Edward, Earl of Clarendon*, prior to its publication, iii. 2-3.

Cambridge, *Ode on the death of a favourite Cat*, written at, i. 10.

Progress of Poesy, written at, i. 28.

The Descent of Odin, written at, i. 60.

portion of the *Elegy*, written at, i. 72.

The Alliance of Education and Government, written at, i. 113.

Couplet on Birds, composed near, i. 139.

views of the colleges, by Loggan, i. 309.

Satire upon the heads (of colleges), i. 134.

Cambridge, Gray unacquainted with the younger tutors of, iii. 58.
likened to a desolation and a solitude, ii. 5.
election of a High Steward (Lord Hardwick and Earl of Sandwich the candidates) will take place in Westminster Hall, iii. 168, 171; Lord Hardwick to come in quietly, iii. 183; appeal to the King's Bench, iii. 200; Lord Hardwick judicially declared elected, iii. 200; points settled by Lord Mansfield, iii. 201.
contest for the Margaret Professorship of St. John's College, iii. 189.
great contest for the Mastership of St. John's College, iii. 190.
St. John's Lodge, old picture in, considered to be Sir Anthony Denny, iii. 227.
Mr. Lyon's chambers destroyed by fire, iii. 301.
as soon as ceremonies are over, Gray will start for Skiddaw, iii. 342.
list of distinguished visitors expected to attend at the installation of the Duke of Grafton as Chancellor, iii. 343, 344.
expensiveness of lodgings in anticipation of the installation, iii. 344.
Camden, Lord, "will soon be Chancellor," iii. 237.
Camelford, Lord (Thomas Pitt), ii. 338.
Candidate, The, a poem by Churchill, quotation from, ii. 289.
Canterbury Cathedral, its choir built by William of Sens, i. 316.
Canterbury, Gray sets out for, iii. 237.
Canzone, its invention, i. 352.
esteemed by Dante the noblest specimen of poetry, i. 352.
Capel, Lady M., attempted suicide of, ii. 274.
Captives, The, a play by Rev. Dr. Delap, ii. 309.
Caractacus, Gray's influence on Rev. W. Mason's, i. 262.
Gray's criticism of, ii. 297, 300-307, 317-318, 332-338, 351-353, 386-387, 391.
Walpole's opinion of, ii. 332.
Gray receives the first act, ii. 384.
Mason issues, and has a fit of affectation, iii. 20.
Gray sends a copy to Rev. J. Brown, iii. 20.
the work of a man, Elfrida only that of a boy, iii. 148.
references to, ii. 341, 371, 379.

Caradoc, a Welsh fragment, i. 130.
probably written in 1764, i. 129.
Caradoc, see Bard.
Caradoc, Caer, mountain in Shropshire, ii. 270.
Cardale or Cardell, Mr., admitted a Fellow of Pembroke College, ii. 203, 288.
Cardinals, frugality of the Roman, ii. 98.
Carew, Sir George, writer of the State Papers of Sir T. Edmondes, ii. 281.
Carey, Henry, his poem of The Moderator between the Free Masons and Gormogons, ii. 166.
Carey, General, reference to his being in Mason's company, iii. 348.
Carlisle, reference to the affair of, iii. 203.
Carlisle, Lady, her altered circumstances, ii. 389-390.
Carlyon, Mr., reference to, ii. 176.
Carnival at Turin, ii. 44.
Casley's Catalogue of the King's Library, i. 306, 312.
Castle of Otranto, by H. Walpole, Gray's account of its reception at Cambridge, iii. 191.
Castlecomer, Lady, her death, ii. 402; iii. 3.
Cat, Ode on the death of a favourite, i. 9.
editorial note on, i. 10.
sent to Dr. Wharton, ii. 164.
Catalina, Crebillon's tragedy of, its success in Paris, i. 193.
Brindley's edition of, i. 194.
Vaillant's edition of, i. 194.
Cavaillac's, Marquise de, Conversazione, ii. 44.
Cavendish, Lord George, attends the university, iii. 385.
the last survivor of those who had known Gray, iii. 385.
Cavendish, Lord John, Chancellor of the Exchequer, ii. 287.
visits Gray at Cambridge, iii. 300.
reference to his visit, ii. 311.
Gray's criticism of Mason's Elegy on, ii. 356.
consults Gray as to the tutorship of his nephew Ponsonby, iii. 57.
recovering from pleurisy, iii. 108-109.
reference to, iii. 67.
Cavendish, Lord Richard, reference to, iii. 297.
description of, iii. 331, 385.
Watson, his tutor, iii. 331.
Winstanley, his private tutor, iii. 331.
Caviche, Gray's receipt for, iii. 81.
Celtic mythology, ii. 351.
Cenci, Cardinal, death of, ii. 84.

Cephalo and Procri, opera of, ii. 133.
Chairs, Gray describes some to H. Walpole, ii. 217.
Chaise, post-, description of a French, prior to their introduction to England, ii. 17.
Chalice of St. Remi, ii. 28.
Chalotais, Louis René de, Gray cannot find the *Mémoires* of, iii. 258.
Chambers, Mr., reference to, iii. 70, 160.
Champneys, Mr. Basil, his remarks on Gray's *Norman Architecture*, i. 301.
Chandos, Duke of, at Southampton, iii. 179.
Chapel of St. George at Windsor, i. 315.
Chapman, Dr. Thomas, Master of Magdalen, ii. 162.
  his Essay on the Roman Senate, ii. 163.
  his marriage to Miss Barnwell, ii. 193.
  his reception of the Duke of Newcastle at Cambridge, ii. 196.
  pamphlet by, ii. 204.
  visits Gray at Studley, ii. 241.
  his death, iii. 50.
  cause of his death, iii. 56, 61, 64.
  his estate, iii. 56.
  references to, ii. 228, 327.
Character, Sketch of his own, i. 127.
Characters of the Christ-Cross-Row, i. 210-213.
  editorial note on, i. 210.
Charles I., his love and taste for the beautiful, iii. 158.
Charles III. of Naples and the excavations of Herculaneum, ii. 277.
Charms of Sylvia, The, by Frederick, Prince of Wales, iii. 73.
Charteris, Hon. Mr., his castle at Hornby, i. 275.
  and at Haddington, i. 275.
Chartreuse Grande, Gray writes an Alcaic Ode in the album of the monks of the, i. 182.
Chartreuse, La, a poem by Gresset, ii. 182.
Chatsworth House, description of, iii. 134, 135.
  Mr. Brown's improvements, iii. 135.
  stateliness of its apartments, iii. 135.
Chaucer, old print by Speed from Occleve's portrait of, i. 305.
  family arms of, at bottom of print, i. 306.
  his portrait in possession of George Greenwood, Esq., i. 306.
  MS. of his Troilus and Cressida in St. John's library, i. 305.
  his portrait by Occleve not in St. John's library, i. 305.

Chancer, the King's library referred to as possessing Occleve's portrait of, i. 306.
  article in *Bibliotheca* by Bishop Tanner on, i. 306.
  alludes to the diversity of writing our language, i. 326.
  examples of his metre, i. 335, 336, 339.
Chaworth, Mr., killed in a duel with Lord Byron, iii. 203.
Chenevix, Bishop of Waterford, insulted in an Irish riot, iii. 26.
Chenevix, Madame, reference to, ii. 124.
Chesterfield, Earl of, purchased the lanthorn from Houghton Hall, ii. 12.
  his friendship for Mr. Dayrolles, ii. 353.
Chevalier de St. George, references to, ii. 68, 76, 84, 94
Child, Epitaph on a, i. 126.
  editorial note on, i. 126.
Chinese possess the art of landscape gardening, iii. 160.
Cholmondeley, General, one of the judges on the trial of Lord G. Sackville, iii. 31.
Christ College, Cambridge, founded by the Countess of Richmond, i. 96.
Christ-Cross-Row, Characters of the, i. 210, 213.
  editorial note on, i. 210.
Christmas dinner in the Duke of Norfolk's establishment in (?) sixteenth century, ii. 296.
Christopher, Mr., reference to, ii. 165.
Chronological table of the works of ancient poets and orators being compiled at Cambridge, ii. 158, 164.
Chudleigh, Miss (Duchess of Kingston), gives a ball to the Conde de Fuentes, i. 40.
  Madame de Mora present at, i. 62.
Churchill, Charles, death of, iii. 187.
Churchill, quotation from his *Candidate*, ii. 289.
Chute, John, Gray asks him to obtain Marivaux' *Mariane*, i. 213.
  at Casa Ambrosio, ii. 126.
  Gray's regard for, ii. 136.
  his return to England, ii. 204.
  visited by Gray at "The Vine" in Hampshire, ii. 264.
Cibber, Caius Gabriel (Danish sculptor), his work at Chatsworth, iii. 135.
Cibber, Colley, his *Character and Conduct of Cicero*, criticised by Gray, ii. 169.

354 INDEX.

Cibber's, Mrs., canary-bird, ii. 360.

Cicero, by Dr. Middleton, ii. 123.
by Colley Cibber, ii. 169.
Ad Familiares, by Rev. J. Ross, ii. 193.

Cinque Ports, Barons of the, their treatment at the coronation of George III., iii. 116.

Circumstance the life of oratory and poetry, i. 393.
Homer the father of, i. 393.

Ciro Riconosciuto, Il, opera by Cocchi, ii. 391, 396.
Dr. Burney's opinion of, ii. 391.

Clare College, founded by Elizabeth de Burg, Countess Clare, i. 95.

Clare, Gilbert de, i. 42, 95.

Clarendon, Edward, Earl of, incorrect edition published of the last seven years of his life, ii. 372.
Life of, announced by the Duchess of Queensberry from his MS., ii. 372.
reference to the Life of, iii. 2, 5.
Mr. Cambridge's premature criticism of, iii. 2.

Clarke, Dr. John, M.D., of Epsom, friend of Gray, ii. 63.
Gray writes him of his return to Cambridge, iii. 60.
reference to, i. 125.

Clarke, Mrs. Jane, Epitaph on, i. 125.
first published, 1775, i. 100.

Clarke, Captain, his Military Institutions of Vezetius, iii. 357.

Cleone, Dodsley's play of, ii. 391.

Clergy, satire on the. Its prevalence, i. 406.
Addison unable to suppress it, i. 406.

Clerke, Dr. John, Dean of Salisbury, ii. 317.

Cleveland, Duke of, his patronage of C. Smart, ii. 179.
story of an attempt to inveigle him in marriage, iii. 33.

Clifford, Hon. Mr., his park on the banks of the Lune, i. 274.

Climate, its effect on nations, i. 118-119.

Clontarf, battle of, i. 52.

Coalheavers at Shadwell, affray of, iii. 29.

Cobden, Rev. Dr., court chaplain, reference to, ii. 327.

Cobham, Viscountess, her house at Stoke, i. 83.
entertains Garrick at Stoke, ii. 323, 324.
Gray visits her at Hampton for two days, ii. 369.
dying at Stoke, iii. 14.
biographical note, iii. 16.

Cobham, Viscountess, Gray attends her from Stoke to Hanover Square, iii. 17.
dying of dropsy, iii. 17.
her death, leaves £30,000 to Miss Speed, iii. 37.
leaves Gray £20 for a ring, iii. 65.

Cocchi, Dr., his opera of Il Ciro Riconosciuto, ii. 391, 396.
reference to, and his music, ii. 127; iii. 157.

Cogitandi, De Principiis, i. 185-193.
fragment sent to Richard West, ii. 104.
familiarly called "Master Tommy Lucretius" by Gray, ii. 121.
editorial note, i. 185.
fragment of the fourth Book sent to Horace Walpole, ii. 172.

Coke, Lady.Mary, reference to and note on, iii. 78.

Coke, Sir Edmund, his residence at Stoke, i. 83.

Colin and Lucy, ballad by T. Tickell, ii. 219.

Colin's Complaint, by Rowe, its origin, ii. 367.

Colleger, vicissitudes of a, iii. 87.

Collins, William, his Odes on several Descriptive and Allegoric Subjects, iii. 150.

Colman, George, his Ode against Gray and Mason, iii. 41, 53.
friend of Garrick's, iii. 41.
his interest in the estate of Lord Bath, iii. 172.

Comédie Françoise, account of the, ii. 22.

Comic Lines, i. 138.
editorial note on, i. 138.

Commerce changes nations, i. 120.

Commines, Philip de, ii. 128.

Common sense thrives better in proximity to nonsense, ii. 339.

Conan, i. 130.
probably written in 1764, i. 129.

Conclave of Cardinals at Rome, and election of Pope Benedict XIII., ii. 63, 67, 84, 93.

Condé, Princess of, Henri IV. and the, ii. 281.

Congresso di Citéra of Algarotti, Gray has read the, ii. 166.

Congreve, Pindaric form first introduced by, ii. 263.

Contades' army entirely defeated, iii. 5.

Conti, the singer, reference to, ii. 125.

Conversazione, definition of a, ii. 64.

Conway, Francis, second Lord Conway (Earl of Hertford), biographical note, ii. 19.

Conway, Francis, Walpole visits him in Paris, ii. 19.
visits Gray in Paris, ii. 20.
at Rheims, ii. 29.
in Geneva, ii. 37.
Conway, General, to take part in a secret military expedition, ii. 321.
Duke of Devonshire gives him a legacy of £500, iii. 183.
Conway, Hon. Henry Seymour, Gray visits him at Henley, iii. 60, 64.
Conway Papers, Gray engaged in deciphering a heap of, iii. 12.
returned to Walpole's house in Arlington Street, iii. 43.
Cook, Mr. (joint paymaster), iii. 293.
Cookery, Verral's Book of, enriched by Gray, iii. 81.
Cornhill, destruction by fire of Gray's house in, ii. 181-182.
rebuilding of Gray's house in, ii. 228.
asks Dr. Wharton to pay his fire policy, ii. 263.
Mr. Ramsay, Gray's tenant in, iii. 208.
Cornwallis, Sir William, his Essayes of certaine Paradoxes, 1617, account of, iii. 312.
Correggio, his works in the churches of Parma, ii. 49.
his picture of Venus in the collection of Sir William Hamilton, iii. 195.
his picture of Sigismonda in the collection of Sir Luke Schaub, iii. 195.
Cors, Lambert li, his poem of the Roman d'Alexandre, i. 357.
Corsini, Lorenzo (Pope Clement XII.), ii. 63.
Corsola, Bishop of, Claudio Tolomei, i. 342.
Coscia, Cardinal Niccolo, Archbishop of Benevento, biographical note, ii. 94.
Costume, Gray's Parisian, ii. 57.
Cotes, Humphrey, friend of Charles Churchill, iii. 187.
Couplet about Birds, i. 139.
Couplet on Dining, i. 141.
Covent Garden, Gray obtains nosegays from, ii. 399.
Coventry, Francis, Gray's friendship with, ii. 163.
his comedy of Pompey the Little, ii. 214.
Coventry, Lady, Elegy on her death about to appear, iii. 65.
Gray's criticism of Mason's Elegy on, ii. 358; iii. 73-75.
Cowley misquoted by Gray in the Progress of Poesy, and by Mitford, i. 32.
Cowley, comparison of his talents with Dryden's, i. 32.
Irregular stanzas introduced by, ii. 262.
Cowper, Mr., residentiary at York, congratulates Gray, iii. 329.
Cradock, Joseph, reports statement of John, Earl of Sandwich, relative to Gray, i. 131.
refers to Gray's use of the mountain of Caer Caradoc, ii. 270.
Cranmer, Archbishop, his portrait in Emanuel College, i. 310.
Craon, Prince of, entertains Gray, ii. 52.
visits Rome, ii. 85.
Crebillon, Prosper Jolyot de, his Lettres de la Marquise, ii. 27.
Gray recommends the romances of, ii. 107.
his Le Sopha, ii. 128.
his tragedy of Catalina, ii. 193.
Crescimbeni, Comentarj del, references to, i. 325, 327, 337, 365, 372, 374.
Creswick, Mr. (the Duke of Cleveland's managing man), iii. 33.
Critical Review, article on Gray's Bard in, ii. 327, 331.
Crofts, Mr., a candidate for the University, iii. 390.
Croma, one of the poems of Ossian, iii. 48.
Cromartie, Earl of, his trial for rebellion, ii. 140.
Cromartie, Lady, supplicates her husband's life, ii. 140.
Crowland Abbey visited by Gray, ii. 366.
Crowley, Robert, printer of Peirce Plowman's Vision, i. 370.
Crusades, History of the, reference to, ii. 229.
Cumberland, Duke of, his entry into Edinburgh, i. 143.
his popularity, i. 145.
his illness, ii. 321.
attended by the surgeons of Marshall d'Etrées, ii. 321.
his resignation after Closter-Seven, ii. 343.
recovered of his paralytic attack, iii. 66.
appears at Newmarket in his chaise, iii. 66.
King George II.'s bequests to, iii. 70-71.
"in a very good way, 'tis strange if he recovers," iii. 183.
his illness at Newmarket and story concerning it, iii. 185.
date of his death, iii. 185.

356

INDEX.

Cumberland, R., his verses on the death of Frederick, Prince of Wales, ii. 119.

Curtall, Mr., reference to, iii. 133.

Curzon, Dr., late of Brazenose, and the Poetical Rondeau, i. 208.

Cyrus, see *Ciro.*

D'Affray, Count, French Ambassador at the Hague, iii. 50.

D'Alembert, M., Gray comments on his *Mélanges de Littérature et de Philosophie,* iii. 46.

Dalston's, Sir W., house at Acorn Bank, i. 250.

Daniel, Arnauld, his decasyllabic verse, i. 334.

his invention of the Sestine, i. 350.

Daniskiold, Count, hereditary Admiral of Denmark, ii. 194.

Dante, *Translation of Canto 33, Dell' Inferno,* i. viii. 157-160.

now first printed from MS. belonging to Lord Houghton, i. 157.

his esteem of the Canzone species of poetry, i. 352.

ascribes the origin of the old prose romances to the French, i. 365.

D'Arcy, Right Hon. Sir Conyers, reference to, and biographical note, ii. 367.

Mason visits, ii. 373.

D'Arezzo, Fra Guittone, inventor of the Sonnet, i. 349.

Darlington, Lady, reference to, iii. 33.

Darradar Liod, an Icelandic poem; see *The Fatal Sisters,* i. 52.

Darwin, Erasmus, his verses on death of Frederick, Prince of Wales, ii. 119.

D'Aubenton, his *Histoire du Cabinet du Roi,* commended by Gray, ii. 199.

D'Auvergne, Cardinal, attends a conclave at Rome, ii. 67.

Davanzati, his translation of Tacitus, ii. 111.

Davenport, Mr., friend of Rousseau and Dr. T. Wharton, iii. 243.

David, C. Smart's *Song to,* ii. 161.

Davie, Mr., reference to, ii. 146, 147.

Davis, Mrs., an English nun in Calais, ii. 17.

Dawson - Turner, his collection of Graiana, the gift of Mr. Mathias, and now owned by Mr. John Morris, iv. 339.

Dayrolles, Mr., intimate friend of Lord Chesterfield's, ii. 353.

Mason christens his child, ii. 353.

Dayrolles, Mr., his daughter elopes with Leonidas Glover's son, ii. 354.

his relation with Mr. Stanhope at the Hague, ii. 354.

De Grey, Lord Chief Justice of Common Pleas, iii. 390.

De Guerchy and the Chevalier D'Eon, iii. 181.

De Honestis Veterum Dictis by Marcellus Nonius, ii. 113.

De la Lande's *Voyage through Italy,* 8 vols., pretty good to read, iii. 344.

Delap, Dr., referred to by Gray, ii. 309.

author of *Hecuba* and *The Captives,* ii. 309.

biographical note, ii. 309.

Gray proposes, through Mason, that a comment should be written on *The Odes* by, ii. 329.

did he write *"Melpomene"* ? ii. 333.

leaves Mason's curacy, ii. 363.

returned to Trinity, iii. 128, 131.

his *Hecuba* and Mrs. Pritchard, iii.128.

and Kitty Hunter, unfounded report of their marriage, iii. 186.

references to, ii. 311, 313.

Delaval, Edward, his tuition, ii. 155.

his disgrace at Cambridge, ii. 159.

a Fellow-Commoner, ii. 203.

Fellow of Pembroke and of the Royal Society, iii. 137.

his skill in playing water-glasses, iii. 31, 124.

attends regularly on the Wilkes case, iii. 89.

visits Gray in Jermyn Street, iii. 132.

his frankness, iii. 320.

his illness, iii. 335.

criticised Gray, iii. 333.

references to, iii. 122, 137, 186.

Delaval, Sir Francis Blake, asks the post of Modern History for E. Delaval, iii. 140.

Delaval, Sir T., reference to a love affair, iii. 256.

Demofoonte, a drama in which Mingotti excelled, ii. 282.

Denbigh, Lady, at Stoke House, ii. 332.

Denmark, Mallet's *Introduction to the History of,* ii. 352.

Denmark, King of, visits Cambridge, his personal appearance, iii. 329.

references to, iii. 327, 330.

Denny, Sir Anthony, old picture supposed to be his portrait, iii. 227.

D'Eon, Chevalier, and Mons. Du Vergy and De Guerchy, iii. 181.

De Principiis Cogitandi, a didactic poem of Gray's, see *Cogitandi,* ii. 104.

De Quincey's invective against Grasmere coach road, l. 266.

De Regimine Principum, Chaucer's portrait by Occleve in the book, l. 305.

Destouches, Néricault, French dramatist, his comedy of Philosophe Marié, ii. 23.

note on, ii. 23.

Devil, History of the, lost fragment of Gray's, i. 142.

Devonshire, Duke of, Head of the Treasury, ii. 292.

appoints Rev. W. Mason Chaplain in Ordinary to George II., ii. 326.

gives a dinner to gentlemen attending coronation of George III., iii. 114.

his seat at Chatsworth, iii. 134-136.

death of William, 4th Duke, and the cause, iii. 176, 184.

value of his estate and his bequests, iii. 183, 184.

Diamantina, La, violinist, ii. 76.

Dickens, Dr., reference to, ii. 118.

Dillon, Mr. John, possessed and added to the Dawson-Turner MSS. of Gray, iv. 339.

Dining, Couplet on, i. 141.

Doctor of Laws, Gray's attachment to Cambridge induces him to decline, from the University of Aberdeen, the honorary degree of, ii. 219-220.

Dodsley, Robert, prints the Elegy written in a Country Churchyard, ii. 211.

the printing of Gray's Odes, ii. 218.

prints a collection of Miscellaneous Poems, including Gray, ii. 219.

Gray offers to Horace Walpole some Odes for insertion in the Miscellaneous Poems, ii. 226, 364.

prints the Elegy with Bentley's designs, ii. 234.

references to, ii. 235, 339.

his conscience settled by Soame Jenyns work on Evil, ii. 310.

how many copies of the Odes has he disposed of, out of the 2000 ? ii. 329.

directed to distribute Gray's poems to certain persons, ii. 344.

his play of Cleone, ii. 391.

printing an edition of Gray contemporary with the Glasgow edition of Foulis, iii. 286-287, 290.

glutted the town with two editions, one of 1500 copies and one of 750, iii. 325.

Dodwell, assists in the Chronological table of ancient authors, ii. 158.

Doncaster, aspect of the country near, ii. 247.

Doria, Andrea, reference to, ii. 48.

Dorset, Ann, Countess of, Gray's extempore Epitaph on, see Pembroke, i. 140.

MS. sketch of her life by Mr. Sedgwick, i. 279.

Dorset, Duke of, his distress on the misfortunes of Lord G. Sackville, iii. 34.

Douániers, dragons of Turin, ii. 43.

Douglas, a tragedy by John Home, ii. 360.

Douglas, Bishop, reference to his Prologue to the 8th Æneid, i. 341.

Dovedale and the Peak, visited by Gray and Dr. Brown, iii. 273.

Doyly, Thomas, Fellow of St. John's, iii. 190.

Dragon, the red, device of Cadwallader, i. 70.

Druidical mythology, iii. 351.

Druidicarum, Historiâ Vettm. Academarium Gallo, reference to, ii. 294.

Druidis, Commentatio de, by Frickius, ii. 293.

Drummond, appointed Archbishop of York, iii. 105.

Drury Lane Theatre, Dr. Johnson's prologue for the opening of, ii. 220.

Dryden, John, compared with Cowley, as a writer of sublime Odes, i. 36.

his license of language in poetry, instances of, ii. 108.

his character disgraceful to the post of poet laureate, ii. 345.

his poems recommended by Gray to Dr. Beattie, iii. 222.

Duclos Mémoires, reference to, ii. 291.

Dufresne, Abraham Alexis Quinault, a member of the Comedie Françoise, ii. 23.

Dunbar, Lord, in attendance on The Pretender at Rome, ii. 85.

Dunciad, The New, Gray's opinion of, ii. 105.

Duncombe, Harry, friend of Rev. Norton Nicholls, iii. 240.

Dupplin, Thomas Henry Viscount, Chancellor of the Exchequer, ii. 354.

Durham, Dr. Richard Trevor, Bishop of, ii. 241.

Dr. Joseph Butler, Bishop of, ii. 241.

fever in, ii. 245.

Durell, Commodore, reference to, iii. 9.

D'Urry's edition of Chaucer's works, l. 306, 325.

describes a portrait of Chaucer at Chastleton, l. 306.

Dutch, probable settlement with, and no war, ii. 392.
Du Vergy, the adventurer, in jail for debt, iii. 181.
Dyce, Rev. A., MS. copy of Gray's *Epitaph on a Child*, i. 126.
MS. note as to the destruction of the autograph of *The Characters of the Christ-Cross-Row*, i. 210.
note on the cause of Richard West's death, ii. 113.
Dyer, John, author of *Grongar Hill*, reference to, ii. 220.
author of *The Fleece*, ii. 345.

EAGLES on Snowdon, i. 43.
Ease, the mother of fine art, i. 119.
Eckardt, J. G., H. Walpole's Epistle to, ii. 221.
his portrait of Gray, ii. 234.
Edmondes, Sir T., State Papers of, ii. 231.
Edouard III., Gresset's tragedy of, ii. 186.
Education, thoughts on, i. 120.
Education and Government, The Alliance of, a fragment, i. 113-117.
editorial note on, i. 113.
first published, 1775, i. 100.
commentary by Gray, i. 117-119.
its duties, i. 119.
Gray sends a copy to T. Wharton, ii. 187.
Edward VI., his restrictions on dress, i. 318.
Effingham, Thomas Harcourt, Earl of, his part in the coronation of George III., iii. 115.
Egmont, Lord, rumour that he will be Secretary of State, iii. 237.
Egremont, Lord, his hanging woods near Ulleswater, i. 254.
Egypt, Travels in, by Captain Norden, ii. 194.
translated by Templeman, iii. 1.
Egyptian architecture, Dr. Pococke's prints on, ii. 255.
Ekkehardus, monk of St. Gall, early authority on Latin rhyme, i. 379.
Election time, letters apt to be opened at the offices during, ii. 249.
Electress Palatine, Dowager, receives H. Walpole at Florence, ii. 54.
Elegy in the Garden of a Friend, by Mason. Gray requests it for criticism, ii. 339.
Gray's criticism, ii. 357.
Elegy written in a Country Church-yard, text of the edition of 1768, i. 71-80.

Elegy, text of the first edition, i. 219-223.
Pembroke text, i. 227-232.
editorial note on, i. 72.
satirical criticism by Professor Young, i. 208.
advertisement to Dodsley's first edition, i. 217.
bibliographical note by Gray, i. 227.
submitted to H. Walpole, ii. 209.
H. Walpole requested to ask Dodsley to print it, ii. 210.
Magazine of Magazines and its publication, ii. 210-211.
printed by Dodsley, with a preface by H. Walpole, ii. 211.
errors of the text, ii. 213.
design by Bentley for, ii. 234; engraved by J. S. Müller and Charles Grignion, ii. 234; the original drawings offered for sale in 1882, ii. 234.
Robert Lloyd publishes a Latin translation, iii. 128.
Elfrida, a drama by Mason, ii. 212, 213; iii. 148.
Elisi, singer and actor, illness of, iii. 77.
excellence of his singing, and his personal appearance, iii. 80.
Elizabeth, Queen, her deportment on receiving Dzialinski of Poland, i. 49.
Elizabethan State Papers, by William Murdin, ii. 396.
Ely visited by Gray, ii. 366.
Emanuel College, portraits in, i. 309-310.
Emile, Rousseau's, Gray's praise of, iii. 151-152.
Encyclopedia, see French.
English language too diffuse, ii. 111.
Engravings, recommends their production in Italy and France, those of England are woeful, iii. 105.
Entail, The, a fable by H. Walpole, ii. 214.
Enthusiast, The, by J. Warton, ii. 121.
Epicurus, ruinous effect of his doctrine to society, i. 120.
Epigram on the company at Cambridge University, 1768, iii. 296.
Epitaph on a Child, i. viii. 126.
Errol, Earl of, his appearance at the coronation of George III., iii. 113.
Erse Poems, publication of the, i. 311.
testimony in favour of their authenticity, i. 311.
Gray charmed with two specimens of, iii. 45.
enquires of Walpole if the authors are known, and whether any more are to be had, iii. 45.

Erse Poems, Gray obtains from Scotland, and reviews a third specimen, iii. 47-48.
said to be translated by Macpherson, but Gray is much exercised as to their authenticity, iii. 51-52.
publication of, iii. 56-57.
David Hume's opinion as to their genuineness, cites persons who believe in their antiquity, iii. 59, 65.
subscription on foot to enable Macpherson to recover further fragments, iii. 59, 65.
Gray more puzzled than ever about their antiquity, iii. 61.
second edition published, iii. 65, 69.
admires nothing but "Fingal," iii. 84.
Hurd writing against, iii. 129.
Gray's scepticism apparently removed, iii. 148.
Erskine, Sir Henry, surveyor of roads, iii. 72.
unsuccessfully endeavours to obtain an appointment for Gray, iii. 72, 136.
his marriage, iii. 104.
Escalopier, Peter L', Theologia Vettm. Gallorum by, ii. 294.
Esher, Cardinal Wolsey's villa at, ii. 253.
Essex, Lady, death of the gay, ii. 401.
dies in childbirth, iii. 3.
Essex, Lord, attempted suicide of Lady M. Capel, his sister, ii. 274.
Estimate of the Manners and Principles of the Times, by Rev. J. Brown, its popularity, ii. 310.
Estrées, Mad. d', and Henri IV., ii. 281.
Eton College, fever among the boys of, ii. 340.
Eton College, Ode on the distant prospect of, i. 15-21.
editorial note on, i. 16.
Etough, Rev. Henry, i. 139.
Etrées, Marshal d', sends his surgeons to attend the Duke of Cumberland, ii. 321.
Ettrick, Mrs., sister to Dr. Wharton, references to, iii. 199, 200, 245, 320, 404.
Euslen, Rev. Laurence, poet laureate, ii. 345.
Evans, Dr., Gray's opinion of, ii. 220.
Evelyn's work on Forest Trees : quotation from relative to locality of the Elm, ii. 247.
Evil, The Origin of, by Soame Jenyns, ii. 310.
Dr. Johnson reviews it, ii. 310.
settled Mr. Dodsley's conscience, ii. 310.

Exhibition of pictures for the first time, ii. 65.
Eyres, Mr., reference to, iii. 319.

Fabian, Alderman, extract from the Prologue to his *Chronicle*, i. 330.
Fairfax, Thomas, Lord, monument of, in Ottley Church, i. 280.
Fall of Princes, see Lydgate.
Farinelli (Carlo Broschi), sopranist, ii. 22, 57 ; iii. 80.
Farnham, Lord, insulted by an Irish mob, iii. 26.
Fashion of the country, the custom and dress of the previous generation of the town, i. 404.
Fatal Sisters, The, an ode, i. 51-58.
editorial note on, i. 52.
paraphrase of "Darradar Liod," i. 52.
Fauchet, President, reference to his Catalogue of Poets, i. 364.
his opinion that the rhyme of the Franks was largely borrowed by other nations, i. 368.
Favonius, *see* West, Richard.
Fawkes, Mr., his residence at, i. 280.
Fellow-Commoners of Cambridge, their riotous conduct, ii. 164.
Female sex, satire on, its gradual extinction, i. 405.
Fen country visited by Gray, ii. 367.
Fenel, Abbé, his *Religion and Opinions of the Gauls*, ii. 362-363.
Ferdinand, Prince, preparing for a battle in Westphalia, ii. 402.
his victory at Minden, ii. 7, 8.
his conduct in Germany, iii. 27.
his reward for Minden, iii. 27.
treatment of Lord George Sackville, iii. 28.
Ferguson, Adam, his *Essay on the History of Civil Society*, Gray's opinion of it, iii. 279.
Ferrera, Lord, his trial, iii. 35.
Mason and Stonehewer present, iii. 35.
burning of his cell during his trial, iii. 35.
Field, Mr, friend of Dr. Wharton and of Gray, iii. 49.
Gray obtains some soap from him as a remedy for gout, etc., ii. 277.
Fielding, Henry, Gray's opinion of *Joseph Andrews*, ii. 107.
and a paper on Message Cards, ii. 143.
Finch, E., appointed surveyor of roads, iii. 72.
Fine Arts, *see* Paintings.
Fischer's concert, and Gugnani, iii. 317.

Fisher, Bishop, supposed portrait in St. John's College of, i. 311.

Fitzherbert, Thos., his second son dies from ampntation of his leg, iii. 272.

Fitzmaurice, Lord William, his rapid military promotion, iii. 76.

Fitz-Osborne's, Sir Thomas, Letters on various Subjects, by William Melmoth, iii. 222.

Fitzroy, Mr., reference to, iii. 76.

Flaubert, his temperament akin to Gray's, ii. 8.

Fleece, The, by John Dyer, ii. 345.

Fleming, Sir Michael, his seat of Ridale-hall, i. 266.

Floods, great, in the country (1770), iii. 387.

Florence, A Farewell to, i. 181.

Floyer, Governor, death of, iii. 249.

Floyer, Miss (cousin to Rev. Norton Nicholls), reference to, iii. 317.

"Fobus," see Duke of Newcastle, references to, ii. 353, 370, 371; iii. 45, 50, 63, 76, 105.

Folcacchio de Folcacchieri, early Italian poet, i. 352.

Foljambe, Francis F. H., note on, iii. 335.

has given Gray a specimen of natural history, which is a "jewell of a pismire," iii. 383.

his disappearance, iii. 384.

Folk-lore, vision seen in Caithness on defeat of Sigurd, Earl of Orkney, i. 54.

Fontenelle, Gray's opinion of his manner of style, iii. 166.

Ford, Miss, a performer on musical glasses, iii. 124.

Foreigners, natural aversion to, iii. 156.

Forrester, Rev. Richard, Fellow of Pembroke, ii. 288.

death of his sister, ii. 318.

vacates his fellowship and goes to Ashwell, Herts, ii. 346.

his patron, Lord Maynard, promotes him from Easton, iii. 140.

mortal foe of his brother "Poulter," iii. 140.

reference to, iii. 63.

Forster, Mrs. (née Pattinson, Gray's cousin), returns from India, ii. 201.

to accommodate some of Gray's lumber, ii. 385.

Gray has kissed her at Dr. Wharton's instance, and forgot old quarrels, iii. 322.

Fortescue, Miss Lucy, afterwards Lady Lyttelton, ii. 180.

Fothergill, Dr., reference to, ii. 252, 259.

Fotheringay visited by Gray, ii. 366.

Foulis, Glasgow publisher of Gray's Poems, iii. 285-287.

Gray's appreciation of him as a publisher, iii. 290, 325.

offers to present Gray with his Homer or the Greek Historians, iii. 346.

new edition of Milton to which Gray wishes to subscribe, iii. 346.

visited by Gray in Glasgow, iv. 343.

Gray admired his academy of painting, iv. 343.

Fountayne, Dean, reference to, iii. 82, 108.

Fox, Mr., unhappily criticises The Bard, ii. 328, 331.

Framlingham rectory in the gift of Pembroke College, iii. 328.

Frampton, Thomas, Fellow of St. John's, candidate for the Mastership of St. John's with support of the Earl of Sandwich, iii. 190.

note on, iii. 190.

France, Abrégé Chronologique de l'Hist. de, by President Henault, ii. 201.

on the brink of a general bankruptcy, iii. 341.

people of the provinces starving on the highways, iii. 384.

Etat de la, Gray commends it, ii. 128.

Gray's Journal in, i. ix. 237-246.

Gray gives detailed advice to the Rev. Mr. Palgrave as to the places he should visit in, iii. 193.

Account of Gray's journey through, ii. 16-35.

references by Gray to towns, etc., in :—

Abbeville, its description, ii. 18.

Abbey of Carthusians, Dijon, ii. 31.

Abbey of Cistercians, Dijon, ii. 32.

Annecy, the residence of the exiled Bishop of Geneva, i. 245.

Ballet de la Paix, description of, ii. 21-22.

Beaune and Nuys, fertility of the country round, i. 242.

Burgundy, description of the country, ii. 31.

united to crown of France, ii. 32.

Calais, description of, ii. 16.

Cenis, Mount, description of, ii. 41-42, 46, 59.

Châlons-sur-Marne, i. 239.

Chartreuse, Monastery of the Grande, its picturesque situation on a mountain near Echelles, i. 241.

reference to, ii. 36-37.

ascent of the mountain, ii. 35-36, 45, 58.

France, references by Gray to towns, etc., in :—
Dijon, road approaching, i. 240.
a beautiful city, i. 241; ii. 31-32, 35.
Abbey of St. Benigne, i. 241.
Chartreuse, The, their chapel and its tombs, i. 242.
Church of the Bernardines, i. 241.
Church of the Cordeliers, i. 241.
Church of St. Michael, i. 241.
Palais des Etats, i. 241; ii. 35.
du Roi, i. 241.
Parc, The, i. 242.
Place, The, i. 241.
Inns, French, description of, in 1739, ii. 17.
Joinville, its fine appearance from the road, i. 240.
Langres, description, i. 240.
Langres, the Bishop of, a Duke and Peer of France, i. 240.
the Cathedral of St. Mammet, i. 240.
Lugdunum (the modern Lyons), ii. 33.
Lyons, description of, ii. 33-35.
view to be obtained of, i. 243.
its situation at the confluence of the Rhône and Saône, i. 243.
Mount Fourvière, near Lyons, antiquities on, ii. 34.
Nuys and Beaune, fertility of the country round, i. 242.
Paris visited by Gray, ii. 20-24.
Paris, burlesque account of, ii. 56-57.
Parisian costume, ii. 57.
Rheims, description of, i. 237; ii. 28-30.
Cathedral of Nôtre Dame, i. 237; ii. 28.
Church of St. Nicaise, i. 237.
Church of St. Pierre-aux-Dames, i. 237.
Church of St. Remi, i. 237.
its ramparts and ancient triumphal arches, i. 238.
its society, ii. 29.
residents known to Gray, i. 239.
Rheims to Dijon, description of road, ii. 31.
St. Denis, its monuments and treasures, ii. 20.
Saône, fine view from Mount Tornus of the river, i. 242.
Savoy contrasted with Geneva, i. 245.
Savoy, description of the vale of the, i. 245.

France, references by Gray to towns, etc., in :—
Sillery, house of the Marquis de Puisieux at, i. 239.
Versailles, description of, ii. 24-25.
Vitry le François, description of, i. 240.
Franck or Francken, Jerome, Flemish painter, Dr. Wharton purchases a picture probably by, ii. 384.
Francklyn, Thomas, of Trinity College, ii. 311.
Franklin, Mrs. Joyce, her portrait in Emanuel College, i. 310.
Franklin, Professor, supposed writer of an article, in The Critical Review, on Gray's Two Odes, ii. 327, 331.
Fraser, H. Walpole asked to influence him on behalf of Dr. Brown, ii. 289.
Gray enquires if he has recovered, ii. 300.
Gray tells Mason he will send a copy of The Odes for, ii. 322.
reference to, iii. 41.
his industry, iii. 224.
Fraser, Sir William, owner of Mason's copy of the Elegy, i. 72.
Frasini, an opera singer, ii. 284.
Frederick the Great of Prussia, his Memoirs of the House of Brandenburg, ii. 229.
Gray's opinion of, ii. 290.
and the King of Poland, ii. 291.
writes to George II. explaining his difficulties (first year of seven years' war), ii. 320.
Gray's opinion centred in, ii. 339.
his contest with Austria, and capture of Silesia, ii. 350.
his account of the campaign, ii. 372.
reduced to the defence of his Marquisate, ii. 376.
victory over the Russians at Zorndorf, ii. 378.
defeat by the Austrians at Hochkirchen, ii. 385.
his poetry, iii. 36.
Frederick, Prince of Wales, his Charms of Sylvia, iii. 73.
Free-thinking, its altered form, ii. 375.
French clergy, Lettres by General Fleury on the, ii. 230.
influence on English poetry, i. 33.
Encyclopedie, Gray purchases the great, ii. 323; criticism of its articles, ii. 331; iii. 235; termination of, ii 17 vols., iii. 235.
French, Mrs., her opinion of Gray's Long Story, and H. Walpole's reply, ii. 228.

Frenchmen, their atheism, iii. 226.
Freret, Mons., his *Dissertation on the Religion and Opinions of the Gauls*, ii. 363.
Frickius, Albertus, ii. 294.
Frickius, Joannes Georgius, his *Commentatio de Druidis*, ii. 293.
Frisby's in Jermyn Street, Gray's occasional place of lodging, ii. 251.
Froissart, a favourite author of Gray, iii. 24.
his history, iii. 392, 393.
the Herodotus of a barbarous age, iii. 389.
Fruits, ripening of, at Stoke during 1755, iii. 96.
Fuentes, Condé de, reference to, iii. 40, 71.
Fuentes, Madame de, and her twelve ladies, iii. 62.

Galuppi, Baldassaro, his operas, ii. 133.
Gardening, Landscape, the only proof of our original talent in matters of pleasure, iii. 160.
not forty years old, iii. 160.
nothing like it before in Europe, although Chinese excel, iii. 160.
the only honour our country has in matters of taste, iii. 166.
Italy or France unable to comprehend it, iii. 166.
Gardens, Gray's, are in the window, like those of a lodger in Petticoat Lane or Camomile Street, iii. 343.
Garrick, David, his popularity, ii. 133.
his farce of *The Lying Valet*, ii. 213.
William Whitehead's verses to, ii. 220.
Epilogue to *Athelstan*, ii. 261.
his verses in praise of Gray's *Odes*, ii. 325.
opinion of Gray's *Odes*, ii. 330, 341.
his dispute with Arthur Murphy, ii. 364.
and Mason, Gray endeavours to allay their quarrel, ii. 376.
his farce of *The Guardian* acted on behalf of Smart, ii. 391; taken from *Pupille* of Fagan, ii. 391.
Mr. and Mrs., visit Lady Cobham at Stoke, ii. 323, 324, 376.
Gaskarth, Joseph, treasurer and Fellow of Pembroke College, reference to, ii. 283, 288.
Gray sends him a copy of *The Odes*, ii. 320.
quarrels with Sir M. Lamb, ii. 346.
at Aston with Mason, iii. 9.

Gaskarths, their mansion of Hill-top, i. 253.
Gaskyn, Mr., reference to, ii. 295.
Gauls, Religion of the Ancient, referred to, ii. 294.
Religion and Opinions of the, Dissertation on, by Fénel and Freret, ii. 362, 363.
Gaurus, Fragment of a Latin Poem on the, i. 179-181.
Gaussem, Jeanne Catherine (La Gaussin), actress at the Comédie Français, note on, ii. 23.
Gautier de Châtillon, a poem of Flanders, i. 357.
Gay, John, the Duchess of Queensberry his patroness and protector, ii. 372.
Gentleman's Magazine, Impromptu on Lord Holland's house, published in, i. 135.
Geoffrey Plantagenet, his part in the construction of York Minster, iii. 145.
George II., his deportment, ii. 154.
and Lord Holdernesse, ii. 321.
account of his sudden death, iii. 69.
his testamentary bequests, iii. 70-71.
George III., his probable marriage, iii. 70.
his reproof to the Court Chaplains, iii. 75.
refuses to expend money on the general elections, iii. 76.
illness of his Queen, iii. 86.
his favourable impression, iii. 89.
description of his Queen, iii. 105-106.
Gray expects to see the coronation procession, iii. 106.
marriage of, iii. 111.
account of his coronation and the banquet in Westminster Hall, iii. 110-116.
paid £9000 for hire of jewellery at coronation, iii. 113.
and his Queen ate like farmers, iii. 115.
said to esteem and understand the fine arts, iii. 158.
Ghirlandaio, Ridolpho, painter, reference to, i. 320.
Gibbon, his praise of *Education and Government*, i. 113.
Gibbons, Grinling, his work at Chatsworth, ii. 135.
Gibside, a seal of Lord Strathmore, iii. 277.
Gil Blas, Edward Moore's comedy of, ii. 213.
Gilmour, Sir Arthur, his conduct in a riot, iii. 339.

Gilpin, his *Observations on the River Wye*, iii. 380.

Gisborne, Dr., President of the College of Physicians, biographical note, iii. 67.

his neglect of the offer of Conservator of Hunter's Museum, iii. 67.

Gray sends a production of Mason's to, iii. 246-247.

references to, iii. 150, 334.

Glasgow edition of Gray's poems; Gray agrees to Dr. Beattie's proposal of publishing a, iii. 285-287.

Gray's praise of it, iii. 325.

its success, sold off in a short time, iii. 346.

Glasgow press, beauty of its type, iii. 165.

Glass, green, not classical, iii. 17.

organist, reference to the death of a, iii. 22.

painted, manufactured at York, iii. 17 ; exhibits at Society of Arts, iii. 102 ; made also at Worcester, and sold by weight, iii. 17 ; failure of the factory there, iii. 102 ; Gray's advice for procuring, iii. 102-103.

Glasses, water, Delaval's skill on, iii. 31, 124.

description of, iii. 124.

reference to various players on, iii. 124.

delights Gray, iii. 125.

Gray knows Mason will be weary of him, because he cannot play them, iii. 147.

Gloucester music - meeting, reference to, iii. 343.

Gloucester Street, Gray enquires of Dr. Wharton if he can stay for a week in, ii. 366.

Glover, Richard ("Leonidas"), his youngest son elopes with Mr. Dayrolles' daughter, ii. 354.

biographical note, ii. 134.

Gluck, a German player on water-glasses, iii. 124.

Glynn, Dr., Gray's Cambridge physician, iii. 296.

"God - willing," Archbishop Potter's proviso, ii. 240.

Golding, Mr., reference to his death, l. 212.

Gondolfo, Castel, a house of the Pope's, ii. 78.

Goodman's Fields, Garrick at, ii. 133.

Gordon, Lady Catherine (Mrs. Charteris), i. 275.

Gordon, Mr., interested in Smart, iii. 163.

Gormogons, note on the, ii. 166.

Gotti, Cardinal Vincenzo Luigi, note relative to, ii. 93.

Gould, T. V., Fellow of New Hall, reference to, iii. 170.

Gout, prescription for the, ii. 267.

Grafton, Augustus Henry Fitzroy, Duke of, Chancellor of Cambridge University, i. 92.

Installation Ode, i. 92.

his descent, i. 96.

Mr. Stonehewer and Mr. Bradshaw, Secretaries to, ii. 94.

Mr. Stonehewer, tutor to, ii. 277.

Gray thanks him for the Professorship of Modern History, iii. 318.

Gray's praise of, iii. 342.

Installation as Chancellor of University, iii. 343-4.

Gray bound in gratitude to write his *Installation Ode*, iii. 346.

Graham, Rev. Mr., the horticulturist, Gray visits him at Netherby, iv. 342.

Graham, Sir Bellingham, dines with Gray, i. 275.

Granby, Marquis of, injured whilst with the troops in Hanover, ii. 378.

Grand Magazine of Magazines, Gray's *Elegy* published by the, i. 72.

Grandval, Racot de, comedian, ii. 23.

Grantley, Lord, *see* Sir F. Norton, ii. 176.

Gray, Mrs. Dorothy (the poet's mother), Gray consoles her on the death of his aunt, Mrs. Antrobus, ii. 208.

her illness, ii. 233.

death of, ii. 237, 250.

Gray's deep affection for, iii. 239.

transcript of her epitaph from the MS. in pencil of Gray, iv. 339.

Gray, Lord, his belief that he was related to the poet, iii. 280.

Gray desires a copy of the Glasgow edition of the poems to be sent to, iii. 290.

Gray, Sir James, may be appointed to Spain, iii. 256.

Greathead, Mr., his residence near Warwick, ii. 258.

Greaves, William, his Pamphlet on Libels, Warrants, etc., iii. 192.

Greece, its early influence on English poetry, i. 33.

Greek inscription for a Wood, by Gray, ii. 115.

religion, the foundation of the Roman, ii. 173.

Green, John, Master of Ben'et, Gray sends him a copy of *The Odes*, ii. 320.

Green, John, requests Dr. Dalguy to preach a commencement sermon, ii. 368.

Green, Matthew, Gray's opinion of his poetry, ii. 219.
note on, ii. 219.
extract from his *Queen's Hermitage*, ii. 223, 224.

Green, Dr. Thomas, Dean of Salisbury, ii. 317.

Greene, Dr. John, Bishop of Lincoln, reference to, iii. 56, 97, 105.

Greenwood, George, of Chastleton, Gloucester, portrait of Chaucer in the possession of, i. 306.

Grenville, G., Paymaster-General, ii. 292.
disinherited by his brother Lord Temple, iii. 123.
his candid refutation of the charges brought against the present ministers, iii. 256.

Gresset, Jean Baptiste Louis, his *Epître à ma Sœur* gave Gray the idea for *The Ode on Vicissitude*, i. 123.
his writings and their influence on Gray, ii. 182.
comedy of *Le Méchant*, ii. 183.
his works enumerated, ii. 184.
tragedy of *Edouard III.*, ii. 186.
Le Lutrin Vivant, ii. 186.

Grey, Walter, Archbishop of York, his part in the building of York minster, iii. 145.

Grey, Dr. Zachary, reference to, iii. 55.

Grignion, Charles, engraved the figures for the design to Gray's *Elegy*, ii. 234.

Grongar Hill, written by John Dyer, ii. 220.

Grotto, The, a poem by M. Green, ii. 219.

Guardian, The, a farce by Garrick, ii. 391.

Gugnani to sing at Fischer's concert, iii. 317.

Gunning, Stuart, Fellow of St. John's, and candidate for Mastership of St. John's, iii. 190.

Guthrie, William, of Brechin, author of the *General History of Scotland*, criticises Walpole's *Historic Doubts* in the *Critical Review*, iii. 313, 314.

Guy Cliff, Warwick, the residence of Mr. Greathead, ii. 257.
its natural beauties, ii. 257.
the cell of Guy, Earl of Warwick, ii. 258.

HABIT, definition of what we call, ii. 374.

Hadden, Ephraim, reference to as a vendor of rope-ladders, ii. 277.

Hadley, Dr. J., of Queen's College, ii. 320.
Gray sends him a copy of *The Odes*, ii. 320.

Halfpenny, William, his popularity and *Useful Architecture*, iii. 110.

Halicarnassus, Dio, his knowledge of the Roman mythology, ii. 173.

Halifax, Lord, appoints Eusden poet laureate, ii. 345.
his boyish days, ii. 115.

Hallifax, Dr., Bishop of Gloucester, note on, iii. 254.
references to, iii. 208, 259, 331, 359.

Hall, Dr., Bishop of Exeter, portrait in Emanuel College, i. 310.

Hall, Joseph, Bishop of Norwich, Gray's opinion of his Satyres, ii. 233.
Virgidemiarium written at Cambridge, ii. 233.

Hall, William, of King's Walden, his daughter Elizabeth marries Mr. Bonfoy, ii. 378.

Hamilton, Mr., Gray recommends Dr. Wharton to visit at Cobham the house of, ii. 254.
his skill in laying out pleasure-grounds, ii. 254.

Hampton, Gray stays with the Cobhams at, ii. 369.

Hardicanute, poem by Lady Wardlaw, iii. 45; second part by Mr. Pinkerton, iii. 46.

Hardwicke, Philip, second Lord, his election as Seneschal of Cambridge University, i. 131.
reference to, iii. 6.
probably will support the Whigs, iii. 76.
author of the King's Speech, iii. 123.
his recovery from illness and election as High Steward of Cambridge, iii. 168, 200.
probability of his becoming Secretary of State, iii. 233.

Hardwick Hall, description of the Duke of Devonshire's seat at, iii. 136.

Harmonica, *see* glasses, water.

Harpe, Jean François de la, his works not to be had in England, note on, iii. 295.

Harris, Samuel, Professor of Modern History, iii. 136.

Hartlepool, Gray visits. Its waters and other attractions, iii. 206, 207.
sturdiness of its inhabitants, iii. 207.
Harvest, progress of, in 1759, iii. 12.
Hasel or Hassle, Mr., his residence of Delnaine, i. 251.
Hatfield, death of Richard West at, i. 2.
church, burial-place of West, ii. 113.
Hatton family, their house at Stoke, i. 83.
Hatton, Sir Christopher, i. 83.
Hauberk, The, definition of, i. 41.
Haveus, Theodore, of Cleves, architect, his portrait at Caius College, i. 309.
Havre-de-Grace, bombardment by Admiral Rodney, ii. 402.
Hawke, Admiral Sir Edward, his unsuccessful expedition to Rochefort, i. 342.
his great victory, iii. 22, 23.
Hawley, General, his defeat at Falkirk, ii. 129.
Hayes, Dr., Gray's medical adviser, ii. 297.
attends Mrs. Rogers, ii. 382.
Haynes, Mr., reference to, ii. 165.
Hayter, Thomas, Bishop of Norwich, translated to London, ii. 105.
death of, ii. 125.
Health, J. Armstrong's poem on, ii. 121.
Hearse-day, appearance of the hearse, iii. 339.
Heberden, Dr., reference to, i. 252, 280.
attends Mrs. Charles York, i. 401.
marries Miss Wollaston, iii. 29.
reference to, and his good dinners, iii. 66.
his son entered as a pensioner of St. John's College, iii. 385.
Hecuba, Rev. Dr. Delap's tragedy of, ii. 309.
Heere, Lucas de, his arrival in England, i. 314.
Helias of Barham, Canon of Salisbury, i. 316.
Heloise, Nouvelle, Gray's opinion of the 6 vols. of, iii. 79, 83.
Hénault, Charles Jean François, President, Histoire de France, ii. 158.
Abrégé Chronologique de l'Hist. de France, ii. 201.
Henley, Rev. John (Orator Henley), allusion to, ii. 15.
Henri IV. of France, effect of his marriage proposals, ii. 281.
character of his court, ii. 281.
Henry VI., founder of King's College, Cambridge, i. 95.
Henry VIII., benefactor of Trinity College, Cambridge, i. 95.

Hens, Supper of, by Francis I., ii. 114.
Herbert of Cherbury, Life of Lord, 200 copies printed at Strawberry Hill, iii. 173.
Hervey, Ashton, fable in Dodsley's Miscellaneous Poems, ii. 222.
Hervey, Frederick, Bishop of Cloyne, Gray laments the loss of his acquaintance, iii. 77.
eats raspberry-puffs with Gray in Cranbourn Alley, iii. 270.
at Durham, his popularity with the ladies, iii. 278.
Hervey, Lord, and Dr. Middleton, dispute as to the Roman Senate, ii. 175.
his admiration of animals, ii. 221.
Hervey, Lady, visited by Madame de Fuentes, iii. 62.
the "Mary Lepell" of Pope, iii. 62.
Heskin, J., verses on the death of Frederick, Prince of Wales, ii. 119.
Hexham, Gray and Dr. Wharton visit, iii. 281.
Hickes, Dr., reference to his Anglo-Saxon Grammar, i. 362.
reference to his Grammar Franco-Theotische, i. 363, 364.
his statement that the Franco-Theotische and the Anglo-Saxon were originally the same language, i. 364.
Hill, Aaron, his play of Merope acted on behalf of Smart, ii. 391.
Hill, Dr. John (the inspector), appointed Master Gardener at Kensington, iii. 89.
Hill-top, the mansion of the Gaskarths, i. 253.
Himers family, i. 262.
Hinchinbroke, seat of Lord Sandwich, iii. 322.
Hinchliffe, Dr., likely to succeed Smith of Trinity, iii. 303, and
Dr. Marriot, reference to, iii. 331.
History of English poetry, contemplated by Gray, i. 53.
History of Hell, A, facetious verses by Gray believed to be lost, i. 142.
Hoadley, Chancellor, Master of St. Cross, iii. 178.
Hodges, his contribution to Dodsley's Collection of Poems, ii. 364.
Hoel, The Death of, an ode, i. 129.
Hogarth's satire on Farinelli, ii. 22.
caricature of Simon Lord Lovat, ii. 146.
his print on The Mystery of Masonry, etc., ii. 166.

Hogarth and Paul Sandby, iii. 65.
exhibition of his pictures in Spring
Gardens, iii. 123.
his periwigs, iii. 123.
introduces Queen Charlotte into one
of his pictures, iii. 123.
Holdernesse, Robert D'Arcy, fourth
Earl of, Gray visits him in Paris,
ii. 20-21.
his interest at Cambridge, ii. 288.
reference to his return to office, ii.
321.
and Mason, ii. 383, 395 ; iii. 9, 50
reference to, ii. 353.
Secretary of State, his premature
publication of General Yorke's
letters, iii. 9.
his residence of Syon Hill, iii. 15.
correspondence with Lord G. Sackville, iii. 23.
obtains a precentorship for Mason,
iii. 82.
named as likely to proceed to Ireland, iii. 91.
going to Yorkshire, iii. 104.
his ghastly smile, iii. 199.
"his ugly face" at York, iii. 283.
Holdernesse, Lady, and Mason, ii. 395.
Holland, Lord, Impromptu on his
house at Kingsgate, i. 135.
editorial note on Impromptu, i. 135.
Gray complains of its publicity,
iii. 334.
his estimate of the character of the
Duke of Newcastle, iii. 42.
his regret of public affairs, iii. 153.
is alive and written three poems,
one entitled Lord Holland's Return
from Italy, iii. 269.
Hollar, neglect of his style, iii. 110.
Hollis, Thomas, presents Gray with a
beautiful set of engravings, iii. 160.
sends Gray Coserella, iii. 198.
Home, John, his tragedies of Agis and
Douglas, ii. 360.
Homer, the father of Circumstance, i.
393.
Essay on, by Rev. John Wood, ii. 395.
Hopson, Major-General, his command
of the Expedition against Mar-
tinique, ii. 385.
Horace, his house at Tivoli, ii. 74.
Commentary of, by Mr. Hurd, ii. 349.
Imitations of, by Thomas Neville, ii.
314.
Hornsby, Thomas, his gout lozenges,
iii. 129.
Houghton Hall, Seat of Sir Robert
Walpole, ii. 11.
its Lanthorn of copper gilt, ii. 12.

Houghton, Lord, his rich collection of
holographs, i. xvii.
possessor of the MS. of Satire upon
the Heads, i. 134.
possessor of Mitford's MS. of Gray's
Dante, i. 157.
Hounslow, residence of Walpole near,
iii. 15.
Housekeeping in the Duke of Norfolk's
establishment (16th century ?), ii.
295-297.
Howe, William Taylor, Fellow of Pembroke, Gray proud of his friendship, iii. 144.
returning from Italy, iii. 143.
channel of intercourse between Gray,
Mason, and Algarotti, iii. 155.
his friendship for Count Algarotti,
iii. 155.
thanked for his testimonies of esteem, iii. 159.
urged not to despair of his health,
will rejoice to see him in England,
iii. 160.
Howlett, Dr. Zachary, see Grey.
Huddleston, Mr., his mansion of
Hutton St. John, i. 251.
Hume, David (historian), believes in
the authenticity of the Erse Poems,
i. 311 ; iii. 59.
History of the Tudors, ii. 396.
Gray considers him a pernicious
writer, iii. 377.
Humorous pieces, recovery of, i. viii.
Hunter, Dr. John, how the College of
Surgeons acquired his Museum,
iii. 67.
Hunter, Kitty, her escapade with
Henry, Earl of Pembroke, iii. 132.
and Dr. Delap, iii. 186.
Huntingdon, the "Wheat Sheaf" Inn
at, iii. 375.
Huntingdon, Earls of, their house at
Stoke, i. 83.
Hurd, Richard, description of, ii. 314.
Gray sends him a copy of the Odes,
ii. 320.
Gray accompanies him to town, ii.
291.
Dr. T. Wharton asks him to be
lenient to Dr. Akenside, ii. 299.
Gray tells him few people admire the
Odes, ii. 325.
at Thurcaston, ii. 326.
allusion to his Moral and Political
Dialogues, ii. 325.
letter on the Marks of Imitation, ii.
339.
his remarks on Hume's Natural
History of Religion, ii. 349.

Hurd, Richard, reference to his *Commentary of Horace*, ii. 349.
Gray enquires of Mason whether he should transmit the MS. of *Caractacus* to, ii. 386.
obliged by Dr. Wharton, ii. 389.
and Warburton's criticism of *Caractacus* called that of Prior Park, ii. 393.
attacking the *Erse* fragments, iii. 129.
obtains the sinecure rectory of Folkton on recommendation of Mr. Allen, iii. 139.
"grown pure and plump," visits Gray, iii. 224.
undergoes a painful operation for something akin to fistula, iii. 335.
reported serious illness of, iii. 353.
is now well, and takes an hour's walk with Gray, iii. 354.
references to, ii. 371 ; iii. 108.
Hutcheson, the disciple of Shaftesbury, ii. 107.
Hutton, Archbishop of York, gives a prebend's stall in York Cathedral to Mason, ii. 250.
Hutton, John, reference to, ii. 82.
his interest with his cousin (the Archbishop) on behalf of Mason, ii. 250.
leaves Mason an estate, ii. 250.
Hymeneal on the marriage of Frederick, Prince of Wales, i. 168.

ICELANDIC LAYS, reference to *Darradar Liod*, i. 52
Vegtams kvida or *Baldrs draumar*, i. 60.
Ignorance, Hymn to, i. 111.
editorial note on, i. 111.
first publication, i. 100.
Imagination, works of, decline, i. 393.
Imitation, Hurd, *On the marks of*, ii. 339.
Impatience, the forerunner of the decline of works of imagination, i. 393.
Impromptus, i. 140-141.
Ingram, Mr., Groom of the Bedchamber, ii. 290.
Ink-fish, iii. 12.
Inscription for a Wood in a Park, i. 193.
Insects, Generick characters *Of the Orders of*, in verse, i. 198-202.
Installation of Knights du Saint Esprit at Chapel Royal, Versailles, ii. 26, 57.
Installation Ode, The, i. 91.
editorial note on, i. 92.

Installation Ode, The, Gray says his worst employment is to write something against the Duke of Grafton's coming to Cambridge, iii. 340.
anecdote relative to Gray's commencement of, iii. 341.
has been rehearsed again and again, iii. 343.
set to music by Dr. John Randall, iii. 343.
sung by Mr. Norris, Rev. Mr. Clarke, Mr. Reinholt, and Miss Thomas, iii. 343.
Gray does not publish it, but *Alma Mater* prints 500 or 600 for the company, iii. 345.
a work of gratitude, iii. 346.
Invasion, fear of a French, ii. 401 ; iii. 3.
King's tent and equipage ready at an hour's warning, ii. 402.
Ireland, Lords Justices offer to resign, ii. 78.
Gray does not know who will go to, ii. 78.
Lord Holdernesse named for, ii. 91.
Irish disturbances in anticipation of a supposed Union and suppression of the Irish Parliament, ii. 25-27.
disgraceful scenes in the Irish Parliament, ii. 26.
Dignitaries of State insulted by the rabble, ii. 26.
tranquillity of the castle authorities and a ball given same night, ii. 26.
riot suppressed by the military, ii. 26.
warning of riot given in England six weeks before, ii. 26.
very intractable, even Lords Justices, ii. 91.
Isocrates should be read with judgment, iii. 363.
Italian orthography co-temporary with Chaucer, i. 325.
language easily acquired by one proficient in Latin and French, ii. 7.
language copious and expressive, ii. 8.
Italians, their magnificent reception of strangers, ii. 97-98.
parsimony of their private life, ii. 97.
Italy, its influence on English poetry during Tudor period, i. 33.
Gray would rejoice to exchange tongues with, iii. 158.
Gray gives detailed advice to Palgrave as to the places he should visit in, iii. 194-196.

Italy, description of Gray's visit to, ii. 40-55, 59-103.
references by Gray to towns, etc., in:—
Albano, description of, ii. 78.
Annonciata, church of the, at Genoa, ii. 48.
Appennines, description of crossing the, ii. 51.
Appian way, description of, ii. 78.
Bologna, description of, ii. 50.
Buchetto, a mountain of green marble, near Florence, ii. 54
Coliseum at Rome, ii. 70.
Doria, Palazzo, Genoa, ii. 48.
Florence, description of, ii. 53-55.
manner of keeping Lent in, ii. 64.
manner of its society, ii. 91.
a gay season in, ii. 97.
statue of the Virgin (Madonna dell' Impruneto) brought into, and devotions paid, ii. 99.
Genoa, description of, ii. 47-48.
Herculaneum, description of, ii. 83.
discovery of its site at Portici, iv. 341-342.
excavations at, ii. 277; iv. 342.
Lanslebourg or Lanebourg, description of, ii. 41.
Lombardy, description of, ii. 50.
Modena, its appearance, ii. 50.
Mount Giogo, description of, in the Appennines, ii. 52.
Mount Radicofani, description of country round, ii. 65.
hunting seat of a Grand Duke on, ii. 66.
Mount Vesuvius, its position, and appearance of the lava, iv. 341.
Mount Viterbo, view of Rome from, ii. 66.
Naples, description of, ii. 81-82.
Feast of Corpus Christi celebrated at, ii. 85.
account of Gray's stay at, iv. 340.
MS. of his excursions, in the collection of Mr. Morris, iv. 340.
Neapolitan dominions, cultivation of, contrasted with Papal, ii. 81.
Palestrina, account of, ii. 75.
Papal dominions, contrasted with Neapolitan, ii. 81.
Parma, paintings of Correggio in, ii. 49.
Placenza, ii. 49.
Portici, description of the adjacent coast, iv. 340.
discovery of Herculaneum beneath the site of, iv. 341-342.

Italy, references by Gray to towns, etc., in :—
Reggio, a fair or carnival at, ii. 102.
Rome, view from Mount Viterbo, ii. 66.
description of, ii. 67-71, 84.
St. Peter's, ii. 67, 68, 70, 71 ; its construction, ii. 79.
description of a ball in, ii. 76, 84-85.
description of an Italian evening in, ii. 79.
inscriptions from, ii. 79.
St. Longinus's spear and St. Veronica's handkerchief exposed to view in St. Peter's, ii. 70.
Sienna, account of, ii. 64-65.
Tivoli, Duke of Modena's palace at, ii. 72-74.
Torre del Greco, description of its appearance, iv. 341.
Turin, visited by Gray and Walpole, ii. 40.
description of, ii. 42-44.
its palace, ii. 44.
Tuscany, description of the country, ii. 65.
Venerie, La, country palace of Turin, ii. 44.
Venus de Medicis of Florence, ii. 55, 61.

JACOBITES, their victory at Falkirk, ii. 129.
slight effect of their successes on the rural population of eastern England, ii. 130.
James the First, 2 lyttel Books tocheing, ii. 128.
James's, Dr., powders recommended by Gray, ii. 244.
Jauncey, Mr., settles his son in a curacy, iii. 102.
Jebb, Mr. (physician), hero of dissent at Cambridge, iii. 325.
Jenyns, Soame, The Female Rake, or the Modern Fine Lady, a play by, ii. 214.
his Origin of Evil, ii. 310.
Gray's opinion of his poetical abilities, ii. 222.
Jermyn Street, Gray's place of lodging either at Roberts's or Frisby's in, ii. 237, 251.
Jersey, Lord, reference to, ii. 328.
Jodelle, Etienne, style of his verse, i. 341.

John of Padua, architect of Somerset House, i. 307.
built Longleat, i. 307.
reference to, i. 317.
Johnson, Dr. Samuel, his poem of *London*, ii. 220.
prologue for the opening of Drury Lane theatre, ii. 220.
reviews in the *Literary Magazine* Jenyns's work on Evil, ii. 310.
not a judge of art, iii. 81.
Gray's repugnance to, iii. 371.
Gray calls him the great bear, *Ursa Major*, iii. 371.
Johnson, Miss, trial of Lord Ferrers for the murder of her father, iii. 35-36.
Johnston, Dorothy, her marriage with Néricault Destouches, ii. 23.
Jonathan, Mr., friend of Dr. Wharton, references to, iii. 17, 83, 87, 173, 219, 237.
Jonathan, Mrs., references to, iii. 152, 173, 219, 35?.
Jones, Inigo, his skill in architecture, ii. 158.
Joseph Andrews, Gray's criticism of Fielding's, ii. 107.
July, 1754 and 1759, records of the weather and condition of the crops in, ii. 398-401.
Juvenal and Persius, Imitations of, by Thomas Neville, ii. 314.

KEENE, Dr. Edmund, Bishop of Chester, *lines on*, i. 140, 141.
at Cambridge, ii. 178.
his interest sought on behalf of Stonehewer, ii. 193, 195.
Gray's acquaintance with, ii. 201.
Master of St. Peter's College, note on, ii. 287.
private ambassador of the Earl of Sandwich, iii. 201.
interview with Mr. Charles Yorke, iii. 201.
refused the Archbishopric of Armagh, iii. 201.
his son leaves Eton for Peterhouse College, iii. 385.
references to, ii. 189, 190, 192 ; iii. 55.
Keene, Mrs., Couplet on, i. 141.
Keith, Marshall, death of, ii. 385.
Kemble, Boaden's *Life of*, quotation relative to Mason, ii. 242.
Kennicott, B., his verses on the death of Frederick, Prince of Wales, ii. 119.
Kennington, harvest just over (1759) in, iii. 12.

Kent, William, the architect, his design at Esher, ii. 253.
Kent, Gray's description of the county.
Visited Ramsgate, Margate, Sandwich, Deal, Dover, Folkestone, and Hythe, iii. 240, 241-2.
contrasts its coast with Hartlepool, iii. 242.
Gray has passed a deal of the summer (1768) in, iii. 320.
Keys, *see* Caius.
Keysler, Johann Georg, his description of Celtic and other antiquities in his *Travels through Germany, Hungary*, etc., iii. 351.
Killaloe, Bishop of, insulted by the Irish rabble, iii. 26.
Kilmarnock, Lord, his trial, ii. 139.
King, Dr., Gray's opinion of his poetry, ii. 220.
King's College, Cambridge, founded by Henry VI., i. 195.
Kingston's Light Horse refused admittance into Edinburgh, ii. 143.
Kinnoul, *see* Viscount Dupplin.
Kinnoul, Lord, his journey to Lisbon and Geneva, iii. 27.
description of his voyage to Lisbon, iii. 30.
Kirke, Miss, executrix of Dr. Newcome, iii. 189.
Knight, Dr. Gowin, M.D., principal librarian of British Museum, iii. 6.
Knights du Saint Esprit, installation of, ii. 26, 57.
Knowles, Mr., elected Fellow of Pembroke College, ii. 188.

Lady, The Modern fine, a play by S. Jenyns, ii. 214.
Laguerre, Louis (Old Laguerre), his work at Chatsworth, iii. 136.
Lakes, Dr. Wharton obliged through asthma to part from Gray, when about to set out for the, iii. 349.
Lakes, Gilpin's *Tour to the*, i. 279.
Lakes, Gray's reason for writing the Journal, iii. 350.
Lakes, Journal in the, i. 249-281.
references to places mentioned by Gray in :—
Ambleside, road from, to Kendal, i. 267.
Appleby, description of the country about, with the river Eden, i. 250.
reference to, i. 140.
Armathwaite-house, residence of Mr. Spedding, i. 262.

Lakes, Journal in the, references to places mentioned by Gray in :—
Bassenthwaite-water, description of i. 261, 262.
Bolton Hill, view of Cartmell-sands and Lancaster from, i. 270, 271.
Borrodale, description of, i. 253, 256.
and Wordsworth's *Yew - Trees,* i. 254.
Botany, excellent ground for, i. 263.
Brough, description of a cattle fair at, i. 249.
Buttermere, charr taken in, i. 263.
Carlisle, Gray and Dr. Wharton visit, iii. 281.
Cartmell sands, i. 270.
Castle-Crag, description of, i. 257.
Castle Hill, view of Derwentwater from. i. 259.
Castle-Rigg, fine view from, i. 264.
Cockermouth, visited by Gray and Dr. Wharton, i. 281.
Cockshut-hill, account of, i. 259.
Craven, description of the district of, i. 278.
Crow-park, i. 259.
Dalemaine or Delmaine, residence of Mr. Hasel, i. 251.
Derwentwater, view of, i. 260.
vale of, called the Devil's Chamber Pot, i. 262.
Druid-Circle at Castle-Rigg, i. 261.
Dunmallert, view of Ulleswater from the hill of, i. 251.
Eagle's-eirie, plundering an, i. 258.
Ehnot, description of the vale of the, i. 250, 252.
Elysium, the vale of, i. 253.
Evening at Derwentwater, i. 258-259.
Gardies and Lowside, valley of, i. 253.
Gordale-scar, description of, i. 276-277.
Gowder crag, description of, i. 256.
Grange, situation of the village of, i. 256.
Grasmere, description of, i. 265.
coach road, i. 266.
Hill-top, a mansion of the Gaskarth's, i. 253.
Holm-crag, i. 265.
Hornby Castle, i. 274.
Hutton or Hatton St. John, the residence of Mr. Huddleston, i. 251.
Ilkeley, i. 280.
Ingleborough, view of, i. 275, 278.
Ingleton, i. 275.
Kent, falls of the river, i. 269.
Kendal, its appearance by night, i. 268.
general description, i. 268, 269.

Lakes, Journal in the, references to places mentioned by Gray in :—
Kendal, its church, with tombs of the Parrs, Stricklands, and Bellinghams, i. 269.
Keswick, botany might be studied to perfection around, i. 263.
visited by Gray and Dr. Wharton, iii. 281.
Kirkstall Abbey, description of, i. 281.
Lancaster, description of, i. 271.
its Gothic gateway, i. 271.
Leathes-water, *see* Thirlmere.
Leeds, aspect of, i. 281.
Levens, the seat of Lord Suffolk, i. 270.
Lodore, account of the falls of, i. 225.
and Wordsworth's *Evening Walk,* i. 255.
Lodore-bank Crags, description of, i. 255.
Lune, valley of, i. 274.
Maltham, i. 278.
Milthrop, iron forges near, i. 270.
Ottley, description of, i. 280.
Fairfax monuments in the church of, i. 280.
Penigant, view of, i. 278.
Penrith, view from the Beacon-hill near, i. 250.
visited by Gray and Dr. Wharton, iii. 281.
Place Fell, view of, from Dunmallert Hill, i. 251.
Poulton, i. 272.
Ridale Hall, seat of Sir M. Fleming, i. 266.
Ridale-head, i. 267.
Ridale-water, description of, i. 266.
St. John's, valley of, i. 253.
Saddleback, effect of clouds on, i. 253.
Sea Whaite, i. 257.
Settle, road between Lancaster and, i. 274-276.
Seven Mile Sands, near Lancaster, i. 272.
their danger and story of a fatal attempt to cross them, i. 273.
Sheffield, its pleasant situation, i. 134.
Shode-bank Hill, steep road over, i. 279.
Skipton, description of, i. 278-279.
Thirlmere, called also Leathes Water or Wythburn-Water, description of, i. 264, 265.
acquired by Manchester as a reservoir, i. 264.
Ulleswater, description of, from the hill of Dunmallert, i. 251.
general description of, i. 134.

Lakes, Journal in the, references to places mentioned by Gray in :—
Wadd-mines, near Sea Whaite, i. 257, 263.
Walla-crag, view from, i. 254.
Water-Mallock, village of, i. 252.
Wentworth Castle, description of, iii. 134.
Wharfdale, description of, i. 279-280.
Widhope-brows and the view of Der-wentwater, i. 261.
Windermere, description of, i. 267.
Wythburn Water, *see* Thirlmere.
Lamb, Sir Matthew, quarrels with J. Gaskarth, ii. 346.
father of the first Lord Melbourne, ii. 346.
Lambertini, Cardinal Prospero, ii. 93.
Landscape Gardening, *see* Gardening.
Langland, Robert, metre of, i. 370.
his birthplace, i. 370.
Langley, Battey, his style of architecture, ii. 253.
biographical note on, ii. 253.
Langley, Thomas, his work on architecture, ii. 253.
Lansdowne, Marquis of, his waterfall at Bow-wood, ii. 254.
Lansdowne, Marquis, William Viscount Fitzmaurice created, iii. 76.
Latin verses, i. viii., xvii.
Latini, Sur Brunetto, his poem of *Il Patafflo*, i. 348.
Lauderdale, Richard Maitland, Earl of, his house of Lithinton or Lenox Love, iii. 209.
Laurel, imported into Europe by Clusius, ii. 174.
Law, Dr. Edmund, Master of St. Peter's College, Cambridge, in succession to Dr. Keene, ii. 287.
made Bishop of Carlisle, iii. 337.
gives up £800 a-year to enjoy it, iii. 337.
Lay of Darts, see *The Fatal Sisters*, i. 53.
Laziness, figurative description of, ii. 119.
facetious account of the effect of, on Gray, ii. 192.
Lee, Dr., his knowledge of college matters, ii. 180.
Lee, Nathaniel, his *Bedlam Tragedy*, ii. 106.
Lee, Sir George, Secretary at War, ii. 203.
Leeds, turnpike riots at, ii. 240.
Legge, Right Hon. Henry, Chancellor of Exchequer, ii. 273, 292.
Leghorn, chaplainship of, formerly held by young Mr. Byron, now suggested for Mr. Temple, iii. 402.

Leicester House, the political arrangements of, ii. 290.
Leicester, Lord, buried in Warwick Church, ii. 257.
Leicester, Lettice, Countess of, also buried there, ii. 257.
Leighton, Mr. and Mrs., reference to, iii. 237.
Leman, Rev. Thomas, Countess de Viry presents him with Gray's MS. of the *Amatory Lines*, i. 137.
presents in turn, Gray's MS. to Joseph Wharton, i. 137.
Lennox, Lord, reference to, iii. 76.
Lenox-love or Lithinton, seat of Lord Blantyre, note on, iii. 209.
Lent, account of a Florentine, ii. 64.
Leonidas, Richard Glover's epic of, ii. 134.
Leonius, Canon of St. Benedict, his Latin verse, i. 137.
his origin of *Leonine* verse discussed, i. 373 375.
Lepell, Mary, *see* Lady Hervey, iii. 62.
Letters apt to be opened at the offices at election-times, ii. 249.
*Lettres de la Marquise M * * * au Comte de R * * *, by Crébillon *fils*, ii. 27.
Liberty of Genius, supposititious *Ode on*, i. viii.
Life, Gray's references to his health, mode and condition of :—
confined at Florence with inflammation of his eyes, ii. 367.
in a good easy sort of state but occasionally depressed, ii. 113-114.
doubts if he should find much difference between living in this world and t'other, ii. 135.
calls himself a solitary of six years' standing, ii. 154.
the spirit of laziness begins to possess him, ii. 192.
his mind unable to keep him cheerful or easy, and the spiritual part is the most infirm, ii. 199.
is listless, old, vexed, and perplexed, ii. 206.
diverting himself for a month in London among his gay acquaintances, then returns to his cell, ii. 229.
suffers from gout or rheumatism, ii. 267, 272, 283, 392.
uses soap prescribed by Dr. Wharton for his complaint, ii. 275.
depressed in mind, ii. 285, 321, 371.
ill of a cold and fever, ii. 329.
is better and more capable of amusement, ii. 330.

Life, Gray's references to his :—
can look back on many bitter moments, partly with satisfaction,
and partly with patience, and forward, although not promising,
with some hope, ii. 347.
almost blind with a great cold, ii. 354.
believes that people take notice of
his dulness, ii. 376.
weary and disagreeable in mind
only, ii. 377.
thinks that he inspires everything
around him with ennui and dejection, ii. 379.
solitary and dispirited, but not
wholly unpleasant to himself, iii. 1.
the British Museum his favourite
domain, iii. 5, 11, 15.
envies Dr. Wharton his country
abode, whilst he will never have
even a thatched roof of his own,
iii. 49.
"racketting about from morning to
night" wears out his spirits, iii.
60-64.
concerts every night at Cambridge,
shall stay this month or two, iii. 124.
has had two slight attacks of gout
after three years' intermission, iii.
130.
long taciturnity owing to the noth-
ingness of my history, iii. 150.
"neglected all my duties in hopes of
finding pleasure," which after all
one never finds, iii. 161.
"nobody contented but you and I,"
iii. 161.
the music of Carlo Bach serves "to
deceive my solitary days," iii 164.
suffered a good deal from a complaint
which has now grown almost constant, iii. 167.
undergoes an operation for the piles,
iii. 170.
travelling through Hampshire, iii. 175.
health much improved by the sea,
iii. 179.
a complaint in his eyes that may
possibly end in blindness, iii. 186.
neither happy nor miserable, iii. 232.
so fat that he suffered more from
heat in 1769 than ever he did in
Italy, iii. 347.
passed six days in Keswick lap'd in
Elysium, iii. 349.
walked about 300 miles through the
lake districts in seventeen days, iii.
350.
have had a cough for above three
months, iii. 392.

Life, Gray's references to his : –
lacks health and spirits all the winter, iii. 401.
travel he must, or cease to exist, iii.
405.
"the gout is gone," but "spirits
much oppressed," God knows what
will be the end of it, iii. 405.
Lighting of the chandeliers at George
III.'s coronation, iii. 114.
Lincoln, Lord, Gray visits him near
Twickenham, and describes his
newly made plantations, ii. 370.
Lisbon, Voltaire's poem on the earth-
quake at, ii. 285.
Lisburne, Lord, reference to, iii. 241.
Rev. Norton Nicholls acts as mediator between him and Mr. Temple,
iii. 287, 289, 332-333, 402-403.
Gray's opinion of the disagreement,
iii. 302-303.
Lloyd, Robert, published a Latin translation of Gray's Elegy, i. 227 ; iii.
128.
author with G. Colman of two Odes
in ridicule of Gray and Mason, iii.
128.
his praise of Gray in the Epistle to
Churchill, iii. 128.
Lloyd, Miss, player on musical glasses,
iii. 124.
Lloyd's Evening Post, G. Colman contributes to, iii. 42.
reference to, iii. 123.
Locke, John, his Essay on the Human
Understanding and Gray's De Principiis Cogitandi, i. 185, 193.
Loggan's views of the Cambridge Colleges, i. 309.
Lotz, L'Esprit des, by Montesquieu, ii.
191, 199.
Lok, the evil being, i. 65.
Lomellini, Genoese family of, ii. 48.
London, Dr. Samuel Johnson's poem
of, ii. 220.
London Magazine, Gray's Elegy pub-
lished by the, i. 72.
London, that tiresome dull place where
all persons under thirty find amusement, iii. 181.
Londonderry, Bishop of, his patronage
in Ireland, iii. 403.
Long, Dr. Roger, Master of Pembroke
College, ii. 14.
his verses on the death of Frederick,
Prince of Wales, ii. 118.
takes Mr. Delaval under his tuition,
ii. 155.
settlement of his dispute with the
Rev. J. Brown, ii. 188.

Long, Dr. Roger, introduces Mr. Bedingfield to Gray, ii. 276.
illness, and recovery from, ii. 289.
referred to in Carey's *Candidate*, ii.
289.
an authority on astronomy, ii. 298.
Gray sends him a copy of the *Odes*,
ii. 320.
his audience at Buckingham Palace
to present a lyricord and a glass
sphere to the king, iii. 152-153.
his mechanical faculty, iii. 152.
agent for the Earl of Sandwich at the
election for high steward, iii. 168.
purchases a zumpe, iii. 267.
his funeral, iii. 387.
reference to his harpischords in the
"old lodge," iii. 391.
references to, ii. 138, 228, 280.
Long Story, see *Story*.
Lort, Mr., a candidate for Professorship of Modern History, and a
worthy man, iii. 320.
note on, iii. 324.
gone to Bath, iii. 335.
Lottery ticket, Gray asks Dr. Wharton
to purchase him one, ii. 370, 376.
wins a £20 prize, iii. 337.
Louth, R., his verses on death of
Frederick, Prince of Wales, ii. 119.
Lovat, Lord, his confinement at Edinburgh, ii. 142.
his execution on Tower Hill, ii. 142.
Hogarth's caricature of, ii. 146.
Love-a-la-Mode, Macklin's farce of, iii.
28.
Lowth, Dr., his wife's recovery, iii. 83.
contributes to Dodsley's Miscellaneous Poems, ii. 221.
Gray's opinion of his *Grammar*, iii.
129.
his pamphlet against Warburton, iii.
224.
Ludlam, Revs. Thomas and William,
Fellows of St. John's College, bio-
graphical note on, iii. 144.
Ludlow's *Memoirs*, ii. 128.
Luna est Habitabilis, i. 171-174.
theme for college verses, ii. 8.
Luttrel, Colonel, insulted at door of
the House of Commons, iii. 338.
Lydgate, John, remarks on the poems
of, i. 337-409.
Lynch, Dr., Dean of Canterbury, his
death, iii. 40.
Lyne, Mr., reference to, ii. 144.
Lyon, James Philip, reference to, iii.
122, 173.
Lyon, Thomas, Fellow of Pembroke
College, iii. 122.

Lyon, Thomas, biographical note on,
iii. 122.
goes to Scotland with Gray, iii. 208.
his chambers at Pembroke College
destroyed by fire, iii. 301.
lost one of his causes in the House of
Lords against Lord Panmure, iii. 317.
Gray breakfasts with him and Lady
Maria, iii. 374.
references to, iii. 101, 238.
Lyon, references to the story of the, ii.
290.
Lyttleton, Dean, satire on, i. 316.
Lyttleton, Mr., Gray's opinion of, ii. 220.
refers to an Elegy by, ii. 225.
Lyttleton, Lord George, his Monody on
death, ii. 180.
his Monody parodied in *Peregrine
Pickle*, and his character portrayed
as " Gosling Scrag," ii. 214.
admires *The Odes* of Gray, ii. 327, 331.
his dialogues of the dead, iii. 42.
Lyttleton, Sir Richard, reference to,
iii. 98.

MACAULAY, Mrs., Mr. Pitt made her a
panegyric in the House, iii. 238.
Machiavel, Gray's opinion of, iii. 299.
Mackay, Major, testimony in favour of
the *Erse* poems, iii. 311.
Mackenzie, Mrs., grossly insults Mr.
L——, iii. 87.
Mackfarline, the Laird of, testimony in
support of the *Erse* poems, iii. 311.
Macklin, his farce of *Love-a-la-Mode*,
iii. 28.
gratifies the king, who sends for a
copy, iii. 29.
Macleod, the Laird of, testimony in
support of the *Erse* poems, iii. 311.
MacPherson, Rev. James, his transla-
tion of Ossian's *Poems*, their publi-
cation, iii. 56-57, *see also Erse*.
Magazine of Magazines, its editor refused permission to publish Gray's
Elegy, i. 72.
publishes the *Elegy*, i. 72.
references to its publication of the
Elegy, ii. 210, 211, 213.
Maggett, Captain, and Lord Lovat, ii. 142.
Mahomet, Life of, li. 128.
Mahomet Second, a tragedy, ii. 22.
Maine, Duchess of, Madame de Stael
her confidante, ii. 291.
Maintenon's, Madame de, Letters, Gray's
account of, ii. 232.
reference to, ii. 287.
Mallet, David, supposed to have writ-
ten Earl Nugent's Ode, ii. 220.

Mallet's, Mons., *Introduction to the History of Denmark,* reference to, ii. 352, 362.

Man-at-arms, Gray's description of a, iii. 394.

Manchester, Duke of, reported to have an ancient genealogy of the English kings, with portrait of Richard III., iii. 309.

Manduit, Mr., pamphlet against the German war, iii. 91.

Mann, Horace, entertains Gray at Florence, ii. 52.
description of his residence, ii. 86.
Gray sends him a parcel of books, ii. 123.
reference to his sufferings, ii. 132.

Manning of Brun, Robert, his octo-syllabic rhyme, i. 353.
translator of Peter Langtoft's chronicle, i. 353, 356.

Mapletoft, John, Fellow of Pembroke, reference to, ii. 288 ; iii. 69, 183.
note on, iii. 69.

Marcello, *see* Delaval, ii. 155.

Margaret of Anjou, foundress of Queen's College, i. 95.

Margaret, Lady, Countess of Richmond, foundress of St. John's College, portrait of, i. 310.

Margate, like Bartholomew fair, flown down into Kent, iii. 240.

Mari, Huon de, *Tournoyement d'Antichrist* of, i. 337.

Maria Theresa, Queen of Hungary, Gray's sympathy with, ii. 129, 134.

Marivaux, Gray recommends the romances of, ii. 107.
his novel of *Marianne,* ii. 128.

Marlborough, Sarah, Duchess of, quarrel with Duchess of Queensberry, ii. 133.

Marriage, the Fatal, tragedy by Southerne, ii. 11.

Marriott, Sir James, Master of Trinity, visits Gray, iii. 182.
notes relative to, iii. 182, 296.
competitor with Gray for the Chair of Modern History, iii. 320, 324.
raises a subscription for a musical amphitheatre, iii. 331.
reference to, iii. 331.

Marsham, Mr., assists in the compilation of the Catalogue of ancient authors, ii. 158.

Martin, Jaques, *Religion of the Ancient Gauls* cited by, ii. 294.

Martinique, command of the expedition refused by seven generals, ii. 385.

Mary, Queen of Scots, furniture used by her at Wingfield religiously preserved at Hardwick, iii. 136.

Masinissa and Sophonisba, story by, ii. 115-116.

Mason, Rev. William, his inordinate vanity, i. xv.
his capacity for writing sublime Odes, i. 36.
opinion of Gray's *Education and Government,* i. 121.
gives the origin of Gray's *Ode on Vicissitude,* i. 123.
Shakespeare verses sent to, i. 133.
Gray sends him some comic lines, i. 133.
elegiacal Epitaph on his wife, improved by Gray, i. 141.
his opinion of the picturesque point in landscape, i. 260.
The Progress of Poetry delayed by a remark of, ii. 111.
Ode to a Water Nymph by, ii. 184.
Gray's opinion of him, ii. 184, 196-197, 212.
Ode on the Installation of the Duke of Newcastle, ii. 196.
Gray's comment on *Elfrida,* ii. 212 ; iii. 148.
Gray sends a copy of *Elfrida* to Walpole, ii. 213.
elected a Fellow of Pembroke College, ii. 158.
contributes an Ode to Dodsley's Miscellaneous Poems, ii. 222.
Essays on church music, ii. 241.
his attainments in the composition of music, ii. 242.
Gray comments on the death of the father of, ii. 242, 243.
his loss of fortune, ii. 243.
death of his friend Dr. Pricket, ii. 244.
his fellowship his sole support, ii. 246.
presented to the prebend of Holme through John Hutton, ii. 250, 261.
on the use of the strophe, etc. ii. 263.
Gray influences the style of *Caractacus,* ii. 262.
gives Gray's reason for changing his college, ii. 279.
publication of four new Odes, ii. 280.
suffering from his eyes, ii. 299, 366, 387, 392 ; iii. 205, 206, 207.
promised Irish preferment, ii. 287.
his interest sought on behalf of Dr. Brown for Mastership of Peterhouse, ii. 288.
resides in Arlington Street, ii. 289.

Mason, Rev. William, his chair given by Mitford to a poet laureate, ii. 299.

Gray sends a fragment of *The Bard*, ii. 312-313.

Chaplain in ordinary to George II., ii. 326.

his proposition to write a comment on Gray's *Odes*, ii. 329.

in waiting, ii. 332.

christens Mr. Dayrolles's child and Lady Yarmouth's son, ii. 353-354.

criticism of his Elegies, ii. 354-358.

and the Duchess of Norfolk, ii. 367.

and Sir Conyers d'Arcy, ii. 367.

his poetical exertion attributed by Gray to rivalry, ii. 368.

his uncle Dr. Balguy, ii. 368.

Dr. Warburton sends his *New Legation* to, ii. 369.

Gray tries to quell his quarrel with Garrick, ii. 376.

goes to Aston for the winter and saves a curate, ii. 383.

and Lord Holdernesse, ii. 383.

his poetical indolence, ii. 394.

plants some roses for Hurd at Thurcaston, ii. 397.

boasts of his skill in planting, ii. 397.

entertains Gaskarth at Aston, iii. 9.

Lord Holdernesse sends him much news, iii. 9.

Syon Hill his place of residence, iii. 15.

sitting for his picture, iii. 31.

present at the trial of Lord Ferrers, iii. 35.

ridiculed by G. Colman and R. Lloyd, iii. 41.

rebuilds his rectory at Aston, and improves its grounds, iii. 44, 368.

Gray doubts if he will succeed Chapman, iii. 50.

caricature of some prominent Cantabs, iii. 55.

referred to by the *Monthly Review*, iii. 57.

consulted as to a private tutor for Lord John Cavendish, iii. 58.

preparing with Paul Sandby a picture of Snowdon, iii. 66, 68.

etches Gray's head. Etching preserved at Pembroke, iii. 68.

walks in the royal procession, and at the coronation of George III. ii. 70, 106.

reproved by Gray for prematurely showing the Elegy on Lady Coventry, iii. 73.

Gray's criticism of the Coventry Elegy, iii. 73-75.

Mason, Rev. William, acquires the friendship of Fred. Hervey, iii. 77.

made a Residentiary of York and Precentor, iii. 82, 108.

established at York, iii. 125.

Letters to Lord D. in *Royal* or *Lady's Magazine*, iii. 131.

his reflections on Kitty Hunter, iii. 131.

Gray staying with him at York, iii. 132.

his position as Precentor, iii. 132-133.

Gray's criticism of *Elegy V. on the Death of a Lady*, iii. 139.

Count Algarotti sends him a panegyric on his *Odes*, iii. 151.

repining at his twenty-four weeks' residence at York, iii. 161.

makes a collection for C. Smart, iii. 162.

his acquaintance with Bedingfield, iii. 163.

Gray's criticism of one of his Sonnets, iii. 163, 199.

Gray recommends the music of Carlo Bach to, iii. 164.

tendency to marry, iii. 168.

modelling antique vases in clay, iii. 171.

reference to "future bride," iii. 183.

reference to his betrothment and note on date of his marriage, iii. 198, 202, 207.

Gray's Sonnet to his servant Mrs. Anne, iii. 205-206.

Gray's reasons for not visiting him at York, but sends his blessing to both, iii. 223.

Mrs., said to be very handsome, iii. 224; by no means in health, iii. 232, 244; Dr. Heberden thinks her irretrievably gone in consumption, iii. 244.

grown extremely fat and his wife lean, iii. 244.

Gray sends in disguise his wickedness to Dr. Gisborne, iii. 246.

opportunity of his obtaining other preferment than York, iii. 253.

Mrs., anxiety concerning, iii. 252; Gray's description of, iii. 258; Gray enquires after her health, iii. 201; Lord Holdernesse offers the use of Walmer Castle for Mr. and, iii. 262; Gray advises Ramsgate for, iii. 263; Gray's letter of sympathy on death of, iii. 265.

his esteem of Gray's letter, 266.

Gray writes part of Mrs. Mason's Epitaph, iii. 266.

Mason, Rev. William, inventor of a musical instrument called a "zumpe" or "celestinette," iii. 267. his derivation of "zumpe," iii. 267.
Dr. Brown and Gray the guests of, iii. 272.
Gray criticises an Epitaph written at the Archbishop's request, iii. 274-275, 278.
remonstrated with upon withdrawal of the Epitaph, iii. 276.
reference to another Epitaph that moved Dr. Wharton to tears, iii. 276.
Cambridge society anxious to see him, iii. 296-297.
with Stonehewer at Queen Street in London, iii. 317.
informed of Gray's appointment as Professor of Modern Languages, iii. 322-323.
rectory of Oddington in his gift, iii. 328.
reported to be married, iii. 331.
complaint of his circulation of Gray's lines on Lord Holland's seat, iii. 334.
Gray cannot visit him from Old Park owing to difficulty of road to York, iii. 348.
Gray tells him of his travels in the western counties, iii. 381.
passes the winter in Curzon Street, iii. 404.
references to, ii. 251, 260, 261, 262, 283, 285 ; iii. 1, 15, 50, 63, 65, 97, 131, 149, 150, 282, 296, 297, 303.
see also Caractacus.
Materialism, discourse on, ii. 373-375.
Mathematics, Gray's aversion to, ii. 5.
Mathias, T. J., first publishes the Essay on Norman Architecture, i. 294.
observations on English metre, i. 324.
his 4to edition of Gray forms the basis of Mr. Morris's Graiana, iv. 339.
Mattei, Colomba, her success as a singer, ii. 80.
Maty, Matthew, M.D., librarian of British Museum, iii. 6.
Maurus, Rhabanus, Archbishop of Mentz in 847, his Glossary of the Bible, i. 363.
May, Ode on, Gray praises Richard West's, ii. 112.
May 29th, Latin poem on the, i. 166.
May, N., quarrels with Dr. Long, ii. 155.
interests himself on behalf of C. Smart, ii. 178.
May, Dr. Samuel, Fellow of Pembroke, ii. 288.

May, Dr. Samuel, reference to, ii. 280.
date of his death, iii. 164.
May, Thomas, precedes Gray as a dramatiser of Agrippina, ii. 106.
Maynard, Lord, his seat near Dunmow, iii. 139.
patron of Richard Forrester, iii. 139.
Mead, Dr. Richard, his corpulence, ii. 117.
Méchant, Le, comedy by Gresset, ii. 183.
Villemain's praise of, ii. 183.
Gray recommends it, ii. 184.
Mediocrity, Gresset's Ode on, ii. 184.
Melara, a favourite of Benedict XIV., ii. 93.
Melbourne, first Lord, a son of Sir Matthew Lamb, ii. 346.
Melmoth, William, author of Sir Thos. Fitzosborne's Letters, ii. 222.
Melpomene, an Ode, Gray enquires who wrote it, ii. 338.
Gray thanks Mason for the history of, ii. 338.
Melton, Archbishop of York, built the Minster nave, iii. 147.
Memoires, Duclos's, ii. 291.
de la Porte, ii. 291.
de Madame Staël, ii. 291.
Memoirs, Ludlow's, ii 128.
Memoirs of a celebrated Literary and Political Character, ii. 293.
Memory, half a word written on or near the spot worth a cartload of recollection, ii. 380.
Merope, by Aaron Hill, acted on behalf of C. Smart, ii. 391.
Mervellie, Arnauld de, his metre, i. 334.
Message-cards, paper in Museum on, by H. Walpole, ii. 143.
Metaphysics, Gray's dislike of, ii. 5.
Methodism, Pembroke College owes its preservation from fire to, iii. 301.
Methodist singing-man, reference to a, iii. 297.
Metre, observations on English, i. 323-409 ; editorial note, i. 324.
use of the Anglo-Saxon prefixes, i. 326.
use of final syllable of verbs, i. 326-327.
termination of "an" or "eon" omitted after settlement of Danes, i. 327.
insertion or omission of initial or final letters intended to perfect the measure, i. 327.
use of the Cæsura, i. 329-330, 332, 333.
example from Milton, i. 332.
example from Lord Surrey, i. 333.
Ryme Dogrell, i. 330, 339.
examples from Fabian, i. 330.

Metre Alexandrines, i. 331, 357.
the decasyllabic measure, i. 333.
 example from Wyatt, i. 334.
 example from Surrey, i. 334.
 example from Spenser, i. 341.
 heroic measure of the Italian, i. 334.
Riding Rhyme, i. 335, 336, 330.
 example from Chaucer, i. 335.
 example from Spenser, i. 339.
 attempt to introduce the hexameter, sapphic, etc., in the reign of Elizabeth, i. 341.
Measures of Verse, i. 343-360.
Rime Plate of the French, i. 343.
Versi Sciolti of the Italians, i. 343.
Ottava Rima of the Italians, i. 347.
Terzetti, or *Terza Rima*, its invention, i. 349.
Sonnet, its invention, i. 349.
Sestine, i. 350.
 Canzoni of the Italians, i. 351.
Octosyllabic, i. 353.
Couue, i. 354.
 of the Vision of Pierce Plowman, i. 369.
Metre of Lydgate's time uniform to the ear, if not to the eye, i. 393.
Michell, Mr., an acquaintance of Dr. Wharton, i. 262.
Middleton, Mr., his residence near Burnley, i. 280.
Middleton, Dr. Conyers, his *Cicero*, ii. 128.
 his work on the Roman Senate, ii. 163, 175.
 presented with a sinecure by Sir J. Frederick, ii. 163.
 his *Inquiry into the Miraculous Power of the Church*, ii. 163.
 his income, ii. 164.
 Gray laments his death, and the loss of an old acquaintance, ii. 199; iii. 151.
 his writings analysed by Mr. Leslie Stephen, ii. 199.
 Thomas Asheton writes against, ii. 210.
 opposes Dr. Waterland's *Doctrine of the Trinity*, ii. 215, 216.
 his *Miscellaneous Works*, ii. 215.
 his influence on the *Essay on the Philosophy of Lord Bolingbroke*, i. 280.
Mildcate, Prince, reference to, ii. 227.
Milbourne, Mr., Fellow of Pembroke, ii. 284.
Mildmay, Sir Anthony, his portrait in Emanuel College, i. 310.
Mildmay, Sir Walter, founder of Emanuel, his portrait in that College, i. 310.

Miller, Philip, gardener and botanist, iii. 363.
Milton, best example of an exquisite ear, i. 332.
 his versification, i. 333.
 creator of poetic language, ii. 108.
 his use of the relative pronouns, ii. 355.
Minden, French storm, ii. 402.
 victory at, iii. 8.
Mingotti, famous singer, ii. 232, 305; iii. 20, 21.
Ministry, probable change of, iii. 153.
 their narrow majorities, iii. 168.
 altogether by the ears, so are the Opposition, iii. 181.
 subversion of, on its last legs, iii. 204.
 position of, in Dec. 1767, iii. 293, 294.
Minorca, reference to its loss by Admiral Byng, ii. 284.
Miraculous Powers in the Church, Free Inquiry into the, by Dr. C. Middleton, ii. 164.
Miraculous Powers, Warburton on, ii. 128.
Mirepoix, Madame de, daughter of Prince Craon, ii. 85.
Mirror of Magistrates, a supplement to *The Fall of Princes*, i. 409.
Mitford relates the cause of R. West's death, ii. 113.
Mob Grammar, The. Lost piece by Gray, i. 142.
Modena, Duke of, his collection of paintings at, ii. 50.
Modern History and Languages, Gray appointed to the Chair of, iii. 318.
 Professorship unsolicited by Gray, iii. 319.
 his competitors for, iii. 320.
 Gray's feelings on kissing hands for, iii. 323.
 worth £400 a year, iii. 326.
Money, its effect, ii. 155.
Mongon, Abbe de, *Mémoires* of, ii. 200.
Monosyllables, their prevalent use in rhyme, i. 396.
Montagu, Duke of, his preservation of Kirkstall, i. 281.
Montagu, Frederick, Gray in town with, ii. 284.
 Gray sends him a copy of *The Odes*, ii. 320.
 proposed visit with Gray to Cambridge, iii. 104.
 obtains the Residentiary of York for Mason, iii. 82.
 appointed an executor to Sir William Williams, iii. 104.

Montagu, Frederick, induces Gray to write an Epitaph on Sir William Williams, i. 128; iii. 109.

Montagu, Frederick, of Paplewick. Did he write *Melpomene?* ii. 338.

Montagu, Lady Mary Wortley, public opinion of her poems, ii. 222.

story of her fictitious gift to Commodore Barnet, iii. 91, 100.

story related by Lord Camelford as to her parsimony, iii. 99-100.

her *Dialogues of the Dead*, iii. 42.

Montagu, Wortley, his death, iii. 90.

his wealth and testamentary bequests, iii. 90-91, 99.

Montesquieu's *L'Esprit des Lois*, its effect on Gray, i. 113; ii. 191, 193, 199.

his *Voix du Sage et du Peuple*, ii. 229.

Monthly Review, matter relative to G. Colman, Mason, and Gray, ii. 57.

Moore, Edward, his comedy of *Gil Blas*, ii. 213.

Moorfields, penny literature sold on the rails of, ii. 258.

Mora, Madame de, at Miss Chudleigh's ball, iii. 62.

Moral and Political Dialogues, by Hurd, ii. 325.

Morceau, first part of Gray's *Bard*, ii. 266.

Mordaunt, Sir John, to take part in a secret military expedition, ii. 320.

his part in the attack on Rochefort, ii. 342.

Morley, his proposed marriage, ii. 165.

Morrice, Gil, or *Child Maurice*, the old ballad of, ii. 316.

Morris, Mr. John, description of his fine collection of Graiana from the Dawson-Turner and Dillon collections, iv. 339-343.

Morris, Lewis, on ancient British poetry, i. 382.

Mortimer, Edmond de, i. 42.

Morton, Dr. Charles, of British Museum, reference to, and note on, iii. 117.

Muffs worn by the countrymen in France (1739), ii. 19.

Mugherino tree, reference to a, ii. 126.

Müller, J. S., engraver of the initial letters in Gray's *Elegy*, ii. 234.

Murdin's, William, *Collection of Elizabethan State Papers*, ii. 396.

Murray, Mr. John, possessor of the MS. of Gray's Journal in France, i. xvii., 236.

Murray, William, Solicitor-General, and Lord Balmerino, ii. 142.

Musgrave, J., his verses on the death of Frederick, Prince of Wales, ii. 119.

Music, Mason's *Essays on Church*, ii. 242.

Music, MS., enumeration of the valuable collection made by Gray in Italy, and sold at Mitford's sale, iii. 164.

Musical composition, English language not adapted to, iii. 158.

Expression, Avison's *Essay on*, iii. 242.

glasses, *see* Glasses, water, iii. 125.

NARES, Archdeacon, his opinion of Lady Hervey, iii. 62.

Natural history, Gray's keen observations in, iii. 383.

Needham, Mr., tutor to Lord Gormanstown, his discovery and interpretation of an ancient inscription, iii. 85.

Netley Abbey, references to and description of, ii. 266; iii. 177-178, 180.

Nevelois, Jean ll, his poem of *La Vie d'Alexandre*, i. 357.

Neville, F., his verses on the death of Frederick, Prince of Wales, ii. 119.

Neville, Thomas, of Jesus College, Gray shows him the *Bard*, ii. 314.

biographical note on, ii. 314.

Gray sends him a copy of *The Odes*, ii. 320.

he and the old musicians do not appreciate Carlo Bach, iii. 164.

New Bath Guide, by C. Anstey, iii. 240, 245.

Newcastle, Gray and Dr. Wharton visit, iii. 281.

Newcastle, Duke of, his journal going to Hanover, one of the lost pieces of Gray, i. 142.

installation as Chancellor of Cambridge University, ii. 195.

laying a foundation-stone at Cambridge, and Gray's desire to avoid him, ii. 259.

probable interest on behalf of Mr. Addison, ii. 288.

called by Gray the *fizzling* Duke, and by Dr. Warner *Hubble-bubble*, ii. 368.

probable visit to Cambridge to open a new library, ii. 368.

Gray does not stay to receive him at Cambridge, ii. 370.

his remark to Bishop Yonge, ii. 371.

effect of his sister's death upon the, ii. 402.

Newcastle, Duke of, attends divine service since the death of his sister, Lady Castlecomer, iiL 3.
his fear of spirits, iii. 3.
Lord Holland's character of, iii. 42.
Gray calls Cambridge "old Fobus's owl's nest," iii. 45.
reference to, as *Fobus*, iL 353; iii. 50, 63, 70, 105.
talks of resigning, iii. 76.
references to, iL 193, 204.
Newcombe, Dr. John, Master of St. John's College and Dean of Rochester, his death and biographical note, iii. 189.
Gray sends him a copy of *The Odes*, iL 320.
Miss Kirke and Richard Beadon his executors, iii. 189.
New Legation, by Dr. Warburton, iL 369.
Newmarket, tapestry of the marriage of Henry VI. in the Red Lion Inn at, iii. 307.
Gray and the King of Denmark at, iii. 330.
Duke of Cumberland at, iii. 66.
Newnham, Lord, in ill health, iiL 224; *see also* Nuneham.
Newspapers in London of 1761, iii. 123.
Newton appointed Bishop of Bristol and residentiary of St. Paul's, iii. 105.
offered the Archbishopric of Armagh, iii. 201.
Niccolina (opera singer), her justness of ear, vivacity and variety of gesture, iii. 157.
her victory over a prejudiced audience, iii. 157.
Nicholls, Dr., expelled from Cambridge for stealing books, iii. 245.
Nicholls's, Rev. Norton, verses on birds composed in his hearing, i. 139.
thanks Gray for Mason's hospitality at York, iii. 191.
illness and recovery of his mother, iii. 238.
at Studley, iii. 240.
Gray's letter of sympathy on loss of his uncle, Governor Floyer, iii. 248.
his probable succession of Dr. Riddington, iii. 254.
advice as to obtaining occupation, and his interim acceptance of a curacy, iii. 254.
presented by his uncles to the rectories of Sound and Bradwell, Suffolk, iii. 260.
rents a seat at Blundeston, iii. 260.

Nicholls, Rev. Norton, Gray congratulates him on his rectory, iii. 284.
Gray advises him as the mediator between Lord Lisburne and Mr. Temple, iii. 287-289, 332-333.
Gray's opinion of the dispute, iii. 302-303.
offered a travelling companionship by Mr. Barrett, iii. 324.
invitation and acceptance to visit Cambridge, iii. 330, 337, 382-383.
congratulated by Gray on having a garden, ii. 342.
agrees to visit Wales with Gray in the summer of 1770, iii. 363.
invited by Gray to go a tour in midland counties, iii. 375.
accompanies Gray thither, iii. 380.
Gray advises him of the French classics, iii. 389.
intention to visit Bonstetten in Switzerland, iii. 394.
urged to curb Bonstetten by his counsel, iii. 401.
Gray asks for minute details of his travels, iii. 406.
his MS. *Recollections of Gray*, in the possession of Mr. John Morris, iv. 343.
Mr. John Morris possesses Gray's MS. letters to, iv. 340.
Niflheimr, the hell of Gothic nations, i. 61.
Niphausen mentions that the King of Prussia will issue an account of his campaign, ii. 372.
Noble, Mr., reference to, iL 294.
Nonius, Marcellus, his couplet on a dimple, ii. 113.
Noontide, an Ode (*Ode on the Spring*), i. 3.
Norden, Frederick Ludvig, his *Voyage d'Egypte et de Nubie*, ii. 194; iii. 1.
tutor to Count Daniskiold, iL 194.
Norfolk, History of, reference to Blomefield's, iL 377.
Norman architecture, *see* Architecture.
Norris, Thomas, soprano, took part in the *Installation Ode*, iii. 343.
Northamptonshire, crops later than in Buckinghamshire, iL 258.
Northington, Earl of (Lord Chancellor), gives a sinecure to Mason, iii. 139.
Norton, Sir Fletcher, Solicitor-General, political opponents shrink under his brazen hand, iii. 172.
anecdote of his parsimony, iii. 176.
Notredame, Jean de, reference to his *Lives of the Provençal Poets*, i. 367.

Nourse, Peter, of St. John's College, Gray sends him a copy of *The Odes*, ii. 320.

Nova Acta Eruditorum, reference to, ii. 294.

November 5th, Latin poem on, i. 167.

Nugent, Robert Craggs, Earl, his elegiac verse, ii. 180.
his Ode to Pulteney, ii. 220.

Nuneham, Lord, Gray's opinion of, ii. 309.
sent by Stonehewer to Gray, ii. 310.
his appearance and conversation, ii. 310.
reference to, ii. 328.

Nunziata, Zoto del, painter, i. 320.

Obscurity and *Oblivion*, two Odes in ridicule of Gray and Mason, iii. 41, 53.

Occleve, his portrait of Chaucer, i. 305-306.

Ode in the Greek manner, see *Progress of Poetry*, i. 28.

Ode (to his embryo muse), i. 205-207.
editorial note on, 205.

Odes, the Pindaric (*The Fatal Sisters* and *The Descent of Odin*), reason for the notes to, iii. 289-290.

Odes, printed by Walpole and published by Dodsley, ii. 319, 321, 322.
public opinion on, ii. 323-326.
admired by Garrick and Warburton, ii. 325.
Gray received forty guineas for, ii. 330.
slow sale of, iii. 53.
meant to be *vocal to the intelligent alone*, iii. 148.

Odikle, Gray's nickname for *The Bard*, i. 40.

Odin, The Descent of, an Ode, i. 59.
editorial note on, i. 60.

Ogden, Dr., his quarrel at the Commons, iii. 63.
his estimation of the Rev. Mr. Ludlam, iii. 144.
candidate for Mastership of St. John's, iii. 190.

Oliffe, Mrs., Gray's aunt, ii. 383.
joint executor with Gray to Mrs. Rogers, ii. 384.
reference to, iii. 375.

Olympiade, the opera of, ii. 133.

Ombre, a game played in Turin, ii. 44.

Onley, Charles, Fellow of Pembroke College, Gray suggests him as tutor to the nephew of Lord John Cavendish, iii. 58.

Onley, Charles, agrees to become tutor to young Ponsonby, iii. 67.

Onslow, Mr. (the Speaker's son), Groom of the Bedchamber, ii. 290.

Opera house, popularity in 1761, iii. 80.
success maintained by a few particular voices rather than by genuine love for Italian music, iii. 157.
opens with Manzuoli, iii. 181.

Opera in Paris (1739), account of, ii. 21-22, 56.

Oroonoko, tragedy by T. Southerne, ii. 11.

Orthography of the text, i. xvi.

Osborn, reference to, iii. 69.

Ossian, *Poems* of, see *Erse* and MacPherson.

Otfrid of Weisenburgh, his paraphrase of the Gospels in rhyme, i. 363.
quotation from, i. 363.

Ottava Rima Measure, its introduction, i. 347.

Ottoboni, Cardinal Pietro, death of, ii. 63.

Owen, The Triumphs of, a fragment, i. 67.

Owl. Gray keeps one, and compares it to himself, ii. 369.

PAGANINI, Signora, her appearance in burlettas, iii. 77.
Gray delighted with her excellence, iii. 81.

Painted glass, see Glass.

Painters, Gray's *Essay to Walpole on his Lives of the*, i. 303-321.
MS. of the *Essay* possessed by Mr. Morris, iv. 340.

Painting and sculpture ; hard to say why they have made no advance in England, iii. 158.

Paintings, Gray's table of subjects, suitable for the style of various old masters, iii. 194-197.

Palgrave, Rev. William, at Scarborough, ii. 378.
Fellow of Pembroke College, and rector of Palgrave and Thrandeston, ii. 379.
Gray writes him a facetious letter enquiring about his Scotch tour, ii. 379.
entertains Rev. J. Brown, iii. 38.
his MS. diaries, iii. 70.
at Geneva, and travelling through Switzerland, iii. 174.
Gray gives him detailed advice of the places he should visit in France and Italy, iii. 193-196.

Palgrave, Rev. William, his return, iii. 208.
visits Glamis and Newby, iii. 256-257, 258.
going to Ranelagh and the opera, iii. 268.
connections of his family, iii. 284.
his elder brother, who took the name of Sayer, dangerously ill, iii. 284.
the strange casualties of his household, iii. 382.
Palma, old, remarks on his skill as a painter, iii. 389.
Panfilio, Prince, his palace at Rome, ii. 97.
Pandore, description of its representation, ii. 21.
Panmure, Lord, reference to, and Tom Lyon, iii. 257.
Paoli, P., Gray's high opinion of, iii. 310.
Paper from silk rags, iii. 40.
Paraphrases from Petrarca, by Gray, i. 194; from Anthologia Græca, i. 195-202.
Paris, Alexandre de, his poem of the Roman d'Alexandre, i. 357.
Paris, Dr. Ayrton, relates the manner in which the College of Surgeons obtained Hunter's Museum, ii. 68.
Park Place, near Henley, residence of General Conway and Lady Ailesbury, ii. 42.
Parker, Mr., lord of the manor of Ingleton, i. 275.
Parmegiano's picture of Moses furnishes a model for Gray's Bard, ii. 313.
Parnell Remains, the dunghill of Irish Grub Street, ii. 372.
Parody on an epitaph, i. 140.
editorial note on, i. 140.
Parrs, chapel of the, in Kendal church, i. 269.
Parry, John, blind harper, his concert inspired Gray to finish the Bard, i. 40.
visits Cambridge, ii. 312.
father of John Parry, A.R.A., ii. 312.
Parthenay, Des Roches de, his translation of Norden's Travels in Egypt, ii. 194.
Pasquier, reference to his Recherches, i. 332, 341.
Passerat, French poet, reference to, i. 341.
Patrizii, Count, great ball given at Rome by, ii. 84.
Patterson, Mrs., friend of Dr. T. Wharton's, ii. 359.

Pattinson, see Mrs. Forster.
Pausanias, a tragedy, by R. West, ii. 103.
Payne, Mrs., a friend of Dr. T. Wharton's, ii. 359.
Pearce, Zachary, Bishop of Rochester, his confusion at coronation of George III., iii. 113.
note on, iii. 113.
Peck, Fellow of Trinity College, iii. 324.
Peele, Theophilus, of Cambridge, reference to, ii. 155.
interests himself on behalf of C. Smart, ii. 178.
settlement of his dispute with Dr. Long, ii. 188.
Pembroke and Montgomery, Epitaph on Anne, Countess of, i. 278.
MS. sketch of her life by her Secretary, i. 279.
Pembroke College, founded by Mary de Valentia, i. 95; ii. 280.
possesses MS. of Ode on the Spring, i. 2; Ode on the death of a favourite Cat, i. 10; Distant Prospect of Eton College, i. 16; Hymn to Adversity, i. 24; The Fatal Sisters, i. 52; Elegy written in a Churchyard, i. 72; A Long Story, i. 82; Sonnet on the death of Richard West, i. 110; by Stonehewer of Gray's Pleasures from Vicissitude, i. 123; A Song, i. 138.
The Bard, finished at, i. 40.
comic lines written at, i. 138.
facetious description of the settlement of a dispute at, ii. 188.
Gray becomes a resident of, ii. 279.
Gray's description of, iii. 150.
Pembroke, Henry, Earl of, deserts his wife and elopes with Kitty Hunter, iii. 132.
Penn, Mr., his residence at Stoke, i. 83.
Perch, receipt to dress, i. 263-264.
Peregrine Pickle, Smollett's, ii. 214.
Pergolesé, Giambattista, his songs, ii. 133.
Ricciarelli sings his Stabat Mater, ii. 282.
reference to his airs, iii. 157.
Gray has a mass of his compositions, all divinity, iii. 163.
Gray's admiration of his compositions, iii. 164.
his Salve Regina performed at the Haymarket, 1740, iii. 164.
Walpole's error that Gray introduced his works, iii. 164.
Perrot, Lord, and the Assizes, iii. 281.
Peru, natural history of, in Spanish, ii. 195.

Pescetti, Giambattista, operatic composer, ii. 133.

Peterborough, visited by Gray, ii. 366.

Peterborough, Lord, story of his bargaining for a canary in Pall Mall, ii. 100-101.

Peterhouse College, *The Bard* commenced at, i. 40.

Hymn to Ignorance, written at, i. 111.

use of iron bar in Gray's window at, ii. 277.

Gray quits it for Pembroke College, ii. 279.

humorous description of its quadrangle, ii. 14.

Petrarch, *L'Abbé de Sade Mémoires pour la Vie de François Petrarque*, Gray has been reading, iii. 236.

Peyriere, Baronne de la, iii. 127.

"Ministress at London," iii. 236.

become a Catholic, iii. 236.

her pets, iii. 236.

Phelps, Mr., about to issue an account of Sicily, iii. 85.

Philips and Smith, reference to, appearing in the same volume, i. 212.

Philosophe Marié, the comedy of, i. 23.

Philosopher, endowments necessary to form a, iii. 361.

Philosophic Dictionary of Voltaire, reference to, iii. 187.

Philosophy, Gray's vindication of, ii. 167.

Philosophy of Lord Bolingbroke, Essay on the, i. 286.

published on Mason's authority, i. 286.

influence of Conyers Middleton apparent in, i. 286.

Piazza, Hieronimo Bartolomeo, Gray's Italian master, ii. 3.

Pictures, first exhibition of, iii. 65.

Pilkington, Mrs. Lœtitia, and Cibber, ii. 169.

her memoirs, ii. 169.

Pinkerton, John, his forgery of the second part of *Hardicanute*, confessed in the *Maitland Poems*, iii. 46.

Pitt, the elder, afterwards Earl of Chatham, paymaster of the forces, his dismissal, ii. 273.

Secretary of State, ii. 292.

ill of the gout, ii. 292.

sold his inestimable diamond for a peerage, iii. 84.

his popularity tottering, iii. 91.

and the Spanish quarrel, iii. 116.

publication of his negotiations with the French, iii. 122.

his resignation, iii. 123.

Pitt, the elder, complains of the inglorious peace, iii. 137.

styled by Count Algarotti "Restitutor d'Inghilterre," iii. 151.

inclination to injure his fame, iii. 167.

report that he lies dangerously ill, iii. 203.

"when he is gone, all is gone," iii.203.

speaks for three and a half hours on the rights of the colonies, iii. 234.

Gray laments his acceptance of a peerage, iii. 243.

breach with Lord Temple, iii. 243.

his restored popularity, iii. 246.

everything is in Lord Chatham's breast, iii. 255.

mending slowly in health, iii. 270.

Pitt, J. (Lord Camelford), his story of Lady M. Wortley Montagu, iii. 99-100.

Pitt, Thomas, afterwards Lord Camelford; did he write *Melpomene?* ii. 338.

proposes to meet Mr. Palgrave at Glamis, ii. 378.

about to marry Miss Wilkinson and £30,000, iii. 406.

Pitt, Mr. (the little), goes with Lord Kinnoul by sea round Spain to Italy, iii. 27.

his return, iii. 85.

his letter to Gray on his travels,iii.98.

Pitt, Mrs. Anne, receives a pension of £500 a year, iii. 78.

Plato, notes on, iv.

Play exercise at Eton, i. 163-165.

printed from Stonehewer collection, i. 163.

Pleasures of Imagination, criticism of, ii. 120-121.

Plummer, Mr., reference to, ii. 239.

Plumptre, Dr. Robert, sits for his portrait to Benj. Wilson, iii. 16.

biographical note, iii. 16.

Pocock, Dr. Richard, Bishop of Ossory and Meath, reference to, iii. 2.

Poems, statement of the source of the present text, i. xiii.-xiv.

Gray agrees to the Glasgow edition in deference to Dr. Beattie, iii. 285-287.

Poésies, Gresset's, ii. 186.

Poetic license, Gray advocates, i. 397.

Poetical Rondeau attributed to Gray, i. 209.

Poet laureate, Gray's opinion of the office, ii. 344-345.

hitherto humbled the professor,ii.345.

Poets, a fig for those who have not been among the mountains, iii. 223.

Poetry, reference to Puttenham's *Art of*, i. 329, 330, 331.
reference to Ronsard's *Art of*, i. 332.
Poetry, the language of the age never the language of, ii. 108.
possesses a language peculiar to itself, ii. 108.
use of the Strophe and Anti-strophe, ii. 263.
the Lyric style in contrast to the Epic, ii. 304-305.
nature of the Lyric, ii. 352-353.
Gray's faculty by no means voluntary, but the result of a certain disposition of mind, ii. 366.
Gray does not know a Scotchman of his own period who could read, much less write, iii. 56.
what its production implies, iii. 156.
Gray once contemplated a history of English; sketch of his design, iii. 365-367.
Poland, King of, and the King of Prussia, ii. 291.
commissions Count Algarotti to purchase pictures, iii. 307.
Political affairs, Gray ashamed of his country, iii. 166.
nation in the same hands as the university, iii. 172.
resembles first years of Charles I.'s time, iii. 172.
reference to, iii. 204.
condition of, in March, 1766, iii. 233-234.
Polymetis, by Joseph Spence, ii. 170.
Pompey's villa, ii. 78.
Pompey the Little, history of; or, *The Life and Adventures of a Lap Dog*, ii. 214.
Pond, Mr., frontispieces supplied by, i. 212.
Ponsonby, William, Lord, his son, iii. 57.
Pope, Alexander, his *Ode on St. Cecilia's Day* compared with Dryden's, i. 36.
his license of language in poetry, ii. 108.
his defence by Warburton, ii. 131.
Odyssey, Essay on, by J. Spence, ii. 170.
Duchess of Queensberry his friend, ii. 372.
Pope Benedict XIV., his election, description of his person, ii. 93, 98.
Pope Clement XII., death of, i. 63.
Porte, Memoires de M. de la, Gray recommends, ii. 291.
Portia, Cardinal, death of, ii. 84.
Portland, William, second Duke of, his eldest daughter marries Lord Weymouth, ii. 395.

Porto Bello, capitulation of, ii. 70.
Portraits, Gray considers it strange that they should be preferred to contemporary descriptions, iii. 24.
Portsdown Hills, description of the view from the, ii. 205.
Portugal, King of, seizes conspirators at Lisbon, ii. 392.
and Tavora family, ii. 392-396.
Post-chaises in France, description of (1739), ii. 17.
Posthumous Poems, i. 99-142.
editorial note on, i. 100.
note on, i. 142.
Potter, Archbishop, his proviso, ii. 240.
Pottinger, Richard, reference to, iii. 41.
Pouilly, Mons. Levesque de, i. 239.
Powell, William Samuel, Master of St. John's College, his candidature, iii. 190.
has the Duke of Newcastle's support, iii. 191.
note on, iii. 190.
Powis, Lord, has 100 copies of the *Life of Lord Herbert of Cherbury*, iii. 173.
Prayer, Treatise on, ii. 217.
Prendergast, Sir Thomas, insulted by an Irish mob, iii. 26.
Pretender, The, James Edward (Le Chevalier St. George), ii. 68.
English correspondence pass through his hands before leaving Rome, ii. 63.
and his family present at a ball given by Count Patrizil, ii. 76-85.
and the Grand Chancellorship at Rome, ii. 94.
his relations with English society in Rome, ii. 187.
Prevôst Abbé, Antoine François, d'Exiles, ii. 21.
biographical note on, ii. 21.
Price, Mr., glass painter of Hatton Garden, iii. 102.
worked at the windows of Westminster Abbey, iii. 102.
Pricket, Dr. Marmaduke, death of, ii. 244.
Pride a sign of folly, ii. 246.
Prince of Wales to have £40,000 a year (1756), ii. 200.
Prince Edward £5000 a year, ii. 290.
Pringle, Dr. Sir J., medical adviser of II. Walpole and Dr. J. Brown, iii. 250.
attends the Prince of Wales, iii. 256.
Pritchard, Mrs., and Delap's *Hecuba*, iii. 123.

Professorship of Modern History, Gray would not ask for it, not choosing to be refused, iii. 21.

Gray's name suggested to Lord Bute but refused, iii. 136-137.

conferred on Lawrence Brockett, in succession to Shallet Turner, iii. 136.

MS. note of Gray relative to Delaval's candidature, iii. 140.

Gray succeeds Brockett, iii. 318.

Progress of Poesy, The, i. 27.

editorial note on, i. 28.

its composition delayed by a remark of Mason, ii. 111.

submitted to Dr. Wharton, ii. 260.

aversion to its separate publication, ii. 262.

Pronunciation, variation between the time of Gray and of Lydgate, i. 393.

Propertius, translations from, i. viii., 151-157.

printed from original MS., i. 144.

sent by Gray to R. West, ii. 111.

influence of the style of Scaliger on, ii. 112.

Prophecy (see *The Bard*), fragment sent to Stonehewer, ii. 268.

Prose as well as verse should have its rhythm, i. 314.

Prose, Gray's posthumous, i. xiv.

Provençal poetry, i. 367.

Prowse, Mr., refused the post office, iii. 256.

Prussia, King of, *see* Frederick.

Public life, obligations incumbent on one desiring to attain position in, ii. 83.

Puisieux, Marquis de, his house at Sillery, i. 239.

Pulpit, Gray's opinion of oratory in, since the Revolution, iii. 81.

Pulteney, Earl Nugent's *Ode to,* ii. 220.

Puppet-Show, *Rappresentazione d'un' anima dannata,* ii. 44.

the Italian, the reigning diversion, iii. 356.

Purt, Rev.-Robert, M.A., i. 85.

Puttenham's *Art of Poetry,* quotation from, i. 329.

his influence on Sir Thomas Wyatt and Lord Surrey, i. 334.

mistaken as to *Riding Ryme,* i. 335-337.

Quebec, compared to Richmond Hill, iii. 34.

siege of, by the French, iii. 44-45.

alarm concerning, conduct of General Murray, iii. 51.

Queen's College, founded by Margaret of Anjou, i. 95.

added to by Elizabeth, Queen of Edward IV., i. 95.

Queen's Hermitage, The, of Matthew Green, ii. 222.

Queensberry, Duchess of, her quarrel with Duchess of Marlborough, ii. 133.

condemns by advertisement a spurious edition of the last seven years of Earl Clarendon's Life, and notifies her early issue of his biography, ii. 372.

friend of Pope and protector of Gay, ii. 372.

her eccentricities, ii. 372.

Quinault, Jeanne Françoise, French actress, ii. 23.

Quintilius Varus, his Piscina at Tivoli, ii. 74.

Raby Castle, Leland's Account of, iii. 294-295.

Racine's *Britannicus,* quotation from, ii. 167.

and reference to, ii. 233.

Radnor, Lord, Gray advises Wharton to see the house of, ii. 253.

Ramsay, Mr., Gray's tenant in Cornhill, iii. 203.

Ramsden, Mr., optician, iii. 373.

Ramsgate, account of, and Sir. E. Brydges's anecdote of Gray at, iii. 263.

Ranby, Mr. (King's Surgeon), Duke of Cumberland sends for and then countermands the attendance of, ii. 321.

Randall, Dr. John, and the *Installation Ode,* i. 92.

composed the music for the *Ode,* iii. 343.

Ranelagh Gardens, non-success, ii. 125.

reference to, ii. 134.

Raphaël, his vision of Ezekiel, i. 42.

figure of God in the vision of Ezekiel furnished Gray with a model for his *Bard,* ii. 313.

Rapin, Nicholas, French writer, reference to, i. 341.

Ratcliffe, Mr., brother to Earl of Derwentwater, his execution, ii. 168.

Reed, Isaac, his note concerning the quarrel between Gray and Walpole, ii. 124.

Reinholt, Charles Frederick, popular bass singer, sung in the *Installation Ode,* iii. 343.

Religion of Nature Delineated, by Wol-laston, I. 290.
Rhyme, Observations on the use of, i. 376-380.
examples of the most ancient rhymes in our tongue, i. 376-379.
children educated at St. Gall in 10th century taught to write Latin rhyme, i. 379.
opinion of the rhyming epitaphs at Canterbury, i. 379-380.
Additional observations from the *Cambri* of Gray, i. 381-386.
ancient names of the Welch, i. 381.
prosodia of the Welch grammar the finest in any language, i. 381.
harmony of the Druidical compositions, i. 381
"Secret of the Poets," i. 382-383.
probability of the English borrowing their rhyme from the Britons, i. 383-385.
suggestion that the Franks obtained their rhyme from this country, i. 385.
rhyme preserved by the common people, i. 386.
Rhyming, greater facility of the ancient poets for, i. 395.
Rhythmus, Observations on the Pseudo-, i. 361-375.
ancient rhyme of the Emperor Adrian, i. 361.
ancient rhyme of the Welch, i. 361.
Anglo-Saxon rhyme, its harmony consisting in alliteration, i. 362.
Anglo-Saxon rhyme, its harmony similarly practised by the Danes, i. 362.
Anglo-Saxon and the Franco-Theotische languages originally the same, i. 364.
earliest extant Romaun or old French verses, i. 364.
earliest Provençal writers, i. 364.
earliest Sicilian poets, i. 365.
earliest English rhyme, i. 365.
German rhyme the oldest extant, i. 365.
Walafrid Strabo and his contemporary writers call themselves *Barbari*, i. 365.
period of Provençal poetry, i. 367.
period of Sicilian poetry, 367.
late retention of the old Saxon or Danish verse without rhyme, i. 368.
Language of the Gauls, i. 369.
the various dialects of the Romaun, Rustica, Romana, Provençal, Valonne, and the Langue Romande, i. 369.

Table showing the period of the introduction of rhyme into various countries, i. 371.
Provençals believed to have borrowed the art of rhyme from the Latin rather than from the Arabs or Franks, i. 371-373.
first appearance of rhyming verses in Latin epitaphs, etc., i. 372.
Latin rhyme, i. 373.
Leonine verse, i. 373; its supposed origin, i. 373-375.
Leonimetes rhyme, i. 374.
Rima alla Provenzale, or verse-rhyming in the middle in place of the end, i. 373.
Rhyme of Bernard of Cluny in his poem *De Contemptu Mundi*, i. 374-375
instance of mixture of different languages in old composition, i. 375.
Ricciarelli, announced to sing the *Stabat Mater* of Pergolesi, ii. 282.
description of his powers, ii. 282.
Richardson, Jonathan, the elder, the painter, iii. 81.
Gray sits to him for his portrait, iii. 81.
Richmond and Derby, Countess of, mother of Henry VII., foundress of St. John's College, i. 96.
Margaret, portrait of, i. 310.
Richmond, Dr. Richard, Bishop of Soder and Man, chaplain to the Duke of Athol, iii. 257.
Ridley, Mr., contributes to Dodsley's Miscellaneous Poems, ii. 221.
Ridlington, Dr., Professor of Civil Law, his recovery from dropsy, iii. 188-189.
gone to Nice, iii. 208.
notes on, iii. 208, 254.
Rigby, Gloster, with Duke of Bedford in Cambridge, ii. 309, 311.
escape of, from an Irish mob, iii. 26.
likely to be one of a new ministry, iii. 153.
to move the expulsion of Wilkes, iii. 332.
Rinuccini, Marquis, visits London, ii. 145.
Rivett, Nicholas, his work among the Antiquities of Athens, ii. 283.
Robbery, liability in London to, iii. 14.
Roberts, Mr., of the *Pell Office*, relates the cause of the quarrel between Gray and Walpole, ii. 124.
Roberts, Rev. Mr., translated and published Gray's *Elegy* in Latin, i. 257.

Roberts's, Gray asks Mason to procure him lodgings at, ii. 251, 284.

Robertson, Dr. William, author of *Life of Charles V.*, Gray sups with him, iii. 209.

History of Mary Stuart and her Son, ii. 396.

Robinson, Rev. Wm., *Impromptu on Lord Holland's house,* written by Gray at his rectory of Denton, i. 135.

at Cambridge, ii. 163.

biographical note on, iii. 15.

Gray makes a list of wild plants native to the neighbourhood of Denton, iii. 15.

his marriage to Miss Richardson, iii. 57, 63.

proceeds to Naples for his honeymoon, iii. 57.

Gray hopes to see him in many new lights, iii. 161.

Gray hopes to be better known to Mrs. Robinson, iii. 162.

visited by Gray at Denton, iii. 237, 242.

description of Mrs. Robinson, iii. 265.

Robinson of Faseley, his house in Killiecrankie Pass, iii. 218.

Rochefort, unsuccessful expedition on, ii. 342.

Rodney, Admiral, his bombardment of Havre, ii. 402.

Roger, Archbishop of York, founder of St. Sepulchre's Chapel, iii. 140-142.

Rogers, Jonathan, uncle to Gray, *Ode to Spring* written at his house, i. 2.

his funeral, i. 72.

Rogers, Mrs. Jonathan, receives a paralytic stroke, ii. 245, 250.

her illness, ii. 366, 377, 381.

recovers her speech after years of unintelligibleness, ii. 382.

her death, ii. 383.

reference to, ii. 185.

Rogers, Samuel, gave eighteen guineas for a letter of Gray's from the Bindley and Reed collections, ii. 344.

Roi, Histoire du Cabinet du, by Buffon and D'Aubenton, ii. 199.

Rolfe, Mr. Wm. J., of Cambridge, Mass., i. xvii.

Rolle, Mr., contributes to Dodsley's *Miscellaneous Poems,* ii. 221.

Romaine, Archbishop of York, built north transept of York Minster, iii. 146.

Roman Senate, Chapman's *Essay on the,* ii. 163.

Romances, purpose of, i. 338.

Romans, foundation of their religion, ii. 173.

Ronsard's *Art of Poetry,* reference to, i. 333.

Roper, Mr., his opinion of *The Odes,* ii. 330.

Ross, John, Bishop of Exeter, ii. 193.

his *Epistles of Tully,* ii. 193.

Ross, Mr., of Cambridge, reference to, ii. 232-233.

Ross, Mr., murder of, iii. 339.

Ross, Dr., obtains the living of Frome, iii. 32.

Gray remembers his kind invitation and in better days hopes to accept it, iii. 161.

his contentment, iii. 161.

said to be made Dean of Ely, iii. 335, 337.

succeeds Dr. Law as prebend of Durham, iii. 338.

Rousseau, his characters do not interest Gray, ii. 329.

Gray has not seen, ii. 389.

his *Nouvelle Heloise,* Walter Savage Landor on, iii. 79; Mason and Hurd admire it, iii. 83.

everybody that has children should read his *Emile,* iii. 151.

Gray sets his religious discourses at nought, iii. 152.

resides near Neufchâtel, iii. 174.

publishes at the Hague and realises considerable sums, iii. 174.

venerated by the people of his district, iii. 174.

his *Lettres de la Montagne,* except the *Contrat Social,* of the dullest, iii. 187-188, 192.

in Derbyshire with Mr. Davenport, iii. 243.

quarrels with David Hume, iii. 243.

quits England, iii. 271.

writes letters to the Lord Chancellor and Mr. Conway, iii. 271.

Voltaire's *Guerre de Geneve* a satire on, iii 271.

Rovezzano, Beneditto da, painter and architect, i. 320.

Rowe, Mrs., letters of the dead to the living, ii. 6.

Rowe, Nicholas, poet laureate, his flowers of eloquence, ii. 167.

reference to, i. 345.

origin of his ballad of *Colin's Complaint,* ii. 367.

Rowley, Mr., insulted by an Irish mob, iii. 26.

Royal family, their frequent visits in society, iii. 89.
Royston, Lord (second Earl of Hardwick), his *State Papers*, iii. 6.
Russia, Account of, by Lord Whitworth, printed at Walpole's Twickenham press, ii. 373.
MS. purchased from Mr. Zolman's library and given by R. O. Cambridge, Esq., ii. 373.
Rutherford, Dr. Thomas, mathematician, ii. 163.
candidate for the Mastership of St. John's, iii. 190.
Rutherford, Mrs., her opinion of Mason's Elegy V., iii. 159.

Sackville, Lord George, his conduct at Minden, iii. 8.
arrival in England, anticipates court-martial, iii. 14.
reference to, iii. 25.
Law-officers declare him amenable to court-martial, iii. 28.
his trial and demeanour : the result, iii. 31, 34, 35.
Sade, Abbé, his *Petrarch*, iii. 235.
St. Andre, Dr. Nathaniel, who married Lady Betty Molyneux, resides at Southampton, iii. 175-176.
St. Augustine, hymn of, its rhyme, i. 361.
St. Bruno, his retirement at Chartreuse, ii. 36, 45.
St. Cecilia's Day, remarks on Dryden's Ode on, i. 36.
Dryden's Ode compared with Pope's, i. 36.
St. Cloit, Pierre de, his joint poem of *La Vie d'Alexandre*, i. 357.
St. Francis, his early attempt to write an ode without rhyme, i. 344.
St. Germain, Count, ex-French general, his visit to England, iii. 50-51.
St. Giles, broad, reference to, iii. 4.
St. Helen's, Fitzherbert, Lord, his recollections of Gray and the great respect held for the poet at the university, iii. 385.
a pensioner of St. John's College, iii. 384.
biographical note of, iii. 385.
St. John's College, Cambridge, founded by the Countess of Richmond, i. 96 ; her portrait in, i. 310.
portraits in library, i. 310-311.
St. Margaret, *Life of,* its age and style, i. 357.
quotation from, i. 366.

St. Sepulchre's Chapel, York Minster, Gray's attempt to identify its site, iii. 140-144.
Salisbury music-meetings, reference to, iii. 343.
Sandby, Paul, R.A., exhibits at the first exhibition of artists, iii. 65.
biographical note, iii. 65.
preparing a great picture of Snowdon. iii. 65, 68.
Sandwich, John, Earl of, squib on, i. 131.
his remark to Cradock on Gray's aversion to himself, i. 131.
his boyish days, ii. 115.
and the High Stewardship of Cambridge, iii. 168.
Dr. Brook, Mr. Brockett, and Dr. Long, his agents, iii. 168-171.
hires a scribbler to write a weekly paper, the *Scrutator*, iii. 171.
whatever seems against him is popular, iii. 201.
engages the Bishop of Chester's interest, iii. 201.
joint postmaster, iii. 204.
Sangallo, Bastiano Aristotile da, painter, i. 320.
Sapphic Ode, i. 174-176.
Sardinian Ambassador's chapel and stables in Lincoln's Inn Fields burnt, iii. 22.
marriage of his son to Miss Speed, iii. 83.
Satire upon the Heads; or never a barrel the better herring, i. 134.
editorial note on, i. 134.
Satyrical prints, their popularity, circa 1746, ii. 134.
Saxe-Gotha, Princess of, reference to, iii. 70.
Saxon Architecture, see Architecture.
Sayer, Mr., elder brother of Mr. Palgrave, reference to, iii. 284.
Scaliger, Julius Cæsar, *The Propertius* of Gray influenced by the writings of, ii. 112.
Sceptic, a professed, can only be guided by his present passions, iii. 378.
Schaub, Lady, i. 82.
Schoolmistress, Wm. Shenstone's poem of the, ii. 219.
Scotch, Character of the, lost piece by Gray, i. 142.
Scotland, Gray about to accompany Lord Strathmore and Thomas Lyon to, iii. 208.
journey from Hetton to Glamis, iii. 209-210.

Scotland, considers its scenery sublime, iii. 219.
returned charmed with the Highlands, iii. 223.
Italy can hardly excel its scenery, iii. 223.
Gray will certainly go again, iii. 224.
a country that gave him much pleasure, iii. 279.
Gray's first visit to, iv. 343.
MS. of his journey in the possession of Mr. John Morris, iv. 342.
reference to places mentioned by Gray in :—
Arbroath, visit to, iii. 219.
Blair of Athol, (proposes to visit, iii. 220.
Braidalbane's, Lord, description of his estate, iii. 216-217.
Dunkeld, its ruined cathedral, iii. 215.
house of Duke of Athol, where Gray stayed, iii. 215.
road from, to Inverness, beauty of, iii. 218.
Edinburgh, visit to the principal sights, iii. 209.
dreads it and the itch, iii. 219.
Fingal, tomb of, iii. 216.
Forfar, Lord Strathmore engaged in draining the lake of, by widening the little river Deane, iii. 212.
Glames, town built of stone and slated, iii. 211.
castle, its position, approach, etc., iii. 210-213.
its nurseries, iii. 213.
Killiecrankie, Pass of, iii. 218.
Mr. Robinson's house at foot of, iii. 218.
Loch Tay, beauties of, iii. 216.
Megill, story of Queen Wanders buried there, iii. 214.
Perth, stay at, iii. 210.
Strathmore, valley of, iii. 210.
Strath-Tay, beauty of, iii. 215.
Tay, the, iii. 210, 214, 215, 216.
Taymouth or Balloch, scenery in neighbourhood, iii. 215.
Tummeli, the, iii. 217, 218.
Wade's, Marshal, road, iii. 218.
Scripture Vindicated, by Dr. Waterland, ii. 215.
replied to by Dr. Middleton, ii. 215.
Seba, Albertus, his Locupletissimi Rerum Naturalium Thesauri, iii. 203.
Secker, Bishop, his conduct as a courtier, iii. 71.

Secretary of State, changes in 1766, iii. 237.
Sedgwick, Mr., secretary to Anne, Countess of Dorset, i. 279.
Selby, Bell, her dream of Mason, ii. 204.
Selwyn, George, present at the execution of Lord Lovat, ii. 142.
Senesino, nicknames of certain Italian singers, ii. 65.
Senhouse, Mr., and his acoustic warming-pan, ii. 295.
Sestine, ascribed to Arnauld Daniel, ii. 350.
Settle, Elkanah, poet laureate, ii. 345.
Seven Years' War, the, fear of a French invasion, iii. 3.
Prince Ferdinand defeats Contades at Minden, iii. 7.
conduct of Lord G. Sackville, iii. 8.
Prussian victory over General Harsch, iii. 9.
expectation of an action between the fleets, iii. 18.
victory of Admiral Hawke, iii. 22, 23.
fear of invasion dispelled, iii. 23.
proposed great expedition to France, iii. 66.
secret expedition, iii. 68.
pamphlet against Mr. Manduit, iii. 91.
treaty of peace, iii. 137.
Sextus V., built dome of St. Peter's, ii. 79.
his obelisk in the great area, ii. 80.
Seward, Thomas, contributes to Dodsley's Miscellaneous Poems, ii. 221.
Shaftesbury, Lord, how the third earl came to be a philosopher, ii. 375.
Shakespeare, creator of poetic language, ii. 103.
beauty of his language, ii. 109.
Shakespeare Verses, by Gray, i. 132.
editorial note, i. 132.
Sharp, Mr., travels into Italy, iii. 256.
Shaw, Dr., his work on Architecture, ii. 255.
Shelburne, Earl of, likely to join the new ministry, iii. 153.
Shenstone, William, his poem of The Schoolmistress, ii. 219.
admires the Odes of Gray, ii. 327, 331.
his contribution to Dodsley's Collection of Poems, ii. 364.
his Letters, Gray's opinion of them and the author, iii. 344.
Shepherd, Miss, reference to, ii. 290.
Sheridan, Mr., advertisement of his lecture on elocution, iii. 124.
Sherlock, Bishop of London, reference to, iii. 125.

Sherman, William, his daughter married to Mason, iii. 193.

Shirley, Mrs., mother of Lord Ferrers, petitions for mercy, iii. 36.

Sicilian poetry, period of its success, i. 367.

Sickness makes us better friends and better men, ii. 206.

Sictryg, his warfare with the King of Dublin, i. 54.

Sidney, Sir Philip, his attempt to introduce the hexameter, i. 341.

and the park of Warwick Castle, ii. 257.

Sidney, Le, comedy by Gresset, ii. 184.

Sigurd, Earl of the Orkney Isles, his expedition to Ireland, i. 54.

Silver boar, the badge of Richard III., i. 47.

Simms, Mr., Mrs., and Madlle. Nanny, reference to, ii. 124.

Simona, Rudolph, his portrait in Emanuel College, i. 310.

Sisters, see *Fatal Sisters*, an Ode.

Sketchley, Mr. R. F., reference to, i. xvii.

Skinner, John, Fellow of St. John's, candidate for the Mastership of St. John's, note on, iii. 190.

Skroddles (Rev. Wm. Mason).

Smart, Christopher, the poet, his debts, ii. 161, 178.

biographical note, ii. 161.

his comedy of a *Trip to Cambridge*, ii. 162.

Duke of Cleveland allows him £40 a year, ii. 179.

committed to Bedlam, ii. 215.

not dead, *Merope* and *The Guardian* acted for his benefit, ii. 391.

collection on behalf of, iii. 162.

Messrs. Gordon and Anguish, gentlemen interested in him, iii. 163.

Smith, Dr. Adam, has heard several of the *Erse* poems repeated from tradition, i. 311.

Smith, his print of Derwentwater, i.259.

visits Maltham and issues an engraving of Gordale Scar, i. 278.

Smith and Philips, reference to, i. 212.

Smith of Trinity is dead, iii. 303.

Snowdon, its name, i. 41.

resorted to by eagles, i. 43.

Somerset, Carr, Earl of, reference to a letter about, iii. 123.

Somerset House, John of Padua, its architect, i. 307.

Somner's Saxon Dictionary, reference to, i. 326.

Song, to an old air of Geminiani, i. 133.

editorial note on, i. 138.

Sonnet, its invention ascribed to Fra' Guittone d'Arezzo, i. 349.

Sopha, Le, de Crebillon, ii. 128-133.

Sophonisba to [Masinissa, story of, ii. 115-116.

Sophonisba to Masinissa, part of an heroic epistle, i. 183.

Southampton, appearance of the coast in its vicinity, ii. 265.

Gray staying in the High Street, iii. 177.

full of bathers, but Gray knows not a soul, iii. 178.

no coffee-house, no bookseller, no pastry-cook, and lodgings very dear, iii. 178.

description of, iii. 179-180, 200.

Southampton Row, once the residence of Dr. Wharton, and afterwards a lodging of Gray's, ii. 397.

Gray takes up his abode at Mr. Jauncey's in, iii. 1, 6.

description of the prospect from, iii. 3, 5.

its surroundings, iii. 4.

Gray about to remove, iii. 102.

Southcote, Mr., offers his house and lands to Dr. Wharton, ii. 252.

Southerne, Thomas, Restoration dramatist, ii. 11.

Southwell, Henry, of Magdalen College, reference to, ii. 76.

goes to Ireland, ii. 104.

Southwell, Mr. and Mrs., reference to, ii. 287.

Gray sends him a copy of *The Odes*, ii. 320.

Spain, quarrel with, about logwood, iii. 116.

and the French, iii. 172.

Spanish War, Gray takes an interest in the, iii. 84.

Spectacles, Gray's aversion to wear, ii. 75-76.

Spedding, Mr., his residence of Armathwaite House, i. 262.

Speed, Miss (Countess de Viry), reference to her attitude towards Gray, ii. 330.

possessed Gray's MS. of the *Amatory Lines*, i. 137.

Gray writes a *Song* at her request, i. 133.

reference to, i. 82.

her legacy from Lady Cobham, iii. 37.

Gray's probable visit with her to Oxfordshire, her uncertainty of mind, iii. 49.

public chatter respecting Gray and, iii. 65.

Speed, Miss, her marriage with the Baron de la Peyriere, iii. 83.
need not change her religion, iii. 83 ; see also Peyriere.
Spence, Joseph, his description of a puppet-show in Turin, ii. 44.
his *Polymetis*, ii. 170-172.
his Essay on Pope's *Odyssey*, ii. 170.
drowned in his own garden at Byfield, iii. 329.
Spence, S., his verses on the death of Frederick, Prince of Wales, ii. 119.
Spencer elected Fellow of Pembroke, ii. 227.
interests himself for Lord Nuneham, ii. 309, 311.
Spenser, Edmund, adopted the hexameter, etc., ii. 341.
Spiletta, portion of a comedy, reference to, iii. 81.
Spleen, The, a poem by Matthew Green, ii. 219.
Spring, Ode on the, i. 1.
editorial note on, i. 2.
Matthew Green's *Queen's Hermitage* furnishes Gray with two thoughts for, ii. 222.
Squibb, Dr. Arthur, M.A., chaplain of Colonel Bellasis's regiment, i. 88.
Squibb, James, of Saville Row, i. 88.
Squibb, James, of Stowe, i. 88.
Squire, Dr. Samuel, Bishop of St. David's, i. 127.
biographical note on, ii. 327.
Dean of Bristol and candidate for St. David's, iii. 78.
reference to, iii. 103.
Staël, Memoires de Madame, ii. 291.
Stamp Act, Bill for the repeal of, gone to the Lords. "Oh that they would throw it out," iii. 234.
Stanhope, Mr.,and Mr. Dayrolles, ii.354.
Stanza on Immortality, i. 141.
State Papers, by Dr. Birch, ii. 194.
Statius, translations from the *Thebaidos* of, i. 145-148.
when printed, i. 144.
Stephen, Mr. Leslie, analysis of Dr. Middleton's writings in *English Thought in the Eighteenth Century*, ii. 199.
Sterne, Laurence, his popularity, iii. 36.
receives £700 for a second edition of *Tristram Shandy*, iii. 36.
his portrait by Reynolds, iii. 36.
publication of his sermons, iii. 37.
Gray's opinion of the sermons, iii. 53.
Stevenson, John Hall, humorous poet, friend of Sterne, iii. 37.
his *Crazy Tales*, iii. 245.

Stillingfleet, Benjamin (*Blue Stocking*), the naturalist, iii. 33.
resides with his friend Mr. Marsham, iii. 83.
his observations on the Norfolk birds in 1755, iii. 95-96.
Stocks, public, are low, ii. 393.
Gray loses £200 by selling, ii. 395.
Stoke Pogis, "West End," residence of Gray's uncle, Mr. Rogers, afterwards of his mother, i. 2.
Ode to Spring, written at, i. 2.
Ode on Distant Prospect of Eton College, written at, i. 16.
Hymn to Adversity, written at, i. 24.
Elegy in a Churchyard, chiefly written at, i. 72.
Sonnet on the death of Richard West, written at, i. 110.
Manor House, Gray's sketch of, i. 82 ; ii. 234 ; the residence of various families, i. 83.
Gray's melancholy reminiscences at, ii. 250.
Stone, John, sculptor, reference to, iii. 135.
Stone, Nicholas, sculptor, reference to, i. 321.
Stone, Mr., obtains a political post, ii. 290.
Stonehewer, Dr., rector of Houghton, ii. 241.
his death, iii. 351.
Stonehewer, Richard, Fellow of St. Peter's College, and secretary to Duke of Grafton, ii. 241.
Gray enquires of Dr. Wharton his opinion of, ii. 187.
Gray seeks the interest of Dr. Wharton and Dr. Keene on behalf of, ii. 197.
proposes to visit York with Gray, ii. 233.
fragment of the *Prophecy* sent to, ii. 268.
tutor to the Duke of Grafton, ii. 277.
goes to Portsmouth to receive a Morocco ambassador, iii. 10.
attendant on his sick father, Rev. Dr. Stonehewer, iii. 46.
busiest creature on earth, except Mr. Fraser, iii. 224.
Gray's oracle of State, iii. 233.
living in Queen Street, London, iii. 317.
induced the Duke of Grafton to recommend Gray for the professorship of Modern History, iii. 322.
health of his father, iii. 350.
Gray's letter of condolence on the death of his father, iii. 351.

Stonehewer, Richard, references to, ii. 144, 181, 188, 230, 264, 268, 273, 307, 373, 390, 395 ; iii. 37, 150, 173, 176.
Story, A Long, i. 81.
  editorial note on, i. 82.
  occasion of its being written, ii. 228.
  not intended for publication, suffered to appear because Mr. Bentley's designs were not intelligible without it, iii. 268, 308.
Strathmore, John, ninth Earl of, his personal appearance, ii. 263.
  returns to College with his brother, ii. 307.
  his coming of age, and biographical note, ii. 369.
  his seat of Hetton, iii. 208.
  going abroad, iii. 21.
  proposed voyage to Genoa, iii. 28.
  ill at Turin, iii. 98.
  takes Gray to Scotland, iii. 208.
  his agricultural operations around Glamis, iii. 212.
  approaching marriage, iii. 245.
  to be married in London, iii. 258.
  interesting condition of Lady Strathmore, iii. 268.
  reference to, ii. 261 ; iii. 276.
Strawberry Hill, bowl with Gray's lines on Walpole's cat at, i. 10.
Stricklands, their family seat of Siserge, ii. 269.
  chapel in Kendal church, ii. 269.
Stuart, Mary, and her son, Robertson's History of, ii. 396.
Stuart, James ("Athenian Stuart"), his work among the Antiquities of Athens, ii. 283.
  Gray subscribes to his Attica, ii. 360 ; to his Antiquities of Athens, and desires a copy for Pembroke Hall, iii. 149-150.
  successful architect, iii. 149.
  proposed to be consulted for Mrs. Mason's monument, iii. 266.
  approves of Mason's sketch, iii. 272.
Stuart, Mr., his duel with the Duke of Bolton, iii. 34.
Stuart of Cambridge, reference to, ii. 159.
Studley, residence of Dr. Wharton, visited by Gray, ii. 240.
Stukeley, Dr., frequents the reading-room of the British Museum, iii. 2.
  note on, iii. 2.
  talks nonsense and coffee-house news at the Museum, iii. 5.
Sturbridge fair, ii. 15.
Sturgeon, Roger, Fellow of Caius, ii.311.
Suard, Madame, an acquaintance of Voltaire's, iii. 173.

Suarez, Countess of, entertains Gray at Florence, ii. 53.
Suffolk, Lord, his seat at Levens, i. 270.
Sully, Duke de, Gray's opinion of his Memoirs and character, ii. 281.
Summers, Mr., recommended by Gray to Dr. Wharton for his skill in planting, iii. 292.
Superstition, Gray's love of popular, iii. 222.
  History of Witches and a History of Second Sight given by Beattie to Gray, iii. 222.
Surrey, Lord, his use of the Cæsura, i. 333.
  his verse, i. 334.
Swift on Money, ii. 155.
Swift's application of Herodotus's passage on feathers, ii. 240.
Swift's history of the Tory administration, ii. 360.
Swinburne, Lady, reference to, ii. 246.
Swithin's Alley, fatal fire in, iii. 22.
Switzerland,
  Arve, river, banks of, at Geneva, ii. 33.
  description of, ii. 40.
  Geneva, its peasantry contrasted with those of Savoy, i. 245.
  Geneva, description of, ii. 37, 38.
  lake of, ii. 38-39.
  its trout, i. 246 ; ii. 39.
  Gray obliged to forego his proposed visit to, iii. 403, 405.
Syon Hill, Brentford, residence of Lord Holdernesse, iii. 15.

Tacitus, Gray's admiration of, ii. 104-105.
  whenever translated into English should be done freely, ii. 111.
  Davanzati's Italian translation of, ii. 111.
Tadcaster, beauty of country south of, ii. 247.
Talbot, Earl, Lord High Steward at coronation of George III., iii. 116.
  and barons of the Cinque Ports, iii. 116.
  and Alderman Beckford, iii. 116.
  his treatment while suppressing a riot, iii. 339.
Talbot, Thomas, Gray sends him a copy of The Odes, ii. 320.
  his part in Rev. William Robertson's marriage, iii. 62.
  reference to, ii. 379 ; iii. 176, 179.
Tale of Sir Thopas, reference to the, i. 338.

Taliessin, chief of the bards, i. 49, 361.
prophecy that Welch should regain
the sovereignty of Britain ful-
filled, i. 48.

Tanner, Bishop, his article on Chaucer
in *Bibliotheca*, i. 306.

Taroc, a game played in Turin, ii. 44.

Tasso, translations from the *Gerus* of,
i. 148, 151.
first printed, i. 44.

Taste, more difficult to restore than
to introduce good taste to a nation,
iii. 158.

Tavistock, Francis, Marquis of, comes
to Cambridge, ii. 309, 311.

Taylor, Dr., attends Mrs. Charles York,
ii. 401.
his opinion of a portrait in St. John's
College, i. 311.

Taylor, J., *Tracts* by, ii. 119.

Temple, Lancelot, *see* Dr. Armstrong.

Temple, Lord, Head of the Admiralty,
ii. 292.
Newcastle and Bute's opposition in
council, cause of his resignation,
iii. 123.
disinherits his brother, iii. 123.

Temple, Mr., allusion to, iii. 241.
Rev. N. Nicholls mediates on his
behalf with Lord Lisburne, iii.
287-289, 332-333.
Gray's opinion of the disagreement,
iii. 302-303.
Gray would wish by all means to
oblige him, iii. 336.
and Lord Lisburne, his distress of
circumstances, iii. 402.
Gray suggests application for chaplainship of Leghorn on behalf of,
iii. 402.
reference to, iii. 401.

Temple of Tragedy, Gray busy in writing the, iii. 187.

Templeman, Dr. Peter, keeper of the
British Museum reading-room, iii.1.
biographical note on, iii. 1.
translator of Norden's *Travels in
Egypt*, ii. 194.

Tenducci, Ferdinando, reference to, ii.
65.

Tent, Ode on a, William Whitehead's,
il. 220.

Tenter-grounds, description of, i. 268.

Terrick, Bishop of London, reference
to, iii. 202.

Thanet, Earl of, his castle at Skipton,
i. 279.

Theatres, common, subject to outrage-
ous riots, iii. 157.

Theirre, Madame de, reference to, ii.128.

Theodulus, his treatise *De Contemptu
Mundi*, i. 361.

Thibaut, King of Navarre, i. 347.

Thomas, Dr. John, Bishop of Lincoln,
translated to Salisbury, iii.105,114.

Thomas, Dr., Master of Christ's College,
rumoured to be Bishop of Carlisle,
iii. 335, 337.

Thomas, Miss, singer, sung in the
Installation Ode, iii. 343.

Thompson, a friend of Gray's, ii. 63.

Thomson, the poet, his fine description
of a spirit, iii. 43.

Thorney, visited by Gray, iii. 366.

Thrale, Mr., the brewer, reference to,
i. 316.

Thrale, Mrs., calls Gray a merciless
critic, iii. 399.

Thurcaston, the living of the Rev. Mr.
Hurd, ii. 326.

Thurlow's *Papers*, ii. 123.

Thurot, hovering off Scotland, iii. 23.

Thynne, Sir John, employed John of
Padua at Longleat, i. 307.

Tickell, Mr. Thomas, his poem on the
peace of Utrecht, ii. 219.
his ballad of *Colin and Lucy*, ii. 219.

Tolomei, Claudio, Bishop of Corsola,
i. 342.

Tophet (an epigram), i. 139.
editorial note on, i. 139.

Torrigiano, i. 319.

Tory Administration, Swift's *History
of the*, in the press, ii. 360.

Tour of the Lakes, Gilpin's, i. 279.

Tour of the western counties, Gray's,
iii. 379-381.

Townsend, Charles, William Whitehead's verses to, ii. 220.
accepts office, but not what he as-
pired to, ii. 292.
refused post of Secretary of State
and a peerage, iii. 238.
reference to his death, 282.

Townsend, General, his relations with
Wolfe before Quebec, iii. 25.
adventure with an Indian boy, iii. 25.

Tractatus, universi juris, published by
Zilettus, ii. 368.

Traigneau, Professor, ii. 122.

Translations, i. 143-160.
editorial note on, i. 144.

Travelling, difficulty of, between Old
Park and York, iii. 348.

Travelling, On the Abuse of, by G.
West, ii. 90.

Trebia, battle of, *Elegiacs* suggested by,
i. 177.

Trevigi, Girolamo da, his style of drawing, i. 319.

Trevor, Dr. Richard, Bishop of St. David's and of Durham, ii. 241.
Trevor, Mr. (Hambden), designs some wall-paper, iii. 121.
Trial of Scotch Lords, ii. 139.
Trinity College,. Cambridge, Henry VIII. its benefactor, i. 95.
Trip to Cambridge, or the grateful Fair, a comedy by Smart, ii. 162.
Trissino, his invention of Blank Deca-syllabic verse without Rhyme or Italian Heroic Measure, i. 343.
Tristram Shandy, popularity of Sterne's, iii. 36.
much humour in, iii. 53.
Triumphs of Owen, The, a fragment, i. 67.
editorial note on, i. 68.
Trollope, Mr., referred to by Gray, ii. 117, 118, 121, 123, 138, 161, 164.
at Dev'reux Court, ii. 159.
Tucker, Dean of Gloucester, Warburton's remark to, ii. 327.
Tudors, History of the, Hume's, ii. 396.
Tully ad Familiares, Epistles of, by Rev. J. Ross, ii. 193.
Turner, Dr. Shallet, of Peterhouse, his declining health, iii. 21.
his death, iii. 136.
Turnpike Riots at Leeds, ii. 240.
Tuthill, Henry, Dr. T. Wharton's in-fluence solicited on his behalf, ii. 145.
biographical note, ii. 173.
elected a Fellow of Peinbroke, ii. 188.
Gray anticipates his success as a Tutor, ii. 197.
indebted to Dr. Keene's interest for his fellowship, ii. 201.
votes for Mr. Spencer at Pembroke College, ii. 228.
references to, ii. 138, 161, 197, 230, 264, 308.
Twitcher, Jemmy; or The Cambridge Courtship, i. 131.
editorial note on, i. 131.
Two Odes, a satire against Mason and Gray, iii. 53.
Tyre, Cardinal Archbishop of, ii. 62.
Tyrrell, reference to young, iii. 203.
Tyson, Mr., of Bene't College, his drawing for Tophet, i. 139.

Ubaldini, Ubaldino, verses by, i. 368.
Union of poetry, music, and the dance with painting and architecture, might bestow the sublimest plea-sure, iii. 155.
causes to hinder, iii. 156.

Union, The, a Scotch collection of poems containing Gray's Elegy, i. 277.
Urry, see D'Urry.
Utrecht, T. Tickell's poem on the peace of, ii. 219.

Vaga, Perin del, reference to the painter, i. 321.
Valence or Valentia, Mary de, Countess of Pembroke, foundress of Pem-broke College, i. 95; ii. 280.
Valet, The Lying, farce by Garrick, ii. 213.
Valkyriur, description of the, i. 55.
Vane, Harry, Impromptu on, i. 140.
journies to the north, ii. 238.
reference to, ii. 178.
Vane, Rev. Mr., the younger, circum-stances of his ordination, ii. 231.
ordained by the Archbishop of York, ii. 232.
Vanrobais, Madame, her famous manu-facture of cloth at Abbeville, iii. 353.
Vauxhall preferred to Ranelagh Gar-dens, ii. 125.
Vavasor, Mr., his residence of Weston, i. 280.
Velleron, Marquis de Cambis, The Pope's Lieutenant - General in France, ii. 27.
Verneuil, Marqse. de, Henri IV.'s pro-posal to marry the, ii. 281.
Verrio, Antonio, his paintings at Chats-worth, iii. 135.
Verse, Table of the measures of, with authorities and the order of the Rhymes, i. 343.
Vertue, George, his MSS. purchased by Walpole, i. 305.
his engravings of Chaucer, i. 306.
known by Burroughs, Master of Caius, i. 307.
discovers John of Padua to be the architect of Somerset House, i. 307.
Ververt, by Gresset, ii. 184.
Verzenay, famous for red wine, i. 239.
Vicissitude, Ode on the pleasure arising from, i. 123.
editorial note on, i. 123.
Victory, popular superstition in Lyd-gate's time of decisive, i. 389.
Villeneuve, Huon de, quotation from the verse of, i. 337.
Villevielle, Marquis de, visits Gray, iii. 372, 374.
Villiers, Lord, his interest for Lord Nuneham, ii. 309, 311.

Vine, The, Mr. Chute's residence, iii. 271.

Virgidemiarium, Bishop Hall's, Gray's opinion of, ii. 233.

Viry, Comte de, marriage of his son to Miss Speed, iii. 83.
value of his estate, iii. 83.
Minister at Turin, iii. 236.

Viry, Countess de, see Miss Speed.

Vivares, Landscape painter, visits Maltham, i. 278.

Voix du Sage et du Peuple, reference to, ii. 229.

Voltaire, Crébillon's Catalina and, ii. 193.
Gray's opinion of, iii. 173, 192.
gains restitution from the Parliament and Court of France for the family of Calas, iii. 173.
his Philosophic Dictionary, iii. 187.
his Lewis XIV., ii. 204.
History of Crusades believed to be by, ii. 229.
his satire on Rousseau called Guerre de Geneve, iii. 271.
his Poeme sur la Desastre de Lisbon, ii. 285.
"He must have a very good stomach that can digest," iii. 378.

WAKEFIELD'S Life of Gray, reference to, ii. 124.

Waldegrave, Lord, Gray dines with him in Paris, ii. 21.
marries Miss Maria Walpole—a handsome couple, ii. 396.

Wales, Frederick Prince of, verses on the death of, ii. 119.

Walker, Dr. Richard, Fellow and Vice-Master of Trinity, his death, note on, iii. 188.

Wall-papers, reference to, iii. 110, 118-119, 120-121.

Walpole, Sir Edward, marriage of his natural daughter Maria, ii. 396.

Walpole, Horace, Earl of Orford, friend and schoolfellow of Gray, ii. 6.
Inspector-General of Exports and Imports, ii. 13.
resigns and becomes Usher of the Exchequer, ii. 13.
travels with Gray through France, ii. 17.
resolves at wish of Sir Robert Walpole to visit Italy, ii. 39.
his spaniel "Tory" carried off by a wolf, ii. 40.
visits the Court of Turin, ii. 44.
entertained by Prince Craon at Florence, ii. 52.

Walpole, Horace, entertained by Countess Suarez, ii. 53.
his epistle to Mr. Ashton, ii. 90, 221, 225.
cause of Gray's quarrel with, ii. 124.
Gray's reconciliation with, ii. 207.
Gray visits him at Stoke, ii. 207.
Gray visits him in Arlington Street, ii. 139.
his disposition towards Gray, ii. 143.
takes a residence at Windsor, ii. 143.
paper on Message Cards by, ii. 143.
Advertisement on Good Breeding, ii. 143.
presents the Marquis Rinuccini, ii. 145.
Gray condoles with him on the loss of his cat and encloses the Ode, ii. 165.
MS. of the Ode on the death of Walpole's cat, i. 10.
elected a F.R.S., ii. 166.
sends Gray a copy of Spence's Polymetis, ii. 172.
Gray's Elegy in a churchyard sent for his criticism, ii. 210.
requested to ask Dodsley to print the Elegy, ii. 210.
Gray's Elegy first published by, with a preface, i. 72 ; ii. 211.
Gray sends a copy of Mason's Elfrida, ii. 212.
his fable of The Entail, ii. 214.
Gray's advice upon the proposed Memoirs, ii. 215.
Epistle to Mr. Eckardt, the painter, ii. 221.
Gray's facetious enquiry concerning the Memoirs, ii. 226.
opinion of Gray's Long Story shown by his reply to Mrs. French, ii. 228.
preserves the fragment of The Characters of the Christ-Cross-Row, i. 210.
letter in which Gray introduced them, i. 212.
requested not to preface the Poems with Gray's vignette, ii. 235.
his opinion of Mr. Stonehewer, ii. 241.
his Gothic residence, ii. 253.
ill of a fever in London, ii. 272.
asked to obtain the influence of Mr. Fraser and Duke of Bedford on behalf of Dr. Brown, ii. 289.
prints Gray's Odes at his Twickenham Press, ii. 319, 322.
prints Gray's Bard for Dodsley, ii. 320.
his opinion of Mason's Caractacus, ii. 332.

Walpole, Horace, prints Lord Whitworth's *Account of Russia* at Strawberry Hill, ii. 373.
description of a new bed-chamber at Strawberry Hill, iii. 11.
nearness of his residence to Hounslow, iii. 15.
slight description of his Mosaic window, iii. 17.
consulted by Gray on the *Erse* fragments, iii. 45, 127.
his *Anecdotes of Painting*, its engravings, iii. 125.
Gray's review of *The Lives of the Painters*, i. 304.
advice upon an editorship offered him by the Court, iii. 126.
visits Gray at Cambridge, iii. 150.
his new gallery all Gothicism, gold and crimson, iii. 150.
purchased in Suffolk a waggon-load of old moveables, iii. 151.
sends Gray a copy of the *Castle of Otranto*, and a pamphlet concerning libels, etc., iii. 191.
his career in Paris, 1765, his health in a deplorable state, iii. 236.
sends Gray the *Historic Doubts*, iii. 303.
Gray's criticism of it, iii. 304-307, 134.
Gray describes the London and Glasgow editions of his *Poems*, iii. 308.
referred to an ancient MS. in Benet Library, iii. 311.
criticised by Guthrie in the *Critical Review*, iii. 313.
his noted copy of Gray's *Six Poems* inserted in the Graians of Mr. Morris, iv. 340.
references to, i. 311 ; iii. 192, 225, 226, 227, 255.
Walpole, Lord, of Wolterton, reference to, ii. 237.
Walpole, Sir Robert, Earl of Orford, his seat of Houghton Hall, ii. 11.
directs his son Horace to go to Italy, ii. 39.
Parliamentary inquiry into his conduct, ii. 134.
Walpole, Lady, death of, ii. 9.
Wanstead, reference to a house of Gray's at, ii. 263.
Want, the mother of inferior Art, i. 119.
Warburton, William, Bishop of Gloucester, anecdote of, i. 127.
his *Reflections on the Miraculous Powers*, ii. 128.
defence of Pope, ii. 131.
admires Gray's *Odes*, ii. 325.

Warburton, William, his knowledge of Druidical and Celtic belief, ii. 351.
his *New Legation*, ii. 369.
his remarks on the Deans of Gloucester and Bristol, ii. 327.
his criticism of Gray's *Odes*, ii. 341.
and Hurd's criticism of *Caractacus* called that of Prior Park, ii. 393.
breaks his arm in Prior Park, iii. 145.
his sermon to the Court against illiterate preferment, iii. 202.
attacked by Dr. Louth, iii. 224.
reference to, iii. 117, 129.
Wardlaw, Lady, her ballad of *Hardicanute*, iii. 45.
Warton Crag, near Lancaster, i. 270.
Warton, Joseph, reference to his poem of the *Enthusiast*, ii. 121.
his *Poems*, ii. 159.
receives MS. of Gray's Amatory Lines from Mr. Leman, i. 137.
Warton, Thomas, Gray's esteem of his talents, and upon request sends him a *Design for a History of English Poetry*, iii. 365.
his qualifications as the Historian of English Poetry, i. 53.
Warwick, description of, and its castle, ii. 256-257.
church, Earls of Warwick buried in, ii. 257.
Water-glasses, *see* Glasses.
Waterland, Dr. Daniel, reference to, ii. 169.
his *Scripture Vindicated*, ii. 215.
Water Nymph, Mason's *Ode to a*, ii. 184.
Watson, Mr., public tutor of Lord Richard Cavendish, iii. 331.
Weather record —
July—August, 1759, iii. 13.
September—November, 1759, iii. 18.
April—June 3, 1760, iii. 54-55.
January 1761, iii. 92.
February—April, 1763, iii. 153-154.
January—March, 1766, iii. 868-369.
November 3—December 14, 1767, iii. 293.
January—April 1770, iii. 368.
Weddell, William, of Newby, reference to, iii. 197.
with Rev. Norton Nicholls, iii. 240.
reference to, iii. 266.
at York, iii. 284.
Welsh fragments, i. 129-130.
editorial note on, i. 129.
language, remarks on, i. 381.
Wemyss, Earl of, his second son takes the name of Charteris, i. 275.

Wentworth, Lady Harriet (Marquis of Rockingham's sister) marries her footman, iii. 163.
embarks for America, iii. 165.
West, Gilbert, reference to *On the Abuse of Travelling*, by, ii. 90.
his contribution to Dodsley's Miscellaneous Poems, ii. 180.
note on, ii. 180.
West, Richard (the Favonius of Gray), effect of his criticism of *Agrippina*, i. 101.
Sapphic Ode sent to, i. 174.
Sapphics sent to, i. 176-177.
Carmen ad C. Favonium Zephyrinum sent to, i. 177.
fragment of a Latin poem on The Gaurus sent to, i. 179-181.
Farewell to Florence sent to, i. 181.
biographical notes on, i. 110 ; ii. 1.
his personal appearance, ii. 45.
loss of his companionship regretted by Gray, ii. 2.
advised by Gray to learn Italian, ii. 7.
his Latin Elegy *Ad Amicos*, ii. 8.
writes an Elegy in reference to the Venus de Medicis of Florence, ii. 55.
assured of Gray's unalterable friendship, ii. 96-97.
his fragment of the Tragedy of *Pausanias*, ii. 103.
sends Gray some hexameters on a cough, ii. 106.
his translation of Tacitus commended, ii. 111.
praise of his *Ode on May*, ii. 112.
his death, and its cause, i. 2 ; ii. 113.
Gray's *Sonnet* on his death, i. 110.
reference to, ii. 167.
note as to the publication of his poems, ii. 171.
his *Monody on the death of Queen Caroline*, ii. 180, 222.
Westminster Abbey, fragment of an Act of Parliament relative to ; one of the lost pieces by Gray, i. 142.
Westminster Hall, Gray's account of George III.'s coronation in, iii. 110-116.
Westminster Theatre, reference to, iii. 270.
Duke of York, Lady Stanhope, the Delavals, etc., play parts in, iii. 270.
Weymouth, Thomas, third Viscount, his marriage to Lady Elizabeth Bentinck, iii. 395.
presents living of Frome to Dr. Ross, iii. 32.
offered Spain (Ambassador ?), iii. 255.
reference to, iii. 294.

Whaley, Dr., reference to, ii. 159.
Wharton, R., advice as to educating his son at Eton, iii. 86-87, 106-107.
death of, iii. 167.
Wharton, Thomas, M.D., Fellow of Pembroke College, his MSS. of Gray, i. xiv.
Gray's *Epitaph* on his infant son, i.126.
note on, ii. 61.
Gray dubs him Sir Thomas and wishes him a great career, ii. 118.
influence solicited on behalf of Tuthill, ii. 145, 185.
asked his opinion of Thucydides, ii. 147.
Gray requests a small loan, and its repayment, ii. 156, 176, 177.
Gray asks the loan of twenty guineas, ii. 195.
contemplated marriage of, ii. 157.
reference to his marriage, ii. 176.
Gray sends him the *Ode* on Walpole's cat, ii. 164 ; i. 10.
interest sought on behalf of C. Smart, ii. 179.
sympathises with Gray on the loss of his house in Cornhill, ii. 181-182.
congratulated on the christening of his daughter, ii. 185.
Gray asks his opinion of Stonehewer, ii. 187.
Gray sends him *The Alliance of Education and Government*, ii. 187.
asked to obtain the influence of Dr. Keene on behalf of Stonehewer, ii. 198.
contemplates a change of practice, ii. 202-203.
Gray sends him a copy of the *Elegy*, ii. 228.
Gray directs that two copies of his *Poems* should be sent to, ii. 237.
birth of a son, ii. 238.
Gray proposes to visit him at Studley, ii. 240.
desires to change his residence, ii. 252-253.
the *Progress of Poesy* submitted to him, ii. 260 ; i. 2.
reference to his politics, ii. 259, 261.
requested to pay the fire policies on Gray's property, ii. 263.
Gray asks to be entertained as an invalid at Wharton's house, ii. 273.
reference to his profession, ii. 274.
Gray asks him to procure a rope ladder to be used in escaping from drunken visitors, ii. 276.
his desire that Mr. Hurd should treat Dr. Akenside leniently, ii. 299.

Wharton, Thomas, told that Gray's *Odes* are not at all popular, ii. 323.

Gray mentions the criticisms on the *Odes* to, ii. 330-331, 341.

congratulated upon recovery of his family, ii. 340.

Gray condoles with him on the death of his son, ii. 361.

his dejection, ii. 365.

residing at Hampstead, ii. 377.

purchases a picture believed to be by old Fran[c]k, ii. 384.

Gray troubles him to accommodate some baskets of china, ii. 385.

Gray sends him same with inventory, and asks that they may be insured, ii. 387-389.

complimented upon owning a "Pieta," ii. 389.

once lived in Southampton Row, ii. 397.

removes to his paternal estate of Old Park, ii. 397; iii. 17, 21, 49, 133.

keeps record of temperature for July 1759, ii. 398.

Gray unable to purchase old tapestry for, iii. 10.

proposes to have a painted window, Gray's proposal for same, iii. 17.

birth of a son, iii. 49.

has recovered his hearing, iii. 64.

illness and death of his sister-in-law, iii. 82, 121.

Gray's advice on an Eton education for his nephew, iii. 86-87, 106-107.

Gray advises him upon coloured glass, iii. 102-103.

Gray advises him upon Gothic wall-paper and its cost, iii. 110, 118-121.

visited by Gray at Old Park, iii. 133.

Gray buys him some *rout-chairs*, their price, iii. 137.

confinement of Mrs. Wharton, iii. 138.

condolement on the death of R. Wharton, iii. 167.

protection of his sister Ettrick from a brutal husband, iii. 199-200, 245.

entertains Gray, Dr. Hallifax, and Dr. Louth at Old Park, iii. 208.

entertains Gray and Dr. Brown, iii. 274.

they accompany him to Barnard Castle, Rokeby, and Richmond, iii. 277.

contemplates with Gray a tour through Westmoreland and Cumberland, iii. 277.

taken ill with asthma while on a visit to the Lakes with Gray, his return home, iii. 291, 351.

Wharton, Thomas, desires a drawing-master for his daughters, iii. 293.

Gray sends books requested, also family presents, who are mentioned by nickname, iii. 291-292.

what does he think of Mason's plans for his grounds? iii. 292.

Gray hopes the asthma has not returned, iii. 294.

Gray, consulted in a tythe dispute, endeavours to dissuade Wharton from pursuing it, iii. 314-317.

Gray relates the manner of his appointment to the Chair of Modern History, iii. 321.

his nephew admitted to Pembroke College, iii. 340.

will visit Mason at York, on horseback, from Old Park, iii. 349.

Gray hopes he got safe home after his troublesome night of asthma, iii. 350.

Gray writes the Journal of the Lakes for his amusement, iii. 350.

sends Gray an object of natural history, iii. 352.

illness of his daughter, iii. 21, 368.

Gray tells him of his journey through the western counties, iii. 379-380.

MS. of *Impromptu* on Lord Holland's house, i. 135.

Whateley, Thomas, his *Observations on Gardening* and account of the Wye, iii. 380.

Wheeler, J., has returned from Lisbon, iii. 238.

Whitehead, William, Gray's opinion of his *Ode on a Tent*, etc., ii. 220.

Birthday Ode for 1758, ii. 390, 391.

Ode for the New Year, ii. 394.

his *School for Lovers*, iii. 128.

Gray pleased with his *Charge to the Poets*, iii. 128.

Elegy against Friendship, iii. 128, 131.

Gray would rather steal his verse than his sentiment, iii. 138.

Whithe[a]d, Francis, reference to, ii. 125, 136, 137, 207.

biographical note, iii. 205.

Whitworth, Lord, his *Account of Russia*, printed at Strawberry Hill, ii. 373.

Wilkes, John, speech by, iii. 39.

his pursuit of Lord Hallifax, iii. 39.

likely to be chose for the city of London, iii. 317.

like to lose his election (in 1771, but returned top of the poll), iii. 406.

Wilkinson, Mr., reference to, ii. 177.

his influence at Pembroke College, ii. 223.

398 INDEX.

Wilkinson, Miss, about to marry Mr.
T. Pitt, iii. 406.
Wilkinson, Mrs., reference to, iii.
274.
William of Sens, built the choir of
Canterbury Cathedral, iii. 316.
William Shakespeare to Mrs. Anne, a
poem by Gray, iii. 205-206.
Williams, Bishop, portrait as lord
keeper, i. 311.
Williams, Mr., friend of Gray and Wal-
pole, iii. 71.
Williams, Sir Charles Hanbury, has he
gone to Berlin ? ii. 227.
death of his daughter Lady Essex, ii.
401, iii. 3.
Williams, Sir William Peers, about to
take part in a secret expedition,
iii. 68.
Montagu one of his executors, iii.
104.
Gray requested to write his Epitaph,
iii. 109.
Gray's first thoughts for an Epitaph,
iii. 109.
Epitaph on, i. 128.
Walpole's description of, i. 128.
Williamson, Mr., friend of Dr. Beattie,
reference to, iii. 278.
visits Gray at Cambridge to which he
walked from Aberdeen, iii. 280.
Willis's *Mitred Abbies*, reference to, ii.
377.
Willoughby's *Book of Fishes*, iii. 291.
Book of Birds, prices realised for
copies, iii. 291.
Wilson, Benjamin, portrait painter,
Dr. Plumptre and Gray sit to, iii.
16.
Wilson, Dr. Christopher, Bishop of
Bristol, his fortunate acquirement
of wealth, iii. 75.
King George III.'s reproof to, iii.
75.
biographical note on, iii. 75.
Wilson, Colonel, his house in Kendal,
i. 269.
Wilson, Thomas, Fellow of Pembroke
College, iii. 384.
Winstanley, Mr., private tutor to Lord
Richard Cavendish, iii. 331.
Winston, reference to, iii. 152.
Winter of 1763-4 hot and unseason-
able, iii. 169.
Winter of 1771, iii. 391-392.
Woburn, residence of Duke of Bedford,
ii. 258.
Wollaston, Wm., quotation from his
Religion of Nature Delineated, i.
290.

Wollaston, Miss, marries Dr. Heber-
den, iii. 29.
Wolsey's, Cardinal, villa at Esher, ii.
253.
Women, frailties of, the favourite
theme of conversation, i. 403.
Wood, Rev. John, curate to Mason, ii.
309.
reference to, ii. 395.
Mason engaged to, iii. 328.
Wood, Robert, author of *Ruins of Pal-
myra*, disappointed at Gray's pro-
ductions, ii. 323, 331.
Duke of Bridgewater's companion in
Italy, ii. 328.
gone to Chatsworth, iii. 124.
Woodhouse, Tytler, Lord, his *Essay on
Petrarch* against the Abbé de Sade,
iii. 235.
Woodville [Widville], Elizabeth, wife
of Edward IV., i. 95.
Wormius, Olaus, his preservation of
the Anglo-Saxon poem of *Ransom
of Eigil*, i. 362.
Wren, Sir Christopher, his opinion
that Gothic architecture is the
Saracen or Moorish, ii. 255.
rebuilt Warwick church, ii. 257.
Writing, Gray on good, ii. 199.
Wroxton, residence of Duke of Guild-
ford, ii. 258.
Wyat, Sir J., Gray's transcript of his
defence offered to H. Walpole, i.
312.
Wyatt, Sir Thomas, his verse, i. 334.
Wyatt, Rev. William, Fellow of Pembroke, reference to, and note on,
iii. 353.
Wye, River, Gray's account of, iii.
380.
Gilpin's *Observations* on the river
submitted to Gray, iii. 380.

Yarmouth, Lady, her son christened
by Mason, ii. 354.
George II.'s bequest to, iii. 71.
Yonge or Young, Philip, Bishop of
Bristol, Duke of Newcastle's remark to, ii. 371.
reference to a caricature of, by
Mason, iii. 55.
translated to Norwich, iii. 105.
York, Mrs. Charles, death of, and one
of her children, ii. 401.
attended by Drs. Heberden and
Taylor, ii. 401.
York, Duke of, his popularity, iii. 89-
90.
anecdote concerning, iii. 90.

York, Duke of, speaks in Opposition on the American question, iii. 270.

his private theatricals, iii. 270.

York Minster, ruin of a Gothic chapel in precincts of, Gray's opinion of its being the chapel of St. Sepulchre, iii. 140-144.

period and style of its construction and architecture, iii. 145-147.

Yorke, James, succeeds to the deanery of Dr. Greene, iii. 105.

Yorkshire, Gray's journey through part of, iii. 133-134.

see Lakes, Journal of.

Young, Professor, author of a satirical criticism on the *Elegy*, i. 208.

ZEPHYRINUM, Carmen ad C. Favonium, i. 177-178.

Zilettus of Venice, publisher of *Tractatus universi juris*, ii. 368.

THE END.

Printed by R. & R. CLARK, *Edinburgh.*

www.ingramcontent.com/pod-product-compliance
Lightning Source LLC
Chambersburg PA
CBHW032318280326
41932CB00009B/860